# THE

## — OF —

# READING

*A Passionate Guide to 189
of the World's Best
Authors and Their Works*

### CHARLES VAN DOREN

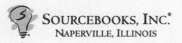

SOURCEBOOKS, INC.®
NAPERVILLE, ILLINOIS

Published by Sourcebooks, Inc.
P.O. Box 4410, Naperville, Illinois 60567-4410
(630) 961-3900
Fax: (630) 961-2168
www.sourcebooks.com

First published in the United States of America by Crown Publishing, Inc., 1985

Van Doren, Charles Lincoln.
  The joy of reading : a passionate guide to 189 of the world's best authors and their works / Charles Van Doren.
    p. cm.
  1. Best books. 2. Books and reading. I. Title.

Z1035.V26 2008
011'.73—dc22

                                2007043270

      Printed and bound in the United States of America.
         BG 10 9 8 7 6 5 4 3 2 1

*For my colleagues, friends, and students at the University of Connecticut*

*and*

*For Gerry*

# Author to Reader

Reading is my favorite thing to do. When I was ten and supposed to go to sleep at a certain time, I read under the covers with a flashlight until my father told me I would ruin my eyes. I didn't stop; I was willing to risk my sight to enjoy the pleasures of reading. In fact he was wrong; after seventy years I can still read, even without glasses if there's enough light.

I have had many teachers. I've learned something important from each of them. This book is partly my attempt to repay them.

My mother first taught me to read, I remember very well. I was not in school; we were living in the country, and she and I had lessons every morning. My first book was *The Little Fir Tree*. It was about a little forest tree that was glad it was cut down for Christmas and taken to the home of a nice boy and girl. I would not let any child read that book now.

Once the door was open, I pushed through eagerly. By the time I entered high school I had read a good deal; more, probably, than most kids my age. My father had fostered my reading (when he wasn't prohibiting it, thinking I should go outdoors and get some fresh air) by suggesting a wide variety of titles and giving me all kinds of books as Christmas and birthday presents. He didn't care if I read them all; he just wanted me to be acquainted with different kinds of books and not to be afraid to read any particular kind. He kept giving me books as long as he lived. I still have many of them, especially those he sent me when I was serving in the Air Force in

World War II. I carried for months in the breast pocket of my fatigues a hard-bound copy of Palgrave's *Golden Treasury*. A tough little book with hard covers, it was a kind of talisman that I thought would stop a bullet and save my life. Maybe it did; at least, no one ever shot at me.

During my senior year in high school I began trying to read some of the classical authors my father said I would have to read in college: Plato, Homer, Sophocles. A friend already in college to whom I revealed that I had read the *Apology* belittled my achievement, saying it was "easy." I've never forgotten my chagrin, but to this day I believe he was wrong. Plato's *Apology* isn't easy, though it's more interesting than many of his other dialogues. Scholars struggle to understand the meaning of the more difficult, later dialogues, but in the long run they are less crucial for the way we live our lives than the humanity of Plato's account of the trial and death of Socrates.

In 1946, I returned to college from the war to find myself in a class conducted by Richard Schofield, who taught me to appreciate Baudelaire and William Blake, among others. I could read French but I was as yet unable to forget it was a foreign language. I learned that language is both a means of and an obstacle to communication—foreign languages, obviously, but one's own language if one's not careful. Blake's utter simplicity can be misleading, hiding depths of profundity that most poets never sound.

I learned other lessons at my college, St. John's in Annapolis. The most important was that I was free to read any kind of book; my father's mentoring many years before was now validated. I gained the confidence to attempt almost any book, in almost any Western language, employing almost any set of symbols. (Of course, I often failed!) For years I thought everyone shared this confidence, but now I know that not too many possess it. One of my main goals in writing this book is to try to instill that confidence in other readers.

I was for a time a professor at Columbia University, where among other subjects I taught the famous "Humanities" course that was then required for all freshmen. That was a whole new lesson in reading, but I didn't stay at Columbia for long. I soon found myself headed for Chicago and Encyclopaedia Britannica, where for twenty-five years I studied under and worked with one of the great teachers of reading,

Mortimer J. Adler. We wrote and edited books together and also taught together a seminar that had originated in the 1940s (when Adler led it with Robert Hutchins). Over the years Dr. Adler and I read about two hundred books together for this seminar, and I never ceased to be astonished by his ability to arrive at the central question a book asks, or that it requires a reader to ask. He died ten years ago, but his spirit still hovers.

Now we are back home from Chicago, Gerry and I. The children have gone away and have children of their own, and we have settled into a life of leisure, which means I have more time since I retired to read than I ever did. I still love reading, best of all when Gerry and I or someone else read the same book, which often happens these days for professional and other reasons (we are both teachers now). When that happens I'm always surprised at the difference of our reactions, even though we have read the same words. The fact that the other reader may be a woman has something to do with this, but not everything. Their minds grasp things mine never will, and vice versa, which is right and proper.

This book contains fifteen chapters, each of which gathers discussions of a group of authors and their works. The chapters are arranged in chronological order, from "The Golden Age: In the Beginning" to "Only Yesterday." All told there are 182 entries, each one about the work or works of a different author (or authors, in some cases). Entries, too, are arranged in chronological order, starting with Homer and Hesiod and ending with Patrick O'Brian and J.K. Rowling. Occasionally it wasn't possible to stick strictly to chronological order within the period covered by a given chapter, since some authors may have had long careers, and others quite short ones; or I may have chosen to discuss a number of books by some authors and only one or two books (or essays or poems, etc.) by others. Nevertheless, the general direction of the book is chronological, as you can see from a glance at the table of contents.

Saying that, I have to admit that my knowledge of and interest in many very recent and popular books and other writings isn't infinite. I have not forgotten Ralph Waldo Emerson's injunction: "Read no book that is not a hundred years old." A century is needed, he thought, for good books to emerge from the throng of titles which, then as now, presented themselves. I have disobeyed him in a few cases but really not many, and when I have done so I may turn out to have been wrong. Will anyone be reading about Jack Aubrey and Stephen Maturin or Harry Potter a hundred years hence? I hope so, but I'm not at all sure. I'm not sure that anyone will be reading *anything* a hundred years hence—but that is another question.

# HOW TO USE THIS BOOK

There are, I suggest, four different ways to use *The Joy of Reading*. The first is as a reference in which a given author or title can be researched, perhaps because it is mentioned in something else you may have been reading. You could look it up elsewhere—on the Internet, for instance—but the book might be more convenient if it's sitting on your desk next to a dictionary and a thesaurus. If you looked up a writer or a work in my book, you would also be assured of the authority of the information, something the Internet does not always provide.

Second, it can be used as an introduction to the history of literature (taking that word in its most general sense, to include history, philosophy, even mathematics and science up to a certain level, as well as fiction, drama, and so forth). Used in this manner it need not be read straight through. The table of contents alone may suggest all you want to know about what I believe to be a reasonable history of literature (in that sense). Or parts of it, for example the Golden Age of Greece or the Romantic Age, might especially interest you, in which case you could read some or all of the entries in those chapters and leave the others for another day. If I myself were new to this book, I might turn first to a chapter about the seventeenth century, if there was one, because that is a period I like and know quite well. (And if I did find such a chapter, I might be annoyed because the author had left out this or that figure.)

Third, the book can be read from cover to cover. I know this is unlikely. My editor, Hillel Black, may turn out to be the only man who has ever done it. His reasons were professional, but he pleased me by saying he enjoyed doing it. (The book has been read from cover to cover by one other person: my computer guru. Her name is Laurel

McKiernan and she too said she enjoyed it. But she may have just been polite. In any case, I owe her a great debt for all she did to make the manuscript presentable.)

Fourth and finally, the book can be used as the basis for a reading program that can be followed for a number of years. In the Afterword that follows the text, I present a program covering ten years. It includes ten books a year, or one hundred all told, which may be too many or too few—that depends on you. If you undertake this program, I wish you the best. I can assure you that almost all the books that are included are really good, so you will not be wasting your time.

# Contents

# chapter one

# The Golden Age

In the beginning ... two thousand seven hundred years ago, more or less. That great beginning led people of later times to call it a Golden Age. It is almost incomprehensible that the first poet about whom we know anything in the history of the Western world is also, as Dante later called Homer, the greatest of all. The same is true of Aeschylus, Sophocles, and Euripides; they are not only the first dramatists but also among the best. Herodotus and Thucydides are, if not the greatest historians, then the most inventive and memorable not only for their stories but also for the judgments they pronounced. And Aristophanes taught us how to laugh at the follies of even the most powerful tyrants.

Homer; Aeschylus, Sophocles, Euripides, and Aristophanes; and Herodotus and Thucydides were all Greeks; that is, they were inhabitants twenty-five hundred years ago of a small, disorderly country at the eastern end of the Mediterranean Sea. Homer predated the others by two or three hundred years, but his presence continued to be felt by all classical Greeks for as long as people thought it meant something special to be Greek. He was not an Athenian, as most of the others were, but he might as well have been. Nor was the language he spoke and wrote exactly the same as theirs, although it was close enough to be understood by them when they read him. The entire population of what could have been called Greece, or Hellas, in the fifth century before the birth of Christ was probably not greater than the population of a medium sized city of today. The total number of persons calling themselves Greeks (or Hellenes) may have represented less than 1 percent of the population of the world. But they had an advantage not shared by any one else at the time. They were fighting for their lives, not just as individuals but as members of a civilization that treasured liberty. They were fighting to be free, and that is a powerful incentive.

# HOMER
## fl. 750-675 BCE ?
*The Iliad*
*The Odyssey*

Almost nothing is known about the author of *The Iliad* and *The Odyssey*. It is only a guess that he lived, probably somewhere on the Mediterranean's eastern littoral or perhaps on one of the Aegean islands, sometime in the eighth or seventh century before the Christian era. It is customary to say he flourished 750-675 BCE. It used to be thought that he, like most of his contemporaries, could neither read nor write, but the latest theories hold that he must have inscribed the two great epics, although no manuscripts dating from that period have ever been found. The language of the poems is a curious mixture of more or less ancient dialects and later versions of Greek, but this doesn't mean the works are merely collections of stories or songs. It now seems almost certain that a single man, whom we call Homer (as did the Greeks twenty-five hundred years ago), wrote the two poems that, for a hundred generations, have continued to move our hearts and souls because of their deep understanding of what it means to be human. It is not surprising, then, that they have also influenced almost every great literary work since.

*The Iliad* is surely the earlier of the two poems. Beginning with the immortal hexameter line: "Sing, Goddess, the wrath of Achilles, Pelias's son," it deals with events that are thought to have occurred three or four hundred years before it was composed, perhaps around 1200 BCE. According to Homer's version of the events, Paris, the second son of King Priam of Troy, eloped with Helen, the wife of Menelaus, king of Sparta. Helen was apparently willing to leave her husband and her daughter Hermione for this handsome stranger, and Paris took her back to Troy where, after a suitable period, they married. They lived there as man and wife for twenty years, Helen in particular enjoying the luxurious life her new husband provided for her in what was then perhaps the wealthiest city in the Mediterranean world. Troy was the capital of an empire that encompassed much of what we now call the Middle East, and Priam seems to have been a benevolent ruler who was loved and admired by his subjects. Mainland Greece at this time was probably primitive by comparison with the civilized world that Paris had described to Helen when he wooed her away from her old home and carried her off to a new one.

But Menelaus never forgot her, and after many lonely years he prevailed upon his brother, Agamemnon, king of Mycenae, to gather an army to retrieve her. This first expeditionary force was beset by bad luck; among other things, the Argives, or Achaeans, didn't know where Troy actually was located. Agamemnon returned with little to show for his efforts except some treasure stolen from small cities along the way, and slaves—males to row his ships, and females to perform their usual services.

Menelaus continued to urge his brother to "make things right," as Homer writes, and another, much larger army was raised about ten years after Helen's abduction. The siege of Troy began and continued for another ten weary years, with neither the Argives nor the Trojans able to claim victory. Victory for the Trojans would mean the destruction of the entire invading army, with perhaps only a handful of refugees able to return to their far-off homes. An Achaean victory would result in the destruction of the city of Troy and the devastation of its hinterland.

In the tenth year of the siege, the Trojan general, Prince Hector, was killed by Achilles, the chief Argive warrior, and shortly thereafter Troy fell, was burned to the ground, its male inhabitants put to the sword, and its women and children sold as slaves.

Things like that happened fairly frequently in the twelfth century BCE, and it is not entirely clear why the Greeks commemorated this tale with religious intensity, as they did no other expedition, successful or not. The Homeric poems were said to have been divinely inspired, and the story they told was interpreted as revealing the true story of the gods in their relation to men.

Later epics—for example, *The Song of Roland* or *The Saga of Burnt Njal*—are primitive, in the sense that they present scenes of heroic warfare unalloyed with profound or subtle emotions. They are about raw courage, raw revenge, and other strong feelings. Homer, in *The Iliad*, deals with these feelings, too, but the poem is not primitive. An astonishing thing about it is, although Homer obviously knew nothing about the amenities and comforts of our life today, he knew most of what we know about the human heart. Maybe even more.

Hector and Achilles are an extraordinary pair. There is a sense in which both are the hero of *The Iliad*, another sense in which neither is. Both Achilles and Hector have their moments of "stardom," as we might call it, in the poem. Achilles is far and away the best of the Greeks, but he is deeply insulted by Agamemnon, who humiliates him in front of the entire army. He retires from the fray to sulk in his tent, surrounded by his followers—his Myrmidons. In his absence, Hector tears through the Achaean army, killing many famous fighters, and finally reaches the Greek ships, which he tries to set afire. Without their ships, the Achaeans will never be able to return home. Win or lose, they will be stranded in Asia. The burning of the ships is therefore a major crisis. Hector is beaten back not by Achilles, who should have been there, but by the giant Ajax, whose slowness of wit then and thereafter deprives him of the honor that should have been his due.

But Hector has overreached himself. He is so certain of victory he ensures his own death and the destruction of his family and his city. In a mad rage he kills Patroclus, the best friend of Achilles, and Achilles, wracked by this unbearable loss, finally returns to the battle. His revenge is terrible. He is like a great scythe slicing through the Trojan ranks. Finally the field is left alone to the two antagonists, Hector and Achilles. The Achaeans fall back to the water's edge; the Trojans retreat within their walls. There is an awful silence on the plain, the only sound the crunch of Achilles' feet and the rasping gasp in Hector's throat as, in heavy armor, he runs for his life. He doesn't make it.

Achilles, still enraged, insults the body, dragging it naked behind his chariot, round and round his Myrmidon encampment. Finally, old King Priam, who has lost both his general and his dearest son, determines that he must retrieve the body. Alone he goes, out into the silence, with a wagon drawn by mules, piled high with a ransom of gold, rich robes, jewels, and ornaments. It is night and Priam, aided by the gods, drives the wagon through the Greek encampment, seeking the tent where Achilles sits, still mourning the death of his friend. The old man enters, kneels down, and "kisses the hands that had slain so many of his sons." Achilles, shaken, moved beyond grief, accepts the gifts and returns the body. Priam, the old king, loads the corpse of his son on the wagon and drives the mules back to the city, where the funeral takes place.

On the twelfth day, when the funeral ends, the war will begin anew. The poem ends here. It does not tell what happens. Everyone knew, and still knows, that Troy will be taken, burned, destroyed, wiped from the face of the Earth, that Helen will run back to the arms of Menelaus and be forgiven, and that many Achaean leaders will be lost or killed on the way home. Agamemnon, the chief Argive general and the king of Lacedaemon, will reach home but be slain there by his wife, Clytemnestra, as he struggles to emerge from a richly embroidered shirt he discovers has no sleeves or neck hole. Before he dies she tells him she has made it as a homecoming gift.

The Greeks thought the siege and defeat of Troy was the most terrible thing to ever happen, and the most wonderful. The gods were involved in it as much as the men and women and children. It was a conflict on every level the Greeks could understand, and yet they also understood—or Homer did—that nobody won. They recognized that the deaths of the three great men—Achilles, Hector, and Patroclus—were all tragic and would define the meaning of tragedy for millennia. Perhaps most astounding of all about *The Iliad* is that its author, writing at the very beginning of recorded history, already knew everything there is to know about the deep folly of war.

People who have never read *The Iliad* but who know of it are often unwilling to open it in the belief that it is unrelievedly sad, a seemingly endless series of bloody battles. In a sense this is true, but in another sense it is not. Homer never fails to tell us what is going to happen, but even so, when it happens, it is a surprise. You hope against hope and are exhilarated by your love and admiration for the three main characters. The deaths leave your heart broken, but the epic is inspiring nevertheless.

And there are many wonderful interludes in the savage brutality of the fighting, moments during which the beauty of peace shines through even though it cannot be enjoyed. The scene where Hector unknowingly says goodbye for the last time to his beloved wife, Andromache, and his little boy, brings tears to the eyes of the hardiest reader. The response of Andromache to the return of her husband's body from the encampment of Achilles is wrenching: she understands perfectly what must happen to her and her child now that her husband can no longer protect them. And the last dirge for Hector, spoken by Helen herself, who remembers that he was always kind to her even though he knew, as did she, that her very presence in his city was a curse, is riveting. You realize you will never forget these remarkable men and women and that you are richer for having known them.

During the German occupation of Paris in World War II, Simone Weil, a French philosopher, published a small book (really only a pamphlet) titled *The Iliad; or, the Poem of Force*. She said that *The Iliad* was a poem without a hero; the dominant figure in the war was force itself, brutal force, the force of bronze cutting into flesh, the force of fate overtaking a human life, the hopelessness of all the characters, great and small, in the face of events they did not and could not comprehend.

The book was a veiled reference to the brutal German occupation of France, but it is as a commentary on *The Iliad* that it achieved permanence. Simone Weil was right about Homer's epic, which is completely without sentiment and is about force, another name for which is *anangke*, the "necessity" that stands between human beings and the realization of their dreams.

The world of *The Odyssey*, although superficially the same as that of *The Iliad*, is really utterly different. The entire action of *The Iliad* takes place in a period of forty-one days on a blood-soaked beach at the foot of the walls of Troy, and within the beleaguered city. The action of *The Odyssey* ranges over land and sea, extends all the way

to Hell and back, and only at the end—ten years after it begins—
focuses on the small island of Ithaca, in the Ionian Sea, where the
crisis and denouement of the poem are played out. The sounds of *The
Iliad* are those of clashing arms and the screams of wounded and dying
men, and finally the hoarse gasp of a single man running from his foe.
Those of *The Odyssey* are the cries of sea birds and the strumming of
a lyre as a harpist sings of a world that is no more. And our memory
of *The Iliad* suggests to us that much of its action occurs at night in
flickering campfire light, whereas *The Odyssey* unfolds in daylight,
high noon, with the sun shining and sea waves lapping against a
white beach, while on the brow of a hill there shines a building,
dazzling, white, a dwelling whether of gods or men we cannot tell.

For more than two thousand years readers have said of *The Iliad*
that it is, or is like, a tragedy; and of *The Odyssey* that it is, or is like,
a comedy. This judgment is, I think, most just.

Not that *The Odyssey* is funny. A man has gone off to war, and
although his side has won he has not returned. For ten years, since
word came of the fall of Troy, his faithful wife has waited for him,
hoping and praying that he is still alive and will come home to her.

Now, a troop of greedy neighboring landowners is trying to force
Penelope to choose among them, beautiful as she still is, her riches
and the kingdom to be the reward of the man who wins her. Her son,
Telemachus, who was a baby when Odysseus went off to war and is
now almost twenty years old, sets out to seek news of his father, in the
faint hope that he can be found and brought back to help them.
Meanwhile Odysseus lies in the soft, illicit bed of the lovely nymph,
Calypso, whose fame is immortal.

The gods are impatient with Odysseus, particularly the dread
goddess Athene, the daughter of Zeus. Athene sends the messenger
god, Hermes, to Calypso, warning her that she must release her lover,
who has remained with her for seven years. Calypso finds Odysseus
sitting by the edge of the sea, weeping, and she begs him to stay with
her; she will make him immortal, and they will live together for
always on her island, Ogygia, the island of the Dead, in the paradise
she has made.

He refuses, declaring that he must go home if she will let him.
Reluctantly, she helps him build a raft. But Poseidon, Lord of the Sea

Waves, angry with him, causes a storm to rise. It destroys the raft, and Odysseus is washed up on the shores of a magic land, Phaeacia. There he meets the maiden Nausicäa, who takes him to her father the king. Odysseus is recognized and tells the story of his earlier voyages, beginning at Troy after the end of the war and concluding with his rescue by Calypso. It is probably the most famous voyage ever described—even though it never happened.

Odysseus leaves Troy intent on going home as quickly as possible, but is waylaid by adventures, mostly of his own making. They arise out of his great curiosity about lands he has never seen and the people who inhabit them. He leads a raid on the Ciconians, which offends the gods. He visits the land of the Lotus-eaters, where all is sweet and delightful and no one seems to be ambitious. Odysseus breaks away from that temptation only to fall into the clutches of the Cyclops, Polyphemus, a son of Poseidon. He nearly loses his life but in the end he blinds Polyphemus, thus incurring Poseidon's wrath.

Onward Odysseus wanders, to the land of the Lastrygonians, and then to Circe's island, Aeaea, where Circe transforms his men into grunting swine. Odysseus once again escapes and, at Circe's suggestion, travels to Hell in order to discover the best way home. There he meets the dead Heroes, including Achilles, who tells him how terrible death really is. Returning to the world of the living, Odysseus avoids the Sirens, manages to sneak through the strait between Scylla and Charybdis, loses all his companions, and finally is rescued from the sea by Calypso at the very moment he is expiring.

The telling of this tale within a tale occupies four whole books of *The Odyssey*. By the end of his story, Nausicäa is more than half in love with Odysseus, and the king of the Phaeacians would like to keep this famous, fascinating man in his kingdom, as his son-in-law. But that is impossible; Athene won't have it. And so the Phaeacians carry Odysseus home to Ithaca after bestowing on him princely gifts.

He has arrived home, but he is not yet safe. If the suitors who are harassing Penelope were to find him, alone and unarmed, they would slay him in an instant. How "wily Odysseus" makes contact with Telemachus, how father and son plan together their revenge on the suitors, and how Odysseus finally triumphs over his enemies, is the real story of *The Odyssey*, and a superb story it is. It is made even more astonishing as we realize, slowly but surely, that the plan is really Penelope's (although she refuses to accept credit for it). His lovely, faithful wife is therefore the equal of her husband, the famous "Man of Many Devices," and deserves as much fame as he does.

Odysseus, who has spent much of the past nine years in the arms of one goddess or another, still has to make his peace with his wife. Athene is fond of him, chastely of course; he is her favorite mortal. Fortunately, the love of this goddess is without jealousy, the proof of which is made clear by the gift Athene gives Odysseus after he has slain all the suitors and taken his wife into his arms.

What do you do when you have been away from home for twenty years (ten in the siege of Troy, ten in the subsequent wanderings)? Do you spend the first night making love? Or sharing the stories of your troubles? Odysseus of course wants both, as he always does. He asks Athene for help and she, smiling at him as *she* always does, extends the night so there is time for both. Such a night there never was before, and perhaps never after.

*The Odyssey* is an adventure story of almost unbearable excitement, but it is also—as countless other poets, as well as ordinary readers, recognize—a profoundly true portrayal of human beings and the relations among them. A mother and a son just growing into manhood, a father learning how much he needs the help of his son; that father and *his* old father, whom he also needs; a man and wife— these human ties are probed with an intensity seldom equaled in the two and a half millennia since the poem was composed. In the end, a wonderful family—father, mother, and their beloved son—emerges from the apparent wreckage of their lives. Homer also understands that in the most difficult human enterprises a mortal has to pass through Hell, and Odysseus does that, too, seeking among the dead for the secrets of life among the living. Meanwhile, on Mount Olympus, the immortal gods recline on golden benches, drink from golden cups, and smile and sometimes weep at the vanity and ambition of those creatures down below, with their loves and hates and desires and fears. And their mortality.

Before leaving *The Iliad* and *The Odyssey*, I want to say a word about translations. There are many, and some are better than others.

I have read at least four different translations and skipped through a fifth—*Pope's Iliad*, as it was called as though he had written it himself. Despite the praise that famous version received when it was published in the eighteenth century I believe it is unreadable today. The versions of the two poems published in the Loeb Classical Library, by A.T. Murray, seem to me even worse, although these were *The Iliad* and *The Odyssey* my father knew and loved and on the basis of which he wrote his superb commentaries in *The Noble Voice*. Translations of both epics by Richmond Lattimore are said to be closer to the Greek than most others but perhaps as a result they are not easy to read. A more passionate version of *The Iliad* by Robert Fitzgerald seemed preferable when it appeared thirty years ago. But none of those, in my opinion, can be compared with the translations of both poems by Robert Fagles that were published at the end of the last century. His *Iliad* is powerful, almost overwhelming, his *Odyssey* utterly charming, and I recommend them to anyone who wishes to read—or reread—Homer's two great epics. I can't imagine any reader not being transported by Fagles into Homer's magical world.

## HESIOD
### fl. 700–650 BCE ?
*The Homeric Hymns*

Very little is known about Hesiod. He probably lived from about 700 BCE to about 650, which would make him perhaps half a century younger than Homer. He wrote a "Theogony"—that is, an account of the history of the gods, starting with Chaos and Night and coming down to the present day (his, not ours). Not all of it survives and what does is rather confusing. The better-known "Works and Days" also survives in lengthier fragments. It contains some good advice about both farming and living, but perhaps not enough to warrant finding and reading it.

"The Homeric Hymns," which may or may not have been written by Hesiod, are well worth the trouble—at least the four that survive more or less intact. One is the famous story of Demeter (or Ceres), the goddess of agriculture, whose daughter Persephone is abducted by Hades (Pluto), God of the underworld. Her mother, in despair, travels the world in search of her, and when she discovers her whereabouts she asks Pluto to let her daughter come back to the light. Pluto, the third brother of Zeus (Poseidon is the second), is a great god and doesn't have to release her, but he relents on condition that Persephone spend one half of the year with him beneath the surface of the Earth, the other half with her mother above it. Demeter must accept this, which explains the origin of the seasons.

Other "Hymns," more or less intact, are addressed to Apollo and Hermes. They tell delicious tales of these gods that were retold by Greek and Roman poets many times in subsequent centuries.

The "Hymn to Aphrodite" is a fine story and is sexy in a way Homer never was. Aphrodite, the goddess of love, has tricked many male gods into falling for mortal women, and Zeus, to punish her, causes her to fall in love with a mortal man. His name is Anchises and he is very handsome; he is also a son of Dardanus, the founder of Troy. At the time Aphrodite falls in love with him, Anchises is herding his father's cattle high on Mt. Ida.

When Aphrodite feels the pangs of love that Zeus has instilled in her heart she flies to Cyprus, to Paphos, where her sweet-smelling temple is located. She enters, closing the glittering doors, and the Graces bathe her with the heavenly oil that blooms upon the bodies of the eternal gods. Then Aphrodite dresses in all her rich clothes, decks herself with gold, and flies to Mt. Ida, accompanied by wild creatures, wolves and lions and bears and leopards, male and female, that she enchants with desire so that they mate, two and two, around the house where Anchises lives and where he is strolling, playing his lyre.

The goddess approaches and stands before him, looking for all the world like a pure maiden, averting her eyes as a mortal girl would do. Anchises, seeing her rich garments that shimmer like the moon over her tender breasts and the rich jewels that sparkle on her wrists and around her lovely neck, is seized with desire. He thinks she must be a blessed goddess, and so kneels and addresses her with respect and awe. But Aphrodite answers that she is no goddess. "I am just a mortal girl," she declares, "and I was playing with the other maidens around the temple of Artemis when the Slayer of Argus took me up and carried me here, saying I should become the wife of Anchises and that I would bear him goodly children. I beseech you by Zeus and by your noble parents," she continues, "take me now, stainless and unproved in love as I am, and show me to your father and mother and to your brothers. And send a message to my parents and they will send you gold and other splendid gifts, which shall be my marriage portion."

Hearing this declaration, Anchises is even more overcome by love and he swears: "If Hermes has brought you here to me to be my wedded wife then neither god nor mortal man shall restrain me until I have lain with you in love right now. Willingly will I go down into Hades, O lady, beautiful as the goddesses, once I have gone up to your bed!"

Whereupon he takes her by the hand. Aphrodite, with face turned away and downcast eyes, moves to the couch, whereon are spread skins of bears and lions Anchises has killed on the mountain. He first takes off all her beautiful jewelry, then loosens her girdle and strips off her bright garments, folds them carefully, and lays them down on a silver-studded chair that stands nearby. "And then by the will of the Gods and destiny he lies with her," says Hesiod, "a mortal man with an immortal Goddess, not clearly knowing what he does."

In the evening, Aphrodite rises and clothes herself again and stands by the couch. Her head reaches to the roof-tree and a radiance shines within the room. Arousing Anchises, she says to him: "Up, son of Dardanus—and tell me whether I look as I did when you first saw me!"

Anchises cannot look at her. Trembling, he speaks: "As soon as I saw you, Goddess, I knew you were divine but you did not tell me the truth. I beseech you now, have pity on me, for he who lies with a deathless Goddess is no whole man after."

Aphrodite does take pity on him, saying he should fear no harm from her or any of the Gods for he is dear to her and to them. And she tells him she will bear a son that she will care for until he is five years old, when she will bring the boy to Anchises, who must say that his mother was one of the Nymphs that live on the mountain. "But if you foolishly boast that you lay with Aphrodite of the rich crown," she warns him, "Zeus will strike you in his anger. Take heed! And name me not!"

The boy's name is Aeneas. He is fated to reign among the Trojans and their children and children's children, time without end. However, years later, Anchises is playing at a game with some other men and, having drunk too much, boasts that he once lay with the Goddess of Love. Of course they don't believe him; nevertheless, Zeus strikes him blind.

# AESCHYLUS
### 523?–456 BCE
### *The Oresteia*

Little is known about Aeschylus. An Athenian, he was the son of Euphorion: he had a son named Euphorion, who also became a dramatist. Aeschylus was born at some time during the last quarter of the sixth century BCE, but the traditional date of 525 or 524 may be too early. Perhaps he was born in 513 or 512, which would have made him about twenty-two when he fought in the victory over the invading Persians on the plain of Marathon (490 BCE). He may also have fought a second time at Plataea when the Persians invaded again and were defeated a second time (480).

Aeschylus won his first drama prize in 484 when he was probably not yet thirty, and he continued to win, often in competition against other dramatists, until the end of his life. (Sophocles sometimes beat him but Euripides never did.) The death of Aeschylus occurred in 456 or 455 BCE. In Sicily, the rich western colonial empire of Greece, a monument was set up by his Sicilian hosts. They were not democrats like the Athenians, but tyrants, and the monument glorified his military service but made no mention of his plays. The titles of some eighty plays are known and fragments of a fairly large number survive. But only seven plays of Aeschylus have come down to us complete.

Drama was probably invented by the Athenians when Aeschylus was a boy. The legendary Thespis, who was honored as the inventor of tragedy, is said to have produced the first true plays shortly before 500 BCE. Those first plays were relatively primitive dramas; they had evolved only slightly from the poetic rituals that had been celebrated in Greek cities throughout the sixth century. Usually they consisted of exchanges on religious themes between a masked actor—often the poet himself representing a god—and a chorus that danced as well as sang. Aeschylus is said to have introduced the device of a second actor, which was an immense change. Henceforth the action of the drama was played out between individual (masked) actors, while the role of the chorus became more and more that of a commentator on the action. Aeschylus may also have been the first to address political issues instead of, or in addition to, religious themes. But of this we actually know very little. What we have is seven stunning plays, which are extraordinarily different from one another.

The Athenian playwright who desired to compete in the annual dramatic competitions in honor of the god Dionysus was usually required to present four plays, not just one, for the judgment of the audience, which consisted of all the male citizens of Athens. Three of those could deal with a single story, often drawn from a body of religious writings centering on the *Iliad* and *Odyssey* of Homer, or could treat separate mythical occurrences. The fourth, a satyr play or farce, provided comic (i.e., Dionysian) relief. Only one trilogy on a single theme survives: the *Oresteia* (story of Orestes). It was produced in 458 and won first prize in the competition that year. The satyr play that must have followed the trilogy is lost.

The *Oresteia* of Aeschylus is based on one of the most famous, bloody, and terrible Greek myths, the story of the House of Atreus. Many surviving Greek plays and even a few Roman dramatic works (as well as some modern plays, by Eugene O'Neill, for example) were written about this myth. The story cannot be told quickly, but it's necessary to know something about it before reading the trilogy, as there are many oblique and glancing references to various aspects of the myth that are not dealt with explicitly.

Agamemnon is the king of Mycenae when Helen, his brother Menelaus's wife, is seduced by Paris, prince of Troy, who takes her home to his city. After years of ineffectual raids against the Trojans, Agamemnon gathers a large army to help Menelaus retrieve his bride.

A flotilla of ships sails to Aulis, but the winds die and the army chafes under the enforced delay. A seer tells Agamemnon the expedition can proceed only if he will sacrifice his daughter, Iphigenia. By a trick he succeeds in getting his wife, Clytemnestra, to bring their child to him at Aulis. There he kills her. The wind springs up, and the army sails on to Troy and finally conquers it. Agamemnon returns to his kingdom to find his wife living with his cousin, Aegisthus. The guilty lovers murder Agamemnon in his bath. This is the subject of the first part of the trilogy.

Agamemnon and Clytemnestra had three other children, notably a son, Orestes, and a daughter, Electra. Orestes returns home from his travels to find his father dead and his mother ruling his kingdom with her paramour. With the help of Electra, Orestes murders his mother in revenge. This is the subject of the second part of the trilogy.

At the end of the second part (*The Libation Bearers*), Orestes flees the stage pursued by Furies who will avenge the death of his mother. Most of the action of the third play of the trilogy, *Eumenides*, consists of a trial on the hill called the Areopagus, in Athens. Orestes is charged by the Furies with murder most foul; he is defended by the god Apollo, on the grounds that the murder of a father is more serious than that of a mother. The jury of Athenian elders—the Chorus in the play—is evenly divided, and Athene appears in all her splendor and casts the deciding vote for acquittal. Feuds must end, she declares, and all must be forgiven. The Furies are changed from hideous hags to gentle, beneficent Eumenides who inhabit the world underground and are propitiated by a promise of respect and honor from the Athenians forever.

Aeschylus's audience would have known the story well—as well as (or even better than) a modern audience would know a familiar story from the Bible. For them there would be no suspense, in the ordinary sense, as they would be aware in advance that Clytemnestra was going to kill her husband on his return from the conquest of Troy and that their son in turn would kill his mother and then seek justification and, ultimately, forgiveness before a court of gods and men. But there was suspense of a sort, as the audience would not know how Aeschylus was going to treat the familiar myth, how he would use it to comment both directly and indirectly on current events, and what conclusions he would draw from it about human life and the relation between humans and their gods.

Aeschylus's conclusion—that a blood feud, particularly within a royal family, cannot be allowed to proceed indefinitely and that society, in order to sustain itself, must develop institutions that can control the anger and hatred of individuals—is of course important. If the *Oresteia* did no more than to present this crucial political idea at such an early date, it would deserve much of its fame. But it does a great deal more than that. It is not only a political treatise in dramatic form, but also a lyric tragedy. As such, in the grandeur of its conception, it is almost unique.

This is particularly true of *Agamemnon*, the first and by far the longest of the three parts of the trilogy. The play has three main characters: Agamemnon, the returning hero; Clytemnestra, who waits with implacable hatred in her heart to kill him when he reenters his home; and the girl Agamemnon brings back with him as a spoil of victory, the princess-prophetess Cassandra, who has given her name to the deepest kind of pessimism about the future in which she sees her own death with awful clarity. But despite the majesty of these masked figures, it is perhaps the Chorus of Old Men of Argos that will endure longest in the minds of readers.

The choral songs in *Agamemnon* are beautiful and moving poems. The Chorus in its odes obeys no common limitations of space or time. Seeming to wander from subject to subject but actually following trains of thought that are inevitable, the Chorus "remembers" the departure of the army under Agamemnon many years before, the brutal murder of Iphigenia in order to placate the impatient troops gathered at Aulis, the seduction of Helen by Paris and the devastation this brings down on Paris's city, the conquest of Troy and the slaughter of its men and enslavement of its women and children, the overweening pride of the conquerors as they run riot through the burning city and their subsequent punishment by the deeply offended immortal gods, and the awful consequences, still to come, of all these events. The Chorus sings of the future and the past, of the distant and the near, and it says things about men and war, about justice and pride, about love and honor, about hatred and shame that for their profundity are hardly surpassed in all of literature.

The original Greek verse of the entire *Oresteia* is antique and difficult, and perhaps no translator is capable of perfectly understanding, to say nothing of conveying, every allusion and meaning. But the reader who will take the trouble to read slowly, carefully, and thoughtfully—and more than once, for this three-part play richly rewards multiple readings—will come to realize that Aeschylus, especially in *Agamemnon*, creates a tragic intensity that has been seldom achieved since.

# SOPHOCLES
### 496?–406 BCE
*Antigone*
*Oedipus Rex*
*Oedipus at Colonus*
*Ajax*
*Philoctetes*

The life of Sophocles epitomized perfection. He won every prize, gained every honor. As a youngster he was the favorite of his teachers because of his exceptional brilliance and personal beauty. He won first prize with the first set of plays he produced. He was president of the imperial treasury and was elected general to serve with Pericles in one of Athens's wars. He was several times an ambassador and managed the city's affairs after the defeat in Sicily, late in the Peloponnesian War. He was the friend and confidant of every Athenian leader from Pericles on. He was also the leader of the cultural life of his city. Best of all, he was born about 495 BCE, just as Athens was emerging from the relative darkness of the sixth century into its short-lived but immortal splendor. He died in 406, just before the final defeat by Sparta, which ended that great age. It can almost be said that Sophocles *was* fifth-century Athens: he was conterminous with it and created more of it than any other man.

In this unbroken string of successes were dramatic moments. A notable one occurred at the very end of his life. He was almost ninety years old when his son sued for control of his father's financial affairs, on the grounds that the old man had become incompetent. Sophocles appeared before the judges with a manuscript in his hands. It was *Oedipus at Colonus*, his last play; he begged the court's leave to read from it. His voice was weak but the words of the superb choral song were rich, strong, and beautiful. His competency was confirmed and the judges chastised his son.

Sophocles wrote a number of plays dealing with the myth of Oedipus, which must have retained a fascination for him throughout his life. Here is the basic story: Laius, King of Thebes and husband of Jocasta, is told by an oracle that their son, Oedipus, will grow up to kill him. In his superstitious fear he takes the boy from his mother and nurses and gives him to a faithful shepherd with instructions to expose him to the elements. The herdsman, his heart touched by the baby, cannot kill the child and gives him to a certain Corinthian, who rears him as his own son. However, during a drunken brawl, a man tells Oedipus he is not his (supposed) father's son, and Oedipus sets out to search through the world for his real father. At "a place where three roads meet," in the lonely mountains between Thebes and Delphi, he is ordered by a noble in a chariot to step aside at a narrow place in the road. Oedipus, in the impatient fury that often overtakes him and is so characteristic, kills the man in the chariot and soon goes on to Thebes. There he learns the king has recently been killed by robbers and that a new husband is being sought for the queen. The oracle has said she should marry a man who can solve the riddle of the Sphinx, which Oedipus has no trouble doing. He marries the queen and rules for many years over Thebes, bringing the city great prosperity. He and his wife have four children, two sons and two daughters, one of whom is Antigone.

Then, in the glory of his middle age when he has achieved all that a man can achieve and looks forward to an old age filled with peace and honors, a terrible plague descends on his city. Oedipus, concerned as always for his people, sends to Delphi for advice from the oracle. The message comes back: there is a frightful pollution within the city that must be removed. With his customary energy the king sets about to discover it. He questions, interviews, threatens those who won't answer his questions. Slowly the truth emerges: he himself is the pollution. Fulfilling the old prophecy, he has slain his father at the place where three roads meet and married his own mother Jocasta who, learning the truth, hangs herself. Oedipus tears out his eyes so he can no longer see her body swinging from a beam.

But the line of Thebes is not yet finally extinguished. The two sons of Oedipus dispute the kingship. One, Polyneices, leads an army against the city; the other, Eteocles, leads the defenders. In a battle before the city's gates both Eteocles and Polyneices are slain. Creon, aged brother of Jocasta, inheriting the city's rule, decrees that the patriot Eteocles shall receive a proper burial but that the body of the traitor Polyneices shall be left on the field to be devoured by dogs and vultures. Antigone refuses to heed the decree and buries her brother, whereupon Creon condemns her to death. So ends the line of King Laius.

*Antigone* is Sophocles' earliest surviving play. It deals with the end of the great myth, with the disobedience of Antigone and her insistence before the tyrant Creon, the uncle whom she once loved, that there is a higher law than that of man, a law that all must obey whether or not temporal rules permit it. Antigone is condemned for her refusal to obey Creon; she will be immured and sealed up in a cave, there to starve to death. Her last speech before she disappears into the cave is inexpressibly moving. She is the beloved of Haemon, Creon's son; they were to be married. Haemon pleads for her life, but his father is relentless; he has the mark of Oedipus upon him. Haemon therefore joins Antigone in the cave and dies with her. Creon learns too late what he has done—and what he should have done.

The critic George Steiner once told me that *Antigone* has been more often played on the stages of the world than any other play, ancient or modern. This judgment of the people cannot be denied. *Antigone* is the perfect tragedy, period. It defines tragedy. Read it first, even though it tells the end of the story.

*Oedipus Rex* is the most perfect Greek tragedy. Aristotle thought so and said so in the *Poetics*. Who are we to disagree?

The play was written during the middle of Sophocles' career, when he was at the height of his powers. Oedipus has sent to Delphi for advice about the plague and when the answer arrives he begins his investigation. Relentlessly, implacably, he approaches the truth. All see the truth before he does. He alone is blind to what has really happened. And all warn him not to go on seeking. But he can't stop, he won't be shunted aside on this or any other road. Finally he too knows everything and tears out his eyes. At the end of the play, a poor, broken, blind old man, he is led off the stage by his faithful daughters, who must share his exile.

The power of *Oedipus Rex* to hold the imagination and, in fact, freeze the blood is undiminished after more than twenty centuries. Or after numerous readings, which is perhaps the more astonishing. You know as well as did the Athenian audience—some play about the Oedipus myth was presented every two or three years—what will happen. But the inexorable fate, the ananke or "necessity," that slowly surrounds the king, a fate entirely of his own making although he doesn't know that, sends shivers down the back again and again.

Aristotle said the play was the most tragic of all because it most effectively served to rid the soul of the two emotions of pity and fear—emotions that stand, he said, in the way of self-knowledge and understanding. Perhaps that's still true. Certainly the penalty for Oedipus's failure to know and understand himself is very clear and very terrible.

*Oedipus at Colonus* was Sophocles' last play and, in a sense, the last play of Athens, for it was presented in the year of the final defeat by Sparta, after which Athens was never the same city.

Sophocles poured his soul into this play, his last creation. Old and blind, Oedipus arrives before Athens. Haughty as ever, he sends for the king to appear before him. The king sends messengers instead, who, upon hearing Oedipus's demands, are shocked. What, allow this vile old man, this pollution of his city and his people who is even more filthy in his soul than in his body, to enter the city? Surely the gods would punish the city for so doing. Oedipus waits, angrily, for King Theseus himself to appear. Finally he does, and in a great colloquy the old man teaches the young one some things about life and the real meaning of the divine. He has been singled out by the gods, the old man says, as a force both for good and for ill. Good and ill are inseparable but now, after so many years of suffering, the good is predominate, and the Athenians should take him in. Theseus is convinced. But Oedipus, struck by a sudden vision, is led off by his daughters. They return to tell of how a god came down and took their father away—or something of the kind occurred; it was hard for them to see, and they didn't understand it. The place, Theseus declares, shall be forever holy.

The place was Colonus, a suburb of Athens. Sophocles had lived there and knew it well. Once it had been beautiful, with its olive trees gray-green in the brilliant Mediterranean light. Now, in 406 BCE, as the play is being produced, Colonus is a wasteland. The Spartan armies have burned it to the ground, houses and olive trees and all. The beautiful choral lines describe another city in another world.

The story behind the play that Sophocles called *Ajax* must be known if the play, which is unlike any other surviving Greek tragedy, can be understood. After the death of Hector, which ends Homer's *Iliad*, Achilles proceeds to decimate the Trojan troops. But he himself is killed by Paris, the abductor of Helen, who shoots an arrow into his most vulnerable spot. The Achaeans mourn the death of their champion, and after a suitable time there is a great funeral. A pyre is raised higher than that of any man who ever died. After the body is burned, a vote is taken to decide who shall receive the greatest honor the Achaeans can give, the bestowal of Achilles' armor. Because he valiantly defended the ships when Hector in his last attack had set them aflame, Ajax assumes he will be honored by his peers. But Odysseus, by a trick, wins the election and gains the prize.

Grief-stricken and mortally insulted by this rebuff, Ajax goes mad. In the insane belief that he's killing Odysseus and all his followers, he instead attacks the cattle of the army, killing every beast. He awakens from his madness surrounded by the bleeding bodies of cows and pigs, and in his remorse he falls on his sword.

The play is a kind of trial, not of a question of fact—the facts are not disputed—but of a question of honor and reputation. Should the memory of Ajax be black or white; should he be honored despite his crime or expunged from men's minds because of it?

Sophocles' answer is curious. What Ajax has actually done, in saving the ships on the one hand and in destroying the food supply of the army on the other, balances out. If it is a question of choosing between the good Ajax did and the bad he did, no choice can be made. But that's not the question. The real question is whether Ajax was a hero. But what is a hero? He—or she—is a man or woman who is called by the gods to do great things. Good things or terrible things these may be, but they must be important and memorable and significant. Both of the things Ajax has done are great in this sense. It doesn't matter, therefore, whether you are for him or against him, whether you like him or loathe him. He has been chosen by the gods, for reasons you can't understand, and so he must be honored and loved with all the devotion due to the gods themselves.

This enigmatic doctrine also applies to and helps to explain Sophocles' feelings about Oedipus. It applies all the more to the hero of the next to last play he wrote, *Philoctetes*.

The story of *Philoctetes* is a strange tale that is not included in any other ancient work. He was known as the greatest Argive archer, having inherited the bow of Heracles from his father. He was drafted by Agamemnon for the expedition against Troy, but on the way he was bitten by a snake and left behind, deserted on an island. His wound won't heal and the smell of it is unbearable to his companions. However, a seer tells the Argives that without Philoctetes' magic bow they will never conquer the Trojans, so Odysseus and Diomedes return to the island.

The action of the play takes place on this lonely island, where the hero ekes out a meager existence with the terrible recurrent pain of his wound to remind him of his hatred of the men who used to be his friends. The deceit of Odysseus in obtaining the bow is brutal and cruel, but the play ends happily when Philoctetes relents and forgives his erstwhile friends and Odysseus, in a rare moment of sentimentality, gives him back his bow. Together the three depart for Troy once more, to end the war.

The idea of the indispensable man with the magic instrument— the bow—and the frightful wound inspired the critic Edmund Wilson's book, *The Wound and the Bow*. Wilson found Freudian psychological depths in the Sophoclean idea. The artist, Wilson said, is often a man like Philoctetes who possesses a gift of immense value but suffers from an incurable psychic wound, a neurosis that can only find relief in artistic creation. It's true that many great writers, painters, composers, and others have been men and women apart, living lives filled with suffering on lonely islands of their own making and finding their only happiness in their art. We must always invade their loneliness, Wilson said, and at the end they can obtain some kind of peace.

Philoctetes thus becomes the symbol of artists everywhere. The theory is credible, I think, all the more because it extends to Oedipus as well, and perhaps to Antigone—to the protagonists of how many other Sophoclean plays we cannot tell, since most of the rest of the one hundred and twenty or so he wrote are lost. Oedipus, too, has both a wound (his crimes, which are a pollution) and a bow (the divine blessing that will descend on the place of his death).

In these two plays, and perhaps in others, was Sophocles consciously suggesting something about art and even about himself? We can't tell, of course, and in the end it doesn't matter. The greatest works of art almost always have more in them than the artist meant to put there.

# EURIPIDES
## 484?–406 BCE
*Alcestis*
*Medea*
*Hippolytus*
*Bacchantes*
*The Trojan Women*
*Iphigenia Among the Taurians*

Euripides was an enigma to his contemporaries, and he remains an enigma today. Aristotle said he was "the most tragic of poets," which in the context was high praise indeed. Socrates never went to the theater unless a play of Euripides was being presented, and he would walk all the way to Piraeus to see it. But Aristophanes and the other comic poets never ceased to ridicule Euripides for his background (his mother was supposed to have been a greengrocer who sold inferior lettuces) and for his supposed lack of a sense of humor, and for this or some other reason he had difficulty winning prizes in the dramatic competitions. He presented plays for fourteen years before he ever won a prize, and he was often defeated by inferior playwrights in the years thereafter. Nevertheless, he acquired a great reputation while alive and an even greater one after his death. He was called "the philosopher of the stage," and more of his works survive than of any other classical dramatist because they were so often copied down by teachers and students. Altogether, as I say, he was and is an enigma. Many readers do not understand him to this day.

Euripides was born in Athens about 484 BCE and died in Macedonia in 406. Nineteen of his plays are extant, out of a total of perhaps eighty-five that he wrote. All are worth reading and seeing performed if you have a chance to do so, but some are better than others. Of special interest are the six plays listed above.

Of the plays that survive, *Alcestis* is the earliest, though it is not a particularly early play in the works of Euripides. Nevertheless, it seems less mature than some of the others—but more playful.

Early in the fifth century BCE, when tragedy was new, playwrights were required to present four plays on a single theme: three tragedies and a "satyr play" or farce. By the time Euripides was composing *Alcestis*, for the Great Athenaeia in 438, these requirements had been dropped, so *Alcestis* is probably a self-contained work. The custom at the time was for the playwright to choose a particular mythical subject or story and write a play about it that adhered more or less closely to the original theme. The basic events could not change, but many minor changes could be made; modifications of emphasis could add up to a substantial alteration of the story's meaning.

In this case, the myth was an old one to the effect that Admetus, an ancient king of Pherae, was informed by Apollo that he would have to die unless he could find someone to die for him. He asked his wife, Alcestis, to do so. She agreed, but at the last moment was saved from death by the intercession of the hero Herakles. A simple story, suggesting the early Greek notion of the responsibilities of a faithful wife, but Euripides made a very different thing out of it. He was fascinated by these questions: What kind of man would ask his wife to die for him? Wouldn't a husband ask someone else, his parents for example, instead? Why did Herakles save Alcestis, and how?

The long conversation in the play between Admetus and his parents is both funny and sad. They deserve him as a son, and he them as parents. The contrast with the nobility of Alcestis is stark. Herakles comes to the house while preparations are being made for her death, but Admetus tells Herakles nothing of this. He is torn between conflicting religious obligations: one to his wife, the other to his guest. He is a good man according to Greek cultural beliefs, which held that a guest was sacred because he might be sent by Zeus, king of the gods. Admetus is brokenhearted but feels he has no other choice.

Herakles, who is drunk, discovers what is happening and, because he loves both Admetus and Alcestis, he sets out for Hell to bring Alcestis back. He wrestles with Death and rescues the wife of his friend, and all ends happily. Except that it doesn't.

He returns with a woman who is wearing a veil that covers her face. Is she Alcestis—or is she another young woman who can take her place in Admetus's bed and as the mother of their children? Herakles refuses to say who she is. He forces Admetus to accept her—which he does, although he's not certain. But Admetus has sworn an oath that he will never take another wife, and when he reaches for the veil he is astonished—but Euripides leaves us to guess. The woman turns her back on the audience, and we are left to ponder the end of the story.

I recommend the translation by William Arrowsmith. His interpretation is brilliant, but I'm not going to tell you what it is. Read the play, which is powerful despite its apparent slightness.

*Medea* and *Hippolytus* also present theses about women, although different ones. (Euripides was fascinated by women, which partly explains why the comic poets mocked him.) Medea has arrived in Athens as the wife of Jason, who led his Argonauts into the wilds of Thrace and there found and wooed her. She fell in love with him and helped him escape from her savage father, killing the latter in order to save her lover. But now, as the play begins, Jason has received an offer he can't refuse. The king has promised that if Jason frees himself from his marriage to Medea he can marry his daughter and become the heir of the kingdom.

Jason tells Medea of the king's promise and is astonished that she doesn't view it as a great opportunity for the family, as he does. A divorce will be easy and painless, he explains, because Medea, as a foreigner, is not a citizen. Nevertheless she needn't worry, because he will always care for her and the children.

He has reckoned without her fury. Medea is a sorceress—this is always a danger when you bring back a woman from a wild country, says Jason. Apparently mollified, she presents him with a gift for the prospective bride. It is a lovely cloak, but when the princess dons it she dies a horrible death. Jason returns home in a fury. "Look, you've spoiled everything!" he shouts.

"You do not know the half of it," Medea says. She stands on the balcony of their house with Jason in the street below. "I have a gift for you, too," she says, and shows him the bodies of their children, whom she has slain. Maddened, Jason seeks to destroy her, but she escapes in a chariot drawn by dragons. Jason is left to mourn the loss of his kingdom, his beautiful new bride, and his young sons.

The pusillanimity of Jason and the magnanimity of Medea, despite her savagery, present a remarkable contrast. The civilized man is the villain of this piece despite the appearances; equally villainous are the laws of Athens, which view foreigners as having no rights. This is a dark and disturbing play.

Hippolytus is the son of Theseus, who is married to Phaedra, the young man's stepmother. (When Racine rewrote this play in the seventeenth century, he changed the name from *Hippolytus* to *Phèdre*.) Hippolytus is obsessively chaste. He has sacrificed his sexuality to the goddess Artemis and is therefore shocked when he learns his stepmother has fallen in love with him. Phaedra, devastated when she realizes she has been refused, commits suicide, leaving a note accusing Hippolytus of having seduced her. Hippolytus flees his father's revenge in vain, neither understanding the other until it is too late. Theseus kills the boy, who lives long enough to die in his father's arms after Artemis has explained everything. Theseus survives, but he has lost both his wife and his son.

The play is about chastity and the dangers of tempting and then refusing the advances of the great and powerful. (The Biblical Joseph, tempted by Potiphar's wife, manages to survive in a similar situation.) Hippolytus is caught in a net of fate, but Euripides doesn't leave the audience in any doubt that he has placed himself there. His fervent devotion to Artemis is at the expense of what should be an equal devotion to another goddess, Aphrodite. Humans should live moderately and avoid excess, even excess of virtue.

*Bacchantes* is the play in which Euripides surprised his audience and showed them he was a devout believer after all, despite his mockery of the gods. Pentheus, king of Thebes, is a rationalist, as Euripides was thought to be. A person claiming to be the god Dionysus comes to his city demanding homage. "Nonsense," says Pentheus. "We can't admit your frenzies, your abandoned singing and dancing, your illegal celebrations here. This is a law-abiding town!" Dionysus departs. His revenge is terrible. A messenger comes to Pentheus: Bacchantes, or followers of Dionysus, are engaging in an orgy in a nearby forest and—horror of horrors—his mother is among them. In high rationalist dudgeon, the king rushes off to put a stop to this, but the Bacchantes, led by his mother, attack him and tear him to pieces. They eat the shreds of his body—his mother among them. Only when he is dead and their terrifying passion is spent do the celebrants realize what they have done—his mother among them.

A strange play, this. Rationalists have often wondered whether Euripides really wrote it. But certainly he did write it: It is pure Euripides. Dionysus is only the symbol, he is saying to us, of something that is in us, all of us, that we mustn't deny. To deny the wild, orgiastic element in our being, to give it no outlet, to dam it up, is to create a force so great it will destroy men and cities. Better—more rational because more human—to allow Dionysus his due.

*The Trojan Women* is Euripides' great anti-war statement. Written toward the end of the glorious fifth century, when Athens was falling to pieces, it reminds us about war's consequences. The Achaeans have won and sacked Troy. Now the captured Trojan women are lined up and counted off prior to being placed on board the ships, where they will begin their slave existence. Andromache, widow of Hector, holds her little boy in her arms. She and her mother-in-law, Hecuba, the widow of King Priam, bewail their fate.

A messenger arrives to inform Andromache that the Greeks have decreed her son must be killed, thrown from the battlements—whether in punishment or in fear of what he may become when he grows up is not made clear. After a heartbreaking farewell, the boy is snatched from his mother's arms.

Menelaus next appears, ordering his servants to go to the tent where Helen, herself one of the captives, is hiding. She is dragged forth, in all her astonishing beauty, so that he may decide whether he will kill her now or later. Hecuba urges him to kill her immediately but, already beginning to feel the strength of "the ancient flame," he spares her and allows her to speak for herself. She argues that she has really done well instead of ill and, besides, the whole thing was not at all her fault. Hecuba is infuriated but can do nothing against such beauty and willfulness.

Hecuba has all the more reason to weep as soldiers appear on the battlements of her city and set it on fire. The play ends with the citadel crashing down in ruins and the line of enslaved women weeping as they move toward the ships.

Because of such scenes as these, the play is hard to stage. For the reader, however, this masterly playwright tightens the screws with each successive scene, each successive revelation: there is no limit to the hatred and fear the winners feel toward the losers in this war, and the losers toward the winners. So it is with all wars, Euripides is telling us. War brings out the worst in us, and its glory is a cheat and a fraud. In war, pitiless, indomitable force is the only reality, for victor and vanquished alike. His message predates Simone Weil's by more than two millennia.

Iphigenia was the eldest daughter of Agamemnon. After Paris has taken Helen to Troy, Agamemnon and Menelaus together raise an army to get her back. They reach Aulis, a harbor on the eastern coast of Boeotia, but there, for weeks, the weather hinders their future progress. Agamemnon, his army melting away before his eyes, is at his wit's end. He asks the seer for advice. "If you will sacrifice your daughter to Artemis," the seer tells him, "the wind will change and you will be able to go on." Agamemnon struggles against his better nature but the worse wins out, and he tricks his wife Clytemnestra and his friend Achilles to get the girl, then kills her on the altar of the gods.

Except that unknown to him he doesn't kill her. She is snatched away by the gods, who can't accept this injustice, and spirited away to the land of the Taurians, a wild and savage tribe who live at the end of the world. There she becomes their priestess, her duty to sacrifice to the gods all Greeks who are captured and brought before her. Now, in one of Euripides' last plays, *Iphigenia among the Taurians*, a young man is brought before her, victim of a shipwreck. In a beautiful and moving recognition scene, she realizes he is her little brother, Orestes. She determines to try to save both him and herself.

She does save them both, but only with the help of Athene and only in circumstances made so absurd by Euripides that you know he doesn't mean it. Great goddesses don't appear in real life and rescue mariners from storms and enemy warships. For that matter, chariots drawn by dragons don't rescue women like Medea from their husbands and the law. As always, Euripides uses the myth on which his play is based to comment on the ordinary lives we all live. There is cruelty and bestiality in the world, and wishing it were not there, or counting on the gods to correct it, will not help us. We must face the humanity within us, fearlessly and frankly, and learn to live the best lives we can. That we will never do as long as we lie to ourselves and believe ourselves to be better than we are.

# ARISTOPHANES
## 450?–380? BCE
*Acharnians*
*Peace*
*Lysistrata*
*Clouds*
*Birds*
*Frogs*

Aristophanes was born circa 450 BCE—certainly, a very long time ago. Curiously, if he had been born in 350, only a century later, it would not have seemed such a long time ago. The reason is that during the century from 450 to 350 the so-called New Comedy was invented, and New Comedy is essentially what comedy is today. In New Comedy boy meets girl, boy loses girl, boy finds girl again, the ingénue is delectable but dumb, the boy is a scapegrace but highly forgivable, there are one or more rascally servants who turn out in the end to have hearts of gold, and the play ends with everybody looking foolish but happy on a stage full of lovers. These formulas were developed in the fourth century BCE, perfected by the Roman comic dramatists Plautus and Terence, further perfected by such "modern" dramatists as Shakespeare, Molière, Sheridan, and Shaw, and adapted in many hit comedies and, especially, present-day musicals.

Aristophanes was a practitioner—the greatest of all—of the so-called Old Comedy. This had a strong religious bent and made full use of a chorus that played an important role. The characters were often gods or demigods, like Dionysus or Herakles, and the dialogue and action were often extremely lascivious and utterly ridiculous. The plays of Aristophanes are deliciously funny if you like that sort of thing. Most people do.

The best way to introduce Aristophanes is to describe the absurd situations of some of his plays. *Acharnians*, his first play (he probably wrote about forty, but only eleven survive), follows a farmer, Dicaeopolis, who, sick and tired of the war that has been going on for years between Athens and Sparta, goes to Sparta to negotiate his own private peace treaty. The fact that such an action is impossible and would be considered treason in the real world only makes the point more strongly: war is folly. The play contains two ironic scenes—skits, we would call them—that take place in the marketplace of Athens, the Agora. In the first, a needy Megarian, impoverished by the war, enters with a bag over his back in which, he says, are two piglets. A buyer sticks his hand in the "poke" and finds indisputable evidence that the contents are two naked little girls, not two little pigs. The Megarian then admits that he's selling his daughters rather than have them starve to death at home. In the second skit a rich Boeotian wants to take back a really typical Athenian item from the fair and ends up buying an informer. The satire throughout the play is heavy but funny.

*Peace* was staged in 421 BCE, several months after both the Spartan and the Athenian leaders of the respective war parties had been killed in battle and shortly before the Peace of Nicias was signed, interrupting but not ending the Peloponnesian War. Peace is a lovely young girl, quite nude, who is immured in a cave. The action of the play involves various attempts to release her. Finally Peace emerges, triumphant in her beauty, and everybody celebrates. What a fine idea!

*Lysistrata* (411) also has a relevant background in the politics of the day. Athens has suffered devastating defeats. A revolt of the Athenian oligarchs has led to a new government that may or may not intend to sue for peace. The heroine, Lysistrata, leads a revolt of the women of Athens, who seize the Acropolis and undertake a sex strike that will not be ended until the men declare peace. The men of course endeavor to have sex with their women without having to pay the price of peace, but (in the play, at least) they fail. Another fine idea.

*Clouds* (circa 423) is a satirical attack on the Sophists, or professional intellectuals and teachers of the day. The hero, named Socrates, runs a Think Shop where young people are taught to win arguments in ridiculous ways. The real Socrates is said to have sat in the first row when the comedy was performed and laughed harder at it than anyone else, although some scholars believe this attack on him by Aristophanes—an unfair attack, they point out, because no one was more opposed to the Sophists than the real Socrates—did him no good when he was later tried and convicted for corrupting the Athenian youth.

Maybe the two best plays of Aristophanes are *Birds* (414) and *Frogs* (415). The birds in the comedy named after them have banded together to create a utopian community, Cloudcuckooland, where there is permanent peace and everyone loves one another. The play is funny yet bittersweet too, because—again—of the evident impossibility of such a good government ever actually existing on Earth. Aristophanes is thought by some critics to have been responding to Socrates' and Plato's ideas in this play: Cloudcuckooland is the comic version of the Platonic Republic. The play is a profound study of utopianism as well as being funny.

*Frogs* takes place in Hell. Dionysus, god of drama (as well as other things), has disguised himself as the hero Herakles and has set out to bring back to life his favorite tragedian, who is Euripides. When

Dionysus arrives in Hades he also meets Aeschylus, and a literary competition is arranged. Aeschylus wins, not Euripides, and so Dionysus returns with Aeschylus in tow, instead. The literary subtleties are brilliant but the play is intelligible to anyone whether he or she knows the works of Aeschylus and Euripides or not.

The combination in Aristophanes of broad farce and dirty jokes, profound satiric themes, and lovely choral songs may be unique in the history of drama.

# AESOP

—

*Fables*

Enough of all this literary seriousness, high or not. The Classical Greeks also had a lot of fun, in the theater and out.

All the evidence suggests that Aesop was not a real person. As early as five centuries before our era the name "Aesop" came to be given to all stories in which animals talked and acted like human beings. Thus it is actually redundant to refer to "Aesop's Fables." A fable is an Aesop, as it were, and an Aesop is a fable.

Let us retain the traditional usage. The question is why fables, and Aesop's fables in particular, are important as well as popular.

Actually, it's not easy to answer the question. It may help to remember the inveterate human habit of treating animals as though they were people. Farmers, pet owners, and other people who live in some sort of intimacy with animals talk to them all the time. Why? The animals don't answer back. What kind of conversation is it that is so completely one-sided and at the same time so satisfying?

Or *do* animals answer back? Every pet owner believes his or her pet not only understands but also responds. People who don't own pets think this is nonsense.

Conversations with animals are not always confined to repartee between one human and one animal. Often a single animal plays an important, though dumb, part in a conversation involving two or more persons. Husbands and wives can converse with one another through or via their pets.

Wife to dog: "Duke, the garbage has to be taken out. Help Daddy take out the garbage." Duke looks baffled.

Husband to Duke: "Let's take out the garbage, Duke." Duke jumps with joy. The garbage is taken out without the wife having to ask the husband to do it. Nor has she called him by his name nor he her by hers. Taking out the garbage is an unpleasant duty which by this round-about device has been made as pleasant as possible. If the wife had said, "George, take out the garbage," she would probably have started a fight.

The fables of Aesop—indeed, all fables—express home truths that in another guise would be hard to accept. Putting them in the form of a fable makes them palatable, even enjoyable, without detracting from their effectiveness. Take the fable of the Wolf and the Dog. The Wolf meets the Dog after a long separation. The Dog is sleek and fat, the Wolf skinny and hungry. The Dog explains that he has found an exceptional situation in which he receives regular meals, a warm place to sleep, and so forth. The Wolf could have it too. The Wolf says, "Let's go!" But as they trot side by side the Wolf notices a worn place in the fur of the Dog's neck. "What's that?" he asks.

"That's where my collar rubs," says the Dog, continuing to trot home.

But the Wolf has stopped in the road. "No thanks!" he says as he runs back to the forest.

The moral of this fable doesn't need to be made explicit. We all know how to apply it to our own lives. None of us is completely free. We all wear collars of one sort or another. Even the Wolf wears the "collar" of necessity. He has to seek his sustenance and sometimes fails to find it. He is almost always hungry. What is your "collar"? What is mine? As you think about this fable you may begin to ask the question in a way you never did before. An explicit discourse on freedom and necessity, about the kinds of deals we make with life— which are different for everybody and even different at various times in everybody's life—might have little effect or none. It would go in one ear and out the other. Distancing the story by putting it in the mouths of animals serves to bring it closer to home. Even more important, maybe, is that these home truths can be immediately perceived by children, who may need them the most.

All of Aesop's fables are like that one. All are wonderful. If there ever were any bad ones, they have long since fallen by the wayside.

# HERODOTUS
### 484?–425? BCE
### *The History*

Herodotus was born about four years after the battle of Salamis, in Halicarnasus in Asia Minor, around 484 BCE. This Greek colony had been subject to Persia for many years and remained so for half of Herodotus's life. The Persian tyranny made free life impossible, and the future historian prepared himself by wide reading of the "classic" literature of his time. In his *History* he shows familiarity not only with Homer but also with Hesiod, Sappho, Solon, Aesop, Simonides, Aeschylus, and Pindar.

More important were his incessant travels all over the world as he knew it, from Sicily in the west to the islands of the Aegean and to Susa in Persia, Babylon, and Colchis, as well as Scythia, Palestine, Gaza, and other places in Asia Minor. He traveled to Egypt and remained there for years, learning the language and discoursing with priests about the history and customs of their ancient land. Wherever he went he continued writing his *History*.

When he was about thirty, the tyrant of Halicarnassus was overthrown with the help of the Athenian navy and Herodotus returned to his home. But not to stay: After less than a year he went to Athens, where he was welcomed into the brilliant Periclean society. He gave readings of his *History* to enthusiastic audiences. Uncomfortable with the fact that he was not a citizen, he left Athens and joined a new colony Pericles had founded at Thurii in southern Italy. From that time forth we know nothing of him. He probably died around 425. We can guess that he never stopped writing until his death.

Herodotus was the first historian: no one before him had ever written a book that could be called a history. And few after him, writing history, have wanted or been able to ignore his work.

Herodotus didn't think of his book as what we might call a finished history. It was not a completely consistent or coherent account of its subject matter, nor did Herodotus really desire it to be that. He preferred to call what he had done "researches," and we may think of him as preparing the way for another, more formal historian, who would write the "true" history of his time. Such a history did not get written for two millennia after Herodotus. Such is the power of a great—even if defective—book!

His time was the first half of the fifth century BCE, the great age of Greece, before it ruined itself in the terrible waste of the Peloponnesian or Greek Civil War. Herodotus tells how Hellas forged a unity against the common enemy—the Persians, how it defeated the Persian army and navy (vastly larger and more powerful than anything the Greeks could pose against them) by adhering to a set of ideas that were radically different from those by which the Persians lived. It is a moving story that still deeply influences how we think about the ancient Greeks, and how we think about ourselves.

Let us take a moment to review the background of the events that Herodotus describes in the *History*. Even late in the seventh century BCE, Greece consisted of small settlements surrounding the north-eastern corner of the Mediterranean Sea, trading and fighting with one another and with neighbors of other races, but having very little conception of "Greekness." Around 600 BCE, Greece emerged as a coherent entity on the world stage, but it was still small and weak compared to the great Persian Empire, which stretched from Asia Minor all the way to India and was, compared to Greece, almost unimaginably rich and powerful.

But the Persians were ruled by a despot. They and their subject peoples were not free. The Hellenes were free, and each Greek thought himself to be the equal of all others. So said Herodotus, ignoring the large numbers of slaves who did most of the work.

The Greek settlements along the Ionian coast of the Mediterranean—in what is today Syria, Lebanon, and Israel—began to irritate the Persians. The emperor decided to punish and control them. He sent expeditions, small at first then larger, but—to the dismay of everyone on the Persian side—these Greeks did not fall down and beg for mercy, as subject peoples were supposed to do. Instead they fought. And often won.

So the Great King (as the Greeks called him, using the word for king that in Greek meant "tyrant") sent a larger force, an army that landed on the plain of Marathon, twenty-six miles across the mountains from Athens. A joint Spartan and Athenian army under Miltiades the Spartan attacked in September 490 and routed the Persians, killing 6,400 with a loss of only 192 men. It is one of the most famous battles ever fought.

Darius, the Persian emperor, died and was succeeded by Xerxes who, infuriated by the defeats, determined to send an army and navy to Greece that no force on Earth could resist. Herodotus tells of the gathering of the soldiers and sailors in the early spring of 480, of the long days it took for the troops to march past certain points, of the thousands of camp followers and others who accompanied the immense horde as it slowly advanced across Asia Minor to the Bosporus, the narrow strip of water that divides (not far from the site of modern Istanbul) Asia from Europe.

Here bridges were constructed for the troops to cross. A storm rose and broke the bridges. Xerxes grew angry and ordered the sea to be whipped. Hundreds of Persians, armed with whips, strode to the shore and lashed out at the waves. Herodotus thought the gods were offended by this act of hubris and decided then and there to punish Xerxes.

New bridges were built. The army crossed the straits and marched on. The Greeks met them at Plataea and defeated them again. The Persian navy, the most redoubtable sea force up to that time, was trapped by Themistocles the Athenian on a lee shore in the Bay of Salamis, just a few miles from Athens. Themistocles sank many of the Persian ships and captured the others. Persia retreated and did not try again to interfere in Greek affairs for a century.

This utterly surprising victory by Greeks—who fought freely, Herodotus said, and not out of necessity (in battle the Persian captains whipped their men into action, as they had whipped the sea)—initiated one of the most creative and innovative half-centuries in the history of Western man: the period from about 480

BCE until the beginning of the Peloponnesian War in 430. Athens became the "school of Hellas," as Pericles would call it. Aeschylus, Sophocles, and Euripides invented and refined the art of the drama; Phidias and Myron carved sculptures that come down to us (for the most part in Roman copies) as among the highest achievements of art; and the Athenians, united by passion and an idea, built the Acropolis and its great shining monument to Athena, the Parthenon. Equally important achievements occurred in the other arts, in mathematics and science, in language and in philosophy. Perhaps there has never been a time quite like it.

The sense of that time and Athenian freedom breathes in Herodotus's book. It is full of wonderful, curious stories, many of which he knows are probably not entirely true—but, as he says, it would be a shame not to tell them, they are so interesting. Equally, it would be a shame not to read the *History*, it is so interesting.

*Nota bene:* Recently a spate of so-called historical films about the classical age of Greece have appeared. They are a sorry lot, which would not be important except that many young people, for example my younger grandson, believe after seeing them that they know everything about Greece in the old days and don't have to read Homer and Herodotus and Thucydides, and so forth. All I can say to them and to you if you agree with them is that you are missing something wonderful.

# THUCYDIDES
## 460?–404? BCE
### *History of the Peloponnesian War*

Thucydides, an Athenian, was born around 460 BCE. He was old enough, as he writes in his history, to understand the importance of the Peloponnesian War when it began in 431 and to foretell that it would probably be a long war. He was of Thracian descent on his father's side, and he had property in Thrace including mining rights in its gold mines.

Thucydides was in Athens during the great plague of 430–29 BCE and was himself infected. In 424, he was elected a general for a year and was given command of a fleet. But, failing to prevent the capture by the Spartan general Brasidas of an important city, he was recalled, tried, and condemned to exile from Athens. He did not return to his native city until the war was over, in 404, and he probably died very soon thereafter, for his *History of the Peloponnesian War* is unfinished. The narrative, in fact, does not continue beyond the year 413. The last surviving book apparently consists of notes for a continuation of the narrative that Thucydides didn't have time to complete.

The sculpture collection of the Vatican contains many famous works from antiquity, but perhaps none is more impressive than the portrait bust of Pericles the Athenian. Pericles ruled Athens as "first among equals"—that is, more or less by the common consent of his peers—during the third quarter of the fifth century BCE. We have the impression, both from the bust with its steady, firm gaze and from what Thucydides says about him, that Pericles was the leader of Athens because he was the most intelligent and capable man in the city. Extraordinary and fortunate city to choose its best man for its ruler!

We meet Pericles near the beginning of Thucydides' account of the travails and tragedy of Athens during the last decades of the fifth century. An Athenian armed force has obtained a certain victory, Thucydides tells us, but at the loss of a number of young lives. Pericles is asked to deliver the funeral oration and takes the opportunity, Thucydides says, to explain not only the immediate cause of the fighting but, more generally, what those young heroes had been fighting for—which, in short, was to explain what Athens was and meant. The speech is one of the half dozen most famous orations. Perhaps only Lincoln's Gettysburg Address is comparable to it.

In the speech, Pericles takes pains to say that Athens is democratic, in contrast to many of its neighbors, and to explain why democracy is the best of all the forms of government. There are perils in democracy, Pericles admits. Democratic citizens do not always do what they are told to do. But that is also democracy's strength. Finally, he says, Athens is the "school of Hellas"—the example that all the rest of Greece should follow and would follow, he suggests, if it were not impeded by tyrants.

The speech is moving to this day, especially when one contemplates the tragic fall that Athens suffered only a few years after the speech was given on that bright day at the outset of the Peloponnesian War.

This celebrated conflict was a civil war between Athens and its followers—the liberal, seagoing, commercial cities and states of Hellas—and Sparta and its followers—the oligarchic, conservative, agricultural, and land-bound cities and states. At war were not only all the men and cities of Greece, but also sets of ideas about how human beings should live and work together.

At first, Athens was successful, but as the war went on its fortunes worsened. The plague of 430–429 killed many in the city, including Pericles himself, and the city was left without a great leader. Furthermore, frightened by the apparent success of Sparta, Athens began to adopt Spartan methods, not only of fighting but also of ruling.

In the end, Athens had become a worse tyranny than its enemy. It was finally defeated and humiliated, after nearly thirty years of intermittent warfare. In its frustrated bitterness and fury, it turned on what was left of its own best self and, among others, executed the philosopher Socrates because he had never ceased to tell it that its only chance to win was to remain true to its ideals.

One of the supreme creations of the Athenians during the half century before Thucydides wrote his *History* was dramatic tragedy. There is no question that Thucydides was influenced by the tragic dramatists of his era and conceived of himself as writing a kind of tragic history or historical tragedy. Certainly "tragic" is the right word to describe the fall of Athens. At the beginning of the war, Athens was the best and the brightest of its time and its world. At war's end, owing to the city's own tragic flaw, it had become a broken shadow of its former self. How this happened, how the city took each downward step without understanding where it was headed, is described by Thucydides in cool, objective, nonjudgmental prose. You wonder how he, an Athenian, could exercise such restraint; you sometimes forget that he loved his country with all of his heart.

In short, he wrote one of the great histories, an inspiration and a model for other historians ever since. It continues to be read for its facts and its insights about the Greece of Thucydides' time. But it is not just a history of those times. Thucydides was the first historian to recognize that "war is primarily a matter of money." This and other cold observations on the life of mankind dot a narrative that is in itself rich and powerful. Underlying all is the book's profound understanding of the role of force in human life. Perhaps that is exemplified most memorably in the series of events that occupies the book's final part. The citizens of a certain island, Melos, one of Athens's allies, inform the Athenian leaders that they no longer desire to be followers of Athens; they have decided to be neutral. Impossible, says Athens; once an ally, always an ally. A dispute ensues, with Melian envoys voicing the very arguments, in favor of freedom and democracy, that the Athenians would once have used themselves. But these latter-day Athenians are unable to heed those arguments, and when they cannot win the dispute in words, they win it by force: They kill the Melian men, enslave the women and children, and, as Thucydides coolly remarks, "occupied the place themselves."

Only a short time afterwards, a large Athenian armed force is surrounded in the harbor at Syracuse, on the eastern coast of Sicily, by a combined Sicilian-Spartan army. The Athenians are defeated and captured, the soldiers put to work in the Syracusan silver mines, sweating and dying in the Sicilian summer at the bottom of deep holes in the ground. The Athenians present the Melian arguments to their captors, but their captors treat them like Melians in return. It is a hard lesson, and all the harder for never having been learned by those who have followed after.

General George C. Marshall, the U.S. chief of staff during World War II, was wont to say that every military leader should read Thucydides, that this little war between the two different halves of a small nation at the end of the fifth century BCE somehow prefigured all subsequent wars, especially all civil wars, and that there was much to be learned from it. Those were essentially military lessons. There is also a deeper lesson to be learned, about the human condition. Is it, after all, irremediable?

# chapter two

# After the Fall

The fourth century before the Christian era was very different from the fifth. Gone was the artistic glory of the fifth century, together with the glow of surprising military inventiveness and discovery in the natural world. Particularly in Athens, the self-elected capital of Hellas for five or six great—indeed unforgettable—decades, the mood was somber and dark. But despite their victory in the civil war that ended just before the turn of the century, Sparta was hardly better off than Athens. The war had sapped the strength and resources of both winner and loser. There wasn't much to look forward to for either in those sad and hopeless years.

Nevertheless, the fourth century had, because it made them, its own glories and successes. In philosophy, Plato and Aristotle achieved greatness of a different kind from that of Themistocles and Pericles. For all practical purposes democracy no longer existed. Athenian drama had fallen on hard times, religion had become secretive, and citizens looked at one another with fear and suspicion, and, despite the valiant (and ultimately self-defeating) efforts of Aristophanes and Euripides on their behalf, women were treated with the same old lack of honor and respect. In Hellas proper it was not a time to look back on with any pride or pleasure. Yet there was a new light blazing in the north, in Macedon, only recently thought of as backward and poor. And by the end of this new century the greatest and most famous of all Greeks had flamed through a world that had belonged to Persia and never would again.

His name was Alexander of Macedon. He was the third to bear a name that in after times would be borne by kings, popes, and emperors. His father, Philip, won the crown that he gave his son, and that his son wore with unexampled brilliance. Alexander was born in 356 BCE and died in 323, still a young man, but in those thirty-three short years he conquered the greatest empire ever seen until that time, defeating Persia, Egypt, and Babylon and the rest of the Near East, and threatening India, which escaped only because he died. His exploits were extraordinary in every sense of the word. If you want to know more about him, read Plutarch's *Life*, in which he is compared to Julius Caesar. Even that would not have satisfied Alexander—he thought there was only one man that ever lived who could rightfully be compared to him, and that was Achilles. When he came upon the supposed tomb of that great hero on the Troad, the beach below the ruins of Troy, Alexander wept because, he said, he regretted there was no poet as great as Homer to tell his own story.

Alexander wrote nothing, nor has his story ever been told as well as it should be. However, there were small triumphs in the era, and some works that deserve their fame. I have chosen five authors to represent the time: Hippocrates, Plato, Aristotle, Euclid, and Archimedes. Any century would be proud to possess five such names.

## HIPPOCRATES
### 460?–377? BCE
*Medical Treatises*

Hippocrates (fl. 400 BCE), "the father of medicine," a friend of Socrates and Plato, was the best physician of his time. He taught medicine as well as practiced it, and he may have written some of the works that were later ascribed to him by the ancients, but this is by no means certain. Instead, these treatises—"On Ancient Medicine," "On Airs, Waters, and Places," "On the Sacred Disease," and so forth—may have been written by anonymous physicians and teachers of the famous fourth-century BCE medical school of Cos and published as the works of Hippocrates, who for at least a thousand years thereafter was the greatest name in medicine. Whatever the truth of the matter, the works ascribed to Hippocrates are important. There are three things to learn from them.

They are full of medical lore—odd ideas and strange practices and treatments. For hemorrhoids, "transfix them with a needle and tie them with a very thick and large woolen thread." For dysentery, prescribe "a fourth part of a pound of cleaned beans, and twelve shoots of madder." For watery eyes, "take one drachm of ebony and nine oboli of burnt copper, rub them upon a whetstone, add three oboli of sapphron, triturate all these things till reduced to a fine powder, pour in an Attic hemina of sweet wine, and then place in the sun." "Persons disposed to jaundice are not very subject to flatu-lence." "Eunuchs do not take the gout, nor become bald." "Persons above forty years of age who are affected with frenzy do not readily recover." And so on.

Those are oddities. But not all the lore of the Hippocratic writings is odd. Much of it is based on sound observation and practical sense. It is evident, however, even to a nonphysician, that we have come a long way since the fourth century BCE. There is some satisfaction in that discovery. What if it were the other way around—if Hippocrates knew vastly more about medicine than we do?

He did know some things that are sometimes forgotten. He (or those anonymous physicians who may have published under his name) never ceases to emphasize the importance of knowing the past as well as the present of the patient, instead of just his disease—of knowing the whole person, that is, instead of that part of him that is affected by the condition concerning which the physician is a "specialist." Even a bad diet, Hippocrates says, can be good if one is accustomed to it, which is to say if one has learned to thrive on it. The circumstances of a patient's life must be known by a physician and will affect the treatment: whether the patient lives in a place where warm winds prevail, or cold ones do; whether the water of his city is brackish or bland. The good physician does not study and treat diseases, but diseased men, women, and children.

Above all, the good physician must strive to do good for his patient. If he cannot do good, then he must strive to do no harm.

This famous injunction, which is included in the Hippocratic Oath that all physicians take even today upon entering the medical profession, is never to be forgotten. Remembering it makes a man—be he physician or not—humble in the face of life.

Finally, the third great lesson of Hippocrates is suggested in this distinctive passage:

> The physician must be able to tell the antecedents, know the present, and foretell the future—must meditate these things and have two special objects in view with regard to diseases, namely, to do good or to do no harm. The art consists in three things—the disease, the patient, and the physician. The physician is the servant of the art, and the patient must combat the disease along with the physician.

The passage has often been commented upon. The great second-century physician Galen, in particular, was struck by two things in it that he considered eminently wise: the injunction not to do harm if the physician could not do good, and the observation that the physician is the servant of his art (or, as some Hippocratic manuscripts have it, the "servant of nature").

The ancients were of the opinion that of all the arts (we would call them professions), three and only three are "cooperative" —but these three arts are the most important and valuable. By cooperative they meant that the art cannot be practiced without the willing cooperation of someone or something else. In the case of agriculture, that something is nature itself; the good farmer does not fight against nature, he works with it to produce his crops. In teaching, it is the student or pupil who must strive to learn, who cannot be forcibly taught, and in whom the learning takes place. It is the learner who acts in learning; the teacher merely assists the process. Finally, in the case of medicine it is the patient who gets well, not the doctor, and the patient's cooperation in this endeavor is indispensable; he cannot be cured against his will or unless he contributes actively to the result; nor can he be cured by unnatural (in the sense of anti-natural) endeavors on the part of the physician or anyone else.

In the modern world we often forget this old wisdom, in all three professions. Modern scientific agriculture—or "agribiz," as it is called—is an offense against nature and its results are predictably bad, if not always disastrous. Many teachers think of themselves as playing the active role in "the learning process" and are surprised when unwilling pupils seem hard to teach. And modern medicine is in danger of becoming "healthbiz," with regimented cures and automated treatments, as like as not dialed up on a computer.

Computers are useful in medicine; Hippocrates would have welcomed them. But he would have warned of the dangers of overdependence on them or on any other instrument or tool. The maintenance of health and the recovery of health from illness are found in the joint efforts of two kinds of wisdom: that of the physician and that of the body itself. The body knows what it has to do and the physician, more than anything else, should not stand in the way.

# PLATO
428?–347 BCE
*The Republic*
*The Symposium*
*The Trial and Death of Socrates*

Plato was born in Athens about 428 BCE, the son of aristocratic parents who traced their lineage, on his father's side, to the god Poseidon, and on his mother's to the lawgiver Solon. Plato's early ambitions were political, but the last quarter of the fifth century in Athens was no time for an honest politician, so Plato instead founded a philosophical school, the Academy, which was in many respects the first university (besides philosophy, it taught and underwrote researches in all the sciences, law, and medicine). Plato's own favorite study was mathematics, and he was closely associated with all of the mathematical discoveries of the fourth century. He had one eventful, and finally dangerous, brush with practical politics. He journeyed twice to Sicily, the leading Greek colony, to try to educate its unruly rulers, but gave up when he realized how little rulers desire to be educated. As to his character and talents, perhaps it is sufficient to quote Aristotle, who declared him to be a man "whom it is blasphemy in the base even to praise." Plato lived to be about eighty years old. His Academy survived him by more than eight hundred years.

Plato wrote dialogues throughout his life. Most of them have as their main character Socrates, who was Plato's teacher. Socrates plays many roles in the dialogues of Plato, but he is always the center of the drama as well as being—we must assume—the presenter of Plato's own views. In his last dialogues (for example, the *Laws*), Plato discards Socrates and replaces him with an "Athenian Stranger" who is surely Plato himself. This protagonist is nowhere as interesting as Socrates, who enlivens the many dialogues in which he appears with his odd mannerisms and his unique way of discussing philosophy. In a sense, Socrates and Plato, although in fact two different men, are inseparable in our minds. Certainly each of them owes most of his fame to the other.

The *Republic*, the greatest as well as the longest of Plato's Socratic dialogues, cannot be dated accurately, but we can guess that Plato wrote it during his middle years. It retains the freshness and charm of his earliest writings but at the same time reveals a profundity of philosophical thought that is characteristic of his later works.

Like all of the Platonic dialogues, but especially the early ones, *Republic* is both a dramatic and a philosophical work. It is written in the form of an account by Socrates, Plato's teacher, of a long conversation that had occurred on the previous day, involving a number of different people of varying opinions, and also involving some very heated interchanges. Socrates had been the main speaker.

The subject of the dialogue is justice, the search for which had obsessed Socrates for years. What does justice mean? Can it be shown that justice is always a good and injustice always an evil, apart from any consideration of consequences? Socrates maintains that this can be done. The *Republic* is Plato's attempt to do it.

In the dialogue, Socrates first describes a conversation with Cephalus, an elderly rich man of Athens who has been Socrates' friend for many years. Like so many others, Cephalus does not care to strive to understand justice. The next interlocutor is Thrasymachus, the Athenian general, who is certain he already understands it:

justice is the interest of the strong. Might makes right, no bones about it. Socrates describes his spirited battle of wits with Thrasymachus, who retires from the fray disgruntled and unhappy.

Socrates is not happy either. He knows that making your opponent look like a fool isn't the best way to win an argument. Two young men, followers of Socrates, agree, and ask their master to take the time and make the effort to instruct them in the meaning of justice. I will do so, Socrates says, if you will help me, and the search begins.

It ranges far and digs deep. Plato has Socrates concede from the start that justice is a hard idea to understand in the life of a man—so hard he proposes to magnify it, as it were, and view it in the context of a state. A state is good, he finds—that is, just—when every member of it takes his rightful and proper place within it and performs his rightful and proper role. Those who are naturally laborers and merchants take those jobs, those who are naturally soldiers find themselves guarding the state, and the most competent and intelligent of all are rulers. When philosophers are kings, Socrates says to Glaucon and Adeimantus, and kings philosophers, then and then only will states be truly just. Once this conclusion is reached it is applied to individuals. The three types of citizens correspond to three parts of the soul, and only when a man is ruled by his intellectual part, with his appetitive and spirited parts playing their necessary but subservient roles, can he be said to be just.

The conversation, which occupied an entire day and the account of which fills three hundred pages, covers many subjects. Two of them are the system of education to be developed in the ideal state—the "republic" of the title—and the place of artistic productions, notably music and theater, in such a state. Socrates'—or Plato's—ideas about education are both radical and modern. Plato held, for example, that education should be the leading concern of the state, that it should be provided free to all, and among the "all" he included girls and women, maintaining that there should be no difference between their education and that of boys and men. He was the first serious thinker in human history to take this position and one of the very few to take it before modern times.

Regarding the place of art in a just society Plato was not nearly so modern; in fact he proposed, and seems to have believed, that works of imaginative artistry—poems, songs, plays, and so forth—should be banned altogether as being essentially subversive of the state's true health. Plato left a loophole in this severe position, and Aristotle took advantage of it in his *Poetics*. It is an interesting, if not a pleasant, theory nevertheless.

The English philosopher and mathematician Alfred North Whitehead once said that "the safest general characterization of the European philosophical tradition is that it consists of a series of footnotes to Plato." He could have said footnotes to the *Republic*, for almost all of Plato's ideas are at least touched upon in this dialogue. Plato puts these ideas in the mouth of Socrates, of course. The real Socrates, on the other hand, may have been the source, or at least the inspiration, of the dialogue's most potent images. No reader who has seriously read this greatest of philosophical books will ever forget the story of the Cave, the account of the Divided Line of knowledge, or Socrates' retelling of the Myth of Er, which closes the dialogue. These and other moments are wonderfully dramatic whether or not they are also profoundly true. (I think the myth of the cave, when properly understood, is true.)

The *Republic* of Plato is far from a mere entertainment for an evening. Purchase or borrow a good translation (I suggest that of F.M. Cornford, with copious notes), block out a period of some consecutive days—ten or more would not be too many—accept no engagements of any sort, prepare a quiet space with a table close by with paper and pencils on it (for your own inevitable notes), and begin the incomparable journey. Everyone who counts for anything has taken it, and in twenty-five hundred years very few, I believe, who have seriously made the effort have been other than glad they did.

Every one of Plato's dialogues is a human drama as well as an intellectual discourse, but none is more entertaining than the *Symposium*, or banquet. Here is what happens on that night when there occurred one of the most famous dinner parties ever held.

The company is large and all male. Some twenty men sit, or rather recline, on couches, around a long, low table. Socrates was not among those originally invited, but he is brought by another guest and warmly welcomed by the host, Agathon, who the day before has won the prize for his first tragedy; the party is in celebration of the victory. The first question asked by the host is whether the company shall drink hard or not. The majority say not, which opens the way for rational discourse unspoiled by drunkenness, and the female flute players, whose activities would also spoil rational discourse, are sent away. A subject is chosen, and it is decided that each guest shall speak in turn, going around the table and ending with Socrates, who all agree is the best speaker.

The subject is love. Fine speeches are made about it, but all are rather solemn until that of Aristophanes, the comic poet. To explain the power of love, Aristophanes says that once upon a time we were not divided into two sexes but instead were wholes, with both sexes in one person; round creatures, we rolled from place to place and were contented with our lot. But the gods, to punish us for some transgression, split us in half and now we go through the world seeking our other half and are not happy until we have found him or her. "A likely story!" the other guests cry. Aristophanes smiles, knowing full well that his tale is worth a dozen of their speeches.

Finally it is Socrates' turn. He is as elusive, and his speech as strange and unexpected, as ever. He tells of a meeting long ago with a prophetess, Diotima, who taught him about love. Love is the desire for eternity implanted in a mortal being; we seek love, she said, in order through our offspring to overcome our mortality and leave something enduring behind us. Thus we can love our works as well as our children, Socrates is explaining, when suddenly the doors are thrown wide and into the banquet chamber bursts a company of half-drunken revelers who insist on joining the party—and who refuse to accept the rule of no hard drinking.

The leader of this ribald band is none other than Alcibiades, the greatest man of Athens (by now Pericles is dead), the hero who has been chosen to command the Athenian expedition against Syracuse that is to embark the next day. Alcibiades, brilliant, handsome, rich, and unpredictable, soon discovers what has been the order of the evening and demands to be heard, whether or not it is his turn. No one has ever denied Alcibiades, and he begins to speak.

His speech is one of the most moving ever made, and it produces a high drama in this dialogue. For Alcibiades discourses not of love itself but of Socrates his beloved friend, the man who above all, he says, has made him what he is but who also above all, Alcibiades admits, disapproves of what he is. For Socrates, says Alcibiades, is the most demanding of teachers and you can never satisfy him; he always wants more from you, indeed nothing less than all you can give.

Alcibiades tells stories about their life together, in the army and out, how Socrates once saved his life in battle, and how his own attempts to seduce Socrates into a life of pleasure and ease have utterly failed. Finally he describes Socrates in an unforgettable image. Socrates, says Alcibiades, is like those cheap little statues of Silenus, the god of drunkards, which are to be found in all the markets—little clay figurines that, when broken open, are found to enclose a sweet within. Socrates is just such a figure, says Alcibiades, with his short, squat body and his rolling gait, his simple courtesy, and most of all his homely manner of speech. But, says Alcibiades, when you break open those simple words and sentences and truly seek to understand them, "you find a delicious treasure at the center that is to be found in the words of no other person and which is, in short," Alcibiades concludes, "the whole duty of a good and honorable man." And, repeating that he will praise Socrates in this figure and drink to him, too, Alcibiades raises his glass and drinks deep. Thereafter he insists that all do likewise, whereupon the party disintegrates into a rout.

It ends hours later in another famous scene. Alcibiades is long gone, together with his companions; most of the other guests are sleeping, on or under the table; but Socrates, together with Agathon and Aristophanes and one or two others, are soberly discussing, as the first light of day shows in the windows, the nature of tragedy and of comedy. Socrates is defending the interesting proposition that "in the deepest sense they are the same."

The banquet, or its consequences, did not end there, as Plato well knew. Alcibiades, on actually leaving this party, went on a drunken revel through the city. As a joke he, or some of his friends, or perhaps some of his enemies (in order falsely to accuse him later), defiled many of the little statues of household gods that stood outside of houses. This caused no comment at the time, and Alcibiades sailed for Syracuse in all the glory of Athenian might. Once he'd gone, however, Alcibiades' enemies became dominant in the government and accused him of impiously destroying the religious icons, and on failing to appear he was tried and convicted in absentia. No longer able to command the expedition, Alcibiades deserted to the enemy and gave over his command to Nicaeus, who shortly suffered the worst defeat in Athenian history. This led to the final defeat of Athens by Sparta in the Peloponnesian War. Socrates, harmed in reputation by his close association with the traitor Alcibiades, was accused of corrupting the youth of Athens—meaning Alcibiades?—and put to death.

Was all this in Plato's mind when he wrote? Certainly. What then was he saying in the dialogue? Did he mean us to understand that when love is transferred from an ideal to a living person—from the idea of eternity to the man Socrates—it really does corrupt the lover? Did he mean that carelessness about solemn things, as exemplified in Alcibiades' interruption of Socrates' speech about love, was the real corruption of Athens and led to its fall? Or did he mean that despite these dire consequences life goes on much the same as ever, for the tragic and the comic are merely different versions of the same scene? It is interesting to speculate about these matters, but of course no final answers are possible. One thing, at least, is certain: Plato's *Symposium* remains one of the great entertainments.

If the Passion of Jesus Christ is the greatest story ever told, *The Trial and Death of Socrates*, as described by Plato in four dialogues, *Euthyphro*, *Apology*, *Crito*, and *Phaedo*, is a close second. Socrates was an important early philosopher in his own right because he was Plato's teacher (as Plato was the teacher of Aristotle), but his memory survives primarily because of his martyrdom. Not a few great men and women have become immortal by dying unjustly at the right time and place.

Let us set the scene. Socrates, an old man (he is about seventy), has been accused by two enemies of corrupting the youth of Athens. It is a trumped-up charge, but much anger and frustration lie behind it. Athens has finally lost the long-drawn-out Peloponnesian War and Sparta, the victor, has replaced Athens as the dominant political and economic force in Greece. The wealth and power of Athens are gone; there is not much to look forward to. Mean-spirited rulers have succeeded the great men like Pericles and Alcibiades who once led the city-state. The artistic force that had produced playwrights such as Aeschylus and Sophocles, painters and sculptors such as Phidias, and thinkers such as Socrates, seems to have played out. Business goes on but no longer with the imaginative brilliance that marked it before. From a growing, confident society, Athens has turned inward upon itself. Bitterness and nostalgic regret are the main emotions of the citizenry.

The trial itself—as was true at the time of all capital trials, for the accusers in this case are asking for the death penalty—takes place in the open, in the central place (or Agora) of Athens, before an audience of hundreds. All present male citizens of the city are jurors who will vote to decide the issue. The entire trial will occupy no more than one day.

The accusers speak first. Their charges are false, hollow. Socrates replies. His magnificent defense is, more than anything else, an explanation and justification of his entire mature life during which he has persisted, as he says, in being a kind of "gadfly" to the Athenians—an insect whose sting has driven the "animal of the state" onward to greatness.

He has been a teacher to the Athenians, he reminds them, and teachers, especially when critical of their pupils, are not always loved. Socrates knows this well. But he will not step out of character and cease to be the severe though caring teacher he has always been. He will not beg for forgiveness; he will not even beg for his life. When the verdict goes against him—by a vote that Socrates declares to be closer than he expected—the question becomes one of punishment. His accusers propose death; Socrates himself proposes a monetary fine, which his friends, he concedes, will have to help him pay. Again the decision goes against him. Death it shall be.

He has one more opportunity to speak to the men of Athens among whom he has lived and played his strange, ironic role. He takes full advantage of it, typically chastising his fellow citizens and telling them how they must live if they are to remain free, telling them to be honorable and good. He wishes them well and bids farewell in the famous, enigmatic words: "The hour of departure has arrived, and we go our ways—I to die, and you to live. Which is better God only knows"

The three speeches of Socrates at his trial, as recounted by Plato in the *Apology*, are among the most moving ever written. No one who has any feeling for the Greece that gave us the arts and sciences, or who has any love for philosophy, can avoid the catch in the throat as he reads them. But there is more. The *Crito* is almost more moving than the *Apology*. Crito is an old man Socrates' age and a friend of long standing, who visits Socrates in prison. He tells Socrates his escape from prison has been arranged. It will be a simple matter for him to leave the city never to return and to sojourn with his friends in some pleasant spot for the rest of his life, discoursing on philosophy. But Socrates refuses to go. Not only would he find it difficult, perhaps impossible, to survive anywhere except in the city that has been his home throughout his life but, more important, what would the Athenians think of him if he were to flee and thereby show his contempt for the laws of his city? Would not their judgment of him at his trial be thus confirmed—that he was a bad man and deserved to be punished with death? Crito and the others attempt to persuade him, to no avail.

Finally, in the *Phaedo*, the last visit to Socrates by his friends, and their last conversation with him, is described by Plato. Not surprisingly the talk turns to death and to the great question of what comes after it. I do not fear, says Socrates, for either I shall cease to exist altogether or, since I have been a good man, I shall enjoy the rewards of virtue in the afterlife. "For no evil," he says, "can come to a good man, in life or death."

The conversation ends. The executioner appears with the poison that Socrates must drink. He does so with the simple grace that has always marked his actions, and lies down to die. It does not take very long.

*The Trial and Death of Socrates* as described by Plato in this series of dialogues presents few problems for modern readers. Consequently many students are assigned the story to read at an early age, an age when they are not yet fully able to comprehend its meaning. It is well enough that the reading of Plato should start here, but it shouldn't stop here. Read the *Symposium* and the *Republic*, and then *Meno and Protagoras* and *Thaeatetus, Sophist,* and *Statesman*—read as much Plato as you can. But keep coming back to the *Apology* and the *Crito*. Here beats the heart and here shines the soul of one of the finest men who ever lived. He can be our teacher too, as he was the teacher of the Athenians many years ago.

# ARISTOTLE
## 384–322 BCE
*Poetics*
*Ethics*

Aristotle was born in the summer of 384 BCE in the small Greek colony of Stagira, in Macedonia—hence he is often called the Stagirite. Coming from a family of wealthy physicians, the boy received an excellent education, with the emphasis on biology, botany, and medical procedures. In his early twenties, Aristotle's father died, and he was sent to Athens to study and work at Plato's Academy. There he remained for twenty years, as the greatest of Plato's many pupils. But he was gathering his forces for the inevitable break. This occurred during the twelve years, starting in 348, that he spent away from Athens, partly because of strong anti-Macedonian feelings there, partly because of his intense curiosity about the world. These were happy years, during which he married, fathered two children, and attempted to teach philosophy to the heir of the Macedonian throne, the young man who would become Alexander the Great. Aristotle is said to have spanked his pupil more than once, but the boy did not learn much from him. Alexander did, however, later rebuild Stagira, after it had been destroyed in one of his father's campaigns. The relationship between the great philosopher and the great conqueror is a matter of conjecture—but irresistible to speculate about nevertheless.

Aristotle returned to Athens in 335. Plato being dead, and perhaps disappointed at not being named to replace him as the head of the Academy, Aristotle established his own competing institution, the Lyceum. There he worked and taught until 323 when, on the death of Alexander, Aristotle, having lost his great protector, was charged with impiety. It appears that condemnation was certain. Aristotle, declaring (in reference to the judicial murder of Socrates in 399 B.C.) that he would not give the Athenians a second chance to sin against philosophy, went into voluntary exile at Chalcis, north of Athens. He died there the next year, in 322, at the age of sixty-two.

The challenge that had been thrown down by Plato in the *Republic* is taken up and answered by Aristotle in the *Poetics*, the short, precious work that has shaped our thinking about theater and drama for more than two thousand years. The pages—only twenty or so, but rich in content—of the *Poetics* are filled with profound insight, and reading them makes going to the theater or the cinema more pleasurable.

Plato—or Socrates—had made the claim that the free exercise of the artistic imagination is a danger to the state, since poets and dramatists (and moviemakers and TV producers) are likely to tell stories that make people feel dissatisfied with their lot in life. Plato therefore proposed banning poets from his ideal Republic—a proposal that has offended nearly all of his readers ever since. Socrates, the protagonist of the dialogue, had left a loophole, however, conceding that though he himself could see no good that poets might do to balance the disruption he knew they could produce, someone else might see some countervailing benefit in poets and therefore allow them to return to the state—where, Socrates also conceded, they could provide much pleasure.

The good that poets can do—especially dramatists, and among them especially the writers of tragedies—constitutes the main subject of the *Poetics*. There are certain emotions, Aristotle says, that are in all people and that are harmful to them—emotions likely to disturb the equanimity of their lives and impede their going about their business with pleasure and success. Among these emotions he particularly mentions pity and fear, but these apparently harmless emotions clearly imply (by his argument) envy and ambition, and the implication also extends to other strong emotions, like anger and overweening desire and pride.

Aristotle's argument goes like this. All art, he says, is imitation, and we delight in a work of art that imitates well—that is, presents to our view the similitude of real things, which in their originals may not be pleasing to our senses but, as imitated, produce pleasure for our minds. A tragedy, Aristotle goes on to say, is "the imitation of an action, complete and entire of itself, having a beginning, middle, and end, and dealing with an event or series of events of a certain seriousness and import."

An action sufficiently important and serious that is well imitated in a play that is well written, according to rules of art that Aristotle lays down, has a profound effect on its viewers, making them share and participate in the great emotions presented on the stage and eventually—when the play is over—exorcising or driving out those troublesome emotions from their souls. The result, Aristotle concludes, is a kind of catharsis of harmful passions, leaving the spectator, as he (or she) departs from the theater and for some time afterward, purified and cleansed, more able to deal with his worldly tasks.

Whether Aristotle is a good psychologist has often been debated, but the question is really irrelevant to our appreciation of the *Poetics* today. The work is not only the first but also perhaps the finest—the most thorough, the most insightful, the most accurate—critique of drama ever written. It remains the basis of all dramatic criticism.

The *Poetics* contains some difficult passages. It is advisable, therefore, to read it more than once. Your reward comes when you begin to think about Aristotle's discussion of types of plays and why some are better than others. Apply these critical guidelines to the next stage play you see; also to films, television shows, and other entertainments. All will become more intelligible and thus more enjoyable.

The surviving texts of Aristotle's works offer an interesting puzzle for scholars. Despite centuries of study and speculation, no one is certain what kind of texts they are. Are they essays or treatises direct from Aristotle's hand? If so, he must have been a careless writer, because the texts are full of contradictions, non sequiturs, and other rhetorical defects. Contrarily, do the texts consist of notes taken down by students from Aristotle's lectures? Or are they Aristotle's own notes, for spoken or for written works? Are the texts collections of various original sources, slapped together by a careless or ignorant editor some years, or centuries, after Aristotle's death? Or are the texts, especially of the political treatises, the result of brutal censorship at some period between Aristotle's death and the fifteenth century, when the texts as we have them were codified and fixed?

No one knows the answers, but there is no doubt that the form of Aristotle's works makes them hard to read. However, not all the works are equally difficult, and compared to most, the Nicomachean *Ethics* is a complete and carefully written book. For this reason, among others, it has often been held to be Aristotle's greatest work.

The *Ethics* is a book about virtue—about good and bad people, and about good and bad actions. "Virtue" is not a popular word today, but the idea it names, and the problems to which it points, are inescapable. We simply cannot avoid asking ourselves whether, in this situation or in that, we are doing the right or the wrong thing. And however blind we may be to ourselves, we are all prone to judge others and to declare that an individual is either a good or bad person. We recognize, too, a combination of good and bad in most people and ask ourselves how we can increase the good and decrease the bad in ourselves.

Aristotle is a great help to us, primarily for the reason that the Nicomachean *Ethics* is such a valuable book. He begins by saying, simply—and sensibly—that virtue is a habit: an habitual disposition, as he calls it, to choose right rather than wrong. The good and the bad, the right and the wrong among actions, of course, not things; one can be an excellent judge of wines or investments and still be a thoroughly bad person. A good person, Aristotle says, is a person who does good things not just once or twice but at least most of the time.

How to become virtuous, if we are not so already? Well, there are rules, to which Aristotle devotes many pages. Mostly they have to do with choosing the mean between two extremes of action. Courage, for example, is a virtue; to lack courage is to be cowardly, and that is one extreme; but to have too much courage, to be rash, is also a mistake, and the habitually rash person is not admired (although he is probably more admired than a coward). Similarly with prudence and temperance: there are extremes of each, and virtue lies in the middle way.

In another sense, Aristotle reminds us, there is no such thing as being too prudent, too temperate, too courageous. When those great virtues are properly understood, we begin to see that courage is a complex thing, not a simple one, involving our knowledge of consequences, control of our bodies and wills, and the recognition that often there is no completely safe choice among evils. When we realize that to be courageous is to choose—habitually, not just once or twice—as a courageous person chooses, and that is never rashly or in a cowardly way, then we comprehend that we cannot be too courageous, although we may be less than we would like to be. And so it is with all the other moral virtues.

But therein lies a great problem, as Aristotle points out. Moral choices are not made in a vacuum. Every situation is almost infinitely complicated, with consequences that reach out to touch the lives of many other persons, now and in the future. So complex, indeed, is every choice we face that we must almost conclude that each choice is unique. Rules are useful but they go only so far; when it comes right down to it, we are on our own, making the best choices we can but never being absolutely certain we are correct. When things are hardest we often ask ourselves: What would so-and-so (a good person whom we admire) do in this situation? And that is quite appropriate, says Aristotle, for good actions are, on the whole, the kind that are performed by good people. The argument is circular, Aristotle admits: although it is true that good actions are ones that are performed by good people, it is equally true that good people are those who perform good actions. So it was in Athens twenty-five hundred years ago. So it is today.

There is a useful aspect of this dilemma, as Aristotle also brings us to understand. If to be virtuous is to habitually choose rightly, then to have that habit is perhaps the most comforting of possessions. To be virtuous is to have a will we can trust. A good person can be happy in doing what he wants, because what he wants is good, not just for others but also for himself. Followers of Aristotle have seen this point and expressed it in their own way. "The greatest and most beautiful thing in the world," says Dante, "is a righteous will." The motto of Rabelais's idealized Abbey of Theleme is "Do As Thou Wilt." Dante and Rabelais mean the same thing. Indeed, we can wish no greater good to anyone than that they have such a well-formed will that when they desire something they can do it in the confidence that that thing is not only desirable but also good.

The last book of the *Ethics* (there are ten in all) is concerned with happiness—what it is, and how to achieve it. Regarding happiness Aristotle says many things that are surprising, but none that, on reflection, do not seem to be true. So it is throughout this book. Perhaps no book ever written has so much to say to us that is really useful.

Aristotle's *Politics* is another valuable book. This work begins with a history of human communities, starting with the family, then the most simple groups, then larger groups created for the sake of life (security and other like goods), and "finally," as he says, "for the sake of a good life." A good life is only possible in a community wherein most members are virtuous. Again there is a certain circularity of the argument, but perhaps this is unavoidable. In any event, to live in a town or city where most people are good, and the bad are kept under reasonable control, seems to be desirable.

Towns or cities are one thing; a nation is another. Aristotle understood this, too, and he concludes the *Politics* with a discussion of the best kind of government. He declares that a nation living under a constitution that is accepted by all or most citizens is the best. Being the eminently practical man that he was, he admitted that such a government is never likely to be perfect and, what is more, may find it difficult to continue to exist. He recognized that, first, the rich are always desirous of governing for their own benefit, and second that the people can always turn against them and become a mob, taking things into its own hands. As always, the mean between extremes is to be sought.

The *Ethics* and the *Politics* contain inconsistencies and seeming contradictions, some apparently missing connections, and other such defects. Thus they are not always easy reading. Choosing among translations doesn't solve the problem. Even a good translation will not supply what is most needed, and that is a teacher to stand by our side and guide us as we read. A living teacher is best. Failing that, such a book as *Aristotle for Everybody*, by Mortimer J. Adler (my own teacher), is almost a necessity.

# EUCLID
## fl. c. 300 BCE
### *The Elements*

Little is known about Euclid. What is known is mysterious. He probably lived and produced his major work around 300 BCE, in Alexandria, the city Alexander the Great had recently founded and that was considered the intellectual and commercial center of the Hellenic world. Euclid probably did tell Ptolemy I, who ruled Alexandria in his day, that "there is no royal road to geometry"—this in response to a question by the king as to whether there was not an easier way to learn the subject that might suit a busy man and monarch. It may also be true that Euclid once gave a coin to a student who, after his first lesson, inquired about the practical value of learning mathematics, saying contemptuously, "He must needs make gain in what he learns."

If Euclid's life is misty and unclear, his book, *The Elements*, known traditionally as *The Thirteen Books of Euclid's Elements*, is clarity itself. Building on the work of all his forebearers, Euclid summed up and collated what was known in his day about geometry and also, as admiring Proclus said, "brought to incontrovertible demonstration the things which were only loosely proved by his predecessors." As a result the *Elements* is both beautiful and right, infused with a brilliance that remains as wonderful today as it was when the book was first published and immediately became a classic.

"Euclid alone," the poet Edna St. Vincent Millay wrote, "has looked on Beauty bare." The statement makes a point about beauty—that it can exist shorn of its incorporation in things—that may be questioned. But the suggestion that mathematical truth is, somehow, the essence of the beautiful is surely interesting. Many, mathematicians and nonmathematicians alike, have felt the same way.

There is indeed something gratifying about a mathematical proof. If we assume this (set of mathematical truths), and if we follow certain rules of operation (i.e., definitions and axioms) that we have ourselves laid down in advance, then that which follows will have a certainty which is no less than that of the circling of the heavenly spheres. No less, I say; but this certainty is even greater. The planets in their revolutions are subject to the inevitable disturbances that affect all physical things. But mathematical entities are not physical. They are eternal, and eternally unchanged. The point which, according to the first Definition of Euclid's First Book, "is that which has no part," will never change and cannot change. Incommensurable magnitudes will remain incommensurable for ever, whatever we do, and the icosahedron (twenty-sided regular solid) inscribed in its sphere will always shimmer in our imaginations, or in that of God Himself, who cannot change it either.

The inscription over the door of Plato's Academy was a warning: "Let no one enter here who has not studied geometry." This was not because geometry was useful, although it was and is: ancient geometers used it for surveying, and modern engineers use it to build computers. Plato meant that geometry—in fact all mathematics—is intimately involved in making a good mind.

Much of what I have said here is no longer true, or no longer wholly true, of modern mathematics, which has its deep intellectual difficulties, as do all other sciences. But those difficulties do not apply to Euclid's *Elements*: It is perfect, right, and true forevermore.

The *Elements* is a difficult, but not impossible, read. You may not want to read all thirteen books, but you should glance at them all, read the definitions at the beginning of each, sample their various propositions. They deal with different mathematical entities. Wander among the pages as if wandering among the galleries of a strange museum full of perfect works of art. Why did this artist create that work? You do not really know, at least the first time you look at it, but you are certain that he had a good reason. And you are aware that the whole museum hangs together, forms a unity unlike that of anything but mental places. Euclid's book is a mental place, and one can do worse than to retreat to it. You will meet many other minds there and you will find them at peace.

# ARCHIMEDES
## 287?–212 BCE
### *Scientific Writings*

When Archimedes was born, in about 287 BCE in Syracuse, Sicily, mankind knew very little about the natural world it inhabited—at least understood very little scientifically about it. The distinction is important. A great deal was known, of course, about the lives of animals and plants, about the weather, about the stars, as well as about the behavior of human beings in all kinds of circumstances: hunger, fear, desire. The fact that societies had survived up to that point attests to their knowledge—rather, their lore—about the world around them. And the works of writers such as Homer, Aeschylus, and Euripides, to say nothing of Plato and Aristotle, attest to the knowledge that the Greeks (as well as other peoples) possessed of the human heart.

But for the most part, this was not *scientific* knowledge. The basic principles according to which things worked and acted on other things were still, for the most part, unknown. Good guesses had been made, as they had to be to get anything more than the simplest things done. But there is a difference between a guess, no matter how inspired, and a scientific principle or law, which is based on knowledge of *why* things work the way they do and that allows the scientist to predict with accuracy future occurrences of the same sort. The patient construction of the structure of natural laws as we know them today has been the major work of Western man for the past twenty centuries. For all intents and purposes, this work was begun by Archimedes. In many and important ways he was the first true scientist, and as a result of his work mankind knew much more, scientifically, about the natural world on the day of his death than it had on the day of his birth.

Archimedes was what we today call a physicist. He was deeply interested in the way simple machines work: levers, balances, inclined planes. He saw the same or similar principles in operation in many different situations. Today we would say he was a master experimenter with gravity.

Perhaps his most famous discovery had to do with the specific gravity of various substances, which he rightly understood differs from substance to substance. His friend, King Hieron of Syracuse, had received as a gift a certain amount of gold. Hieron has his goldsmiths fashion it into a crown. When he received the crown, he began to suspect the goldsmiths had alloyed the original gold with silver, which of course had less value. But how was he to prove this? He asked Archimedes, who puzzled over the problem for a long time. One day, as he was stepping into the public baths of Syracuse, Archimedes slopped the water in the bath over the edge—and immediately was struck by an idea. His body displaced water from the bath; gold and silver would also displace water if placed in a full basin; and since given amounts of gold and silver were different in weight, they should therefore displace different amounts of water. Archimedes was so excited by this idea that he jumped out of the bath, quite naked (he had forgotten to put his clothes back on), and ran home to experiment, shouting "Eureka!," which in Greek means "I have found it!"

Archimedes' hunch turned out to be correct, and so did the king's. When Archimedes tested the metals in a water bath he found that a certain weight of silver displaces more water from the bath than the same weight of gold, because the gold is heavier, for the same amount of volume, than the silver. Archimedes therefore carefully weighed the crown and measured out an equal weight of pure gold. The gold displaced less water than the crown; thus, the crown contained silver (or some other metal, not gold). What happened to the goldsmiths is not, as far as I know, a matter of history. They certainly came to no good.

Archimedes was intrigued by this problem, but not because of the king's concern about his crown. Rather, Archimedes was interested in the mathematical and physical principles involved, and after further study he discovered the important principle that is named after him: that a body immersed in a fluid loses as much in weight as the weight of the fluid it displaces. He wrote a treatise on this, *On Floating Bodies*, and I suggest that you read Book I of this work.

Archimedes' most important discoveries, in his own view, involved the so-called method of exhaustion, whereby a sought-after goal is achieved by a succession of approximations, each closer than the last. This method, which he carried further than anyone before him, is closely akin to integral calculus. He wrote two treatises on this subject, *The Method* and *Measurement of a Circle*. Read the latter and the first two propositions of the former.

I recognize that you may not find it easy to read these and other short works of Archimedes, either in the famous edition of Sir Thomas Heath, in the slender paperback from St. John's College Press (Annapolis, Maryland), or in the volume of Greek mathematicians and scientists in Great Books of the Western World. But I recommend that you try hard to read one short treatise by Archimedes that is highly suggestive in its implications. Called *The Sand-Reckoner*, it survives in the form of a letter to one King Gelon, who has asked Archimedes how many grains of sand would be required to fill the entire universe. Archimedes takes the question seriously but immediately recognizes the fundamental problem, which is not to estimate the number of grains of sand but instead to create a number system capable of expressing such large numbers.

The Greeks, with all their wit, were crippled in their scientific work by the lack of a convenient number notation, which made it not only impossible to express large numbers but also very hard to conceive of them. The Romans were similarly hampered. The creation of a workable number system is an achievement of the past few centuries to which we owe much of the scientific progress that is our civilization's proudest boast. But Archimedes was on the track of a workable number system nearly two thousand years before the modern scientific period.

He had made significant progress toward it, as shown in *The Sand-Reckoner*, when he died. His death was a ridiculous accident. Syracuse fell to the Romans in 212 after a protracted siege. A general massacre followed, but the Roman general Marcellus gave specific orders that the great sage Archimedes should not be harmed. However, during the rout, a Roman soldier came upon an old man drawing a mathematical figure in the sand. Exactly what happened between them we shall never know, but according to a two-thousand-year-old story, the soldier asked Archimedes what he was doing. The old man didn't look up at him, saying only, "You are standing in my light," whereupon the soldier stabbed him. That was the demise of Archimedes.

# chapter three

# The Silver Age of Tyranny

Virgil tells us in the *Aeneid* that, after the victory of the Achaeans and the destruction of Troy, Aeneas, fruit of the illicit coupling of the divine Aphrodite and the human Anchises, escaped from the burning city. After many adventures he reached Italy, where he had been fated to found a city and eventually a new Troy. This happened at the time of the Trojan War—and many interesting events followed in the next ten centuries. Things became even more interesting during the last century before our era, and during the first after it began; and this period we know more about.

After the defeat of Carthage and the final defeat of what remained of Greece (although Greeks continued to be the teachers of the Romans), civil war broke out over the question of which should rule Rome, a Senatus of wealthy and powerful men or a Popolus of lesser but more numerous persons. (The famous motto of the Republic, SPQR, stood for "Senatus Popolusque Romanus," which, translated, means the Roman Senate and People.) There were several factions, one led by Julius Caesar and Mark Anthony, another by Pompey, a third by Brutus and Cassius and other senators. Caesar and Pompey were both generals, but Caesar captured Pompey and killed him. Brutus and Cassius then assassinated Caesar, whereupon Antony and Octavian, the young adopted son of Caesar, and a third man, Lepidus, who was not very powerful but was very rich, "elected" themselves a Triumvirate ruler of what was by now the largest, richest empire in the world. But Anthony and Octavian could not rule together, especially after Anthony went to Egypt, fell in love with its queen, divorced his wife (who was Octavian's sister), and married Cleopatra—incidentally obtaining control of her enormous treasure. This turned out to be just what Octavian needed, and with a ruse he trapped Anthony's and his wife's separate navies at Actium, a harbor on the western coast of Greece. Cleopatra abandoned her lover suddenly, for a reason that has never been clear. Anthony, defeated, committed suicide; Cleopatra did the same.

Octavian, now in possession of Cleopatra's treasure and therefore enormously wealthy, returned to Rome, paid off his debts, discarded Lepidus (but without killing him), changed his name to Caesar, pulled in all his strings, and declared himself—nothing very great, just "the first man at Rome." He was cunning. He let people from all walks of life decide to accept him as their leader. Then as their ruler. Then as their dictator. Finally, under his new name of Caesar Augustus, as their god. The Republic was dead, and the Roman Empire had come into being.

It began better than it ended. A Silver Age, so-called, of Roman literature was inaugurated by Lucretius, included Virgil and his friends Horace, Ovid, and Catullus, and played out in less than a century. None of it, with the possible exception of Ovid's works, was really original—not even the philosophical writings of Cicero, who admitted he was simply trying to teach the Romans what the Greeks knew and what the Romans had always been too busy fighting wars to learn.

Virgil was the greatest of imitators. His *Eclogues* were based on the *Pastorals* of Theocritus, although several of them had a considerable charm; he wrote them to show that a Roman could write Eclogues. Virgil's *Georgics* were based on Hesiod's *Works and Days*, although they too had an ulterior purpose. The unending civil wars had impoverished the Roman countryside as peasants were drafted before every campaign by one side or another. Virgil had been a farmer; his *Georgics* tried to teach Roman youth how to farm in the way he and his father had. And of course even *The Aeneid* was a frank imitation of Homer's two great epics, with the first half of the Latin poem based on *The Odyssey* and the second half on *The Iliad*. Virgil was the greatest Roman poet. His imitations were elegant and beautiful, but they lacked the passion and humanity of the Greek originals. Of all the Latin poets Ovid may have been the best (apart from Virgil, of course), but he fell afoul of the Emperor and was banished

# LUCRETIUS
## 96?–55 BCE
### *On the Nature of Things*

The only biography of Titus Lucretius Carus is two sentences long and was written four hundred years after his death by a man who had little cause to like him. Here it is, from the *Chronicles of Saint Jerome*:

> 94 B.C. Titus Lucretius is born. He was rendered insane by a love-potion and, after writing, during intervals of lucidity, some books which Cicero emended, he died by his own hand in the forty-third year of his life.

This may be true, but there is no evidence either to confirm or deny it. Saint Jerome would not have approved of Lucretius's Epicureanism, which may invalidate the account; on the other hand, love potions were so common in Lucretius's day (roughly the first half of the first century BCE) that there were Roman laws against their use. Whether Cicero amended Lucretius's great poem is also not known, although Cicero does say in a letter to his brother that the poem was being read in Rome in 54 B.C. Lucretius may have died the year before.

Scholars may favor the story of the love potion because they detect in Lucretius's work an ardent interest in love. *On the Nature of Things* begins with a very beautiful invocation to Venus, goddess of love. But there were other reasons for dedicating such a poem to Venus. She was the mother of Aeneas, the founder of Rome, and thus the primal ancestor of all Romans, and Lucretius was writing in Latin (not in Greek, the more common "literary" language of his time) for Romans who, in his opinion, needed the kind of instruction his verses could impart.

More important is the role that the invocation plays in the poem itself. Lucretius sings of the delights of love and of the beauty of a world that is made by the love that is in all things; but this is merely to emphasize his true doctrine, namely that all of the visible world is merely an appearance. All of its color and charm and motion are nothing more than an illusion, for the only reality is atoms and the void—"first bodies, [from which] as first elements all things are."

The shock of this message as conveyed in the very first pages of *On the Nature of Things* is not soon forgotten. Reach out and touch the cheek of your beloved—in fact you touch nothing but tiny pellets, indestructible and persisting from the beginning of the universe, some with hooks and some without, flying hither and yon at great speed within the emptiness of space. But do not weep; your fingers are made of atoms, too, as is your heart and also your mind, with which you delude yourself. Strange doctrine for a man who was supposed to have been driven insane by a love potion!

The theory of atomism had been first proposed by the Greek scientists Democritus and Leucippus early in the fifth century BCE. The reality we think we see, they contended, is an appearance only. In fact, all things are made of tiny elements, of which there are only a small number of types, but which in various combinations produce all the material things that we observe. Democritus had said there are two kinds of atoms, corporeal ones and soul ones, and that the two are mixed within us. The Greek atom could not be split; its very name indicated that it was primitive, the beginning and basis of all other things.

The atomic theory as proposed twenty-five hundred years ago and as kept alive by poets, philosophers, and alchemists until it was finally triumphantly confirmed in our own century, is really a very simple idea. It is much harder to believe that things are as they seem than to believe they are underlain by a more intelligible substratum of entities that cannot be seen and that we can therefore speculate about with relative impunity. Reality, in short, is always the hardest thing for human beings to face. It is therefore not surprising at all that Democritus, Leucippus, and Epicurus held to the theory long before there was any "scientific" evidence for it. What is really surprising is that it took two thousand years to prove it.

One reason for that long delay is a serious mistake made by the early atomists. They imagined a universe composed entirely of atomic particles constantly in motion in a space without limit, and they furthermore imagined that the motion of the particles was utterly unpredictable, ruled by chance alone. Their first idea was sound, but their failure to see how useful it would be to suppose that the motion of the particles was governed by natural laws proved a great error. Only when the laws of that motion were discovered within the past two hundred years were we able to confirm the theory.

It was also a mistake, I think, for the old atomists to deny the freedom of the will, which they did when they said that all was ruled by chance. It was not necessary to suppose that there were no imma-terial entities in the universe. And if there were and are such they could have been and could still be free—like you and me, when "you" and "me" refer to entities that are not material (I do not know about you, but I know about me!).

Be that as it may, the theory came down to Lucretius via the offices of the Greek philosopher Epicurus, who taught a kind of Stoicism in a school he established in Athens in the third century BCE. For the Epicureans all was calm and peace because nothing was really important except the soul, and nothing could hurt that. The gods were very far away. They didn't care about men, or maybe they laughed at them. Pain was an illusion, as was pleasure, but of the two pleasure was the greater good, so why not follow it? A moderate life ended by a composed and peaceful death was the greatest pleasure of all.

That is the doctrine of Lucretius's long philosophical poem, combined with the atomism that, in his view, somehow strengthened the moral implications of Epicurus's teaching. As such it seems a curious subject for a long poem, and an impossible subject for a great poem. But the poem is great nevertheless.

It is very beautiful in its antique Latin, with a beauty the best translations retain. It is also imbued with passion, which Epicurus might have disapproved of but to which no reader can object. Lucretius was indeed a passionate man who saw no contradiction in his passionate attempts to convince us that we should be free of passion. Maybe there is none.

*On the Nature of Things* has much to say about love, but no less to say about death. It begins with love and ends with death; the last book (unfinished, as it turns out—as though Lucretius had died in the writing of it; and if he did kill himself, maybe he did so because he could not finish it) describes at awful length the horrors of the plague at Athens that had killed Pericles and so many other noble souls and left Athens vulnerable to the high tide of Spartan tyranny. From an invocation to Venus, lover of "increase," to a paean to Mars, the provider of death and dissolution—that is the road Lucretius leads us down.

# VIRGIL
## 70–19 BCE
### *The Aeneid*

Little more than a century ago, most educated people knew Virgil reasonably well, had read some Virgil in school—in the original Latin—and could quote Virgil on appropriate occasions. They also knew Homer, of course, but they did not like Homer as much as they liked Virgil. Homer, in their view, was somewhat primitive and quite indefensible as far as his morals went, while Virgil was in all the important respects impeccable. Today the pendulum has swung the other way. We tend nowadays to appreciate Homer much more than we do Virgil; in fact, we sometimes find it hard to see much good in Virgil at all. He has become a poet who is paid more lip service than real affectionate attention and regard.

The modern judgment regarding the relative merits of Homer and Virgil is, I believe, correct. Homer is the greater poet, and Virgil has serious defects that are hard for us to accept. But this doesn't mean the works of Virgil, especially *The Aeneid*, should no longer be read. *The Aeneid* is a wonderful poem, although it is not as wonderful as *The Iliad* or *The Odyssey*, both of which it often imitates closely. Nor are the reasons to read *The Aeneid* merely antiquarian. Virgil's poem retains life and meaning for us in the twenty-first century. It also contains beauties that are rare if not unique in all of poetry.

Publius Vergilius Maro was born on a farm near the town of Mantua, in Italy, in 70 BCE. (Because of his birthplace he has been called "Mantovano" by later poets.) He came of good peasant stock, but his genius must have been recognized very early because he received an excellent education and soon came to the attention of important men in Rome. Virgil's youth was a troubled and chaotic time. When he was twenty, Julius Caesar swept down across the Rubicon from Gaul into Italy and carried the civil war with Pompey close to home. Caesar was the victor, but war erupted again after his assassination in 44 BCE and continued until the final victory by Octavian (later called Caesar) over the combined naval forces of Antony and Cleopatra at Actium in 31 BCE. Virgil was, in short, nearly forty years old before peace came to his country, peace which he and most living men and women had never known. It was an enormous relief and Virgil, like most Romans, felt indebted to the man who had brought it about—to Augustus, now the single ruler of the Roman world.

Virgil was well known as a poet long before the final triumph of Augustus, who later became his friend. Virgil's *Eclogues*, a collection of ten pastoral poems composed between 42 and 37 BCE, were much admired for their limpidity and perfection of tone. One of them, the *Fourth Eclogue*, brought to Virgil great fame at a later time, when most Roman and pagan poets were almost forgotten. In it, Virgil prophesies in mystic verse the birth of a child who will banish sin, restore peace, and bring back the Golden Age. The poem can be dated to 41–40 BCE, a time when the civil war seemed to be drawing to a close (in fact it did not end for ten years). Virgil was probably referring to the expected child of Antony and Octavia, sister of Octavian. In any event, Christians later read it as prophesying the birth of Christ and this kept the name and works of Virgil alive when other pagan reputations withered and died.

The civil wars, besides keeping the Roman cities in a state of continuous political turmoil, also nearly depopulated the countryside as farmers everywhere were forced to leave their farms and go to war. Virgil's *Georgics*, a didactic work pleading for the restoration of the traditional agricultural life of Italy, was written in the period between 36 and 27 BCE. It is filled with the deep and sensitive love of the country of Italy that marked everything Virgil, once a farmer, wrote.

Virgil began *The Aeneid* almost immediately, it seems, after Augustus's victory at Actium had made peace possible at last. His theme—the founding of Rome by Aeneas, the last of the Trojans and the first of the Romans—made it possible for Virgil to operate on a double time scale. The poem could be and was read as describing an antique world, that of the heroes in the mythical past, but also the world of today (that is, of the late first century BCE), when Roman virtues had finally been proven triumphant and would now ensure peace forevermore.

Virgil was a shy, timid man, although he must have been a charming one, too, for he had many loving friends including the poet Horace, the emperor Augustus, and the art patron Maecenas, who supported him financially for most of his later years. But despite his success Virgil was not happy. He had been born under the Roman Republic and he died under the Empire, unable for personal as well as political reasons to express his growing sense that the change, for all it had to recommend it, was for the worse, and would become more and more so with the passage of time. I think it is obvious Virgil felt so; nothing else accounts for the persistent note of sadness and melancholy that imbues the *Aeneid*. The poem is about glory, duty, and sacrifice for the sake of a great aim, but it is also pervaded by what Virgil in one of his most unforgettable phrases called, "the tears in things." That there are tears in things, that there is a deep sadness at the very heart of reality, was not an ordinary Roman idea.

*The Aeneid* begins with the fall of Troy. Aeneas, carrying his old father Anchises on his shoulders and leading his little son Ascanius by the hand, escapes from the burning city, silhouetted against the lurid light of the flames. It is one of Virgil's unforgettable word pictures. Aeneas then takes a ship and sails across the sea to Carthage, where he meets and seduces Queen Dido. The seduction is necessary—Aeneas must have help for himself and his men—and so, he feels, is his departure from the queen. As he sails away never to return, Dido stands upon the shore, knowing in her heart (despite his protestations) that she will never see him again. She then immolates herself upon her funeral pyre. This image, of the ship sailing away into the distance and the flames leaping up high above the cliff, is also unforgettable. These huge, sad, heartrending scenes have shaped the imaginations of men and women for two thousand years.

Aeneas is drawn, or driven, by a sense of duty—not by love or desire or ambition or pride or even plain curiosity, as was Odysseus. Duty, though indispensable to the success of large enterprises, is no longer a lovable virtue; it seems to be a cold, sad obligation. This is a defect that Virgil never overcomes.

All the antagonists of Aeneas in the poem—Dido; Turnus, who fights for his homeland and his bride against the invading Trojans; Camilla, the lovely leader of the Volscians (allies of Turnus) whom Aeneas slays in battle—all of these share a humanity Aeneas himself lacks. He is a gigantic marble figure, glimpsed through the smoke of a burning city or in the murk of battle, a symbol, representative of Rome in all her greatness but not really recognizable as a man. This central fact makes *The Aeneid* essentially inaccessible to many modern readers. We want our heroes to be made of flesh and blood, with their vices as well as their virtues as large as life, so we can see them clearly.

Virgil's *Aeneid* hangs in the balance when we say these things. On the one hand, there are grand, unforgettable images; on the other hand, the cold inhumanity of its central figure. Virgil's magnificent verse finally tips the scales. Tennyson, in a famous tribute, proclaimed:

> *I salute thee, Mantovano, I that loved thee since my day began,*
> *Wielder of the stateliest measure ever molded by the lips of man.*

The stately measure of the verse of Virgil moves inexorably, like an enormous, benevolent giant, marching one large, solemn step at a time, over mountains, plains, and seas. The Latin hexameter line is, in Virgil's hands, wonderfully flexible; he can say anything serious in it (comedy is not much heard in *The Aeneid*). The verse is so fraught and burdened with symbolism that hundreds of lines can be detached from the poem and applied to other contexts. Thus when people still knew Latin as a matter of course, books of quotations were full of tags of Virgil. This Virgilian verse, however, is not easy to translate. Try to get hold of a good modern translation; for example, Robert Fitzgerald's or Robert Fagles's. Then, to obtain a sense of what Virgil sounds like in Latin, read a few pages of an older translation—for example, that of John Dryden, published in the 1690s. Dryden wrote in sonorous heroic couplets that are said to be the closest to Latin hexameters that English verse permits.

Do not expect to be exalted by Virgil, especially at first. The verse is an acquired taste. But give it a try. In the end, remember the image of Aeneas fleeing Troy, leaving it burning behind him, carrying his father on his shoulders, leading his little boy by the hand. Bernini sculpted it in marble, and a dozen painters have depicted it. It's not easy to forget.

Why? Perhaps because every father would like to have a son like Aeneas and every son a father like Aeneas. As long as there is war and the desolation war brings, so long will that young man stand as a symbol of hope for those who are too old or too young to escape war's destruction. Would that all such people on Earth had a young Aeneas to lead them to a new home.

# OVID
## 43 BCE–17 CE
### *Metamorphoses*

Publius Ovidius Naso was born in a small town east of Rome in 43 BCE. "Naso" in Latin means nose—why he acquired this nickname, as it were, is not known. He came of a comfortable family and received a good education at home, then moved to Rome for the training in rhetoric and other arts required for a professional life. But from an early age he knew that what he most wanted was to be a poet and, despite many troubles, he was, for the rest of his relatively long life.

He was a brilliant, witty man, and his poetry reveals those qualities. In his youth he wrote love poems and a mock didactic "treatise" on love and sex called *Ars Amatoria* (*The Art of Love*). This and other poems like it won him friends as well as readers, which both amused and pleased him, although he knew he needed a greater challenge.

He found this, in his middle age, in the large body of Greek mythical tales that Romans liked to read although they generally disapproved of the lack of Roman moral values in the stories. (Or maybe they disapproved of them because they knew the emperor did.)

Ovid began to compose the *Metamorphoses* when he was nearly forty and completed it in the year 1 BCE. The poem consists of a collection of stories, more or less based on familiar Greek myths, but really just stories about people—men and women, brothers and sisters, fathers and children, every kind of relationship both within families and without. The stories are strange, brutal, sad, funny, mocking, surprising, and wonderful. *Metamorphoses* is certainly a great book. And when it was finally published it established Ovid as the preeminent poet of Rome, since both Horace and Virgil now were dead.

Almost everyone loved the book. One man did not, and his opinion was the only one that counted. Ovid was vacationing on the famous Isle of Capri, in the Bay of Naples, when word came that Caesar Augustus wished to see him. It was an unavoidable journey, not pleasant. When Ovid arrived at Rome he was invited into the Emperor's presence, where the two men met privately. No one knows exactly what was said except that Augustus was apparently not pleased by something Ovid had done, by an "error" of some sort that the poet had committed. After the private audience, Ovid was tried by a private imperial court, convicted, and sentenced to banishment. He was not harmed; nor was he fined or deprived of his possessions; nor were his writings officially proscribed, except that they mysteriously disappeared from all the libraries and bookshops.

His banishment was terrible indeed. He was carried in an imperial ship through the Dardanelles and across the Black Sea to Tomi, a small city in the northeastern corner of Pontus, as the Romans called it. Tomi was totally bereft of everything Ovid held dear: there was no culture, no books or plays or any kind of public entertainment, and the people did not even speak Latin. (Their language was called Getic and I think no one speaks it now.) For years he remained an outcast in the town but was finally accepted as some kind of strange anomaly, and in a way he came to accept his fate. His wife, whom he loved, remained behind in Rome and never ceased to try to soften the Emperor's mind, but to no effect. When Augustus died in CE 14, she petitioned his successor for mercy, but again failed, partly because everyone else—even her closest friends—were afraid to join her pleas lest they be tarred with the same brush. They never saw one another again, although Ovid never ceased to write letters to her. He lived for three more years and died at Tomi in CE 17 in the middle of one of its dreadfully dark, cold winters.

He might not have been surprised to learn that all the efforts of Caesar Augustus to wipe his name and his writings from the memory of man were unsuccessful. For a while his books had to be secreted in cellars and barns and country houses, but many survived and before long came to be openly admired. With the ascension of the Christian Constantine to the imperial throne, his books were again banned but not destroyed. Within a few hundred years they were again popular, and during the English renaissance were among the most popular books of all, thanks to a translation of *Metamorphoses* by Arthur Golding that was quoted by everyone from Shakespeare on down.

A good translation by Rolfe Humphries captures the wit, brilliance, and pathos of the original. Another book that I recommend, if you can find it, is *The Last World*, by Christoph Ransmayr. This extraordinary book seems to be written about the present day, but at the same time the action takes place in Tomi, two thousand years ago, where the people of the town find themselves playing out the adventures and the fates of the characters in Ovid's great book. I read Ransmayr's book fifteen years ago and I have never forgotten a word of it.

# TACITUS
56?–120?
*Annals*
*Histories*

We know a good deal about first-century Rome—the first century of the Roman Empire. Records have survived, historians have recorded the facts, and archeological study has added its not inconsiderable part. But what we think about that famous age is largely owing to Tacitus

Cornelius Tacitus. He was a fine writer as well as a great historian—indeed, one of the most influential historians of all time.

Eleven emperors ruled Rome during the eighty-two years from the death of Augustus in 14 to the death of Domitian in 96, and four of them are among the most famous—or infamous—men who ever lived. Tiberius. Caligula. Nero. Domitian. The blood runs cold at the mere mention of their names, thanks to Tacitus.

Tiberius may have deserved a better report. During the first half of his reign, at least, he tried to be a good ruler and a worthy successor to Caesar Augustus. Like Augustus, Tiberius had to make up a great deal as he went along; the Romans weren't used to being ruled by a king, having enjoyed a Republican constitution for centuries. There were few precedents to follow. At the same time there were great temptations; the Senate threw power at Tiberius even when he wasn't sure he wanted it. During his last years he did, and he used it. Suffering from a disease that made him hideous to behold, he retired to his heavily guarded villa on the island of Capri, near Naples, and there ruled through subordinates, indulging himself in cruelty and vice. Or so Tacitus says. We do not really know.

Tiberius was succeeded by a madman, Caligula, whose cruelty made everyone regret the murder of Tiberius. But Caligula only lived for four years before he too was assassinated, to no one's displeasure. His successor was Claudius, in many respects a successful ruler; his only real mistake was in taking the last of several wives, Agrippina. She was a devil, and she brought with her a devil of a son whom she persuaded Claudius to adopt as his heir before poisoning him.

The son, Nero, was only seventeen when his mother handed him the throne. He was already practiced in cruelty and in every form of vice. He particularly enjoyed torturing people to death and forcing the wives of Roman senators to prostitute themselves at the elaborate parties that he threw and that helped to exhaust the imperial treasury. His leading passion was the theater. He loved to act and to hear himself applauded. He acted often, his soldiers roaming the audience, beating onlookers who applauded for the wrong actor or didn't applaud at all. Nero said he was surprised that he always won the prize as the best actor. His soldiers told him it was because he was so good. No one dared to puncture the deception.

Nero was acting one evening when a great fire began to sweep through Rome. The worst fire in the city's history, it destroyed half of all its buildings, including many government structures as well as Nero's own house. There were rumors that Nero had started the fire himself to destroy the city so he could rebuild it after his own plan and perhaps even name it Neropolis. He did build a new palace, the Domus Aurea or Golden House, on the ruins of the central city, thus further impoverishing the state. The rumors would not die concerning his own involvement in the conflagration and concerning the fact that he refused to stop his performance even though word of the fire had reached the theater (he was not, however, fiddling, despite the popular belief), and so he decided to shift the blame to a scapegoat. For this nefarious purpose he chose a burgeoning sect, the Christians, who were disliked by most people anyway. Nero arrested many thousands and killed them in cruel and humiliating ways. He disguised himself as a commoner and wandered among the crowds who were whipped into being present at the executions. His delight in the pain he inflicted led some among the spectators to begin to have sympathy for the Christians, a novel development at Rome.

Nero was assassinated in 68, when he was thirty-one. He had earlier murdered his mother, his brother, his wife, and his tutor and guide, the philosopher Seneca. Following each of their deaths, and the deaths of hundreds of other eminent and noble victims, he required of the Senate that it not only thank him for saving the state from traitors but also that it thank the gods. The Senate never failed to do so—but they were sincere when they thanked the gods for the death of Nero.

Since Nero left no heir and had killed every member of his family, his death was followed by civil war. It raged for more than a year, during which three men occupied the principate; finally a fourth, Vespasian, ended the carnage and reestablished imperial rule. He was succeeded by Titus and he by Domitian, another in the Tiberius mold; what began well ended, in the case of Domitian, with a reign of terror—during the middle 90s—that may have exceeded for cruelty and madness anything that had gone before.

Tiberius was in fact a somewhat better man than Tacitus gave him credit for being; Domitian may not have been as bad as Tacitus said he was; and Claudius and Vespasian, at least, were relatively good as emperors went. This was not, however, what really interested Tacitus. He was interested in tyranny—in the effect it has on those who suffer under it and what it does to the tyrant himself. The *Annals*, covering (with lapses—unfortunately, much of the work is lost) the period from the death of Augustus to the death of Nero, and the *Histories*, covering (again with lapses due to missing pages and whole books) the period from the civil war of 68-69 to the death of Domitian in 96, are among the most powerful indictments of absolute power ever written. There is nothing quite like them.

The world today has its share of tyrants, as it has always had. Probably the great majority of all rulers who have ever lived have been despots and only a very few of them have been benevolent. But there have been men like Tacitus, too—and there still are—who hate tyranny, bravely confront it, and eloquently describe it in its true colors. And who therefore make us truly understand what Tacitus called "the rare happiness of times"—namely, the times of those emperors immediately following the death of Domitian when Tacitus was able to publish his books—"when we may think what we please, and express what we think."

That happiness is very deep; it is the immemorial dream of all men and women who know the difference between being ruled well and being ruled badly. Such happiness is worth any effort, any sacrifice. If you have any doubt of that whatsoever, read Tacitus. Even if you do not doubt it, read him. The story of that first century of the Roman Empire is one of the best true, instructive stories in the history of the world

# PLUTARCH
## 46?–120
### *Lives of the Noble Greeks and Romans*

Plutarch was born in the small Theban city of Chaeronea in Boeotia and spent most of his life there, apart from a few years in Athens as a student and several visits to Rome and to other places in Greece.

During the turmoil of the first imperial century—he was born in 46 and died in 120—he was obviously content to remain far from the metropolis and its temptations and perils. His reward was that he seems to have been one of the happiest of the great writers. A number of his letters survive; in one, to his wife, whom he loved, he wrote that he found "scarcely an erasure, as a book well written," in the happiness and contentment of his long life.

He wrote a great deal, besides occupying many political offices in his little town, directing some kind of school there that was known for miles around, and serving as a priest of Apollo at Delphi (which is not far from Chaeronea). In this last capacity he may have written to the emperor Trajan to try to revive the waning faith in the oracle. This may have led to a meeting with Trajan when Plutarch was in Rome, which may in turn have led to an honorary title of ex-consul. All of this is far from certain. It *is* certain that the stories of his having been Trajan's tutor and of his having been named by him governor of Greece are fabrications—although the honor and respect in which this provincial schoolmaster was held both near and far is no fabrication at all. He was one of the best-loved authors in the world for nearly two thousand years, until the French Revolution ushered in an age with a romantic passion for the expression of emotion as contrasted with the classical passion for its control and regulation by morals and law.

Such respect for the laws of god and men imbues Plutarch's *Lives of the Noble Greeks and Romans*, biographies of the men of both Greece and Rome who were considered great not only for their achievements but also for the nobility of their characters, particularly in adversity. The *Lives* were written in pairs, one Greek, one Roman, the pairs being chosen by Plutarch as far as possible on the basis of similarities in his subjects' lives and careers. Thus two men who betrayed their country, but for noble reasons, are compared in the lives of Alcibiades and Coriolanus; two commanders who lost important campaigns because of their timidity are compared in the lives of Nicias and Crassus; two renowned rebels are compared in Agesilaus and Pompey; two great revolutionary figures in Alexander and Caesar; and two notable patriots in Dion and Marcus Brutus. The comparisons of these *bioi paralelloi* ("parallel lives") are sometimes forced, but the lives themselves are always fascinating and what is more, always inspiring. To inspire the men of his day with the ideals of the virtuous men of old was certainly one of Plutarch's main purposes in writing his book, although he admitted that as he wrote he was deriving profit and stimulation himself from "lodging these men one after the other in (my) house."

Plutarch's *Lives* were based on solid research and they are still an important resource for scholars studying the period with which they mainly deal—from about 300 BCE to about CE 50. But it is not as history that they have been primarily read, and loved, down through the ages. Plutarch himself saw a major difference between history, which he thought of as chronology, and biography, which he thought of as drama. And dramatic his lives certainly are. They are full of anecdotes and stories, of quotations that are more or less verbatim, and of wonderful background notes that tell us what it was like to live in those far-off times. But the high drama—in many cases the high tragedy—of these lives is what in the long run attracts us most. That, together with the nobility that so many of the subjects show in meeting their tragic end: The death scenes in Plutarch's *Lives* are beautiful—and unparalleled.

Plutarch's book has had an enormous influence on other writers, notably Shakespeare, who was not above quoting or at least paraphrasing whole passages from Thomas North's brilliant translation, which had appeared in Shakespeare's youth. Plutarch's prose description of the first meeting of Antony and Cleopatra is only outshone—if indeed it is outshone—by the splendid Shakespearian verse that describes the same meeting, so fraught, as Plutarch and Shakespeare both knew, with the doom of men and empires. But it is ordinary readers like you and me who have loved Plutarch most. Here is the best way to read him.

Wait for a cold night, or one of driving wind and rain. Light a fire in the fireplace (if you don't have a fireplace, imagine one). Place your chair so you are warmed by the fire and protected from the dark shadows in the rest of the room. Draw the light forward and open the book, to the lives of Romulus and Theseus, respectively the mythical founders of Rome and Athens, or to those of Aristides and Marcus Cato, each of them moralists of the old school, or to Pericles and

Fabius, noble losers, or to Demosthenes and Cicero, the eloquence of the one exceeded only by that of the other. Or indeed any other lives; it doesn't matter which. Start to read.

Soon, very soon, you will have traveled far away from your fireside. The electric bulb will have turned into a candle and the sounds of automobiles will have faded, to be replaced by the sounds of horses' feet and the creak of harness. Only the passions and the perils, the temptations and the falls from grace, will be familiar. You will not be sorry to take this journey and you may not want to come back when the present calls.

# EPICTETUS
## fl. lst-2nd century
### *Discourses*

Epictetus was born in the middle of the first century and as a boy was the slave of a follower of the emperor Nero. Epictetus's owner was sometimes cruel to his slave and once, perhaps playfully, he twisted Epictetus's leg. The boy smiled. The master twisted the leg harder; he wanted Epictetus to admit that it hurt. But Epictetus only said, "If you do that you will break it." The master twisted the leg harder and it broke. "I told you so," said Epictetus. He was lame for the rest of his life.

The story, whether true or not, is utterly typical of the man, who gained his freedom while in his twenties, was exiled from Rome by the tyrant Domitian because he laughed at tyranny, and went to the city of Nicopolis, in northern Greece, where he lived for the rest of his long life and taught his philosophy to men who came from all over the world to learn it from him.

He was poor, possessing only, as he said, earth, sky, and a cloak. He sat on the ground, not writing anything but only talking to his visitors, who considered themselves his disciples. One of them, a certain Flavius Arrian, took notes and published them as the *Discourses of Epictetus*; he was careful, he said, to copy the exact words and very

language of Epictetus and to preserve "the directness of his speech."
Indeed, the *Discourses* read like a man talking.

What did he talk about? Courage, and freedom, and that condition of the will that makes a man free—these were his main subjects.
"He is free who lives as he wishes to live," Epictetus says over and
over; and how should you wish to live? Why, in such a way that no
one can hinder you. And how is that? Desiring those things that are
yours alone and that no one can take from you. Are there such
things? Yes, one: the freedom of your own will. You can be deprived
of everything you possess: your wealth, your wife and children, even
your life. But you cannot be made to desire what you do not desire.
You alone are able to corrupt your own will.

"Only consider at what price you sell your own will," Epictetus
warns; "if for no other reason, at least for this, that you sell it not for
a small sum." But do you have to sell it at all? Like Socrates, you can
refuse and put your tormentors and executioners to shame. You will
still die. Yes, none shall avoid that fate. It is better to live long and
then die. But in the end, what is the price of this long life? Epictetus
himself apparently lived to about eighty.

It is a hard doctrine, that "to study philosophy is to learn to die,"
and hard men adhered to it, the noble Romans most of all. It is difficult not to admire them; not to know about their courage is to fail to
know how good men can be. In reading Epictetus, ponder the relevance of his sayings to your own life. Pay attention to his admonitions about the will. The next time you justify a mean or cowardly
action by saying, "I couldn't help myself," ask whether Epictetus
would have accepted that explanation.

At the same time, ask yourself whether the Roman philosophy
of Stoicism, of which Epictetus was one of the most eloquent
spokesmen, is enough, whether it lacks something important. Why,
for example, did the early Christians, who were all attracted to
Stoicism, all without exception turn away from it and deny its
teachings? Is it enough, to gain freedom, merely to desire only those
things that no one can take away from you? Or is there not also a
more positive aspect to freedom, a striving after goods, both human
and divine, that requires a reaching out, a daring, and another kind
of courage?

# MARCUS AURELIUS
## 120–180
### *Meditations*

⌒

Epictetus was a slave; Marcus Aurelius, a Roman emperor. Their philosophies were similar. In fact the emperor was a disciple and follower of the slave, living, as he did, only half a century after him. But for which of these two men was it more difficult to be free?

The answer is the emperor. It is harder for a ruler over all mankind to be free than for his meanest subject. The meanest subject might be imprisoned, might be hung in chains at the city gate; in another sense he would certainly not be free. But, Epictetus and Marcus Aurelius agreed, in the most important sense of freedom such a prisoner might still be free, that is, his will might still be his own and not at the whim of another. The question is: Is it harder for an emperor or a slave to be free in this sense? It is harder for the emperor, because he lives in a palace and is subject to every temptation, can follow every whim. Perhaps there is not any greater slavery than that.

Epictetus, after he was exiled from Rome, went to Greece and taught philosophy. Marcus Aurelius had to remain at Rome and rule it. When the troubles started that, unknown to him, were the beginning of the fall of the Empire, he had to go where the troubles were and confront them, be they human disasters or natural ones like floods and earthquakes. His life, in short, was more subject than Epictetus's was to necessity—but only because he was a good man and a good ruler; a bad one would have "fiddled," like his predecessor Nero, while Rome burned.

It is curious and ironic that Marcus Aurelius, the best man among all Roman emperors, was beset with troubles that he could not control, while Nero, among the worst of men and emperors, handed down to his successors a relatively thriving state. After all, such ironies may be the best confirmation of the value of the Stoic philosophy. If we cannot control the world in which we live—and certainly we cannot—then we should learn to live with that fact and content ourselves with controlling what is in our power. And the only thing that is within our power is our own will.

We do not read the *Meditations* of Marcus Aurelius to learn the Stoic doctrine, which is better stated in the *Discourses* of Epictetus. We read Marcus Aurelius instead for the light he throws upon his own life and upon the life that must be led by a man such as himself, who was responsible for the peace, safety, and prosperity of all mankind (as he saw it). We read him and are touched by his weakness, which he is very frank to confess. (Probably he never expected anyone to read these private thoughts, which he put down while in his tent, at night, awaiting a battle or resting up from one.) There were even days when he did not want to get out of bed:

> In the morning when thou risest unwillingly, let this thought be present—I am rising to the work of a human being. Why then am I dissatisfied if I am going to do the things for which I exist and for which I was brought into the world? Or have I been made for this, to lie in the bedclothes and keep myself warm?—But this is more pleasant.—Dost thou exist then to take thy pleasure, and not at all for action and exertion?

We read him, too, for his good advice. Every once in a while, he tells us, when you are doing this or that unpleasant task, "pause and ask yourself, if death is a dreadful thing because it deprives thee of this." And we remember his famous injunction, "to live every day as if it were your last."

Most of all, we are curious about what it is like to be an emperor, to be rich beyond limit, powerful beyond limit. Very few men, or women, have handled absolute power and riches well. Marcus Aurelius did. He was acutely aware of the problems of power and he contemplated what was, for him, the greatest obstacle to his living a good life. In the first book of the *Meditations* he speaks of the good fortune that gave him the strength to overcome his—good fortune! It is a famous and beautiful passage of which I shall quote a small part:

> To the gods I am indebted for having good grandfathers, good parents, a good sister, good teachers, good associates, good kinsmen and friends, nearly everything

good … Further, I am thankful to the gods that I was not longer brought up with my grandfather's concubine and that I preserved the flower of my youth, and that I did not make proof of my virility before the proper season but even deferred the time; (and) that I was subjected to a ruler and a father who was able to take away all pride from me, and to bring me to the knowledge that it is possible for a man to live in a palace without wanting either guards or embroidered dresses, or torches and statues, and such-like show; but that it is in such a man's power to bring himself very near to the fashion of a private person, without being for this reason either meaner in thought, or more remiss in action, with respect to the things which must be done for the public interest in a manner that befits a ruler.

Imagine this man, who could possess any woman, buy any honor, own any thing, desiring above all to live as much as possible like a private person. Surely that is the proof of virtue. If not, then what does virtue mean?

# chapter four

# The Middle Age

W hen did the Middle Age begin? When did it end? These are interesting questions and, as Sir Thomas Browne, that great old seventeenth-century antiquarian said, "not beyond conjecture."

A little numerology may help us. For example, Plato's Academy was founded in the year 387 BCE. It was closed by the Emperor Justinian in 529. Hence it endured for 916 years, longer perhaps than any other school, college, or university in the history of the world. The year 529 was notable for another event: the promulgation of the "Rule" of Saint Benedict, which inaugurated the epoch of the monasteries, which may be said to have ended around 1450, give or take a generation. From 529 to 1450 is 921 years.

The convenient date of 1450 corresponds to the passage of the Renaissance, which began a hundred years before in Italy, to France and thence to England, Spain, and finally Germany, where its arrival was delayed by the devastation of the Thirty Years War.

When did it begin in Italy? Dante died in 1327; in many respects he was the last great truly medieval man. Bits and pieces of medievalism endured for a century or two beyond his death, but they were only fragments that the spirit of the Renaissance succeeded in wiping out as time passed. By 1550 they were almost all gone.

Petrarch and Boccaccio were the first to undertake this great change, which they believed had to happen. Neither was interested in the great cultural tradition they were seeking to displace. Oh, they admired Dante of course, and they remembered fondly some of the works of the troubadours, which they considered charming but primitive. But they saw a new world (actually an old one, because the Renaissance really was the rebirth of an old world that had passed away a millennium before).

The nine hundred years, more or less, that can be called the Middle Age is sometimes divided into two parts: the first half, which was considered a Dark Age, and the second half, which seemed to be full of light, but a strange light that was different from anything that existed before or since. In what follows I have allowed four figures to stand in some way for that darkness, which of course was mainly brought about by the fall of the Roman Empire, which didn't really fall but only moved from Europe to Asia, from Rome to Ravenna to Constantinople. These four figures were Ptolemy, who lived in the second century; Boethius, who lived at the end of the fifth; Saint Augustine, who lived mostly in the fourth; and finally the author, whoever he was, of *The Song of Roland*, who wrote that great poem some time before the year 1000.

The second half is on the whole more interesting because it includes Aquinas, Dante, and Chaucer. But there were other, lesser lights, several of them anonymous because only at the end of the medieval age did it become customary for poets, especially, to sign their works. This anonymity also applied to most of the architects who built the great cathedrals of France during the late twelfth and thirteenth centuries. Almost all of these astounding buildings were dedicated to the Virgin Mary; indeed, the Mother of God was the inspiration for most major works of art of all kinds in those waning years of the Middle Age. The two centuries were hers and hers almost alone. When you read the little story, "The Tumbler of Our Lady," you will see why—or if you read the *Divine Comedy* or visit Chartres. It was a wonderful and beautiful time.

# PTOLEMY
fl. 2nd century
*The Almagest*

"Almagest" means "the greatest" in Arabic. When Ptolemy's work on astronomy (written by Claudius Ptolemaeus in the second century) came to be used by the Arabs of the early Middle Ages as a textbook of the subject they honored it with that name, and the *Almagest* it is to this day.

Its greatness can be attributed to the fact that it was the most complete and satisfying of all the ancient astronomical texts. Complete because it dealt with everything that such a book should deal with: the Earth, the Sun, the Moon, the planets, and all the fixed stars. It described their motions and showed how to predict astronomical events like eclipses of the Sun and Moon.

It was satisfying because it explained every astronomical phenomenon according to a unified theory. "Phenomenon" comes from the Greek word for "appearance." All that any scientist has to go on are phenomena, or appearances. His theory of why the appearances are the way they are must adequately "save" the appearances, as the Greeks said. Ptolemy's theory saved all the astronomical appearances that were evident to the men of his day, and of a good many days after him—his theory prevailed for more than a thousand years.

Ptolemy's theory was simple and, therefore, beautiful. In the sublunary world—the world beneath the Moon, the one in which we, who inhabit the Earth around which the Moon revolves, find our home—motions are complex and difficult to measure and understand. Above the Moon, Ptolemy believed, all motion is regular, uniform, and circular, as Aristotle had said. It was a fine idea.

The hypothesis of regular circular motion, whereby all celestial bodies revolve around one central point, which is the center of the Earth, does not actually save the appearances. The Moon does not seem to simply orbit the Earth, nor do the planets. But the hypothesis does not have to be abandoned. It will still save the appearances if we make some small adjustments. These involve allowing the Moon and the planets to revolve around points that in turn revolve around the Earth. All celestial motion is still uniform and circular, and that is the main thing. All is right with the world.

Why these adjustments have to be made, and indeed why the Earth must be supposed to be the unmoving central point of the cosmos, and why (for example) the great sphere that surrounds us and on the inside of which the stars appear to be placed (and which was therefore referred to as the Sphere of the Fixed Stars) must also be supposed to revolve around it once every day, is all explained in Ptolemy's book. It is not only explained, it is also proved mathematically. The whole system is still satisfying in its way.

The Greeks invented science; that is, they were the first people to believe what the majority of humankind now believes, that the universe is intelligible and that we can understand how it works. When men like Pythagoras and Archimedes and Ptolemy first said this was so, the vast majority of mankind still thought the world was essentially unintelligible, at least to them, and therefore unpredictable. We live more comfortably today because we have come to recognize that those old Greeks were right. And among them Ptolemy was far from being the least right, even though in certain respects he was absolutely wrong. The Moon revolves around the Earth, all right, but the Sun does not, and neither do the fixed stars, which are not fixed after all but instead are speeding at enormous velocities away from us. The apparent motions of all these objects are better explained, because more simply explained, by supposing that the Earth rotates, not the cosmos around it. But when I say that, it is obvious that I am doing the same thing Ptolemy did—saving the appearances. That is still and forever will be the major task of science.

All of this will become clearer if you read, or read in, Ptolemy's *Almagest*. Something else will become clear as well, and that is the enormous complexity and difficulty of the astronomical work done by Ptolemy—and by his predecessors, to whose observations and theories he constantly refers. He obviously considered himself but the latest in a long series of patient laborers in the vineyard of astronomy. Perhaps he was, after all, the greatest such laborer so far, but there would be even greater ones after him, he knew. That too is a noble idea, and at the very heart of science.

I had a philosopher friend who used to speak of what he called "The Great Academy." There were only seven members of this august group: three poets, Homer, Dante, and Shakespeare; three philosophers, Plato, Aristotle, and Aquinas; and one scientist, Ptolemy. Ptolemy belonged, my friend said, because, more than any other scientist who ever lived, he had a clear conception of the fundamental task of science, which is to explain everything and to include everything in one great system. With no exceptions.

Exceptions in science do not prove the rule, they spoil the theory. If Galileo had never built a telescope, we might still believe in Ptolemy's system of the world. And we might be better off; but then again, maybe not.

# BOETHIUS
### 480?–524
### *The Consolation of Philosophy*

This is a book that only a hard heart can read without shedding a tear.

Boethius was born toward the end of the fifth century, when the Roman Empire in the West was falling apart. The emperors were brutal savages, and the institutions that survived were mere vestiges of the system of law and government that had made Rome great. Ignorance was everywhere, in high places and in low, and it was not hard for anyone with half an eye to see that a long dark age was coming, perhaps to endure forevermore.

Boethius had more than half an eye. A member of an old, distinguished Roman family, he received an excellent classical education and set himself, while still a young man, to translate and adapt the Greek works of philosophy into Latin so they might survive in some form, even if civilization did not. He translated Porphyry's *Introduction* to Aristotle's logical treatises, and then began to translate the *Organon*—the collective name of these treatises—itself. He may have completed the work but only parts of it are extant. Nevertheless, they were the only versions that could be read by monks and scholars in the West for more than eight hundred years.

Boethius's father had served as consul and now Boethius came to the notice of the Ostrogoth king Theodoric, who had usurped the imperial rule. Boethius became consul in his turn and a few years later was named by Theodoric *magister officiorum*, or head of all government and court services. As such Boethius was one of the most important men in the Roman world.

If you serve a despot, however, you are important only so long as you continue to please. Boethius ceased to please Theodoric some time around CE 522. He was accused of treason on grounds that are unintelligible to us now, and of practicing magic or sorcery, a charge he strenuously denied. He was tried, convicted, and imprisoned, probably in Pavia, to await his execution.

The wait was long, perhaps as much as two years. Boethius was continuously tortured to remind him of how far he had fallen from the grace of his lord. But he had extraordinary strength of heart and will, and he wrote a book, *The Consolation of Philosophy*. Whether the manuscript was spirited out of his cell before or after his execution we do not know; at any rate it survived and became the most widely read book during the early Middle Ages, after the Holy Scriptures as translated into Latin by Saint Jerome.

In the book Boethius makes little mention of the torments he suffered: it is enough to say that he has once been a great man and is now in prison, awaiting death. As he lies on his narrow bed in his dark cell a beautiful lady appears to him, dressed all in white, with radiance in her hair: this lady is Philosophy, and she speaks to him and soothes his pain. She reminds him that the true Good is not any earthly thing but is instead the being of all good things, existing in that higher and better world to which he perforce will go. Fortune and misfortune, she tells him, are subordinate to a greater Providence, a *summum bonum* (greatest good) that "strongly and sweetly" rules the universe. There is no real evil, and virtue is always finally rewarded. Boethius, the suffering prisoner, thus consoled by the hope of reparation and reward after his death, is able to die in peace.

Boethius's family had been Christian for a century before his birth and he was almost certainly a Christian himself. Nevertheless, the *Consolation* contains little or no hint of Christianity. Instead the work, with its Platonic insistence on the real existence of such ideal forms as Being, Truth, and Good, is a kind of pagan version of a Christian tract. It possesses a clear, cool eloquence that is rare in such works, and all the rarer considering the hideous circumstances under which it was written.

# AUGUSTINE
## 354–430
### *Confessions*

Augustine's *Confessions* is not only the first real autobiography in the history of literature, it is also one of the best. Maybe it is the best. It is astonishing how often the first example or examples of a genre turn out to be the best examples. *Don Quixote* may be the first novel, and few novels compare to it. *The Iliad* and *The Odyssey* are the first epics, and no subsequent works in that genre have surpassed them. No tragedy has surpassed Aeschylus's *Oresteia*; if the tragedies of Shakespeare are equal to the *Oresteia* they are so different as almost to constitute a new genre—in which they, in turn, are unsurpassed.

The question is not, however, whether the first examples of a genre are relatively so good, but *why* they are. Is innovation sufficient by itself to guarantee excellence? Certainly not. Are the greatest artists naturally drawn to the creation of new forms? Perhaps, although some great artists have been followers rather than leaders, inspired imitators rather than breakers of new ground. Or is it only that, as with a field that has lain fallow for a long time or never been planted to crops, the first crop is often the richest, so with a new field of artistic endeavor the first crop is also the richest and best.

Augustine seems to have known almost everything there was to know about writing an autobiography despite the fact that he had no prior autobiographies to read and compare with his own. He started his *Confessions*, as is perhaps natural, with his childhood and youth, with his life within the bosom of his family and then as a student in Rome and Milan (he was born in CE 354 at Hippo, in North Africa, near present-day Tunis). He does not conceal the fact that he was a brilliant student of rhetoric, of history, of languages, and of philosophy; after all, we know from many other sources that there never was such a student as this young African, probably never such a brilliant young man in the whole history of Rome.

But Augustine does not conceal his failures, his inability to understand very important things about human life, and, most important, his inability for many years to accept the apparent contradictions of Christianity. We love him for his admissions of what he considered to be sins (but only in later life), most notably the time when as an adolescent he stole some pears, not because he wanted the pears, not even because it was exciting to break the law, but mainly because he was "ashamed to be ashamed"—that is, it was easier to go along with the other boys than to say to them that he was ashamed of what they were all doing. Many of us may remember similar occurrences from our own childhoods! And then, just as notably, his admission that for years he was unable to overcome his desire for women and had even kept a mistress for many years while praying most fervently for the strength to control these desires, but without his heart really being in it. "Give me chastity!" was his prayer—"but not yet." Few readers have failed to recognize the humanity in those six words.

The heroine of Augustine's *Confessions* is not that mistress, whom in fact he never names—she is one of the lost women of history—but instead his mother, Saint Monica, who was a Christian (her husband was not) and who prayed and worked to bring about the conversion of her son. Augustine was studying under the renowned theologian Saint Ambrose, in Milan. Monica came to Ambrose and pleaded for his help. "The son of these tears," he comforted her, "will not perish." But there were still many difficult philosophical and theological obstacles for Augustine to overcome. Finally he had resolved all doubts, but he still felt that something essential was missing. He could accept Christianity with his mind, he said, but not yet believe with his whole heart.

It is one of the famous scenes in the history of the Christian religion. Augustine is sitting in a garden, struggling to believe, unable fully to understand the Holy Scriptures which he holds in his lap. He dozes off in the sun. Suddenly he hears a voice saying, "Take up and read." He asks himself whether that is a cry ordinarily heard in children's games—there are children all around him, playing in the garden. No, he thinks, there is no such cry in a children's game. He hears it again: "*Tollete lege*," "Take up (the book) and read." He opens the book and reads a passage, and at that instant his heart is filled.

Like all the greatest books, this one possesses great images. The pears, the prayer for chastity (but not yet), the conversion in the sunny garden. The greatest of all is the Window at Ostia. Monica is dying and her son, who has long since accepted Christianity, journeys to Ostia, the seaport of the city of Rome, to be with her in her last days. She lies in a room with a window on the sea. Augustine often stands at the window, listening to the sounds of the sea as it breaks against the shore. One day shortly before her death Monica is able to join him at the window, and they stand there together, he supporting her, she leaning on his arm, and talk of the life they have shared and of the life to come. Suddenly they grow silent, and the world grows silent, the sea becomes silent, there is no sound whatever, and then they hear or seem to hear the Universe itself, turning on its great center, turning by the will of God, and they hear, very faintly in the distance, the angels singing in praise of Him and of all His works. Monica dies soon after, happy in her dying because of her son and because of her vision of that life beyond death—"when we shall all be changed."

The last part of the *Confessions* of Augustine is not autobiographical in the strict sense; rather, this part of the book consists of some profound philosophical discussions of the nature of time. Many readers stop at the end of Book Ten of the *Confessions*, but I urge you to go on, to read to the end, even though the last three books are not easy, requiring considerable care and attention to follow and understand. The reason is that the discussion of time in this book written more than fifteen hundred years ago is one of the most probing and interesting in all of literature. Note: There are many translations of the *Confessions*, but in my opinion the only really readable one is by Francis X. Sheed. Most other translations are hard to follow because of Augustine's habit of interspersing biblical quotations in his text. Sheeer alone makes it clear.

Augustine wrote many other books besides *Confessions*. Toward the end of his life he prepared a list of his writings: as well as he could remember, there were more than two hundred and fifty different titles and that did not include several hundred letters, some of them very long, and perhaps thousands of sermons delivered before and especially after he became Bishop of Hippo. Two among this enormous number of works deserve mention here.

One was *On Christian Doctrine*, a relatively short (only a hundred pages or so) treatise seemingly for young priests or other neophytes. If you are interested in knowing what a good Catholic Christian was supposed to believe in the fourth century, try to find a copy of this (it is reprinted in Great Books of the Western World). The work is interesting for two reasons. First, you will find that not much has changed in the last sixteen centuries. That is either shocking or reassuring, depending on your point of view. Second, the treatise contains a long section on the difference between signs and symbols. The distinction interests me, although it may not interest you.

The other work is a very great book of several hundred pages. Called *The City of God*, it draws a distinction between two "cities," as Augustine called them, one of God, the other of man. The book was completed near the end of Augustine's life, in the year 430. Twenty years before, in the year 410, Rome had been sacked by marauding barbarians, and the pagan Romans who survived that defeat blamed the Christians. Augustine began to write *The City of God* immediately, to counter that charge and to show that the real culprit was the so-called gods of the Greco-Roman pantheon, whose worship had been the work of the Devil. As he lay dying in Hippo in November 430, word came that his own city was under siege by another barbarian tribe. The destruction of his home, and then of the city of Rome itself a few months later, has been taken as a convenient date by which to begin the Middle Age. It is true that his Catholic doctrines had enormous influence for the next thousand years and were held by many to be an alternative orthodoxy to the system of St. Thomas Aquinas.

# ANONYMOUS

—

## The Song of Roland

No one knows who gave the *Song of Roland* its final form. Undoubtedly many poets and troubadours made contributions to it: in a sense it was the product of an entire age, that of the ninth and tenth centuries in Western Europe. Nothing expresses the beliefs of that age better than this poem.

Composed over a period of perhaps a century and a half—from 850, say, to about 1000—the poem describes an event that had occurred long before, during the reign of Charlemagne, Holy Roman Emperor and king of the French, who died in CE 814. Charlemagne was a real man but he was also mythic: he attracted legends as a pot of honey attracts flies. This, the best of all his legends, is the story of the heroic champion who was known as his nephew Roland, or as he later came to be called by Italians, Orlando.

There are many stories about Roland, and one of them even calls in question whether he was actually the nephew of Charlemagne. At Sutri, near Rome, stands an ancient castle that now serves as the home of a farmer who lives with his family in the thousand-year-old barn. Friends who live in the castle itself say that in what is now the barnyard and was once the courtyard of the castle Roland met Charlemagne during Charlemagne's visit to Latium in A.D. 790, when he convened with Pope Adrian I for political discussions that changed the course of European history.

During ceremonies after the meeting, Charlemagne enquired formally whether any of his followers would ask of him a boon. A certain lovely woman advanced to the throne: she was one of the handmaidens of the Queen. She had a son, she confessed, though she was not married, and because of her faithful service to the Queen she asked that the King recognize her son and take him into his band of closest followers. He was already, the woman claimed, a valiant fighter. "His name?" the King asked. "Roland," the boy's mother replied. The King accepted him, both legitimizing and honoring him in one act. The boy may have been his own son by this handmaiden of his Queen.

Roland grew up and became the King's right hand, the first among the Twelve Peers of the realm, the leader of Charlemagne's armies in a hundred battles. Brave and stubborn, fierce and unyielding, ready to defend with his life any slight upon his own honor or that of his King, Roland was the epitome of the medieval knight, the vassal faithful to his lord until death and demanding equal loyalty from those who followed him. A simple man in the extreme, he saw all things as black or white; there were no shades of gray, no difficult moral problems. He was right and the enemy wrong. God was his ally and against his enemies.

*The Song of Roland* tells of how Roland is betrayed by his stepfather Ganelon, whose name betokens treachery to this day; of how Ganelon arranges it so that Roland commands the rear guard of Charlemagne's army as it moves through the deep passes of the Pyrenees, leaving Spain after seven long years of warfare against the Infidel; of how the treacherous Paynim, egged on by Ganelon, attacks Roland and the Twelve Peers along with twenty thousand men, in the defile of Roncesvaux; of how Roland and all his followers are slain and of how Charlemagne revenges Roland's death and punishes Ganelon. The story is straightforward, simple, and predictable. Roland refuses out of pride to call for help when he and his men are attacked and when he finally blows his famous horn it is too late for Oliver, his friend, and all his followers, and for Roland himself, who dies on the field stretched out upon his sword Durendal.

The poem's primal simplicity does not detract from it. Roland is not a modern man nor is his world the modern world. His world died centuries ago. Good riddance to it, we may say, it was a world in which the only honorable occupation was fighting, killing, or being killed, a world in which butchers were exalted to the highest places among men. But it was also a world in which honor was clear and clean and palpable, apparent to all. There were no doubts about what a man ought to do with his life, no second thoughts, and no regrets if one's career was ended by an early death as long as the death was noble and one died on the battlefield facing the enemy.

Men and women shared these beliefs even if they were not knights. Duke William of Normandy had a troubadour, the best in the world as he thought, named Taillefer. Taillefer had grown old in the Duke's service and when William invaded England in the famous year 1066 and met King Harold the Saxon at Hastings, Taillefer asked a boon. "Lord," he asked, "let me lead the charge against the enemy." "You cannot lead the charge," the Duke replied. "You are not a knight and besides, you are not armed." "As for being a knight, you can change that with the tip of your sword," said Taillefer. "And as for being armed, your other knights are well armed and will win the day."

Duke William told him to kneel and knighted Taillefer on the spot. And Taillefer led the charge, riding on his horse and singing at the top of his voice the great verses of *The Song of Roland* that tell of the death of Roland and the revenge of Charlemagne. Taillefer was struck down the moment the armies met but we know, because he was a medieval man to whom chivalry was real, that he had obtained his dearest wish.

If you can understand how Taillefer felt you will have no trouble understanding this splendid old poem out of another age.

# ANONYMOUS

—

*"The Tumbler of Our Lady"*

I don't believe anyone knows the name of the author of this story, but it is nevertheless one I love. It was one of a collection of stories gathered by Gautier de Coinci, a monk of St. Medard, near Soissons in France. Once a royal abbey of the Frankish kings and the goal of many pilgrimages, hardly a trace of it now remains. The manuscript which includes the stories, now in Soissons, is a lovely example of the thirteenth-century art of bookmaking. Each story has its appropriate illustration on a background of gold, blue, and red. The stories were translated from Latin into French and were often based on Eastern originals, some brought by Crusaders, others by traders and travelers. Whatever their original source they were all dedicated to Our Lady, *advocata nostra* as St. Bernard called her. And again, whatever their original sources, they were all turned into simple tales for simple, pious folk, whether monks or peasants. And of course they all told of wonderful miracles wrought by the Virgin, the Mother of God.

This one, "The Tumbler of Our Lady," could hardly be simpler. It seems that a certain man, weary of the world and having relinquished his horses, his clothes, his money—all that he had—and desiring never to return to his old life, has entered the great Monastery of Clairvaux, intending to spend the rest of his days in devotions to the Mother of God. The Abbot, the famous St. Bernard, has not examined very carefully into his background or abilities, content, the story suggests, with the gifts the man has offered and moved by his evident love of the Virgin, a love shared by the abbot himself.

For a while all goes well enough, except that the man is totally unschooled and does not even know how to pray to the Virgin or to God. He was a tumbler in his former life, a famous minstrel, and had performed in the courts of nobles as well as the king, always to great applause. But in the abbey there is no call for his skills, no place to perform. As time goes on he becomes at first embarrassed and then ashamed of his ignorance, which is laughed at by the monks (behind their hands). The man, growing desperate, seeks a quiet place and finds one in the crypt where there is an image of the Virgin, before which he kneels in supplication. He hears the bell ring for Mass and his heart assails him. He cannot attend Mass because he does not know any of the responses, but there is one thing he does know how to do. He strips himself of all but a belted tunic, lays his clothes on the altar beneath the image, and, saying "Lady, to your keeping I commend my body and my soul," he begins to turn somersaults, now high, now low, first forwards, then backwards. When he is exhausted he kneels and says: "Lady, the others serve, and I serve also. Do not despise your servant, for I serve you for your diversion. I do homage to you with my heart, and my body, and my feet, and my hands, for naught beside this do I understand."

From this time forth, whenever he hears the bell for Mass he dances and jumps and leaps until he falls to the ground from sheer fatigue. This goes on for a long time until, one day, he is discovered by a young monk who blames him because he does not come to matins, and following, finds him dancing and capering, as he thinks, just for his own pleasure. The young monk goes to the Abbot and tells him what he has seen.

The Abbot, Bernard of Clairvaux, swears him to silence and goes himself to the crypt. Lo, he sees the man leaping and jumping until he falls to the ground in a swoon. And then the Abbot observes descend from the vaulting so glorious a lady that never has he seen one so fair or so richly crowned. Her clothes are adorned with gold and precious stones. She is accompanied by angels who solace and sustain the tumbler. The sweet, noble lady takes a white cloth and with it gently fans her minstrel before the altar, but of this the man knows nothing nor does he perceive that he is in such fair company.

Not long afterward the Abbot sends for the man. He is fearful because he believes he must have wronged God and his Mother. The Abbot examines him and requires him to tell everything that he has done. The man does so, then falls weeping and kisses the Abbot's feet. The Abbot, weeping himself, raises him up and tells him he should never fear and adds, "Fair, gentle brother, pray for me and I will pray for thee." The man is so overcome with joy that he can no longer devote himself to Our Lady, and in a short while he dies.

I will not tell you how this lovely story ends because I hope you can find it in a book edited by Jessie Weston called "The Tumbler of Our Lady," published in the year 1900. There are other miracles in the book because the time—the twelfth century of our era and the thirteenth also—was a time when such miracles were believed by everyone. I think it is a shame that this is no longer so. Note: For more about this, read the entry on Henry Adams's *Mont-Saint-Michelle and Chartres*.

At the same time it is important to remember that this kind of simple faith was not shared by all in the twelfth century. For example, the famous and again anonymous "Ballad of Aucassin and Nicolette" tells a very different kind of story. Aucassin loves Nicolette with all his heart, but his adoration is not rewarded, at least at first. He even rebels against the warnings of a great churchman who declares that his illicit love threatens both him and his lady. He responds:

> In Paradise what have I to win? Therein I seek not to enter, but only to have Nicolette. For into Paradise go none but such folk as I shall tell thee now: Thither go those same old priests, and halt old men and maimed, who all day and night cower continually before the altars, and in the crypts; and such folk as wear old arnicas and old clouted frocks, and naked folk and shoeless, and covered with sores, perishing of hunger and thirst, and of cold, and of little ease. These be they that go into Paradise, with them have I naught to make. But into Hell I would fain go; for into Hell fare the goodly clerks and goodly knights that fall in tourneys and great wars, and stout men at arms, and all men noble. With

these would I liefly go. And thither pass the sweet ladies
and courteous that have two lovers, or three, and their
lords also thereto. Thither goes the gold, and the silver,
and cloth of vair, and cloth of gris, and harpers, and
makers, and the princes of this world. With these would
I fain go, let me but have with me Nicolette, my
sweetest lady.

In the end he doesn't have to make this choice. He overcomes all
obstacles, wins Nicolette, marries her, and all is well.

# JOSEPH BÉDIER
### 1864–1938
*The Romance of Tristan and Iseult*

Joseph Bédier was born in Paris in 1864. He was a distinguished
scholar who made contributions to our knowledge of medieval literature. His major scholarly work, the four-volume *Les Légendes Épiques*
(1908-21), advanced a theory that is now widely accepted about the
old French epic poems, the *chansons de geste*. These were composed
by the troubadours, according to Bédier, on subjects and themes
proposed by the monks who traveled on pilgrimages from various sites
in France to the shrine of Saint James in Spain, Santiago de
Compostela. The troubadours traveled with the monks on these long,
slow journeys from the cold north of France to the warm spring of
Galicia at Easter time, singing as they rode. One imagines the sun
glinting on the armor of the knights who, for protection, rode along
with these bands of pious travelers, the banners waving in the gentle
breezes, the birds singing in the trees and the fields full of flowers....

The favorite of all the *chansons de geste* was the story of Tristan
and Iseult. Many poets sang the tale and so it took a number of
different forms, but the basic events in the story were these: Iseult
of Ireland was to marry King Mark of Cornwall. Her mother
prepared a potion of exceeding strength for her daughter and the

bridegroom to drink, a potion that would ensure their everlasting love. King Mark sent his nephew, Tristan, to Ireland to accompany his bride to her new home. They took ship to cross the Irish Sea but during the voyage, by accident the story says, they drank the potion. They were thus bound together in love forevermore, a love that could only end with their deaths.

They tried to remain loyal to the king. They slept with a drawn sword, naked and shining, between them in the bed. King Mark somehow understood and forgave them. Iseult married the king. Tristan left England and crossed the sea to Brittany. There he met and married another woman, Iseult of the White Hands, "for her name and beauty," but the marriage was a formality; the symbolic sword was still drawn in the bed. Nevertheless Tristan was betrayed by his enemies at the court of King Mark and, wounded by a poisoned arrow, was dying. It was agreed that Iseult of Ireland should be sent for since she possessed the arts of healing. She came, but the lovers were betrayed by Iseult of the White Hands and died in one another's arms.

The original versions of the tale were harsh and unforgiving: adultery was both a crime and a cruel joke. During the twelfth century, the Anglo-Norman poet Thomas produced a softer, more romantic version. Gottfried von Strassburg wrote, around 1200, an even later version that is the jewel of German medieval poetry; it was on this version that Wagner based his opera *Tristan und Isolde*. Bédier preferred the version of Thomas and produced an adaptation of it in modern French in 1900; the English title is *The Romance of Tristan and Iseult*.

Bédier, besides being a good scholar, was also a good writer and his version is one of the most beautiful of prose poems. The journey across the windswept sea from Ireland to Cornwall, the drinking of the potion and its immediate, terrible effect, the drawn sword in the bed of love, the gift given to Iseult by Tristan when he must leave her, the treachery of Iseult of the White Hands—all of these episodes possess an almost unearthly loveliness and sadness that in my opinion are rare indeed. Above all the tale, as Bédier tells it, is unmarked by any hint of scandal, duplicity, or shame: the lovers try to be loyal to their rightful lord and their fall from grace is noble. The story is a tragedy of love in which the end result is death.

Bédier had deep sympathy for the star-crossed lovers; he under-stood them, too. In their hearts the love they felt for each other was the greatest gift the world could give, and if it was accompanied by unrelenting pain, this, as it was for Taillefer, was a price they were willing to pay.

# THOMAS AQUINAS
## 1225–1274
### *Summa Theologica*

Thomas Aquinas was born in 1224 or 1225 in the town of Aquino, south of Rome. His parents possessed a modest feudal domain, and they were ambitious for their son, whom they destined very early for a career in the Church. When still a boy, Thomas was placed in the monastery of Monte Cassino near his home in the hope that he would some day become its abbot.

In 1239 Thomas was required to move to the University of Naples, where he became interested in the teachings of the Dominicans, which order he joined. The Dominican fathers decided to send him to Paris, the center of theological research and speculation at the time. He set out in the spring of 1244 but was abducted on the road by his family, who did not want him to go to Paris and undertake a teaching, instead of a political, career. After a year of captivity he was allowed to leave. He went to Paris to the convent of Saint-Jacques for study under the great teacher Albertus Magnus. He was immediately plunged into a controversy that was rocking the Church.

Three fundamental positions were vying for dominance in the theological thought of the time. First, there was the spiritual Christian Platonism that had been injected into Catholic thought by St. Augustine in the fourth century and that was the traditional conservative view. Second, there was the position of the Arab scholar Averroes, who held that there were two truths, the one of reason and the other of faith. Finally, there was the new position of the Aristotelians, who maintained that there was only one truth

and that there was no basic conflict between nature, if rightly interpreted, and religion.

Aristotelianism represented a radical new departure, and Thomas
was attracted by the novel doctrine. He was soon involved in the
controversy and became known as the leading spokesman of the
Aristotelians. He engaged in public disputes with various traditional-
ists, defeated the Averroists, and lived to see Aristotelianism's official
triumph, although the fundamentalist spirituality of the Augustinians
has never died out of Catholic Christianity.

Thomas wrote many works. He was often writing more than one
book at a time, which he would dictate to different scribes, sending still
other scribes or students to search out and check references and citations. He sometimes employed as many as twenty assistants at a time.

Without their help it seems unlikely that he could have composed
the more than fifty volumes of theology that are known to have come
from his hand. His greatest work is the *Summa Theologica*, on which
he worked from about 1265 until his death in 1274. It fills some
twenty-five volumes in the complete edition translated by the
Dominican Fathers.

Despite its enormous size the *Summa* is, as Thomas makes clear at
the beginning, no more than a primer of Catholic theology for the
instruction of beginning students. The *Summa* can therefore be read,
or read in, by anyone.

The *Summa Theologica* is organized in the form of "questions"
concerning God and man and their relation, the Angels and their
relations to both God and man, virtue and vice, politics and art,
knowledge and ignorance, teaching and learning—indeed, almost all
of the matters of importance to mankind. One fascinating question
deals with the aureoles—the golden circles that surround the heads
of saints in medieval paintings. Several questions deal with escha-
tology, the science of "last things"—the Day of Judgment, the means
whereby the dead will rise from their graves, the mode of corporeality
that they will enjoy, and the orders of punishments and rewards.

The book has great authority and to read it is very exciting. But
only if you know how to do so.

The *Summa* as a whole is divided into several Parts, these Parts
into Questions, and these into Articles. Examination of the opening

of the first Part of the first Part, on God, reveals the interior organization of the work.

The first question of all is "Whether God exists." The Articles are
then presented in contradiction to the truth. That is, a wrong answer
is stated as a subject and this is then disproved and shown to be false:
the opposite is therefore true.

Article I is: "It seems that God does not exist." Arguments are
given to support this contention. The prosecution, as it were, then
rests, and the defense takes over. The first rebuttal is always a quotation from Scripture. In this case, the text cited is:

"On the contrary, God says in His own person, I am that I am."

Other arguments, not from Scripture but from reason, follow,
Thomas stating all the major ones. Finally, in his own voice, he says:
"I answer that ... " and responds to the false arguments that were
listed earlier in support of the false premise of the Article.

Having established in this exquisitely cumbersome way the existence of God, the *Summa* then moves on to other theological questions. The form is always the same, and the truth always emerges in
the same tortured way.

Tortured perhaps, but also dramatic. The form of the Disputation,
the major conflicts of will and reason that marked the late Middle
Age, is always at work in the *Summa Theologica* to produce a living,
almost throbbing work of literature.

It is not a book to read from beginning to end. That would take
years. But the *Summa* is always interesting, wherever you start to read.
Begin with a subject that especially intrigues you. Practice reading
the queer, inverted form of the Articles. Learn and enjoy.

Thomas Aquinas was summoned by Pope Gregory X to the
second Council of Lyons in 1274, where he probably would have
been chastised. But he died on the way, at the Cistercian abbey of
Fossanova. Several of his theses were thereafter condemned by the
masters of Paris, the highest theological jurisdiction of the Church.
But the modified realism of Thomas Aquinas was important and
valuable, representing as it does the reasonable middle position
between excessive spiritualism on the one hand and excessive
rationalism on the other. Thomas was canonized a saint in 1323,
officially named a doctor of the Church in 1567, and proclaimed as

the leading protagonist of orthodoxy during the nineteenth century.

All that need not concern you too much. The important thing about Thomas Aquinas, and particularly about his *Summa Theologica*, is that the book is a pleasure to read despite the strangeness and unfamiliarity of its form.

# DANTE ALIGHIERI
## 1265–1321
### *The Divine Comedy*

Dante called his masterpiece a "comedy" because it told of the passage of the soul through Hell and Purgatory to Heaven and the vision of God—that is, it ended happily. If the journey had been in the opposite direction and ended badly he might have titled it *The Divine Tragedy*. Dante's understanding of these terms was not profound; it depended upon an abbreviated Latin synopsis of the *Poetics* of Aristotle. Neither Dante nor anyone else in Italy during the thirteenth century could read ancient Greek; there were no original texts of Greek classical authors in the West until after Dante's death. The word "Divine" in the title was added later, by critics and readers who thought the poem was so good Dante could not have written it without God's help. They may well have been correct.

Dante Alighieri was born in Florence in 1265, of a petit bourgeois family. He was ambitious to excel both in politics and in poetry. His first book, *La Vita Nuova* (*The New Life*; 1293), an allegorical amalgam of prose and verse, ensured his literary reputation. He was not so fortunate in politics. The year 1301 was his undoing. He was elected in that year to an important post, but while he was on a diplomatic mission outside the city enemies managed to have him condemned for various crimes. He was exiled from Florence and never set foot in his city again. He died in 1321, in Ravenna. Of course by this time he was famous and Florence, which had banished him, petitioned for the return of his body. Ravenna refused, as it does to this day. There are many memorials of Dante in his native city, but his remains are not there.

For the remaining twenty years of his life Dante wandered from city to city throughout Italy, surviving on the undependable generosity of a succession of wealthy men. He learned how salty is the taste, as he wrote, of another's bread, and how steep are another's stairs.

*La Divina Commedia* is in one hundred verse chapters, or cantos, which are assembled into three canzone, or parts. (The first canto is an introduction to the entire poem; each of the three parts then contains thirty-three cantos, for a total of one hundred. Dante is always careful about this sort of detail.) The first part, called *Inferno* (Hell), relates Dante's meeting with the Roman poet Virgil, who is to guide him through the Underworld, and their subsequent journey together through Hell. According to Dante, Hell is shaped like an enormous cone of concentric circles, going from greater to less as you descend (as the souls of the sinners punished there grow smaller and meaner). These great circles of Hell correspond more or less to the Seven Deadly Sins. All of these sins are deadly; that is, they all entail remorseless damnation and punishment without relief throughout eternity, but they vary in seriousness and intensity, from Lust, the least serious, through Greed, Avarice, Spiritual Sloth, Anger, and Envy, to Pride, the worst of all.

As Dante and Virgil move down through the circles of Hell they meet real people, many of them historical personages, others personal enemies and even some friends of Dante. In the years at the beginning of the fourteenth century, when Dante was writing his poem, most readers recognized these people encountered in Hell, and they appreciated the satirical revenges wrought by Dante upon enemies who had harmed him in his real life. Today, we have to read the notes that accompany any good edition of *The Divine Comedy*. These notes are often a bore but they have to be read. They are the price that has to be paid to read Dante.

Not only does Hell become smaller the farther Dante descends with Virgil at his side, but it also becomes colder. In the last circle the souls of traitors are frozen in ice, signifying the coldness of their hearts when they were still alive on earth. At the very bottom of

Hell, which is also the dead center of the earth, stands the dread figure of Satan, the proudest of all sinners, frozen in the ice up to his waist and grinding in his teeth the arch traitor Judas, who betrayed his friend and master. Having endured all the levels of Hell, Dante is able to pass through its center and emerge on the other side, at the base of the Mountain of Purgatory.

Dante's and Virgil's journey through Hell is one of the most famous events in literature. It has been the source of innumerable drawings and paintings and the subject of endless commentaries and critical appreciations. It is true that Dante's major poetic strengths are much in evidence in *Inferno*: his skill at characterization, his ability to describe a concrete scene in just a few lines or even a few words so that it suddenly is realized before our very eyes, the power, grace, and flexibility of his verse. It is also true that *Inferno* contains wonderful and memorable scenes: Paolo and Francesca, guilty lovers doomed forever to enjoy only one another and not God; the Gluttons, gnawed eternally by the teeth of their hunger; the Fallen Angels and the Furies, and the Heavenly Messenger who rescues Dante from them; the great heretic, Farinata degli Uberti, who "entertained great scorn of Hell"; Dante's old teacher, Brunetto Latini, doomed to run forever in payment for his sexual tastes; the Simonist Popes, already in Hell though not yet dead; Ulysses and his moving account of his own death; the Giants, looming terrible in the half-darkness of deep Hell; Ugolino, with his chilling story of his death and that of his children, immured in the Tower of Pisa.

It is not surprising, then, that so many readers enjoy *Inferno* and think, when they have finished it, that they have read enough of *The Divine Comedy*. Alas, they have not! To stop reading there is to miss another side of Dante that is even more wonderful than the tough, graphic realism of *Inferno*. Some of the most beautiful scenes in poetry are purposely placed by Dante in *Purgatorio* to balance the horrors of Hell, and the flights of thought and imagination that mark the third part of *The Divine Comedy*—*Paradiso*—possess a grandeur and luminosity seen in no other poem.

*Purgatorio* and *Paradiso* are no more difficult to read than *Inferno*, although some readers seem to believe they are. (None of *The Divine Comedy* is easy to read.) Perhaps this is because evil has come to seem more real than goodness, or it may be that scenes of pain and suffering have a fascination not possessed by scenes of bliss. There is plenty of pain and torment in *Purgatorio*, too, the difference being that here the suffering is not endless. It is a cleansing not a punishing fire that burns these souls. They will eventually reach Paradise—in a shorter or, perhaps, a longer time, but what matter how long the wait considering the good that is to be found there?

I myself am no longer able to read *Inferno*. Even though I am the first to concede its incomparable power, emotionally I can hardly stand it. In its place *Purgatorio* has become my favorite part of *The Divine Comedy*. I have reached the age when my own death no longer seems impossible, as was the case when I was young. I wonder, these days, about what is likely to happen afterwards. I cannot hope for bliss, certainly not immediate bliss; but I do hope that something like Dante's Mountain of Purgatory is there to climb. I would be content to spend the necessary time and effort in the climbing in order finally to attain what can be found at the summit.

Virgil, the pagan poet and the symbol, in Dante's scheme, of enlightened reason without the gift of Grace, is able to guide Dante only to the border of the Earthly Paradise, which surmounts Purgatory. There, Virgil must depart. He can go no farther, for he was not a Christian. The moment when Dante turns to exclaim with pleasure at what he sees, as he has done many times before—and finds Virgil gone—is one of the most affecting in literature.

> I turned me to the left with the trust with which the
>    little child runs to his mother when he is
>    frightened or when he is afflicted
> to say to Virgil: "Less than a drop of blood is left
>    in me that trembleth not; I recognize the tokens
>    of the ancient flame."
> But Virgil had left us bereft of himself, Virgil
>    dearest Father, Virgil for whom for my weal
>    I gave me up;
> nor did all that our dearest mother lost, avail to
>    keep my dew-washed cheeks from turning
>    dark again with tears.

Dante is alone now, in a beautiful garden, but he is soon astounded by the appearance of a magnificent medieval procession complete with chariots drawn by heraldic beasts. Out of the last chariot of all steps a veiled woman. This is the lady Beatrice.

The story of Dante and Beatrice is well known but bears retelling. Beatrice Portinari was a girl in Florence when Dante was growing up. He met her first in the street when he was nine years old and she about five. The extraordinary thing is that he fell in love with her instantly and carried the love within him until his death. He married another woman and had seven children with her; Beatrice married another man and died, very young, in childbirth. Dante's love for Beatrice was no secret. He proclaimed it in his early autobiographical work, *La Vita Nuova*, and told the world about it in *The Divine Comedy*, which was dedicated to the memory of Beatrice and in which he said of her "what was never yet said of any woman." Dante thus made Beatrice world famous as his inspiration and his muse.

The date of Dante's journey through Hell, Purgatory, and Heaven is Easter weekend of the year 1300, although he was working on the poem until his death in 1321. On that assumed date of 1300 Beatrice was already dead and, Dante also assumes, in Heaven. Now, in the poem, she has journeyed down from Heaven to the Earthly Paradise to meet him on his journey upward. At first she refuses to raise her veil. When she does, he is taken aback by the sternness of her look. She chastises him for having fallen away from his youthful innocence and purity of heart. He weeps, she forgives him, and she smiles. He feels within him all the force of *l'antica fiamma*, the ancient flame of love for her, and she leads him on his way to the throne of God.

*Paradiso*, the third part of The Comedy, is unfortunately where many readers stumble and lose their way. Theology, with which this part of the poem is deeply concerned, is no longer ordinary fare and there are pages, too, on which even Dante's powerful poetic imagination may have flagged. But if you will give *Paradiso* a real chance, reading it slowly and thoughtfully, not feeling pressed, above all not feeling that you must understand everything the first time through, you may find—as others have—that *Paradiso* contains moments that transcend even *Inferno* and *Purgatorio*, that transcend, indeed, any other poetry. The last half dozen cantos are the finest of all.

The occasion is the Beatific Vision of the Living God, and Dante rises to it.

A sign that you have approached that vision in your own right is that you have understood a conversation between Dante and a certain Piccarda, whom he meets in the third canto of *Paradiso*. Piccarda is "low down" in Heaven, a great distance by our mortal measure from God, for reasons having to do with her late repentance for sin while she was in life. Dante asks if her position in the heavenly scheme troubles or disappoints her. "No, of course not," Piccarda replies. "I am content to be where He has placed me, for," she adds, "in His will is our peace." This famous statement comes close to summing up the meaning of *The Divine Comedy*.

The poem is more than the sum of its meaning. It is also the supreme creation of medieval art. Its words are strange, haunting, and beautiful. Its images implant themselves on the screen of the memory. It rewards any amount of time devoted to reading it

## GEOFFREY CHAUCER
### 1340?–1400
*The Canterbury Tales*
*Troilus and Criseyde*

Geoffrey Chaucer was born about 1340, probably in London, of prosperous middle-class parents who were able to provide him with a good education. He married a sister of Catherine Swynford, the third wife of John of Gaunt, the son of Edward III and, as Duke of Lancaster, the leader of the Lancastrian faction in the fifteenth-century civil Wars of the Roses. Through him and probably others, Chaucer obtained at various times throughout his life important and lucrative official posts. He might be described in modern terms as a senior civil servant who was also a great poet. He seems to have possessed a singularly moderate temperament and an exemplary character, for he had many friends and few, if any, enemies. He loved books, as he tells us in several places in his works, and was well read;

for example, he may have been the first Englishman to know the writings of Dante and Boccaccio, with whose works he became acquainted during several trips to Italy on diplomatic missions—the king's business, as he called it. But he also loved human beings and was able to forgive them their follies; although he knew everything about human wickedness he was never indignant or censorious. He was, in short, a nice man.

As late as 1850, even 1900, most persons even in the rich countries of the world were cold in winter and usually spent the long winter nights in darkness. They were used to it, one is inclined to think; cold is partly a state of mind, and eyes grow accustomed to the dark. But in northern Europe and England the nights in winter are very long and very cold, and no amount of "getting used to it" can overcome the discomfort that, today, we can only imagine. Occasionally a power outage or an empty fuel tank or a bill unpaid reminds us of what life was like for almost everybody throughout most of the history of mankind. (I am reminded of an account by the historian Fernand Braudel of a certain January dinner party at Louis XIV's palace at Versailles. That night, reports Braudel, the wine froze in the glasses on the magnificently appointed tables. The King of France was the richest man in the world and if he was cold, then everybody was.)

A healthy dose of cold and darkness might be the best possible preparation for reading Chaucer's *Canterbury Tales*. Written at a time—the end of the fourteenth century—well before the discovery of fossil fuels and electric power and the other conveniences of modern life, the poem evokes for us overwhelmingly the sense of spring, when cold, dark winter is replaced by light and warmth, and everyone, not just young lovers, can venture out once more.

> *When in April the sweet showers fall*
> > *And pierce the drought of March to the root, and all*
> > *The veins are bathed in liquor of such power*
> *As brings about the engendering of the flower,*
> > *When also Zephyrus with his sweet breath*
> > *Exhales an air in every grove and heath*
> *Upon the tender shoots, and the young sun*
> > *His half-course in the sign of the Ram has run,*

*And the small fowl are making melody*
*That sleep away the night with open eye*
*(So nature pricks them and their heart engages)*
*Then people long to go on pilgrimages*
*And palmers long to seek the stranger strands*
*Of far-off saints, hallowed in sundry lands,*
*And specially, from every shire's end*
*In England, down to Canterbury they wend*
*To seek the holy blissful martyr, quick*
*To give his help when they were sick.*

The only thing that might be puzzling about those famous, wonderful lines that begin the "General Prologue" of *The Canterbury Tales* is the statement in the last seven of them. Perhaps it would not occur to you to go on a pilgrimage for your spring break. But, like everyone else, you want to go somewhere and it might not be so difficult to accept an invitation to ride with an interesting and joyous company through the countryside of southern England, from dark, dirty London to the lovely cathedral town of Canterbury, with birds singing in the trees and flowers blooming in the fields along the way. That, at any rate, is the invitation that Chaucer tenders us. Hardly any reader has ever been anything but grateful.

*The Canterbury Tales* was Chaucer's last and most ambitious work. It is unfinished; not half done, according to the plan he lays out in the "General Prologue." That hardly matters. The poem could be longer or shorter and still be as good because it is mainly a collection of separate stories, most of them interesting, some of them among the funniest stories in English literature. Chaucer may not have made up any of them from scratch, but that doesn't matter either. The genius of Chaucer was not originality.

He was a funny man who must have smiled easily and often. This was probably one reason why people liked him. And he liked them. Some thirty persons join him on his imaginary poetical pilgrimage to Canterbury and he likes almost all of them, although some more than others; the Pardoner he may not have liked at all. His favorite may have been the Prioress, who was called Madame Eglantyne and who spoke French "after the scole [school] of Stratford atte Bowe"—that is, with an English accent. She was a worldly ecclesiastic and wore about her neck a locket that revealed her motto: *amor vincit omnia*, "love conquers all," a sentiment that indeed may be understood in a religious sense but probably not by Madame Eglantyne. Or Chaucer's favorite may have been the Knight, with his ceremonial manners and deep solemnity, or the rambunctious Wife of Bath, still seeking Mr. Right after burying eight husbands. These are joined by a Reeve and a Priest and a Miller and … well, when you read the "General Prologue" you will know all who were there and you will wish you were of their number.

When you have finished the "Prologue" begin on the tales themselves. Read as many, or as few, as you wish. Chaucer would not have cared.

*The Canterbury Tales* was written before modern English came into existence. Chaucer wrote in the common, ordinary language of his day—although enriched by his learning and his wit—with no intent and certainly no desire to be antique or to pose problems for his readers. But the Middle English, so-called, of his time and place changed rapidly in the century after his death in 1400, and even learned Englishmen found it difficult to understand and appreciate his poetry two centuries later, to say nothing of six centuries later where we are today. It is therefore the better part of valor to begin reading Chaucer in a modern version (for example, the one by Nevill Coghill, which I quoted above) that smoothes out some of the roughest places and replaces obsolete words with familiar ones. If, however, you decide you really like Chaucer you may wish to try him in Middle English, preferably in an edition that prints the original text on one page and a modern redaction on the facing page. Also, try to find some learned person who knows how to read Middle English aloud so you can have an idea of what it sounded like. (It's beautiful.) After a while, with a "pony" or glossary by your side, you will be able to do all this yourself.

Chaucer wrote many works besides *The Canterbury Tales*. Probably the best of them is his retelling of the classical love tragedy of *Troilus and Criseyde*. It is a superb story, superbly told by Chaucer, but again it was not original with him. He took it from Boccaccio, in many ways improving on it.

Troilus is a noble young Trojan, one of the many sons of King Priam; Criseyde is a charming Trojan widow, somewhat older than Troilus, considerably more experienced in the ways of the world, and even, be it said, a trifle flighty. Troilus falls passionately in love with her and, through the good offices of his close friend, Criseyde's uncle Pandarus (from whose name we get the word "pander"), presents his suit and wins her favors. But as the war drags on and seems to go against the Trojans, Criseyde's father deserts to the Greek enemy. Criseyde accompanies him into the Grecian camp. There, as one of the few women and almost the only pretty young one, she is vehemently wooed by several Greek warriors. Criseyde genuinely loves Troilus, but he is far away and she may never see him again. She finally becomes the mistress of Diomedes, one of the Greek generals.

Troilus, of course, is in despair. He sallies forth, not caring whether he lives or dies, and is killed in battle. He is swept up into heaven (he being a hero of love and thus having a special dispensation) and looks down upon the Earth. At the close of the poem he expresses his deep pity for mortal humankind.

Shakespeare also wrote a version of the story of Troilus and Criseyde. His play is remarkable for its cynicism and coldness; the heroes are all villains (especially the Greeks) and the lovers are fools. That is very far from the tone of Chaucer's work, which possesses a sweetness that has endured for six centuries and is likely to endure for six more. The love of Chaucer's Troilus for Criseyde is misguided, but then Troilus is really still only a boy. In happier circumstances Chaucer's Criseyde would not have betrayed her young lover. That is why Chaucer's version is a tragedy of love, while Shakespeare's is a hard comedy that leaves a bitter taste in the mouth. *Troilus and Criseyde* is one poem I think you will definitely want to read if you find yourself becoming one of Chaucer's devotees.

# chapter five

# The Renaissance, Part One

It is an odd fact that some people do not know what the word "renaissance" really means. To them it is simply a term that describes a period in Western literary history—the period from Dante to Shakespeare, maybe. But the word has a definite meaning and it is important to know and remember it.

A renaissance is a "rebirth." Perhaps most people more or less clearly recognize that. But the question is, what is the Renaissance a rebirth of?

At the beginning, in the fourteenth century, it meant the rebirth of Classical learning. It was not the birth of something entirely new, but instead the rebirth of something very old. Two men were among the first to realize that something that had been lost could be found again, and together they set out to find it.

Francesco Petrarch, who was born in 1304 and died in 1374, and Giovanni Boccaccio, who was born in 1313 and died in 1375, hoped to find something they knew very little about although they believed it was important and beautiful. This was the great tradition of Latin and especially Greek Classical literature that was referred to in a few texts they knew but that existed in very few actual examples. There were synopses of *The Iliad* and *The Odyssey*, but no texts of the complete poems. There were a few letters of Cicero that referred to many more that were lost—or perhaps not, Petrarch and Boccaccio thought. One or two Greek plays had come down in obviously very corrupt editions, but there were hints that many more could be found. And the philosophical works of Plato and Aristotle were somewhere, because certain Arabic philosophers were said to know about them, but the Italians could no more read Arabic than they could read Greek, and these hints were simply not good enough.

Some things they did know, one of which was that in the Classical world that fascinated them because of its remoteness and mystery it had been the custom to crown poets with laurel leaves. Petrarch was a poet and a very good one, and he suggested to Boccaccio that they ought to find a way to crown him as poet laureate of the "new" world. This was arranged, Petrarch was crowned on the Capitol at Rome, and he then laid the crown at the marble feet of St. Peter in his great church. This ceremony was big news. But the lack of ancient texts was still a serious problem. Petrarch and Boccaccio together traveled around Italy, searching in the archives of old monasteries for any texts that might be lying around and unreadable by the monks themselves. In this way they discovered many of Cicero's letters that were important not so much because of what they said but because of the Latin in which they were written. It was quite different from the Latin of the Church, the language priests spoke and in which they celebrated mass. And so Petrarch, especially, began to try to write in this old Latin. But the very few examples of Greek were still unreadable.

This remained the fact for nearly a century after the deaths of our two wily and hopeful Italians, despite unremitting efforts on the part of others to seek out ancient manuscripts written on parchment that was very much the worse for wear. But in the year 1453 everything changed, and in a sense the Renaissance began.

What brought it about was a tragic event, from a Christian point of view. For centuries the city of Constantinople had remained as the capital of what was left of the Roman Empire, but it was situated in a part of the world that was surrounded on all sides by Ottoman Turks. In that fateful year the Turks finally captured Byzantium, as the city had been called for centuries, renamed it Istanbul, and celebrated by praying in the great basilica of Hagia Sophia, at the time the largest church not only in Christendom but also in the world.

For weeks and months before the city's fall refugees had begun to flee the city and travel westward. Many of them were scholars and most of them read and spoke Greek as their native language. And they carried with them priceless manuscripts written not on parch-ment but on paper, which Muslims had been using for centuries unbe-knownst to Christians in the West and which, among other things, was much easier to transport. Of course the refugees came first to Italy bearing their priceless treasures: complete texts of the Homeric poems, of many plays of Aeschylus, Sophocles, and Euripides, of the dialogues of Plato and the treatises of Aristotle. What was at first only a trickle soon became a flood, and our world began to take shape.

# FRANÇOIS RABELAIS
## 1483?–1553
### *Gargantua and Pantagruel*

François Rabelais was a doctor and like many of the best doctors he possessed an earthy sense of humor. Doctors, like lawyers, do not usually see us at our best; we are in physical (or legal) trouble when we visit them. The response of many lawyers is to become cynical; the response of many doctors is to become jovial. There is so much pain and so little they can do about it that the only thing to do, they seem to be saying, is to smile. Or even to guffaw—to react with a belly laugh directed at that old bully, the world.

This, at least, is the kind of doctor Rabelais was. He was probably born about 1483 and he took holy orders (he was a Franciscan priest) as well as receiving his doctorate from Montpellier, the best medical school in France. He never conducted a general practice, instead serving as personal physician to several members of the Du Bellay family, one of the most powerful families in France because of its closeness to the king. He possessed a great deal of medical knowledge, which keeps showing up in *Gargantua and Pantagruel*, the strange, wonderful book to which he devoted the last half of his life. Of course other kinds of knowledge also appear in the book: medieval versions of geography, astronomy, alchemy, and history, and much Renaissance lore as well. Rabelais was as cognizant of the new learning as anyone in the France of his time.

But humor, not learning, characterizes this book. Rabelais was one of the funniest men who ever lived; he clearly thought all the basic things that doctors know more about than anyone else are hilariously funny. He knew sex was a great pleasure but he also thought it was vastly amusing; he thought defecation was terribly funny; he thought micturation, breaking wind, and eructation were terribly funny; he even thought death was funny. Nor would he have used any of the pretentious euphemisms that I used in that sentence. He would have said pissing and farting and belching, and in fact he did use those and scores of other funny, weird words for things that are never mentioned in polite society but are nevertheless thought about there just as often as anywhere else. In this respect he was irrepressible. If these graphic words offend you, do not bother to read Rabelais. He is an X-rated author.

You should also not bother to read Rabelais if you believe that alcohol, instead of being one of God's greatest gifts, is the bane of man's existence. For Rabelais was a drinker and a lover of drinkers, and after laughter he surely thought that wine was the sovereign remedy for the ills of the world. Everyone in *Gargantua and Pantagruel* (except a few churlish priests) drinks all the time, and a great deal. If at any time they are not drinking this is probably because they are eating, which they also do frequently and in large quantities. Rabelais is the patron of all societies of eaters and drinkers, especially in France, and that is as it should be, for if you are going to eat and drink excessively you might as well have fun doing it, and Rabelais had fun doing everything.

*Gargantua and Pantagruel* is in five books, written over a period of twenty or thirty years. Book Two was composed before Book One, a fact that mostly concerns scholars. Together, Books One and Two are about the jovial, benevolent giant Gargantua and his equally enormous and good-hearted son, Pantagruel. In Book One Gargantua receives several different educations, and you can choose among them. First, he is "educated" by the puppies and kittens in his father's barn. Then he is given a medieval education by Master Tubal Holofernes, but this is soon followed by the Renaissance education administered by the scholar Ponocrates. The latter is demanding, but he provides the kind of humanistic education that survived in good colleges until quite recently. It includes, by the way, a lot of physical exercise, which helps to distinguish it from Holofernes' regimen, which takes place entirely indoors with the lads bent over dusty tomes.

Book One (which follows Book Two) ends with a fine and foolish war won by Gargantua with the help of the scruffy monk Friar John for whom, in gratitude, Gargantua builds the Abbey of Theleme. Here the monks and the nuns have friendly dinners together and wear colorful modern dress (i.e., fifteenth-century) instead of black habits. The motto of the abbey is "Do as thou wilt." All the inmates are excellent persons, says Rabelais, so it is both safe and a great promoter of happiness to allow them to do what they want instead of telling them how to do it or to do something else. The Abbey of Theleme is one of literature's most beguiling resorts: it deserves three stars in the Michelin guidebook of imaginary places.

Book Three (which follows Book One) belongs not to Gargantua or Pantagruel but to their scapegrace friend and penniless follower, Panurge, the perennial student of the University of Paris. Panurge is one of the most delicious villains in literature. He is a very bad young man but you cannot help smiling at the things he says and does—for example, at his plan for reinforcing the walls of Paris or his account of his revenge on a certain lady who refused his advances. Panurge engages in a ridiculous scholastic debate conducted entirely in sign language and performs many other scurvy tricks and bawdy entertainments for the benefit, as Rabelais says, of all good Pantagruelists everywhere. Indeed, by the end of Book Three it is clear that the author of this strange, unique work knows that he has created not just a book but also what the Germans call *Weltanschauung*—a special way of looking at the world.

Book Four is not as good as Book Three, and Rabelais probably did not write Book Five. It can be skipped. But no Pantagruelist can afford to skip Books Two, One, and Three (in that order).

Rabelais wrote at a time when French was not yet a fully formed language (just as Shakespeare wrote when English was not yet fixed in its grammar and vocabulary). Rabelais's bent was fantastical anyway, and *Gargantua and Pantagruel* contains hundreds, maybe thousands, of neologisms—words that Rabelais made up just because he liked the sound of them, or because there was no French word yet that meant what he wanted to say, or because there were only two or three French words and he wanted five or six. How, then, to translate such a work?

One of the miracles of literary history is that Rabelais found his ideal translator in Sir Thomas Urquhart, who produced a version of Books One and Two and part of Book Three (published 1653, 1693) that is fully as fantastical as the original. A second miracle: Urquhart did not complete his task; Pierre Motteux came along to finish it (in 1693-4) and if anything was better at the job than Urquhart. All good modern translations are based on their work, which you may read if you wish. In places, however, it is now rather antique, and so I recommend the fine modern redaction of Urquhart and Motteux prepared by that remarkable Pantagruelist Jacques LeClercq and published by the Modern Library.

# NICCOLÒ MACHIAVELLI
## 1469–1527
### *The Prince*

The life story of Niccolò Machiavelli is a sad one. Fortune, "that great strumpet" whom he described in colorful terms at the end of his little book, *The Prince*, did not deal with him either well or courteously.

Machiavelli was born in Florence in 1469, the son of an impecunious lawyer who was unable to give him a good education. As a consequence Machiavelli was largely self-educated, reading the many tattered old books in his father's library and being forced, through lack of teachers, to decide for himself what they meant.

He had been born in the year when Lorenzo the Magnificent, the greatest of the Medici, came to power in Florence, thus inaugurating a period of wealth and splendor in the city but also subverting its civil liberties. In 1498 the Medici were exiled, and a new government appointed Machiavelli, now twenty-nine, to be Florentine Secretary—in effect the ambassador of the city-state to the other city-states of Italy and to the great European powers. Machiavelli's family had always been civil servants, and he performed well in this post. He visited France three times and Germany once, writing reports on those countries that are still read. And he came to know Cesare Borgia, the son of the Borgia pope Alexander VI, at the time when the young man was attempting, at his father's behest, to unify the Papal States. Machiavelli was struck by the skill and ruthlessness with which Cesare controlled his followers and eliminated his enemies. Niccolò learned another kind of lesson a few months later. He was present in Rome when Cesare suffered ruin and disgrace following the death of his father, the Pope, and the elevation to the papal chair of an enemy of the Borgia family.

In 1512, after fourteen years as Florentine Secretary and many signal achievements for his native city, Machiavelli was himself deposed and exiled when the Medici returned to power. Exile was not the worst of it; he was also suspected of being involved in a plot to overthrow the new government and was tortured on the rack and imprisoned. The strumpet Fortune, having carried him high on her wheel, had now brought him low.

He was released from prison and, with his wife and children, retired to a small farm close to Florence. There, in the last part of his life, he worked in the fields by day but in the evening, after dinner, took succor from his memories not only of the great men he had met and talked with, but also of those he had known only through books. He would repair to his study, where, he wrote:

> At the threshold I take off my work-day clothes, filled with dust and mud, and don royal and curial garments. Worthily dressed, I enter into the ancient courts of the men of antiquity, where, warmly received, I feed on that which is my only food and which was meant for me. I am not ashamed to speak with them and ask them the reasons of their actions and they, because of their humanity, answer me. Four hours can pass, and I feel no weariness; my troubles forgotten, I neither fear poverty nor dread death.

Alone in his study, he "conversed" with Livy, Aristotle, and Polybius, and considered the reasons of human history and of the rise and fall of cities and states. He composed a long book, a commentary on the first ten books of Livy's *History*, and a short one, *The Prince*. The latter is one of the most famous books ever written.

Machiavelli attempted to use these works to regain the favor of the Medici in Florence. Curiously, it was not his brilliant political writings that brought him again to their attention but his comedies, one of which, *Mandragola*, was even performed before the Medici pope, Leo X, in 1520. He was asked to give advice and to write a history of Florence and a later Medici pope, Clement VII, exacted from him a plan for a national militia to defend Italy against the invaders from the north, most notably the King of France and the Emperor Charles V.

"I compare [Fortune] to one of those raging rivers," Machiavelli wrote in *The Prince*, "which when in flood overflows the plains, sweeping away trees and buildings, bearing away the soil from place to place; everything flies before it, all yield to its violence, without being able in any way to withstand it." Such was the descent into Italy in 1527 of the troops of Charles V who, mutinous and their pay in arrears, sacked Rome. There and then ended Machiavelli's hopes, as well as many other beautiful things. He died a few weeks later.

*The Prince*, understood in modern terms, is a book about management. A prince, of course, differs from a corporate executive in a number of ways, most notably perhaps in that if he fails the prince is likely not just to be dismissed but to have his head cut off. But the similarities are many, too. For the prince and the executive alike the hardest problem is trying to get people to do what he wants them to do and not what they want to do.

Machiavelli views mankind as under the control of two overriding passions, fear and love (or desire). The successful leader balances these two passions, manipulates them, and so controls his followers. In modern terms, the leader must balance the conflicting claims of the carrot and the stick, of reward and punishment. He who only rewards fails to retain the loyalty of his servants/employees; a high salary is not enough by itself to make a worker do his best for you. But threats alone do not avail, either; the organization of the most brutal tyrant is not thereby more efficient—in fact, such institutions are notoriously inefficient.

If the prince must choose between being loved and being feared, Machiavelli says, he should choose to be feared. This was but one of the judgments that led readers to say publicly that they despised this wily Italian, this "Machiavellian" adviser to rulers—while they read him in secret and heeded his advice.

Are such dismissals of Machiavelli fair? Was the author of *The Prince* himself Machiavellian? I do not think so. He was a sad and lonely man seeking to curry favor with rulers—the Medici—who he may have thought to be even more cynical than they really were. But one basic belief of Machiavelli may justify the disgust that his name evoked throughout the Renaissance—his belief that most men, and women too, are, for the most part, bad: greedy, selfish, untrustworthy, fickle, and as cruel as their circumstances allow them to be. Was Machiavelli right about this? Is it, in short, merely sentimental to say he was wrong? That, finally, is for every reader, indeed every human being, to decide. The decision is one of the most important that people ever make, guiding and directing their relations with other human beings at every turn.

# NICOLAUS COPERNICUS
### 1473–1543
*On the Revolutions of the Heavenly Spheres*

The life of Nicolaus Copernicus was very neatly divided into almost equal parts. Of his seventy years, the first half was spent getting educated. For Copernicus this was a very serious business. Born in Poland in 1473, he attended first the University of Cracow, devoting his time to liberal studies but concentrating in mathematics. He then went to Italy where, at the University of Bologna, he completed the course in canon law preparatory to a career in the Church. He gained a doctorate in this subject, but he also studied for four years at the medical school at Padua. When he returned to Poland in 1506 at the age of thirty-three he was not only a humanist learned in Greek, mathematics, and particularly astronomy, but also a jurist and a physician.

The second half of the life of Copernicus was essentially devoted to the writing of a book that would radically change men's thinking about the order and structure of the world. The book was titled *On the Revolutions of the Heavenly Spheres*, and although it existed in its basic parts as early as 1520, Copernicus was reluctant to publish it and did not do so until the very end of his life. Indeed, he died on the very day that an advance copy from the press was delivered to him—May 24, 1543. Many date the beginning of the modern world from that day.

It is important to understand what Copernicus did and also what he did not do. He did not discard the Ptolemaic idea that the planets are carried around their orbits on transparent, crystalline spheres—in other words, that it is the spheres that move, and the planets only because they are attached to the spheres. He did not discard the Ptolemaic idea that the motion of the planetary spheres is both regular and circular—because, as he wrote, "the motion of a sphere is to turn in a circle; by this very act expressing its form, in the most simple body, where beginning and end cannot be discovered or distinguished from one another, while it moves through the same parts in itself." Nor did he discard the basic Ptolemaic idea that, with the above assumed, it was necessary, in order to "save the appearances," to suppose many regular circular motions in the heavens rather than a single one for each planetary sphere. In these assumptions and retentions of the Ptolemaic system, Copernicus laid himself open to the corrections of Kepler a half century later.

But Copernicus did not retain all of Ptolemy. He made two extremely important changes. The first was to assume that the Sun and not the Earth was placed at the center of the universe, which is to say that the center of the Sun was the point around which the planets (including the Earth), together with the great sphere of the fixed stars, revolved. The second was to assume that the diurnal movement of the Sun and Moon, of the planets and of the fixed stars, around the Earth—from east to west—was not a movement intrinsic to those bodies (or spheres) but instead only an apparent movement caused by the daily rotation of the Earth on its axis.

Ptolemy had "proved" that the Earth is stationary by stating that if it rotated (as, he admitted, certain of his Greek predecessors had believed), at the great speed necessary to bring it around on itself once a day, then everything would fly off into space and there would be complete chaos in the sea and in the air. But such chaos is not observable, he said, and therefore the Earth does not rotate.

Ptolemy, however, had also held that the sphere of the Fixed Stars was so far away from the Earth that the Earth could be considered, for all practical purposes, as a mere point in relation to the size of that great sphere. This meant, of course, that as rapid as would be the motion of the Earth if it turned on its axis, so much the more rapid would be the motion of the great sphere of the Fixed Stars if the Earth did not turn. Ptolemy, like most men before and after him, believed the crystalline sphere of the Fixed Stars to be somehow divine, so this did not bother him too much. At any rate, he found this enormously rapid motion of the great sphere to be more credible than the rotation of the Earth itself on its own axis.

Copernicus reversed the credibilities. In a brilliant argument at the beginning of *On the Revolutions* he shows how it is not at all hard to believe that the Earth rotates, for such motion is quite natural and a motion that is natural is not violent and chaotic. What is impossible to believe, said Copernicus, is that the enormous sphere of the Fixed Stars revolves around the Earth at almost unimaginable speed once a day.

These two radical changes made by Copernicus had the effect of greatly simplifying astronomy. To place the Sun and not the Earth at the center of the planetary spheres allowed for great progress in explaining the apparent motions of the planets. The Earth turning on its axis, rather than the universe turning around it, also made sense to thinking minds. But not all minds in Copernicus's day, or in any day (including our own), were "thinking." Copernicus's new suppositions about the heavens contradicted what people had taught and believed for centuries. Worse, they contradicted the conclusions of Aristotle.

But if one were to contradict Aristotle on two important points, on what other points might one feel free to contradict him—or his great follower, Thomas Aquinas? The early sixteenth century was not a time when most people enjoyed or looked forward to change in their beliefs and ideas about the world. They preferred to have things stay pretty much the same. Copernicus knew that the publication of his book would create a great controversy, at the best—and at the worst might result in severe attacks upon him. He therefore held off publishing it until the end of his life—and died before he could see the changes its publication would produce.

Copernicus's book need not be read through from beginning to end. There are, for example, many complex geometrical theorems whose demonstrations are hard to follow. The main argument, though, is clear and set forth in lucid prose.

# WILLIAM GILBERT
## 1540?–1603
### *On the Lodestone*

William Gilbert was a famous physician who carved out a prosperous London practice for himself during the last half of the sixteenth century. Born at Colchester in about 1540, he was named in 1601 physician to Queen Elizabeth and thereupon moved to court. The Queen died shortly thereafter but her successor, James I, reappointed Gilbert royal physician immediately. Gilbert took considerable satisfaction in the fact that the only personal legacy in the Queen's will provided a fund for the prosecution of his experiments. But all these high hopes came to an end with Gilbert's death, probably of the plague, in 1603.

Gilbert's reputation as a physician was local, but he was famous throughout England and Europe for a book, *De Magnete* (*On the Lodestone*), which he had published in the year 1600. This book, which remains highly readable today, is full of things that were wonderful to Gilbert's contemporaries and that are still of interest.

Gilbert was not the first to recognize the existence of lodestone (that is, magnetic iron oxide). The Greeks and the Chinese, among other peoples, had known of the magnetic properties of this iron ore compound since at least 500 BCE. But he was the first to conduct careful and duplicable experiments with lodestone. Most important, he was the first to recognize that the Earth itself is a great lodestone and that there is no difference except in size between a simple spherical magnet held in the hand and the great globe on which we stand.

As a young man, Gilbert had traveled on the Continent and had there met many persons who later became notable in science. He corresponded with them throughout the rest of his life. In his London house he possessed a large collection of minerals, instruments, and books, and he held regular meetings of other Londoners interested in scientific subjects, where his experiments were presented and discussed and where he reported on discoveries made abroad. These meetings, which are thought to have anticipated the later organization of the Royal Society, helped to create a wide respect for Gilbert and his ideas not only about lodestone but also about the Earth and its place in the universe. Thus, when Gilbert accepted without a murmur the revolutionary assumptions of Copernicus about the structure of the cosmos, it was easy for learned Englishmen to do likewise. This is one reason why English science during the seventeenth century—the century following Gilbert's death—was the best in the world.

Gilbert's most vigorous arguments in *On the Lodestone* are reserved for his demolition of the Ptolemaic hypothesis of the so-called *primum mobile*, or first mover. According to Ptolemy, the second-century astronomer, the Earth stood still at the center of a nest of concentric spheres, each bearing a planet (or the Moon and the Sun), all of which revolved once every day around the Earth. But why did the spheres move? What provided their motive force?

For Ptolemy there were nine material (though quintessential) spheres that turned around the Earth: the spheres of the Moon, of Mercury, of Venus, of the Sun, of Mars, of Jupiter, of Saturn, of the Ecliptic, and of the Fixed Stars. Each of these spheres had its specific motion or motions—some of them very complicated. But they all shared a common diurnal motion as they were swept around from east to west by the primum mobile. This was a tenth sphere, material but invisible, that surrounded all the other heavens and whirled them around with inconceivable force and, as Copernicus noted, inconceivable speed.

For Gilbert, this primum mobile was sheer nonsense. It "presents no visible body, is in no wise recognizable; it is a fiction believed in by some philosophers (i.e., scientists), and accepted by weaklings."

> Surely that [notion of the primum mobile] is superstition, a philosophic fable, now believed only by simpletons and the unlearned; it is beneath derision; and yet in times past it was supported by calculation and comparison of movements, and was generally accepted by mathematicians while the importunate rabble of philophasters egged them on.

What chance had the Ptolemaic geocentric theory against such fierce eloquence—and such good sense?

Gilbert's hard-headed insistence that scientists look not at books but at things helped to shape the future of English science. It also helped to shape the future of all science. The year 1600, which saw the publication of *De Magnete*, was crucial in human history. Before that, the world was primarily medieval. After it, the world was becoming modern.

# JOHANNES KEPLER
## 1571–1630
### *The Epitome of Copernican Astronomy*

Johannes Kepler was a German who, unlike his predecessor Copernicus, had to struggle to obtain an education. He was born in Wurtemburg in 1571. His father was a soldier of fortune and a tavern keeper, but he himself was a sufficiently brilliant student on the rare occasions when he was allowed to go to school that influential persons noticed him. The Church, that discoverer of talent wherever it might exist, determined that, if properly trained, Kepler might become a faithful servant. He was sent to seminary and college and finally (in 1589) to the University at Tubingen, where for the first time he was introduced to the astronomical theories of Copernicus. He very soon decided that he could do better, although it was many years before he was willing to publish his theories.

His most important book was both a paean of praise of and an apology to the memory of Copernicus. Entitled *The Epitome of Copernican Astronomy* (1618–21), it hewed to the Copernican line wherever its author felt he could. But it made substantial and significant departures from Copernicus at crucial points.

Kepler agreed with Copernicus (and disagreed with Ptolemy) in holding that the planets, including the Earth, revolve around the Sun, which is the center of the universe, and that the Earth rotates on its axis from west to east thus producing the apparent motion of the heavens around the Earth from east to west. He agreed with Copernicus on many minor points as well. But he disagreed on three main points.

The first had to do with the supposed crystalline spheres that both Ptolemy and Copernicus—and everyone else—had believed to carry the planets around their orbital center (for Ptolemy, the Earth; for Copernicus, the Sun). No one before Kepler had thought of the planets as bodies moving through empty, or nearly empty, space (in fact, Kepler could not conceive of empty space and so assumed the existence of an "ether" through which the planets moved). For, as they said, what would move them? Why would they not fall into the Earth, or Sun, as center? Only if they were supported on the great transparent spheres that in their turn revolved around the center would the planets be held in their places in the cosmos. The crystalline spheres were thus necessary in order to "save the appearances."

But they do not do that! wrote Kepler. In the first place, if there were such spheres, they would refract the light from the Fixed Stars—but we observe no such refraction. In the second place, the crystalline spheres of certain planets would at certain times have to intersect the crystalline spheres of other heavenly bodies—but how could this be? Finally, the hypothesis of the crystalline spheres is unnecessary—and that is the worst thing about it!

The second disagreement had to do with the supposed regular circular motions of the heavenly bodies (or their spheres). This too is incorrect, said Kepler. Assuming that the Moon, say, or Venus always moves at the same speed in a perfect circle around its center of revolution will never save the appearances. Instead, the planets—as bodies in space—move in elliptical rather than circular orbits around the Sun, which remains fixed at one focus of the ellipse. Nor do the planets always move at the same speed; the farther away from the Sun they are, the slower they move, and the closer, the faster. This assumption about elliptical orbits much simplified the computations of astronomers everywhere.

These two disagreements would have been in vain without a third. To the question, why do the planets move around the Earth (the Sun)? Ptolemy and Copernicus had given the same answer: because the planets are on great crystalline spheres that revolve around their center, and it is the natural movement of a sphere so to move. Kepler had discarded the spheres and also the regular circular motion. He needed something to replace them. In seeking it he came very close indeed to being the greatest astronomer who ever lived. He just missed it—that honor belongs to Newton.

Kepler supposed that there must be some sort of invisible, but still physical or material, relationship between the Sun and the planets such that the Sun causes the motion of the planets around itself. Taking his clue from Gilbert's *On the Lodestone*, he realized that this relationship must be allied to the force that causes things on the Earth to fall, but he did not discover the simple inverse-square law of gravitation that is Newton's glory. Instead, Kepler thought of the Sun's light as somehow reaching out and sweeping the planets around in their elliptical orbits. It was a noble effort and all the more astonishing when you consider that Kepler had probably never looked through a telescope when he died in 1630.

Kepler's *Epitome* comprises five books. Only the last two need to be read; the first three are Kepler's homage to the memory of Copernicus. The fourth book discusses the motions of the heavenly bodies, viewed in a new way. The fifth book deals in more detail with the orbits of the planets and shows how these may be much more easily understood on the new assumptions.

These two last parts of the *Epitome* are not hard to read—Kepler himself did not approve of "boring demonstrations"—and they are fascinating. Kepler went so far and came so close, but he was unable to take the next steps that led to Newton and Einstein.

# GALILEO GALILEI
## 1564–1642
### *Two New Sciences*

Galileo Galilei was born in Pisa in 1564, the son of a mathematician and musician who had had bitter experience of the impecunious nature of both those professions. He therefore determined to make of his son a doctor and sent him to the University of Pisa to study medicine. But Galileo, sitting in the chapel one day in 1581, began to notice a certain lamp that hung from the ceiling and was swinging in the wind. The wind blew harder and softer and the lamp swung through longer and through shorter arcs—but, Galileo observed, the time it took to swing through its arcs was always the same. At the age of seventeen he had discovered, without at the time naming it, the isochronicity of the pendulum (he later worked out its use in clocks) and, what is more, had become hooked on mathematical physics.

Indeed, he had *discovered* mathematical physics. Until his day, mathematics and nature were held to have no connection; mathematics was philosophical speculation and had no basis in reality. Galileo was the first man to put them together, to declare, as he did in one of his works, *Saggiatore*, that the "book of Nature is …written in mathematical characters."

Galileo's mathematical bent was confirmed, and his reputation made, soon after the episode of the lamp when he disproved Aristotle's ancient dictum that heavy bodies fall faster than light ones. At twenty-five he managed to obtain a position that supported his scientific researches. He taught mathematics first at Pisa, then at Padua, from 1592 to 1610, where he was a popular lecturer.

In 1609 he learned of experiments being conducted by Dutch lens makers to construct a telescope, and he immediately sent for information. He combined the lenses as directed by them but was disappointed in the result. He soon saw what the trouble was, corrected it, and produced a telescope having ten times the magnifying power of any other. That very night he took it outdoors and pointed it at the Moon. The surface of the Moon, he discovered, was not smooth but rough and pitted; there were mountains and valleys just as on Earth. This was extraordinary. Everyone believed that the heavenly bodies were made out of a special stuff, the quintessence, which was immutable. But the surface of the Moon as seen through Galileo's telescope showed clear signs of having changed, as the Earth's surface changes. Aristotle, Galileo concluded, was wrong again.

The battle between Galileo and the Aristotelians continued throughout his life. His discoveries with the telescope confirmed Galileo in his belief that the Copernican hypothesis, that the Sun and not the Earth is the center of the solar system, was not just a hypothesis but was true, and in several works he defended this position. The Aristotelian teachers complained to the Inquisition, which recognized the danger in a man who did not care where truth led him. Galileo was tried, convicted, and forced to recant. The picture of the greatest living scientist being forced to declare in public that everything he knew to be true was false, and that he had been foolish to believe it, is terrifying. It is one of the worst things the Church of Rome ever did, and even a number of Galileo's clerical friends believed his condemnation inexcusable.

Galileo's completed *Two New Sciences* in 1634, only a few months after his trial and condemnation. He had been confined to his house, where he remained for the rest of his life, but he never stopped working and experimenting, and writing. *Two New Sciences* has the surprising form of a conversation among three persons, one of whom represents Galileo himself, a second the intelligent layman, and a third—Simplicio—the naive common man. The two sciences, on which Galileo had worked throughout his life, are statics and dynamics, and together they comprise what was known of mechanics in the early seventeenth century. The book presents many new and surprising theorems, and the dialogue form turns out to be an effective way of explicating them.

One reason to read *Two New Sciences* is because of the book's charming naïveté. Galileo was looking at the world when it was new; he was like a child finding pretty pebbles and bringing them to his mother to be appreciated. Science as it is conducted today is for the most part unintelligible. The mathematics that underlies it is difficult for everyone to understand, and the results of experiments are processed on computers and presented in a form totally lacking in romance. From time to time a great scientist calls a press conference and earnest science writers try to understand his announcements and find a way to present them to readers of the early edition. The scientist, if he writes at all, offers the results of his labors in papers that are readable only by a handful of other specialists in his field. Probably this is the way it has to be now that all the easy truths have been discovered.

But they had not been discovered yet in Galileo's day. He was learning astonishing things about nature just by looking at it, thinking about it, conducting experiments on it. No one had done that before. It is the sense of wondrous discovery in *Two New Sciences* that makes the book so attractive and so moving. Reading it, you learn more about the scientist than about the nature he studies and attempts to control. And if you are of a scientific bent I think you cannot but envy Galileo despite the crudity of his instruments, despite all the things he did not know, despite his shameful punishment.

# FRANCIS BACON
## 1561–1616
*Novum Organon*
*The Advancement of Learning*
*Essays*

Francis Bacon was born in London in 1561, the younger son of Sir Nicholas Bacon, Elizabeth's Lord Keeper. After studying law he entered Parliament in 1584. He met the Earl of Essex, the royal favorite, who attempted to advance Bacon's career. When Essex fell, Bacon was willing to be his official prosecutor, a fact that has always disturbed Bacon's admirers. Under King James I his career was meteoric, and he rose from Solicitor-General to Lord Chancellor in a mere ten years. But in 1621 he was charged before the House of Lords with having accepted bribes. He confessed and was convicted and condemned. The king was lenient with him, but Bacon never held office again, instead devoting himself to revising his many literary works until his death in 1626.

The life of Bacon remains an enigma. About few men living in the Age of Elizabeth do we know more facts: facts about his long struggle for political influence, facts about his career as James's chief advocate and the defender of the royal prerogative against Parliament, facts about his trial and conviction and his fall from grace, facts about his philosophical career and publications. But we do not know his heart.

Sir Francis Bacon, Baron Verulam, Viscount St. Albans ... Strictly speaking, he was not Lord Bacon, but Lord St. Albans. It is one of his great distinctions that he rose above a mere title and is called simply Bacon to this day.

His contributions to the history of thought are important and extensive. In a letter to his friend, the Prime Minister Lord Burleigh, he wrote, in a famous phrase, "I have taken all knowledge to be my province." The claim was not, for Bacon, so all-encompassing as it would be today; he did not mean what we would mean if we said it. Put the emphasis, when you say those words, on "knowledge"; "I have taken all knowledge to be my province"—knowledge as distinct from and opposed to poetry, religion, and practical experience. Formal knowledge, in short, or science, as Bacon called it. He not only took it as his province but also defended it against the numerous attacks that were common in his day. And he wrote a fine book about it, to which he gave the overall title *The Great Instauration*. It is a special book even though unfinished; in fact, only small pieces of it were completed by Bacon. No single man could have written it all.

*The Great Instauration* is comprised of a number of parts, only some of which were written by Bacon. First, there is magnificent introductory matter—a few pages only, but breathtaking in their eloquence and scope. Second, there is the "Novum Organon," or "New Logic," an account of a new method, as Bacon conceived it, of acquiring knowledge—the so-called inductive method—together with warnings about the obstacles that stand in the way of knowledge. Third, there is "The Advancement of Learning," a classification of the sciences based on an analysis of the powers of the human intellect. Finally, there are a group of chapters, papers, and fragments dealing with particular questions in philosophy and the sciences that, if expanded indefinitely, would have been the exemplification of all that Bacon thought and of what he planned to do—or wanted the human race to do.

Much of this makes for excellent reading, and there are pages of both the "Novum Organon" and "The Advancement of Learning" that soar. Of particular note in the "Novum Organon" is the analysis of what Bacon called the Idols, or deep fallacies of mind, that hinder clear sight and understanding. Of these, the "Idols of the Tribe," or fallacies incident to mankind in general, are probably the most important. Humans, as Bacon knew, are inclined to believe what they want to believe, to see what they want to see, to assume more regularity in nature than they have reason to assume, to lend credibility to the evidence of their senses more than they have reason to do. There are also "Idols of the Cave," as Bacon said, which are the fallacies caused by individual quirks and fancies. Words, too, though necessary for discourse, make discourse difficult, and systems of thought and received methods of investigation make it difficult for new ideas to be accepted. All of this is excellent and true.

But Bacon knew that, hard as it is to comprehend the world of external nature—which can be controlled, as he was one of the first to observe, only by obeying its laws—it is even harder to comprehend man himself. His attempts to do so, and to convey his comprehension and understanding, in short his wisdom, are incorporated in his famous *Essays*, undoubtedly his most popular and most loved book. In the introduction to this short work he wrote that, unlike his philosophical and scientific works, his essays would "come home to men's business and bosoms." And indeed they do.

They are full of trenchant and memorable statements or aphorisms that sum up Bacon's thinking on a subject and often sum up our own as well. In the "Novum Organon" he had made the revolutionary proposal that there are in nature a small number of "forms," or essential natures, or—as we would call them—fundamental laws that govern all of nature's operations and that must be understood if we are to understand nature as a whole. In the *Essays* he is suggesting something similar about human nature, and the first sentences of the *Essays*, most of which appear in books of quotations because of their pithiness and truth, are the forms that Bacon has discovered in a long life of observation of both people and things.

"A mixture of a lie doth ever add pleasure," he states in the essay "Of Truth." "Men fear death as children fear to go in the dark." "Revenge is a kind of wild justice." The essay "Of Parents and Children" begins with this cryptic remark: "The joys of parents are secret, and so are their griefs and fears." Parents who have been forbidden by the rules of common politeness to boast of the achievements of their children and who have had to resist the temptation to bore others with an account of their children's troubles know well the truth of that aphorism; its truth, in fact, is confirmed by the fact that the parent who disobeys these rules may be shunned and ridiculed.

"He that hath wife and children hath given hostages to fortune; for they are impediments to great enterprises, either of virtue or mischief." So begins the essay "Of Marriage and Single Life," whereas the essay "Of Love" begins: "The speaking in a perpetual hyperbole is comely in nothing but in love," which is, I believe, the closest to a smile that Bacon ever takes us. The essay "Of Seditions and Troubles" offers this down-to-earth advice: "Money is like muck [manure], not good except it be spread." "Of Innovations," which Bacon feared less than most men of his time—and most people of any time, perhaps— he had this to say: "He that will not apply new remedies must expect new evils; for time is the greatest innovator." "Of Friendship" contains this observation: "A crowd is not company, and faces are but a gallery of pictures." The essay begins with a profound comment upon a famous statement of Aristotle's: "It had been hard for him that spake it," says Bacon, "to have put more truth and untruth together, in few words, than in that speech: "Whosoever is delighted in solitude is either a wild beast or a god." "Virtue is like a rich stone, best plain set," begins the essay "Of Beauty," and—to conclude this litany—"Of Gardens" begins thus: "God Almighty first planted a garden; and, indeed, it is the purest of human pleasures." What gardener will disagree?

# MICHEL DE MONTAIGNE
## 1533–1592
### Essays

Michel de Montaigne had a wonderful upbringing. Born near Bordeaux, France, in 1533, he was never beaten or treated severely, as was the custom in his time; his father waked him each morning with music. To reveal to him more clearly the character of the humble people of his country he was given peasants for godfather, godmother, and nurse. He learned Latin from a German tutor who knew no French; Montaigne did not speak his own language until he was six. The Latin authors remained his closest literary friends throughout his life.

That life was exciting and full of incident. One of his closest friends was Henry, King of Navarre from 1572, who became Henry IV of France in 1589. Only at the end of his life (he died in 1592), when he was suffering from kidney stones, was Montaigne permitted to retire from business and political affairs. He had been writing his book of *Essays* off and on for years; now he devoted himself to it.

The book is about himself. "I want to be seen here in my simple, natural, ordinary fashion, without pose or artifice; for it is myself that I portray … . I am myself the matter of my book." What does he mean by that famous statement? And was Montaigne such a great man that a book about him should be great, too?

We know different things in different ways and with different degrees of certitude. We do not know very well what happened yesterday in Bangkok even if we have seen a news show about Bangkok. We know better, but still not very well, our own city or town. Better still, the news of our own family. We know best what we ourselves did, felt, suffered, feared.

That is a truism, except that most of us do not take advantage of the opportunity afforded by our closeness to our own selves. We live with ourselves with a unique intimacy, yet we do not know ourselves. Socrates, who was Montaigne's hero and exemplar, insisted that to know oneself was the hardest thing to do, as well as the most important.

Why do we resist knowing ourselves? It must be because we don't want to. We are unwilling to admit that we are no more beautiful, no wiser, no richer, no more successful than we actually are. Concerning ourselves we are steeped in a brew of illusions; what we wish we were is more important than what we are, and in fact we don't want to face what we are because that would mean accepting that we are not what we would like to be. Such illusions are well nigh universal. Very few men or women have ever been able to escape them, to look at themselves, in a mirror on the wall or in the mirror of the mind, truly and frankly face to face.

Montaigne was one of those few. Perhaps it was in some way because of his strange education, perhaps it was just because he was a genius, but he did not care to be anything other than what he was. This did not mean he did not strive to be better, to be more moderate, prudent, kind. No one should ever stop striving for those qualities. But he was able to forgive himself for his failures, to accept himself.

Most of all he could forgive himself for being human. This is much harder than it seems. As human beings, we are animals as well as spiritual creatures; but we deny the animal in us. Or deny the spiritual—which is equally foolish. Most of all we find it difficult simply to live. We think we must always be busy at something in order to justify ourselves, to validate our existence. But life itself is sufficient justification.

> We are great fools. "He has spent his life in idleness," we say; "I have done nothing today." What, have you not lived? That is not only the fundamental but the most illustrious of your occupations. "If I had been placed in a position to manage great affairs, I would have shown what I could do." Have you been able to think out and manage your own life? You have done the greatest task of all ... Our great and glorious masterpiece is to live appropriately.

What does it mean to live "appropriately"? As a man should, says Montaigne; that is, moderately, sanely, wisely, enjoying all things but nothing too much, eating, drinking, making love, but also conversing, reading, and thinking well. These are the appropriate things to do, and a few more. Actually, we all know what they are, but we do not do them. Montaigne did.

He first began writing his *Essays*—they were the first "essays" ever written—when he was about forty. He did not know how to write them at the outset, so the book grew and changed as he worked on it. At first he tried to be clever and "interesting" and to show off his learning. But he soon realized that he himself was the most interesting of subjects if he could only manage to present himself honestly to his reader, and so he more and more concentrated on that. The last of the essays, coming at the end of Book III, is called "Of Experience." It is entirely about Montaigne, what he is, what he thinks, what he feels, what he knows to be true.

Many of the essays are well worth reading; most are much more than that. "Of Idleness," "Of the Education of Children," "Of Cannibals," "Of the Inconsistency of Our Actions," "Of Giving the Lie," "Of Repentance," "Of Vanity," "Of Experience"—that is just the beginning of a list of recommended selections. Read those first, perhaps, or start with Book I and read all the way through to the end of Book III.

Montaigne wrote about himself, but you will recognize *yourself*. That is the mystery, the secret of his greatness. He knew himself so well, he looked at himself so honestly, that he saw through himself to the general human nature, which is ours as well (it has not changed much since the sixteenth century). He knew other men, and women too, I think, in high places and in low, and he also forgave them. For they too were human. He would forgive you—even you!

This is the way the book ends. It is Montaigne's gift to all of us.

> It is an absolute perfection and virtually divine to know how to enjoy our being lawfully. We seek other conditions because we do not understand the use of our own, and go outside of ourselves because we do not know what it is like inside. Yet there is no use our mounting on stilts, for on stilts we must still walk on our own legs. And on the loftiest throne in the world we are still sitting on our own behind.

# WILLIAM SHAKESPEARE
### 1564?–1616?
*Plays*

I confess to believing that the biography of William Shakespeare is a great puzzle. It is hard to believe in "the man from Stratford"; to accept that the provincial actor who is ordinarily put forward as the author of the greatest poetic works ever written actually wrote them. It is possible, I admit, to think that "William Shakespeare" was a pseudonym and that the actual author of the plays was quite a different sort of man. Or perhaps a man named William Shakespeare, who did exist, allowed his name to be placed on the plays for purposes not fully understood but that can be surmised. Some people think the author of Shakespeare's plays was Edward de Vere, seventeenth Earl of Oxford. Though I once believed this, I no longer do. Nor do I believe Francis Bacon wrote the plays, nor Christopher Marlowe, nor the Countess of Pembroke, nor any of several others who have been suggested. Feeling thus, I cannot recite the traditional version of the so-called facts of Shakespeare's life. For that you will have to turn to a biographical dictionary.

And after all these years—four centuries more or less—it hardly matters. Someone wrote the plays, certainly one person—they are too alike in too many ways to have been the work of a committee. And whoever he was, he was possibly the most thoughtful man and probably the greatest writer who ever lived. And since genius is always a mystery, he may have been that "man from Stratford" after all.

The plays of Shakespeare fall into four quite distinct categories, although the First Folio recognized only three. There are tragedies, comedies, and histories, as the First Folio has it, but there are also romances, and they are quite different from the others. One must therefore approach Shakespeare from at least these four points of view. (And then, of course, there are the sonnets and the other scattered lyric poems—but among such riches how can we taste all?)

The categories sometimes become confused. Is *Antony and Cleopatra* a history or a tragedy? What about *Richard II*? Or *Julius*

*Caesar*? Or *Timon of Athens*? There is a lot of history in all of these plays. Yet they are tragedies, too—the special kind of tragedies that Shakespeare wrote (which is to say very different from the kind that Aristotle approved).

*Hamlet* may, like the others, have a historical core, but if so it is very remote and finally unimportant. No play of Shakespeare is more purely tragic than *Hamlet*. No play so touches the heart, which is why the work has enjoyed an almost uninterrupted run, somewhere or other on this Earth, since it was first written in London around the year 1599.

*Hamlet* is about loss: loss of a father and loss of love, loss of beauty, charm, and wit, loss of life. The play's great subject, therefore, is heartbreak.

It is heartbreaking that this glorious young man, "the glass of fashion and the mold of form," should have had to dress in tatters and play the fool. It is heartbreaking that he had to lose his love and that she, Ophelia, had to lose her young life before she had more than just tasted its sweetness. It is heartbreaking that Denmark had to suffer any king but young Hamlet who, his rival Fortinbras said, "would have proved most royal if he had been put on."

The play is heartbreaking but it is not sad. It is funny, sharp, challenging, full of movement and extraordinary changes. Only when we think back on it do we realize how much we miss our young friend, Prince Hamlet.

I don't think that in all of literature there is any person more interesting. Perhaps Odysseus is his equal, but no other. That being so, how can anyone ever decide not to go to the trouble to meet him? After all, that's easy enough; he's there, waiting, between the pages of his book. Hold out your hand.

The tragedy of *King Lear* is even more intense than that of *Hamlet*, but Lear is an old man and perhaps we don't feel his loss so bitterly. The tragedy of *Othello* is, if possible, even more intense than that of Lear. We cry out at the end of it, hoping that what we have seen is not so. As plays, *Lear* and *Othello* may be better than *Hamlet*, which is flawed in ways that scholars have been pointing out for two centuries. But Lear and Othello are not, as men, as interesting as Hamlet. Read their plays second, after you have read Hamlet's. There is the incomparable place to start.

Not only do the plays of Shakespeare fall into four distinct categories (categories that, nevertheless, sometimes overlap), but the literary career of their author also falls into four distinct periods. The dates are not at all certain, but the sequence is fairly clear. During the first period, Shakespeare was trying his hand at various types of drama current during the last third of the sixteenth century in England: comedies, often based on classical originals, histories, and outrageously ranting tragedies.

During this first period, or perhaps the second, Shakespeare also composed the 154 sonnets that, alone and if all the plays were lost, would ensure his fame. Numerous attempts have been made to discover a narrative or plot or secret message in the sonnets. Maybe it is there, but I have never been convinced of it. What is there is incomparable poetry, verses that possess a grandeur of thought and a perfection of execution not surpassed in the language. Curiously, most of the sonnets also have a major defect: their last two lines, usually a couplet, are often artificial and banal. Usually it's prudent not to read the last two lines but to assume the sonnet ends after the twelfth, instead of the fourteenth, line.

The best-known comedy of Shakespeare's first period is *The Taming of the Shrew*; the best-known history is *Richard III*. One tragedy originates in this period: *Titus Andronicus*, which only a devoted Shakespearian can love.

The second period produced five luminous comedies, the four best histories, and one more tragedy, the captivating *Romeo and Juliet*. The comedies were *Midsummer Night's Dream*, that thimbleful of moonshine which gives us two delicious quotations: "The course of true love never did run smooth," and "What fools these mortals be!"; *The Merry Wives of Windsor*, written, according to tradition, at the request of Queen Elizabeth I, who wished to be presented with the spectacle of Falstaff in love; and *Much Ado about Nothing*, which is only exceeded in grace, charm, and wit by the greatest of all Shakespearian comedies, *As You Like It*, with its incomparable heroine, Rosalind. The four histories constitute a tetralogy, four plays that tell a continuous story from the reign of Richard II to the final triumph of Henry V.

The first of these four is *Richard II*, which tells of a weak king, albeit a marvelously poetic one, who is overthrown by his sturdy, courageous, treacherous, and cunning cousin, the future Henry IV. *Henry V* tells of the final victory over all odds of the son of Henry IV, who justifies and vindicates his father's misdeed at Agincourt, one of the most important battles in western European history. Between fall the two parts of *Henry IV*.

Shakespeare had been writing, or rewriting (to accord with official court prejudices about the past) the history of England for several years before he undertook the story of Henry IV. By this time he was impatient with history alone and desired more action, fun, and frolic than reality could provide. At the same time he did have a good story to tell: of how the son of Henry IV, Prince Hal, had been a daredevil and a scapegrace while his father was alive, but settled down to be a good and beloved monarch when he inherited the throne. It would be an even better story, Shakespeare felt, if he could show Prince Hal in the company of some amusing villains. It's not certain whether Sir John Falstaff is based on the life of a real person, known to the prince; but Shakespeare was perfectly capable of inventing what he needed.

There was another good story to tell, of the rivalry between Hotspur, a legitimate claimant of the throne and a man known far and wide for his courage, and Prince Hal, about whom little that was good was known by anybody. Nevertheless, Prince Hal must be the hero of the tale because he became king and was an ancestor of Elizabeth, the reigning monarch. Shakespeare had to modify history in some respects to make it all come out, but few readers have ever complained of these liberties. *Henry IV* has its own reality, of a distinctly higher sort.

Hotspur is a magnificent character; in many respects he anticipates Hamlet, although he is more narrow-spirited than the young Dane. *Henry IV, Part I* reveals how Prince Hal rises to the occasion and defeats Hotspur in battle. But it also introduces the villainous Falstaff, the whoremongering, blaspheming, thieving friend of the prince who is nevertheless beloved of every reader and playgoer. How indeed can you not love Falstaff, for he is not only witty in himself but "also the cause," as he says, "that there is wit in other men." He is the greatest comic character in English literature, and perhaps that is enough to say about him. Read *Henry IV* to find out why.

*Henry IV, Part II* ends sadly, although it could not have ended any other way. Henry IV dies, and Prince Hal becomes King Henry V. Falstaff hears the news while on a recruiting mission in the country, far from London, and immediately drops everything to ride as fast as possible to the capital, where he expects that his friendship with the prince will be convertible into high and lucrative office. But King Henry V is a different man from Prince Hal; he is very aware of his responsibilities as a monarch and he knows he must put his past life well behind him. Falstaff is crushed to hear from the King's lips that he is to be punished rather than rewarded and, although this may be right and proper, hardly any reader or viewer fails to be shocked and also hurt by this denouement. Justice is a very great thing in the world, but laughter is also great, and we hate to see the one fall victim to the other.

The purest comedy leaves no doubt about who is good and who is wicked. The good are more than good; they are angelic. And the wicked are devilish. But the wicked are incapable of doing real harm, nor are the good prudish and unlikable. The comic world is a fairy-land in which all receive their just deserts, or a little bit more; punishments are bearable; and at worst a man is forced to marry a maiden he has betrayed. In the end love conquers all. If only life were really like that.

*As You Like It* discharges the obligation that its title implies. This is the comedy that audiences want and it shall not fail in any respect. Audiences have been delighted for four centuries.

The play is based on a perfect comic theme. A Duke has been deprived of his dukedom by his usurping brother; the former is good, the latter wicked. The good Duke has fled to the Forest of Arden, a better place than ever was, where he lives in peace and contentment, at one with nature and his fellow man. He has a daughter, Rosalind, and the usurper also has a daughter, Celia. The daughters are insepa-rable friends. Rosalind, in particular, is sharp of wit and tongue, although Celia is not far behind her. But suddenly Rosalind falls in love. Unfortunately, the object of her affections is distrusted by the usurper and banished; then Rosalind herself is also banished, for the usurper suspects she would always be faithful to her banished father. As indeed she would.

Celia will not let Rosalind depart by herself, but how will two girls travel alone through a dangerous world? Rosalind, who is tall for a girl, decides to dress as a boy and pretend Celia is her sister. They head for the Forest of Arden; but Orlando, the banished beloved of Rosalind, is also there. They meet, but Orlando does not know that Rosalind is his Rosalind; he thinks she is a young man. Rosalind, partly for her amusement and partly because she can't bear to be apart from Orlando, forces him to pretend to woo her as if she were Rosalind. Orlando does so and of course it all comes out right in the end.

Rosalind is a charming young woman, at the beginning and end of the play; she is an even more charming "young man" all during the middle of it. Never did a woman mock love so thoroughly at the same time that she is practically dying of it. From time to time she gets herself into verbal difficulties, but she always squirms free. Her comic ruses appeal to everyone. It is one of the great parts for an actress to play.

There are other fine parts, especially that of the old fool, Jaques, he of "All the world's a stage, and all the men and women merely players," and the young one, Touchstone, a professional Fool who has accompanied Rosalind from the court into the forest and has there met the bewitching Audrey, whom he confesses he will marry, although he would have her if he could without benefit of clergy. Touchstone is amused at his own folly; this is the first time the Fool has ever been a fool. "I press in here, sir, amongst the rest of the country copulatives, to swear and to foreswear, according as marriage binds and blood breaks. A poor virgin, sir, an ill-favour'd thing, sir," he adds, producing the gorgeous, simpering Audrey, spilling out of her bodice, "but mine own; a poor humour of mine, sir, to take that no man else will." And so they are all married— even Celia has found a mate—and the usurping Duke, to make all perfect, is converted to a life of religious penitence and gives up his stolen title to its rightful owner.

All of this is consummate silliness, of course; there is no honesty in it, as Touchstone would say. And yet it is also just and true. When Rosalind says, "The poor world is almost six thousand years old, and in all this time there was not any man died in his own person, videlicet, in a love-cause," we know she is right; and when she adds that "Men have died from time to time, and worms have eaten them, but not for love," we know that is right, too. And yet in no play of Shakespeare, or in hardly any other play, is love so potent, do we feel its great power so deeply. If Rosalind can be so much in love, she the mocker, the sprite, the free woman, then love must be strong indeed. Which is, after all, as good a moral as one is likely to get from a comedy.

Around the year 1600, the author of Shakespeare's plays—whoever he was—seems to have undergone a radical change in temperament and outlook, which ushers in the third period of his career. Gone, never to be found again, is the delicious merriment of *Much Ado* and *As You Like It*, the inspired foolishness of Falstaff, even the warmly touching love-tragedy of *Romeo and Juliet*. "Shakespeare" continues to write comedies, but of a very different sort; there is a bitterness in *Troilus and Cressida*, in *Measure for Measure*, and in *All's Well That Ends Well* that has not been seen before. Indeed, this third period is not noted for comedy. It is the period of the great tragedies, from *Julius Caesar* and *Hamlet*, both about political treachery, to *Antony and Cleopatra* and *Coriolanus*, about political failure. In between lie *Othello*, *Lear*, and *Macbeth*, which plunge the reader-viewer into depths of feeling and experience not equaled in any other works in any language.

One of the many miracles of Shakespeare's career is that he did not founder in despair, but lived and worked his way through it and came out, safe and sound, on the other side. The fourth period is almost the best of all. Five plays mark it, one rather boring history, *Henry VIII*, and four wonderful romances, *Pericles*, *Cymbeline*, *The Winter's Tale*, and *The Tempest*. Of these my own favorite is *Cymbeline*, partly, I admit, because it is probably the least known and most infrequently performed.

*Cymbeline* is a long, immensely complicated play; I would not try to outline the plot in fewer than ten pages. Suffice it to say that it is about all of Shakespeare's favorite subjects: love, loss, and treachery; the unequal conflict between the good and the wicked; the fragile balance between men and women. The love story here is particularly moving; Imogen and Posthumus are one of Shakespeare's finest couples, and Imogen especially is a magnificent creation; she is another Rosalind, but on a higher and more dangerous plane. The treachery is also devastating, as it is in *Othello*, and the friendship of Posthumus and Pisanio reminds us of Hamlet and Horatio. But none of these things, rich and fine as they are, defines or orders the play.

When you have written thirty plays and know everything about writing plays, and in particular know that your skill will not allow you to make any really bad mistakes, you may be willing to take some very big chances and try things that have never been tried. This is what Shakespeare does in *Cymbeline*, and it is the reason above all why I love the play.

Aristotle was the first to observe that the denouement, or unwinding, of the plot is the test of a good playwright. If this is awkwardly or ineptly done the play cannot be good, no matter what other merits it has. In most plays, the denouement occupies only a portion of the last act; even when it is well done it does not take much time to do it. But the denouement of *Cymbeline* dominates the play; it is the reason for the play's existence.

The complexities of the plot are all set forth in the first few scenes, and they are many and various. Once the basic complexities are presented, changes are rung upon them so that the audience, to say nothing of the characters themselves, are simply bewildered. Everyone on the stage during the denouement is under one misconception or another, and these misconceptions are serious matters; if they continue, almost all the main characters will go to their deaths. But Shakespeare doesn't want such an unhappy ending to his lovely story. Slowly, one by one, he unties the knots, picks apart the web of confusions and mistakes, and reveals everyone to everyone else: daughter to father, husband to wife and wife to husband, sister to brothers, master to servant, friend to friend. At the end the poetry of the play, which has never been base, rises to heights. And Cymbeline himself, the old King of Britain to whom is now restored all that he has ever loved and lost, sums up the theme in these lines:

> *Never was a war did cease*
> *Ere bloody hands were wash'd, with such a peace.*

This is the great peace of Shakespeare's last plays. This peace, in the solitary certainty of a task superbly done, is what Prospero refers to in the famous speech that closes *The Tempest*:

> Let me not
> Since I have my dukedom got,
> And pardon'd the deceiver, dwell
> In this bare island by your spell;
> But release me from the bands
> With the help of your good hands.
>
> As you from crimes would pard'd be
> Let your indulgence set me free.

# MIGUEL DE CERVANTES
## 1547–1616
### *Don Quixote*

It would be good to know more about Miguel de Cervantes, but records are sparse. He lived long ago, not an important man as importance was measured in the Spain of four centuries ago. In another sense, of course, he was more important than anyone else in Spain, including King Philip II, and his only peer in Europe and, indeed, the world, was an Englishman who was writing plays for the Globe Theatre when Cervantes was composing *Don Quixote*. In fact, some reference books still report Shakespeare and Cervantes as dying on the same day, April 23, 1616, and that is very pleasant to think about, although it probably is not true. At any rate, we can imagine the two of them arriving together at Saint Peter's Gate, perhaps even hand in hand, but more likely arguing about the relative merits of plays or novels, of comedy or tragedy, or whatever.

We do know that Cervantes had an eventful life before he sat down in the kitchen of his little house in Esquivias and wrote the first part of *Don Quixote*. He had been born in 1547, in the university city of Alcala de Henares, the son of an itinerant barber-surgeon. He received little or no formal education but read all the books he could get his hands on. While still a young man, he was stage struck to the extent that he spent much of the rest of his life dreaming of success as a playwright. When he was twenty-four he sailed from Messina, in Sicily, on board the *Marquesa* in the armada led by Don John of Austria against the Turks, and he fought valiantly at the Battle of Lepanto, receiving three gunshot wounds, one permanently maiming his left hand—"to the greater glory," he said, "of the right." Recovered, he served in other campaigns and was an effective soldier, a fact confirmed by letters of commendation given him by Don John and the Viceroy of Sicily. He left Naples with these letters in hand to return to Spain in the fall of 1575.

A few days later, off Marseilles, his ship was taken by Turkish pirates. Cervantes, because of the important letters in his possession, was considered to be a valuable prize; consequently a high price was set for his ransom. It was five years, full of adventure, before his family could raise the large amount needed, but they finally did so. On September 19, 1580, Cervantes, already on board a ship that was to take him, as a slave, to Constantinople, instead received his freedom.

Once more back in Spain, he tried various occupations, including several attempts to write for a living. His first efforts were plays and a pastoral poem, "Galatea," which gained him some small reputation but no riches. For the next fifteen years he struggled to support his wife and several female relatives by what we would call today civil service activities for the Spanish navy. He was not, however, very adept at keeping accounts, and he was imprisoned more than once during these years for not being able to make a proper accounting of funds that had been given him in charge.

According to tradition, Cervantes began to write *Don Quixote* around 1600, in the house in Esquivias whose two small rooms provided both living and working space for Cervantes and four or five women relatives. Doubtless he began by simply sitting and dreaming in the kitchen of the house, or so it is said. The women stepped around and over him, going about their business, and perhaps he told them stories of his adventures in the great world, but at any rate he pondered his life and the failure of his hopes. What could he look forward to, at the age of fifty-three, but penury, illness, and death? He laughed at that, for he was a great comic spirit.

For years he had read voraciously the popular literature of chivalry—the romances of that day—and he loved the old stories, just as everyone did throughout Spain. At first he thought he might write a chivalric romance, but then he decided to make fun of those foolish popular stories. And so he created Don Quixote, an elderly knight, as poor as a church mouse in all but books, whose brains had been addled by the reading of romances to the point where he had come to believe they were real.

The work thus began simply; Cervantes cannot have had any idea, at the beginning, of the majesty of his conception. Don Quixote sets out on his first sally, meets with a few adventures, manages to get himself made—according to his own crazy lights—a knight, and returns home again. The whole episode fills twenty pages.

Did Cervantes read the story to his womenfolk, and did they like it? At any event he determined to proceed. Don Quixote needed someone to talk to on his travels. So Cervantes created the squire, a certain Sancho Panza, a man of the neighborhood with his head screwed on tight and his feet on the ground, and sent him out to watch Don Quixote and to bring him home safely should he get into too much trouble.

The greatness of the book *Don Quixote* begins here, when the two, the one tall and gaunt, a dreamer, the other short and round, a realist, ride the roads of a Spain of long ago. These two immortal figures talk to one another about all the really important subjects: life, death, and immortality; the whole duty of a man; the meaning of kingship and the reality; the rules of art and poetry. Meanwhile they have adventures, in all of which Don Quixote is bested and beaten and betrayed. Finally, at the end of the book that Cervantes published in 1604, the poor old man is brought home in a cage, close to madness, and deposited before his own door. Sancho returns sheepishly to his family, but he knows that real life was out there and not here in his little village.

*Don Quixote* was an immediate success, being reprinted several times the first year and attracting two pirated editions in Portugal from which Cervantes, of course, received no revenues. In fact, he received almost nothing from the legitimate editions of the work. But he was pleased with himself because all Spain, and soon all Europe, was talking about the Knight of the Woeful Countenance and his faithful squire who spouted proverbs as he rode his donkey behind his master.

Cervantes did not know it, but the best was yet to come; he was not through with Don Quixote. Just as Cervantes had imitated the popular romances of the day, so now another author imitated *Don Quixote*. In mock rage and indignation Cervantes responded with his own genuine Second Part. This, the longer of the two parts and the greater, tells of the third and last sally of Don Quixote and Sancho Panza and shows how they come truly to know one another for what they are, and to love one another, too, although each is so different from the other.

In the First Part, Cervantes had not been sufficiently confident of his characters to let them run on as he would have liked, and instead interrupted their conversations, and the narrative, with extraneous stories and unnecessary literary exercises. But now he knows that the best thing is simply to let his characters be what and as they are and so, more and more as the book progresses, they talk to one another, endless conversations that run on through day and night so that neither is able to sleep for fascination and interest.

Finally, they come to share not only friendship but an equal vision. They meet a band of wandering actors, and they reach the same conclusion, although in different words: We are, all of us, but a band of strolling players, who take our roles and play our parts as well as we can, but we take our exits, too, as our great Author wills. Thus has Sancho taught Don Quixote about the real world, and Don Quixote has taught Sancho how to dream.

At the very end of what may be the best of all books, their roles are reversed. They have returned from the third sally and Don Quixote has become ill. His illness seems to be mortal and Sancho is desolate. "Master," he cries, "come with me yet another time, and we shall have adventures together and teach the world to love and respect knights!" "No, Sancho," replies Don Quixote gently, "for there are no birds in last year's nests." It is the saddest of all the wonderful proverbs that are sprinkled throughout Don Quixote. (But heretofore it has always been Sancho Panza who has remembered the proverbs.) And so the old man dies of a broken heart because he thinks he has been a fool.

He is not a fool, of course; to find real adventures in this workaday world is the signal achievement of a noble and great spirit. Such is Don Quixote. There has never been anyone else like him. Nor has there been such a pair as those two, the old knight on his tall, skinny horse, and the short squire on his fat donkey. They wend their way, forever, in our imaginations. I wish we could call them back.

# chapter six

# The Renaissance, Part Two

We are not done yet with the Renaissance, which, soon after the fall of Byzantium in 1453, took on a life of its own and became not just the rebirth of the Classics but the invention of a new world with new ideas, fears, and hopes.

It is both right and proper to begin with Descartes because he spent his life fighting against the restrictions imposed by the Aristotelians on the freedom of thought. Descartes believed that the Classical worldview that Petrarch and Boccaccio had hoped to re-create had turned out to be closed and narrow, and he rebelled against his teachers as so many young men would in the following centuries. He was a good but not obedient student, which his teachers misunderstood as stupidity and punished with chastisements at which he could only laugh. In some respects he was a very modern man. Other Frenchmen followed his example, and some Englishmen as well. I will let them speak for themselves in what follows. An important thing about all of them is that they did their best work in the seventeenth century, which is one of the most fruitful since— well, since the world began.

# RENÉ DESCARTES
## 1596–1650
### *Discourse on the Method of Rightly Conducting the Reason*

René Descartes (his name in Latin was Renatus Cartesius, hence the adjective "Cartesian") was born in La Haye, France, in 1596. He received a good Jesuit education and was the kind of student that teachers both love and dread. He was a brilliant pupil who understood everything quickly. He asked challenging questions. But he was also surly and rebellious, and he seemed to doubt everything his teachers believed. His questions seemed to shake the foundations of the learning they were trying to instill in their brilliant pupil, and this was a fearful thing—for what if he were right?

When he was twenty, Descartes took his degree in law. Two years later joined the army of the Prince of Orange in Holland. Up to this point his career was uneventful, at least outwardly. Inwardly the young man was fomenting an intellectual revolution based on his perennial questioning.

Descartes was not alone in this. Francis Bacon, in England, had felt the same grave doubts, as had Galileo in Italy. But no one doubted more systematically than young Descartes and as a consequence no one did more to bring down the ancient edifice of learning that had stood for more than a thousand years.

Descartes described the reasons for his doubts, and the extent of them, in the *Discourse on the Method of Rightly Conducting the Reason* of 1637. Once you begin to doubt systematically, he says, the questions become: Where do you stop? Do you ever stop? Is there anything that cannot be doubted, that is undoubtedly true? Yes, one thing: the doubter himself exists, else he could not doubt or, as Descartes put it in a famous phrase, *cogito, ergo sum* ("I think, therefore I am"). Once this is established it is possible to start afresh, on solid ground, and to build up a new structure of knowledge, different from the old, and having the character, as Descartes asserts, of indubitable certainty.

Descartes called the method "geometrical." You lay down the minimum number of assumptions and then, using them as building blocks, patiently build up a new edifice that will stand the test of time and of doubt. But the geometrical method, for Descartes, was not just a matter of taking careful logical steps. It also involved taking the smallest steps possible, because small steps are safer than big ones. And each small step, each element in the solution of the problem, ought to have the kind of certainty that numbers have. In the world of numbers, clear and distinct ideas are possible: $2 + 2 = 4$, there is no doubt about that. In the process of developing this line of thinking Descartes invented analytical geometry, whereby a one-to-one relationship is established between the infinite points of the plane and (pairs of) the infinite numbers from minus infinity to plus infinity. The invention of analytical geometry is one of the milestones in the history of thought, and Descartes deserves much credit for it.

Essentially, the geometrical method, as Descartes described it in the *Discourse on Method*, consists in first reducing any problem to geometrical form (a system of axioms and propositions) and then making a further reduction to numbers as in analytical geometry. This works very well for problems in physics, but Descartes wanted to apply his method to everything—to philosophy as well as physics, to ethics as well as astronomy. He did not live to discover that the method works better in some fields than others—for example, the physical sciences, and that there are other fields, for example, philosophy, ethics, even history, where it does not work as well or not at all. He did live to see his method adopted by many young and vigorous thinkers who began to feel, as he may have felt himself, that those fields in which the method does work were more important to study and develop, and those in which it did not work should be relegated to second-class status and perhaps be ignored altogether.

Unfortunately, that prejudice persists to this day, and it may be called the characteristic disease of modern thought. True, science has made fantastic progress in the three hundred and fifty years since Descartes wrote his *Discourse*, and our world would be vastly different, and much more uncomfortable, if he had not discovered his method. But other realms of knowledge have languished in the bright glare of those sciences that can be mathematicized. Science, we have even come to think, is what can be mathematicized, and what cannot be mathematicized must be called something else—"humanities," say.

But "science" means knowledge, and thus what we are really saying is that we can know about the sciences that are mathematical—and that deal mostly with material things—but only have opinions about nonmathematical, spiritual things. And as we all know, one man's opinion is as good as another's.

What is even worse, we then take the further step of declaring that because we know mathematically about material things, they are more important than spiritual things. (Alternatively, we try to use mathematics in realms where it is does not really apply—in ethics, for example; see Spinoza.) As a result, our whole knowledge structure is skewed toward the material and away from the spiritual.

The knowledge structure that Descartes had doubted and then attacked, and that he helped to bring down, had been skewed the other way and this was not good either. What is needed is still another knowledge structure that discards neither Cartesian, scientific, mathematically based knowledge nor the kind of knowledge that is obtainable by other methods in other fields—by intuition, experience, or common sense. In the best of worlds both kinds of knowledge would be honored equally.

For the moment, we have what we have, and what we have is Cartesianism up to our eyebrows. Thus I cannot think of any book that is more useful to read, if you want to understand the intellectual world we live in, than Descartes' *Method*. Read it, and ask yourself whether it too can be doubted. Is there a hole in Descartes's argument? Does he go off the track partway to his goal? How would you put him back? And if you did that, would it change the goal?

# JEAN DE LA FONTAINE
### 1621–1695
*Fabliaux*

The literature of France, taken altogether, is not surpassed by that of any other European nation. Yet France lacks what several other nations possess, a single preeminent poet. This lack is made up for by a number of poets of the second rank—a very high second rank, after all. La Fontaine is one of these very good poets who just miss being great.

The seventeenth century in Europe, especially in France, was the century of magnificence, when the Sun King, Louis XIV, ruled at Versailles over a populace that was the richest in the world at the time. However, grandeur is far from the leading characteristic of the two best writers of the century, La Fontaine and Molière. Molière wrote plays that made fun of wealth and magnificence; the *Fabliaux* (*Fables*) of La Fontaine do the same thing in a more modest way.

Jean de La Fontaine was born in 1621. It was an age of patrons, and he was expert at finding and retaining them. As a result he never had to work at anything other than his poems and stories; he always managed to be supported by somebody. This was important because, although most of his works are short, they are extremely polished and it took him a long time to write them. In fact, he was a hard worker, although he enjoyed giving the opposite impression.

The *Fables* are perfect small poems, each, however, carrying an electric charge of meaning. La Fontaine possessed a microscopic eye that was uncomfortable with large vistas. He much preferred a pinhole view of the world—through which he nevertheless was able to see everything that was important. The fable of the fox and the grapes, the mountain that gave birth to a mouse, the ant and the grasshopper—these little stories, with their big meanings, fitted his temperament and sensibilities.

A fable, of course, is a story in which the characters are animals that talk to one another, like human beings, and act like human beings, too. The form goes back to the Greek fables of Aesop, and many of La Fontaine's fables are retellings of Aesop's. Some are retold from other sources, a few are original. Whatever their source, all emerge from La Fontaine's pen with the same character and quality: he changes them all into something richer and stranger than they were.

It is hard to choose a best among the *Fables*, but one of the most famous, and most typical, is the Fable of the Grasshopper and the Ant. The grasshopper sings happily all summer long while the ant works from morning to night storing up food for the winter. When winter comes the grasshopper goes to the ant's little house and asks for something to eat. The ant refuses; the grasshopper should have stored up his own food. Where were you, the ant asks, while I was working? I was singing, replies the grasshopper, to entertain you! Well, says the hardhearted ant, start dancing, then!

This fable is certainly not a simple one. There are readers who feel the ant is perfectly justified. She has worked hard all summer, refusing to rest, to take her pleasure; why should she not enjoy her wealth now instead of having to share it with the careless, happy-go-lucky grasshopper, who has done nothing but sing in the sunlight? If you wish to read the fable thus, of course you may.

I don't read it that way, nor, I think, did La Fontaine mean it that way (although he was not entirely unsympathetic to the ant). The grasshopper is a symbol or representative of the creative artist, the man or woman who is driven, at any cost, to write or draw or sing or dance for the entertainment of mankind and as a consolation for our heavy burden in the world. The cost to the artist is often very great: not seldom it is poverty and loneliness, disease and the failure of hopes, and an early death. Yet what would our life be without these indigent, thoughtless creators? How shallow, how barren, how dull! Merely to store up sustenance against the winters of our lives is not enough. Our minds and imaginations need another kind of food as well, the rich, spiritual food that only great artists can provide. We owe them nothing; the ant is right; but she is also wrong, for we owe them everything.

The argument between the grasshopper and the ant goes on and on in our imaginations, and so with a dozen other fables, or a hundred of them. Most are good, many are wonderful, all have the same odd, sideways view of things. La Fontaine himself is nowhere visible in them; they have the sheen of polished anonymous works. Nor are they merely French. If anything in French literature has the quality of universality, it is the *Fabliaux* of Jean de La Fontaine.

There are several good English translations of the *Fables*, for example, those by Marianne Moore. However, almost any will do, if the English and French texts lie side by side. That is usually desirable when reading lyric poems written in another language. But you should not feel deprived if you have a plain English translation. La Fontaine, generous grasshopper that he was, will entertain you anyway.

# MOLIÈRE
1622–1673
*Plays*

———

Jean-Baptiste Poquelin was born in Paris in 1622, the son of a prosperous merchant with an appointment as a furnisher to the royal household who gave his son an excellent education at one of the best schools in France and expected him to inherit his court position. But in his teens young Poquelin was already fascinated by the theater and when he was twenty-one he renounced his inheritance and, with nine others, formed a theatrical company. His stage name, Molière, dates from 1644.

The theatergoing audience in Paris in the middle of the seventeenth century was not large, and there were already two established companies presenting plays on a regular basis. Molière's troupe therefore took to the provinces, where they made a meager living touring for thirteen years. They were hard times, but it was during those years that Molière learned everything there was to know about the stage. Finally the opportunity came for the production of a play in Paris, before the king. The year was 1658, the show was a success, and from that time on Molière never left Paris.

His first Paris play—only two insignificant plays from the touring years survive—was *Les Precieuses Ridicules*, in which two absurdly affected young ladies are contrasted with two commonsensical servants. This play, a hit, was followed by other successes. The king soon gave his patronage, and the company began to perform in a theater built for it by the great Cardinal Richelieu. But there was trouble to come: it began with the first performance, in 1662, of *The School for Wives*.

Many consider this play to be Molière's masterpiece. The plot is delicious. A pedant, Arnolphe, is so frightened of women and so certain they will make a fool of him (and cuckold him) that he decides to marry an absolutely simple and uneducated girl whom he can shape to his heart's desire. Under his tutelage the girl grows to consciousness both of herself and of society. Arnolphe slowly but surely falls in love with her and has to learn lovers' talk. Both educations are wonderful, touching, and funny. But the play was a scandal. It suggested too much about the liberation of women from the slavery of their ignorance, as enforced by men, and about the absurdity of men's illusions about themselves. Molière was attacked and, for a time, the play was taken off the boards.

For the next ten years he was constantly harassed by the authorities. He struggled to keep the company going and wrote play after play, although he was often ill both in body and soul. The year 1665 saw the premiere of *The Misanthrope*, which from the first was viewed as a masterpiece by the critics. An extraordinary comedy, it is as close to black comedy as the seventeenth century could allow. Molière himself played the hero, Alceste, a new kind of fool, a man of such probity and candor that he can never keep his mouth shut when he should. He constantly criticizes everyone else, always for good reason, but he can't understand why this makes him unpopular.

Alceste's beloved, Célimène, is just as upright and discerning as he, and has as sharp a tongue. But she is willing to make an accommodation with society. At the same time that she recognizes fools and makes fun of them, she also charms them out of their shoes. One of the great characters in the history of drama, she also represents a home truth. Plain speaking, no matter how correct, will always offend if it is not accompanied by a certain social grace, a certain courtesy. The insistence on the part of Alceste that all, or at least he, should always speak their minds, is finally seen as overweening pride. Célimène is vain and beautiful, but she has the humility that comes from being able to see other people as real and needful, like herself. Alceste can't see this. He retreats into his dark corner, an almost tragic figure. Yet a comic one, too—the play is very funny, and Célimène is superb.

Molière wrote *The Doctor in Spite of Himself* the year after *The Misanthrope*. It was a time of distress for the company and for Molière personally, who was very ill, but none of his plays has a sunnier disposition than this foolish farce about a peasant who admits to being a doctor in order to avoid being beaten. He gets everything wrong; when he is taken to task for seeking the heart on the right side of the chest he explains, in the immortal phrase: "We have changed all that!" He also cures his patient with some down-home common sense. He knows when a girl is sick and when she is in love, and this one is in love; if so, he knows how to make her well. He rearranges things so that the lovers have each other and everyone else is happy, too, and there is thenceforth no more illness on this stage. Molière played the part of the doctor; he had been treated by many quacks and he knew all their tricks.

Six years after returning to Paris from his years of touring in the provinces, in 1664, Molière presented at Versailles, to a royal audience, the first version of his extraordinary play *Tartuffe*, or, *The Imposter*. This first version, in three acts, tells of a "holy" man who worms his way into the household of a good bourgeois and rewards his benefactor by attempting to seduce his wife. When he is caught in the act he reproaches himself with such aplomb that the bourgeois ends up not only forgiving him but insisting that he spend as much time with his wife as he can.

It was the custom during the seventeenth century in France for "directors of conscience," who were usually pious laymen, not clergy, to be placed by the Church in families where they were supposed to reprove and reform conduct. Obviously this practice could lead to all kinds of hypocrisy. But it was a recognized religious procedure, and Molière's attack on it in *Tartuffe* enraged the ecclesiastics of Paris. The play was banned and he was charged with several crimes.

Molière was acquitted of the charges but it was five years before he was able to free his play, which he liked very much, from the grip of the censors. He twice petitioned the king and published a "Letter on the Comedy of the Imposter" that reflected his deepest views of the essence of comedy. "The comic," he wrote, "is the outward and visible form that nature's bounty has attached to everything unreasonable, so that," he went on, "we should see, and avoid, it."

To know the comic we must know the rational, of which it denotes the absence, and we must see wherein the rational consists ... Incongruity is the heart of the comic ... It follows that all lying, disguise, cheating, dissimulation, all outward show different from the reality, all contradiction in fact between actions that proceed from a single source, all this is in essence comic.

These arguments apparently persuaded the king to allow Molière to present the play again. In the meantime he had doubled its length and added a depth of character seldom achieved in comedy. Orgon, the deceived bourgeois, has become a complex man, a fool for a while, but one who is eventually capable of seeing the light. His wife, Elmire, is a woman of much common sense. Their daughter, Mariane, and Mariane's maid, Dorine, are a superb pair, and the lovers' quarrel that Dorine first promotes between Mariane and Valère and then attempts to stop once it has gone on too long is one of the funniest scenes in theater.

Molière understood the power of hypocrisy and knew that common sense and reason are often helpless against it except in the imaginative world of the stage. Tartuffe, the imposter, wins everything in the final version of the play. Orgon and his wife and children are only saved by the miraculous intercession of His Majesty, who sees all and knows all in this good world of justice and truth. That was a very nice compliment to the King, but the audience departed from the theater realizing full well that kings do not in fact know all, and that evil is a real and present thing.

Molière won his battle for *Tartuffe*; it ended up being his greatest stage success. He did not win in the case of another of his best plays, *Don Juan*. At the end of this play, which influenced Mozart's *Don Giovanni*, an atheist is consigned to hell in a spectacular outburst of words and fire, but before his punishment Juan has had the temerity to mock the priests and charm the audience. The Church found this intolerable. *Don Juan* was banned and never played again during Molière's lifetime.

Many productions of Molière in English attempt to make an English playwright out of him. Such productions overemphasize the farcical elements, ignore the formalisms in his plays, run over the scene breaks, present the actors in modern dress, and the like. The best place to see him played—if you know a bit of French (it need not be a lot)—is at the Salle Molière of the Comédie Française, in Paris, where the plays of this greatest of French writers are presented with all due decorum, love, and respect. Short of that they should be read—for example, in the translations by the splendid American poet Richard Wilbur—slowly and with delectation of the comic situations.

## BLAISE PASCAL
### 1623–1662
#### *Pensées*

Among the thinkers and writers of the seventeenth century in France, Blaise Pascal, the most modest and retiring of all, takes second place to none. Born in 1623, in Clermont-Ferrand, he was a youthful prodigy. He was from childhood fascinated by mathematics, but his father destined his brilliant son for the law and consequently forbade him to study mathematics and removed all mathematical books from his library. Pascal thereupon made up his own system of geometry, using different names: a circle was "a round." The father, coming upon this work of original creative genius, gave the boy his intellectual liberty. Pascal went on to invent truly new things in mathematics—among others, he founded the modern science of probability. His later work on that distinctive curve, the cycloid, made him famous throughout Europe. His correspondence with another mathematician, Fermat, contains much that remains of interest today. And to help his tax-collector father with his computations, Blaise Pascal, at the age of twenty, constructed a calculating device that has been termed the first digital computer.

Mathematics was not demanding enough by itself. Pascal's restless mind sought other challenges, notably in physics, especially in the study of that illusive entity, vacuum. He invented the syringe, improved Torricelli's barometer, and published important papers on the weight and density of air.

But when he turned twenty-three, in 1646, his father being ill, Pascal underwent a kind of conversion from the easy-going, latitudinarian Catholicism practiced by his family to the much stricter Catholicism of the Jansenists, a sect whose leadership was centered in the convent of Port Royale, in Paris. In 1652, when he was not yet thirty and after a mystical "night of fire" that seared his soul, Pascal entered Port Royale and thenceforth wrote and worked according to the dictates of the fathers of the convent.

He was almost at once swept into controversy, writing a series of "Provincial Letters" in defense of the Jansenists against the more lax (as he viewed them) Jesuits. During the course of two years spent writing the eighteen "Provincial Letters," Pascal not only developed his mature thinking on religion but also created modern French prose. Before those interesting and readable letters, French prose had often been heavy, bombastic, and tedious. Pascal's prose, especially as he neared the end of the series of letters, attained those qualities of lightness, variety, and flexibility—*souplesse*, as the French say—that are so much admired today.

Having completed the "Provincial Letters," Pascal decided to write an important work on religion, an *Apology for Christianity* that would emphasize the importance for salvation of God's grace rather than good works, and would compare in the most graphic terms the abject condition of man without grace to the bliss of those possessing it. This book was never finished, but what he wrote of it—some notes, some longer paragraphs, a few "chapters" of several pages in length—was collected by Pascal before his final illness and published soon after his death at thirty-nine under the title of *Pensées* (*Thoughts*). By this title it has been known, and published and republished, ever since.

The surviving fragments of Pascal's original concept are more eloquent about the abjectness of a life without grace than about the bliss of a life with it. If, indeed, "eloquent" is a strong enough term to describe the potent language of these scattered thoughts, which are certainly the greatest collection of *apercus* ever composed. Man unredeemed, without the grace of God, is like a caged animal, constantly seeking a freedom that he does not know how to use, requiring "diversions" of all kinds but unable to face himself.

All the unhappiness of men arises from one single fact, that they cannot stay quietly in their own chamber … Nothing is so insufferable to a man as to be completely at rest, without passions, without business, without diversion, without study. He then feels his nothingness, his forlornness, his insufficiency, his dependence, his weakness, his emptiness … As men are not able to fight against death, misery, ignorance, they have taken it into their heads, in order to be happy, not to think of them at all.

What is to be done? In response to the challenge of skeptics, Pascal proposes a wager, which his study of probabilities has made it easier to explicate. Believe in God, he says; why not? If God does not exist what have you lost? It is not so great a burden to fall upon your knees. But if God does exist, think what you have gained! And if God does exist and you do not believe, think of what you will lose—an eternity of bliss exchanged for an eternity of pain. No gambler would refuse these odds, says Pascal; why should you?

There are two kinds of intellects, Pascal tells us: the geometrical and the intuitive (*l'esprit de géometrie* and *l'esprit de finesse*). The one thinks with the mind; the other, as it were, with the heart. In a famous apothegm he describes the difference between them: "The heart has its reasons," he writes, "which reason will never know." (*Le cœur a ses raisons, que la raison ne connait pas.*) The most important insights, the most valuable knowledge, come to us through intuition; we apprehend directly, by a power essentially mysterious, as opposed to thinking things through. "I can never forgive Descartes," Pascal writes, and although the reason given is a metaphysical one, it is clear that Pascal's philosophy is fundamentally opposed to Cartesianism. Descartes's *Discourse on Method* had advocated just the sort of geometrical thinking that Pascal is here declaring to be of secondary importance. Pascal's distinction between two kinds of thinking remains influential to this day. Probably no one can read the *Pensées* without asking himself which kind of mind he has, and on which kind of thinking he is accustomed to depend.

The invention by Pascal of a digital calculator—the first "real" computer—seems relevant here. One of the great controversies of our time swirls around the question of whether a computer will ever be able to "think like a man." A test often proposed is whether a computer can "jump to a conclusion." (This phrase may beg the question: is "jumping to a conclusion" intuition, or is it just reasoning with suppressed, unconscious steps?) There is no doubt that computers can reason, after a fashion, but will they ever be able to do what a person does when he "has an idea" or "has a flash of inspiration"? Whatever is really meant by the two phrases it seems to be closer to the intuitive than to the geometrical mind.

Even if the subject matter of Pascal's *Pensées* were not so interesting, you might still want to read them because of their beauty and pellucid clarity. These qualities come through in most English translations, which has helped to make this collection of scattered observations one of the all-time bestselling books. Read a little or a lot at a time; Pascal will not only delight, but also improve your mind and help you to contemplate reality.

"The last act is tragic," he concludes, "however happy all the rest of the play; at the last a little earth is thrown upon our head, and that is the end forever."

# JOHN DONNE
## 1572–1631
### *Poems*

It is widely believed (by persons who are neither) that it is impossible to be both intellectually brilliant and deeply emotional—passionate, as it was called. John Donne is the proof that this belief is not correct.

Donne was one of the most brilliant men of his time, and it was a time of brilliant minds: Bacon, Descartes, Galileo, Newton, to say nothing of Shakespeare and Cervantes. Donne possessed a powerful, cool wit that helped him, in his later years, to attract huge throngs (including King James I) to his sermons in St. Paul's Cathedral, the premier pulpit of England in his day. His sermons are among the finest in English and his last sermon, preached when he knew he was dying and entitled "Death's Duel," is, I believe, unequaled.

Brilliant as he was, he was even more a man of passion, of feelings, of emotion. Sometimes the depth and power of his feelings overcame his intellect, or wit, and then he was wild, like a powerful spring popping out of a watch. When this happened his sermons became bizarre, almost unintelligible, and his poems became almost unintelligible, too. They seem to burst the bonds of their form, their rhythm and meter; they are trying to say more than a person can say, in poetry or otherwise.

Donne was like a walking bomb, ready to explode at any time. Born in London in 1572, the son of a prosperous merchant, his early career was very successful. But in 1601, when he was nearly thirty, he eloped with the niece of his patron, Sir Thomas Egerton, who was the Keeper of the Great Seal, an extremely important government post. Ann More's father was also a member of the Egerton household, and he seriously disapproved of the marriage partly because Ann was, at fifteen, still a minor. The result of this was that Donne lost his position and was left without any means of making a living. He was pardoned and the marriage was declared legally valid—they were madly in love with one another—but Donne had to spend the next ten years as an outcast, without steady employment, without prospects.

He retrieved his fortunes in the end, partly because his sermons were much admired by King James and by his successor, King Charles I. But even his best friends were a little afraid of him and of the sudden passions that darted through him. Ben Jonson, one of his closest friends, said that Donne ought to have been hanged "for not keeping of meter," and although this applied primarily to his undisciplined verse, it also applied to his life, which was as undisciplined and chaotic as his poetry.

The passionate, unpredictable character of John Donne is very much apparent in his poems. They are rough, awkward, often obscure, sometimes absurd. But when they work, when everything fits together, they are as good as any lyrics in English. Donne only misses being counted in the very first rank of poets because he failed to write an epic or "major work." (Perhaps he would have written such a poem if he had not devoted his efforts in his later years to preaching.)

The poems fall into three categories. First, there are the many love poems, written before he met Ann More and while he was courting her. A dozen or more of these are among the best love poems ever written. But they are "difficult"; that is, they require careful reading and intense study—an odd requirement for a love poem!

The second category is religious poems—the "Holy Sonnets," and others. One begins:

> Death be not proud, though some have callèd thee
> Mighty and dreadful, for thou art not so.

Not all the Holy Sonnets are as famous as that one, but a choice dozen are nevertheless very fine. They have a deep, throbbing note, like this one, about the Day of Judgment:

> At the round earth's imagin'd corners blow
> Your trumpets, Angels, and arise, arise
> From death, you numberless infinities
> Of souls, and to your scatter'd bodies go.

"At the round earth's imagin'd corners" is so typical of Donne. Four great Archangels will blow their trumpets on the Last Day to wake the living and the dead. But Earth is round, so where will the four Angels stand? (Do angels have to stand anywhere?) Why, at the world's "imagin'd corners"! If you try to imagine what he means the effort will show you what is necessary when reading Donne.

Finally, there is a third category, the so-called "Anniversaries." Donne had another patron after 1611, the death of whose young daughter occasioned a series of overwrought poems celebrating her and "anatomizing" the world: taking it apart and examining it. Donne's vision of the world in the "Anniversaries" is not delightful. Like all good poets he was unsentimental; what is more, his time was no better than ours and maybe worse. It was above all a time of change, of intellectual revolution. Donne was deeply disturbed by that, but he understood it as well as anyone.

When reading lyric poems it is always appropriate to start by reading out loud. Read the poem again silently, more than once, as many times as necessary to understand it—and then read it aloud again to see the difference and to test your comprehension. Does it sound "right"? I say "always," but it is truly difficult to do this with many poems of Donne. Coleridge, in a remark, gave the hint that should be heeded: "To read Dryden, Pope, etc., you need only count syllables, but to read Donne you must measure Time, and discover the Time of each word by the sense of Passion."

Among the love poems of Donne, the following are not to be missed: "Song (Go and catch a falling star)," "Love's Deity," "The Funeral," "The Good Morrow," "The Blossom," "The Undertaking," "The Canonization," "Love's Alchemy," and "A Valediction: Forbidding Mourning." Among the religious poems, read these: "Good Friday, 1613. Riding Westward," "Hymn to God My God, in My Sickness," "A Hymn to God the Father," and Holy Sonnets numbers 1, 5, 7, 10, 14, and 18. The Third Anniversary is the most interesting of the series, although deeply flawed. Read all this, and then read on. These lists are far from exhausting the poetical interest and beauty of Donne.

Finally, you may wish to have a taste of Donne's extraordinary sermons. "Death's Duel" should at least be looked at: try to discover what is happening in it. And the "Devotions upon Emergent Occasions" contain many wonderful things, including these famous lines:

> No man is an island, entire of itself; every man is a piece of the continent, a part of the main. If a clod be washed away by the sea, Europe is the less, as well as if a promontory were, as well as if a manor of thy friend's or of thine own were. Any man's death diminishes me because I am involved in mankind, and therefore never send to know for whom the bell tolls; it tolls for thee.

# GEORGE HERBERT
1593–1633
*Poems*

The great events of George Herbert's life took place within him, not in the outside world.

His career, such as it was, was undistinguished. Born in 1593 and a member of an important and influential English family in the early seventeenth century, he was neither rich nor important nor influential himself. However, with the help of his family and particularly of his mother, a great lady who was also a close friend of John Donne's, Herbert attained an important university post at Cambridge and appeared, while still in his twenties, to have worldly success within his grasp. But this was dependent on the patronage of the old king, James I, and when James died in 1625 Herbert was left adrift. More importantly, he had made the decision to leave the outer world and concentrate on the inner, and to resolve the struggle between his will and God's. He was ordained and became a country parson in the little church at Bemerton, in Wiltshire. He died a few years later, in 1633, at the age of thirty-nine, leaving a sheaf of poems with a friend, "to be published or not, as you see fit." The friend saw fit to publish the works of George Herbert in a volume that he called *The Temple: Sacred Poems and Private Ejaculations*, and so we have them today.

The devotion and humility of Herbert in his post at Bemerton became legendary. He gave himself entirely to his parishioners, exhausting himself in their behalf. But he continued to write poems in his last years and to practice the lute, his only diversion.

Izaak Walton, author of *The Compleat Angler*, wrote a biography of Herbert and one of the stories Walton told is well known. When Herbert took up his duties in Bemerton he realized he needed a wife to share the work and the loneliness. But he had never had anything to do with women and was perplexed about how to find a wife. He did remember, however, that an older friend, also a clergyman, had had six young daughters whom Herbert had liked when he was young.

He wrote the friend and told him he needed a wife and wondered if he—the friend—would choose one of his daughters (if any remained unmarried, Herbert added delicately) for him. In fact, all were as yet unmarried. The friend chose one (the second oldest) and sent her to Bemerton, where she shortly became Mrs. Herbert. The couple were said to have been extremely happy for the few years they had together before Herbert died.

In a letter that accompanied the manuscript of his poems, Herbert had described them as "a picture of the many spiritual conflicts that have passed between God and my soul, before I could subject mine to the will of Jesus my Master, in whose service I have now found perfect freedom." The description is accurate regarding the greatest of the poems in *The Temple*. They record a neverending struggle, fought in the silence of the heart and waged against the temptations of worldly ambition and of spiritual lassitude—*accidie*, or sloth. Herbert's claim that he had finally triumphed in this struggle and had won "perfect freedom" may or may not have been true. The reader of his poems can decide for himself. Certainly they have the ring of sincerity; their power, which is great, derives from the strength of the feelings they describe and with which they deal.

George Herbert has often been likened to John Donne, with justice, but there are differences between them. Herbert wrote no passionate love poems like those of Donne, but on the other hand the intensity of his spiritual striving is probably even greater, and more affecting, than that of Donne. In short, there are hardly any greater religious poems in English than George Herbert's.

These poems, therefore, are not to be read lightly. They demand attention and care, and a willingness of the heart. Give this to them, just the slightest bit, and they will lead you to give more of yourself. It is astonishing how they are able to draw even reluctant readers in. Read "The Collar," "Love," "The Pulley," "The Flower," "Denial," and "Man." Then read "Prayer," "The Temper," "Employment," "Sighs and Groans," "Whitsunday," "The Star," and "The Rose." Finally, read "The Sacrifice," with its heartbreaking refrain of Christ on the Cross: "Was ever grief like mine?" You must be strong to read this one.

Finally, read "Virtue," which begins:

> *Sweet day, so cool, so calm, so bright,*
> *The bridal of the earth and sky;*
> *The dew shall weep thy fall to-night,*
> *For thou must die.*

And think of that young poet who died so many years ago and who felt so deeply the loss of one day, as deeply as you feel the loss of any day of your own.

# ROBERT HERRICK
## 1591–1664
### *Poems*

Robert Herrick led an entirely uneventful life of little note. Born in London in 1591, but for most of his life a country parson, he seems to have gone down to London only once during the last half of his life, to arrange for the publication of the collection of poems he had been writing for many years. They were published, under the title *Hesperides, or Noble Numbers*, in 1648. It was not the best time for such a volume to appear. England had only recently been embroiled in a desperate civil war, which had ended with the ritual execution of the king, Charles I, and the mood of the time was passionate and serious, or passionately serious. Herrick was not serious at all, at least not like the Puritans who took over the government after the death of Charles, and his poems presumed the existence of readers who could enjoy pleasures of an older style, before politics had become so important. As a consequence hardly anybody bought or paid attention to his book. He returned home, wrote more poems, and may have licked his wounds—we know very little about him. Nearly two centuries later, in the early nineteenth century, the gentle critic Charles Lamb discovered a copy of *Hesperides* among some old books, read it, and began to tell everybody that this Herrick had been a great poet. As indeed he was.

Knowing that, and understanding why Herrick is a great poet, is not easy. Many readers, even relatively practiced readers of poetry, fail to see more in him than a graceful skill at describing minor country matters. But look deeper and you begin to recognize a profound melancholy, which is after all the stuff of much of the greatest poetry. At the same time that he is always light and graceful, Herrick struggles in his poems with the most important of poetic ideas: the fact that beautiful as the world is, it is not permanent, it will die. More than any other idea, that is the central one that poets understand and write about.

Both parts of the idea, or all four parts, in fact, are present in the best lyrics. First, that the world is beautiful. If you do not think so, you cannot be a poet, for all good poets share the belief in the exquisite loveliness, charm, and desirability of the world as it is—even though it is also bad and ugly in many respects. Now the beauty of the world is various, and poets have seen it from many points of view. Herrick saw it from the point of view of a country parson in the middle of the English civil war. He saw fields and meadows, flowers and young girls, children and old gnarled people. And he found them all good.

Second, that the world's beauty is not permanent, that it must pass. The world is always changing, its beauty always diminishing—ever since that first morning when God made it perfect, long, long ago. Why does this beauty lessen? Well, there are various theories, having to do with original sin, entropy, and such concepts. Poets do not always bother their heads about the reason. They only know it is so.

Third, that this beauty will not only diminish, it will die. Every living thing that is beautiful in itself and adds to the sum total of the world's beauty will die, sooner or later, and for most living things, very soon—like flowers and butterflies and this very day, which must come to an end tonight. "Everything" includes, of course, both the poet and the reader, who are conceived by the poet to be single: one-on-one is the essential poetical relationship, one writer, one reader, and the poem in between, holding them together with a grip that is firmer than death.

This is the fourth part of the idea: that despite the death of the world and its beauty this poem will endure, will survive both writer and reader and will help readers in other times and places to endure the melancholy facts of human life.

All of this is present in the best poems of Robert Herrick, which are not few, although his most valuable work is not vast, either. All of it is present in what may be his best poem, "To Meadows." He addresses the meadows:

> Ye have been fresh and green,
> > Ye have been filled with flowers;
> And ye the walks have been
> > Where maids have spent their hours.

It is now autumn, the grass is brown, the flowers and the maidens have departed, and the meadows are left to beweep their fate:

> Like unthrifts, having spent
> > Your stock and needy grown,
> You're left here to lament
> > Your poor estates, alone.

The gentle suggestion that it is the meadows' own fault (they have spent all their "stock," all their capital), that they are now deserted where once they have been so rich, is the heartbreaking note of the poem. Indeed, it is not the meadows' fault, it is the fault of the world itself, of things, of the conditions of life. But as we say that, as we defend the meadows from the charge that is implicit in those last lines, we come to understand the point Herrick is making. "Yes, you are right," he nods, "it is not the fault of the meadows, it is the conditions of life and of man of which I am speaking here, and I am glad you have come to understand it."

Here is a suggested list of poems by Herrick that I believe you should read: "The Argument of His Book," "An Ode for Ben Jonson," "To Live Merrily and to Trust to Good Verses," "To Daffodils," "Upon Julia's Clothes," "Sweet Disorder," "Grace for a Child," "To the Virgins, to Make Much of Time," "The Mad Maid's Song," "To Meadows," "A Thanksgiving to God, for His House," "His Litany, to the Holy Spirit," and "To Death." You may wish to read more, but these are often anthologized and are therefore fairly easy to find.

# THOMAS HOBBES

1588–1679

*Leviathan*

In April 1588 rumors were rife in England concerning the approach of the dreaded Spanish Armada. Mrs. Hobbes, wife of the vicar of Westport, in Wiltshire, was beset with fears, as were all of her neighbors. She was pregnant, and because of her fear and distress she gave birth prematurely. The boy, Thomas, was not adversely affected, for he lived in good health and with the full possession of his faculties until the age of ninety-one.

He was slow to mature although he entered Oxford at fourteen, but he learned little or nothing, he later said, from the scholastic program based upon Aristotle that was offered there. Rather, he learned from other men, and not least from his friends and benefactors, the family of Cavendish, Earls and Dukes of Devonshire, with whom he was connected as tutor, fellow traveler, and companion throughout his long life.

It was as the companion of a nobleman that Hobbes found himself in Paris in 1628, when he was forty years old. There he came upon mathematics for the first time and a great revelation it was to him. His friend John Aubrey described it:

> Being in a gentleman's library ... Euclid's Elements lay open, and it was the 47th Prop. Lib. I. So he reads the proposition. "By G-," says he, "this is impossible." So he reads the demonstration, which referred him back to another, which he also read, and *sic deinceps*, that at last he was demonstratively convinced of that truth. That made him in love with geometry.

The forty-seventh proposition of the first book of Euclid's *Elements* is the famous Pythagorean Theorem, that the square on the hypotenuse of a right triangle is equal to the sum of the squares on the other two sides. It is typical of Hobbes 1. that he had never heard of this geometric truth before; 2. that he crustily denied it until he had determined its truth with his own eyes and mind (in other words, he was distrustful of any intellectual authority); 3. that he did follow up the train of demonstration to its beginning, and was convinced by it; and 4. that he ever after loved "not the theorems," as he said, "but the method of geometry, its art of reasoning."

Crusty, stubborn, willful—that is Hobbes to a T. But these are not intellectual vices when combined with a good mind, much experience, and a long life. In fact, they then may turn into virtues, the fruit of which in Hobbes's case was a number of works, one of which was the very important book, *Leviathan*. Its full title was *Leviathan; or, the Matter, Form, and Power of a Commonwealth, Ecclesiastical and Civil*.

The full title is both accurate and instructive. The book is in four parts, the last two of which are closely connected. The first part deals with the matter of a commonwealth, which is to say with human beings. The second part deals with the form of a commonwealth, the traditional differences in which—as between monarchy and democracy, say—Hobbes thought were trivial. The third and fourth parts deal with the vexing problem of the relations of the laws of man and of God in a commonwealth.

Ever mindful of the lessons of the forty-seventh proposition of the first book of Euclid, Hobbes begins his discourse with a presentation of his thoughts about first things: sense, imagination, speech, reasoning, and the like. In a series of short chapters, some of them no more than a paragraph in length, he offers the kinds of sound conclusions that are usually associated with the philosophical school of British Empiricism, of which he may be counted a founding member. He then goes on to examine man in his essence, without sentimentality. Mankind is physically weak but vain and full of desires, Hobbes says, which creates difficulties for him: he is a quarrelsome creature who always wants what he does not have. In the absence of law and government, this natural propensity leads to a condition of war, which is described by Hobbes in one of the most famous passages in the literature of political theory.

> Whatsoever therefore is consequent to a time of war,
> where every man is enemy to every man, the same is

consequent to the time wherein men live without other security than what their own strength and their own invention shall furnish them withal. In such condition there is no place for industry, because the fruit thereof is uncertain: and consequently no culture of the earth; no navigation, nor use of the commodities that may be imported by sea; no commodious building; no instruments of moving and removing such things as require much force; no knowledge of the face of the earth; no account of time; no arts; no letters; no society; and which is worst of all, continual fear, and danger of violent death; and the life of man, solitary, poor, nasty, brutish, and short.

The last three adjectives only are usually quoted, which spoils the wonderful rhythm of the passage; and the word "nasty" is often misunderstood: in the seventeenth century it simply meant "dirty."

Given these facts about the "state of nature," it is not surprising, says Hobbes, that men everywhere are willing to give up their individual liberty for the sake of the security that a commonwealth alone can guarantee. They do this by handing over their individual sovereignties to a single sovereign, who may be an individual (a king) or a legislative body (a parliament).

This done, the multitude so united in one person is called COMMONWEALTH; in Latin, CIVITAS. This is the generation of that great LEVIATHAN, or rather, to speak more reverently, of that mortal god to which we owe, under the immortal God, our peace and defense.

Hobbes lived through troubled times, the English civil war (including the execution of King Charles I) and its aftermath. He was perhaps more willing, as a consequence, than he would have been in more peaceful circumstances, to give up all his sovereignty for the sake of security. He was also a stalwart Loyalist and follower of the King throughout the war. In any case, he did suppose that it was necessary to give up more sovereignty than it is. And the reason for this is that he did not see how sovereignty could reside in anything other than a person or persons. "That great LEVIATHAN," he wrote, "... is but an artificial man, though of greater stature and strength than the natural, for whose protection and defence it was intended."

The idea, in short, of a government of laws, instead of a government of men, escaped him. He thought all government was necessarily of men and he could not imagine such a commonwealth as that of the United States of America, in which the Constitution rules (or is supposed to), and all men and women obey it, even the president, who is (supposed to be) the servant rather than the ruler of the people.

Maybe he was able to imagine such a government but could not believe it would ever be a reality. He did believe that good governance exists only where there are good rulers, and that is certainly true whether the state be constitutional or not. At any rate he was able to imagine almost everything else, and to discourse upon it in his book, in his customary brusque, direct, down-to-earth, commonsensical manner.

It is this manner that is the greatest value, I think, in Hobbes's book. Most of his major conclusions and ideas are better stated by Locke and Rousseau and other political philosophers who followed him. But his comments about all sorts of ordinary things are rich and memorable.

Hobbes is a man to read and ponder over: concerning this sentence or that—is he correct in what he says or not? The pondering leads to a deeper understanding of that commonplace subject. Much of what he has to say deals with the words that were then used to name important philosophical and political ideas. Some of these names have changed since 1651 when *Leviathan* was published. See if you can detect these changes. When you are able to do so, you have learned an important lesson, for the old name often throws much light on the modern idea, which you knew and understood in another dress.

# JOHN MILTON
1608–1674
*Paradise Lost*
*Selected Poems*
*Areopagitica*

Much is known about the life of John Milton—vastly more than about Shakespeare, for example—but this has not added to Milton's reputation. For the fact is that Milton was, if not an unpleasant, then certainly a difficult man. A very hard worker and a man of absolute integrity, he nevertheless suffered from traits that do not recommend him to moderns: stubbornness, inflexibility, impatience. Even so, his genius was so great that, like Beethoven, who was fully as difficult, we end up admiring him if not loving him as we love Shakespeare and Mozart.

At any rate, Milton was incomparably brilliant; no young man was ever more so. Born in 1608, he excelled in all of his studies, at school and at Christ's College, Cambridge, learning the three ancient languages—Greek, Latin, and Hebrew—and several modern ones as well. After years of postgraduate study he journeyed to Italy to polish his Italian and there wrote poems in Italian that were hailed by the cognoscenti. He was sharpening his tools, readying himself, as he felt, for the great task that faced him: the task of writing the English epic, as Homer had written the Greek one, Virgil the Latin, and Dante the Italian. The subject would be the so-called matter of Britain, that is, the grand old stories about the half-mythical court of King Arthur and his Round Table of famous knights. Milton returned from abroad in July 1639, apparently ready to begin his work. But great events intervened.

England had been entangled in religious controversy since the beginning of the seventeenth century, now threatening to break out in civil war. Milton, with the certainty that attached to all his moral choices, knew on which side his sympathies lay: with the Parliament and the Puritans, against the King and the established church. He set to with a will to defend those that the King called rebels from the charges of political illegitimacy that flew from all sides. Milton's superb knowledge of Latin—the international language of the seventeenth century—was a considerable help to the Puritans, who were soon led to victory after victory by the astounding adventurer Oliver Cromwell. The King was defeated, captured, tried, and condemned; Milton justified all of these actions to the world, and when King Charles I was beheaded at Whitehall on January 30, 1649, Milton justified that, too. He worked day and night in his capacity as Latin Secretary, what we might call today press secretary, particularly for communications with foreign governments.

The hard work, combined with a probable congenital weakness, cost him his eyesight. By 1652, when he was only forty-four, Milton was blind. He continued to labor, but with the death of Oliver Cromwell in 1658, the cause was lost. Within two years Charles II had returned from France to be a new king of England. The question for Milton was not so much what he would do now as whether he would be allowed to live at all. Only generosity on the part of the new government—prompted, it is said, by the pleas of another poet, Andrew Marvell, Member of Parliament for Hull—made it possible for him to survive.

That hurdle overcome, the decision for Milton was, as usual, clear-cut: he would return to the work he had abandoned in order to throw himself into the defense, as he saw it, of English liberty. But the "matter of Britain" no longer seemed attractive to the experienced man of fifty. A greater story needed to be told in heroic verse, the story of mankind himself, the story of his fall from grace in Eden, that singular event that had made man what he was (and woman, too) and had led to the inexpressibly loving act of God in sending His only begotten Son to purchase man's forgiveness with His blood.

Milton was at work even before the Restoration, as early as 1655 or 1656, often waking early in the morning—at three or four o'clock—and composing lines in his head. He sometimes wrote a hundred lines or more and then waited, impatient as always, "to be milked" by one of his nephews who took down the old man's dictation. Thus was *Paradise Lost* written, being slowly built up, day by day, by the blind bard, on a gigantic plan that Milton had been forming for many years.

By 1665 the poem was finished, all ten books of it. (A second edition of 1674 divided the work into the present twelve books.) It was praised, albeit with some coolness: Its author had been a rebel and had justified the murder of the king, and Milton had chosen to write in blank verse instead of the established heroic couplets of the time. What is more, the Miltonic blank verse is different from anyone else's; it possesses the grandeur but also the excessiveness of the baroque in art, and for some of Milton's contemporaries—as for some of us—it was often hard to read.

With all this against it, *Paradise Lost* nevertheless was soon recognized for what it is: the greatest long poem in the English language, containing descriptive passages of such force and loveliness—and horror—that the blind poet makes you shiver as you read. And this despite an even greater defect, as some view it: the inability of Milton to make his hero, Christ, more interesting than his villain, Satan (Adam and Eve are pawns in the grasp of greater powers). William Blake, who loved Milton, said he was "of the Devil's party without knowing it." Whatever the justice of that remark, it is true that Satan possesses a doomed, dark splendor, especially at the beginning of the poem. However, if you read carefully, you perceive the transformation of this archfiend from a classic tragic figure into his final form as an enormous bloated worm, thrashing about in the squalid mud and darkness of Hell. At the end Satan is a loathsome figure, the despised of God, condemned to eternal misery and awareness of his loss.

The story of Adam and Eve, read as a love story between two very human (though rather large) people, is deeply affecting. Adam is devoted to Eve from the first time he sees her, a devotion so enveloping that Eve is led to plead with her husband to be allowed to go off by herself for a day so that she may learn to be more independent, and so be a more useful helpmeet. Reluctantly Adam agrees. Satan takes advantage, of course, seducing Eve into tasting of the Tree of Knowledge of good and evil. The Devil's arguments are masterful, the temptation is irresistible, and we forgive Eve at once: she is confronted by a power of which she can have no comprehension.

As soon as she returns Adam realizes what has happened and almost immediately forgives her, although he knows better than she the consequences of her fall. She offers him the apple and he eats, knowing full well that he will lose Paradise but knowing, too, that without Eve there is no paradise for him anywhere. And so they are punished, after first having the future of mankind foretold them by the Archangel. They look back at the flaming sword over the gate and then turn away from Paradise and toward their new life:

> Some natural tears they dropped, but wiped them soon.
> The world was all before them, where to choose
> Their place of rest, and Providence their guide:
> They hand in hand with wandering steps and slow
> Through Eden took their solitary way.

It is surely one of the most beautiful partings in poetry.

The story of Adam and Eve is more than just a biblical tale. Every newly married couple has something like the same experience to undergo and something like the same suffering to endure. *Paradise Lost* is therefore much more than the greatest of all baroque literary monuments. It is a story for all people at all times. In addition, it is a profound apologia for the Christian religion capable, I believe, of softening even the hardest heart.

At the end of his life Milton wrote a kind of sequel to *Paradise Lost* that he called *Paradise Regained*. It is not much read today except by Milton scholars and their students, yet it is an interesting work. Paradise was to be regained, of course, through the intercession of Christ for all mankind. Satan knew very well what the birth of Christ meant, so he set about the task of tempting the Son of God as he had tempted Eve. Temptation was Milton's great subject: as a young man he had written a masque, or musical show, *Comus*, about temptation; *Paradise Lost* was about the temptation of both Adam and Eve; in his tragic play *Samson Agonistes*, Milton reveals Samson tempted by Dalila; and here at the end Christ is tempted by Satan in many and diverse ways. Christ, like the Lady in *Comus* but unlike Samson and Eve and Adam, is proof against temptation, and so man will be saved and ultimately find Paradise again. The verse of *Paradise Regained* is heavy and ornate, with little of the graciousness and beauty of *Paradise Lost*, but the conception of the work is fascinating.

*Samson Agonistes*, too, is but a partial success. It is too long and insufficiently dramatic: one imagines Shakespeare handling the scenes between Samson and Dalila. On the other hand, not even Shakespeare, perhaps, could have outdone the magnificence of the final moments of Samson, as he brings down his enemies in his own fall. His epitaph is spoken by his father:

> *Nothing is here for tears, nothing to wail*
> *Or knock the breast, no weakness, no contempt,*
> *Dispraise or blame; nothing but well and fair*
> *And what may quiet us in a death so noble.*

Shakespeare is unquestionably the greatest English poet and Milton is almost certainly the second greatest, although there are some who might claim the latter distinction for Chaucer or Wordsworth or Yeats—no others, probably. The reason Milton's claim is so secure is that he not only wrote the magnificent long works of his old age—*Paradise Lost, Paradise Regained, Samson*—but that he also composed, at various times in his life, a collection of lyric poems that, taken all together, constitute an achievement that would earn him a high rank even without *Paradise Lost*.

Even Milton's juvenile poems are worth reading if you would know the beginnings of this mighty poet, but at any rate do not skip over "L'Allegro" and "Il Penseroso." This pair of lyrics—the one about the charms of life and happiness and comedy, the other about melancholy and deep thoughtfulness and tragedy—is the best example of an academic exercise ever written. In the dainty four-foot meter that we usually associate with poets like Marvell, rather than Milton, they prove that the great baroque poet had a light side, however difficult this may sometimes be to believe. The best way to read both "L'Allegro" and "Il Penseroso" is to read them out loud, rather softly, while playing Vivaldi's "The Seasons," also rather softly, in the background. The combination is dynamite.

Do not try to read "Lycidas" while listening to Vivaldi; the greater weight of Bach (say, the Brandenburg Concertos) is needed for this bigger, more serious poem. An acquaintance of Milton's, a young and aspiring poet and clergyman, has been lost in the Irish Channel and

Milton contributes to a slim volume published in his memory. But the poem goes far beyond mourning for Edward King. It also mourns for Milton himself, for his lost youth, and for the waste of his time in other deeds and activities when he should be writing his great poem.

The lines in which Milton reminds us of the chanciness of life are justly famous—but so are many others in this poem, which stands as one of the greatest English lyrics:

> *Fame is the spur that the clear spirit doth raise*
> *(That last infirmity of noble mind)*
> *To scorn delights, and live laborious days;*
> *But the fair guerdon when we hope to find,*
> *And think to burst out into sudden blaze,*
> *Comes the blind Fury with th' abhorrèd shears,*
> *And slits the thin-spun life.*

"And slits the thin-spun life"—did ever a line of poetry more perfectly sound what it means?

Do not pass over, either, the sonnets of Milton. Half a dozen are among the finest sonnets in any language.

Finally, try some of Milton's prose, though it is often antique and clumsy to our modern ear. At least read *Areopagitica*, Milton's passionate plea for the freedom of the press. Do not censor books, he cries:

> As good almost kill a man as kill a good book; who kills a man kills a reasonable creature, God's image; but he who destroys a good book, kills reason itself, kills the image of God, as it were in the eye . . . A good book is the precious life-blood of a master spirit, embalmed and treasured up on purpose to a life beyond life.

Every lover of books also loves those lines. In *Areopagitica* Milton also writes about temptation and the need to face it, to overcome it frankly and fearlessly, and not to shrink away:

> I cannot praise a fugitive and cloistered virtue, unexercised and unbreathed, that never sallies out and

sees her adversary, but slinks out of the race, where that immortal garland is to be run for, not without dust and heat.

It was a hard man who wrote that, who had lived a hard life.

# ANDREW MARVELL
## 1621–1678
### *Poems*

Andrew Marvell was born in Hull, Yorkshire, in 1621 and enjoyed an exceptionally fortunate life throughout his fifty-seven years; all his clouds had silver linings.

He attended Cambridge but had to leave without a degree when his father died; however, to gain his living, he then traveled on the Continent as a tutor and thus missed the civil war. He was at first opposed to Cromwell's government, but the character of Cromwell won him over and he became Latin Secretary (succeeding Milton). This might have caused him grave difficulties, but he was elected a Member of Parliament from his native city in 1659. When Charles II was restored, in 1660, it was thought prudent to allow MPs to continue in office (else there might have been another civil war), so Marvell weathered the transition. He served in the Commons as the Member for Hull for the rest of his life.

During the 1660s and 1670s he wrote a number of engaging political satires, in verse and prose, and was a well-known man in London and throughout the realm. He did not publish any of his serious poems, but they were published after his death by a woman claiming to be his wife, although they had probably never been married. Thus the few superb poems of Marvell survived. They are very few; perhaps only three short poems belong in the great canon of English literature.

"An Horatian Ode upon Cromwell's Return from Ireland," written in 1650, shows Marvell's growing admiration for Cromwell but it is most famous for its lines describing the death upon the scaffold of King Charles I.

> *He nothing common did or mean*
> *Upon that memorable scene ...*
> *But laid his comely head*
> *Down, as upon a bed.*

The poem expresses the way many Englishmen must have felt about "that memorable scene," when the king stood upon the scaffold erected at Whitehall on Tuesday, January 30, 1649. That is, they approved of the act in principle but deeply regretted the death of this man whose last moments were the best of his life.

"To His Coy Mistress" is an example—perhaps the best example in literature—of the so-called carpe diem poem. "Carpe diem" means, in the Latin of the poet Horace, "seize the day"—that is, take advantage of the present moment, for it will pass and with it youth and beauty. Carpe diem poems were written by the cartload by young men desiring to seduce young women, who are—or were in those days—deeply affected by the idea that once their beauty has passed no one will want them. Often enough, the young beauty was compared to a flower, usually a rose, which would soon wither and die. The girl was supposed to take that fact to heart and act accordingly, but when the poems were really good they rose above the occasion.

Marvell's "To His Coy Mistress" is almost unique in being at once a serious carpe diem poem and at the same time a kind of parody of such verses.

> *Had we but world enough, and time,*
> *This coyness, lady, were no crime.*
> *We would sit down, and think which way*
> *To walk, and pass our long love's day.*
> *Thou by the Indian Ganges' side*
> *Shouldst rubies find: I by the tide*
> *Of Humber would complain. I would*
> *Love you ten years before the flood*

> *And you should, if you please, refuse*
> *Till the conversion of the Jews.*

"For, lady, you deserve this state, Nor would I love at lower rate," the poet says. However, he adds:

> *But at my back I always hear*
> *Time's wingèd chariot hurrying near,*
> *And yonder all before us lie*
> *Deserts of vast eternity.*

That is of course the carpe diem reminder. Yet here it is advanced to a level seldom if ever seen before. Not only is this woman whom Marvell is addressing not just some young thing with a rising bosom but instead a lady of deep and wide intelligence; in addition, the carpe diem warning is extended to the entire race. Marvell not only deepens the relations between the sexes but also uses the ancient traditional form to say something profound about human life in general. Altogether a remarkable poem, in which you will certainly find much more than I have suggested.

"The Garden" is probably the most admired of Marvell's poems. Written in the same rapid octosyllabic couplets as "To His Coy Mistress"—couplets of which Marvell is the acknowledged master in English—it is a good deal more mysterious than its surface suggests. In fact, what the poem is finally saying about the conflict between society and solitude, between busyness and quietude, between the great world and the proscribed one of the secluded garden, is not, at first sight, entirely clear. The poem contains symbols, as well, that are difficult to interpret. But it weaves an incomparable spell:

> *The mind, that ocean where each kind*
> *Does straight its own resemblance find*
> *Yet it creates, transcending these,*
> *Far other worlds, and other seas,*
> *Annihilating all that's made*
> *To a green thought in a green shade.*

T.S. Eliot admired those lines, and spoke of Marvell's unique ability to turn thoughts into concrete things, and things into thoughts. Perhaps that is what Marvell was doing. At any rate, it was quite wonderful.

# BENEDICT DE SPINOZA
## 1632–1677
### *The Ethics*

In his story "The Spinoza of Market Street," I.B. Singer tells of an old Jew who, after a lifetime of scholarly devotion to the philosophy of Spinoza, falls in love with a crude young woman and marries her, to the amused scorn of his friends. It is not long, of course, before he begins to contemplate the quiet peacefulness of his past life as compared to the turmoil of his present and, doubtless, his future. He goes to the window to gaze up at the cold, circling stars. "Forgive me, great Spinoza," he whispers. "I have become a fool."

Reading Spinoza's *Ethics* is no guarantee against folly—there is none such—but if any book will help, this one will. It is about the passions, or emotions as we not too accurately call them now, and how to deal with them. The reason why "passions" is a better word than "emotions" for anger, envy, scorn, fear, and so forth is that it declares its derivation from a Latin word that also gives us "passive," and it is precisely because our passions act upon us and we are passive with regard to them that they make us unhappy. Spinoza's advice to us in his *Ethics* is to learn to be active toward our passions; in other words, to control them and not allow them to control us. It is good advice, although not exactly new.

Benedict de Spinoza (his Hebrew name was Baruch) was born in Amsterdam in 1632, the son of Jewish parents who provided him with a good education in traditional religious subjects. He studied philosophy, modern languages, and physics and mathematics on his own, and from the time that he discovered Descartes, in the 1650s, he was a rebel against almost all intellectual tradition. A queer, inward-turning man, he gave up his inheritance and became a grinder and polisher of lenses for microscopes and telescopes. He died at forty-five from consumption brought on by the inhalation of glass dust in his shop.

Spinoza worked on his *Ethics*, his masterpiece, for the last fifteen years of his life, but he knew it would never be published while he was alive; he therefore arranged for its posthumous publication. The book describes a world system that in one sense is God and in another sense has no need of God for its existence, and the doctrine was radically unacceptable to Spinoza's contemporaries. We read the *Ethics* today not so much for its metaphysical system as for its solid common sense—and for its extraordinary form and style.

In fact, Spinoza had two styles, very different from one another. The first is his standard prose style, which he adopts in only a few places in *Ethics*—alas, too few! Paragraphs of notes and commentaries are sprinkled throughout the text and they are always welcome because of their special charm and humanity. The Fourth Book of *Ethics*, with its famous title "Of Human Bondage," is particularly rich in prose comments and asides. The book deals with the power our passions hold over us; our passions enslave us, says Spinoza, hold us in bondage. In the Fifth Book, the last, titled "Of Human Freedom," Spinoza shows how, by the intellect's understanding alone, without the help of anything outside the mind (without the help of God—it is no wonder that he was excommunicated by the Jews and his works declared anathema by the Christians), the passions can be overcome and happiness found in a quiet life of peace and contentment. All this is summed up on the last page of the work, in a paragraph that for its sweetness is justly famous:

> I have finished everything I wished to explain concerning the power of the mind over the affects and concerning its liberty ... If the way which, as I have shown, leads hither seem very difficult, it can nevertheless be found. It must indeed be difficult since it is so seldom discovered; for if salvation lay ready to hand and could be discovered without great labor, how could it be possible that it should be neglected almost by everybody? But all noble things are as difficult as they are rare.

Spinoza's other style is astonishing to those who come upon it without warning. Descartes had said that all knowledge was, if not mathematics, then based on mathematics, and his "method," to put it very simply, was to mathematicize everything. Spinoza concluded that metaphysics and ethics, like physics and the other natural sciences, ought to benefit from the Cartesian way of looking at things, and the *Ethics* is therefore in geometrical form. Axioms and definitions are laid down, propositions are stated and proved, and each proof ends with "Q.E.D." But the text does not treat such simple entities as points and lines, triangles and circles. Instead, it deals with God and His creation, the angels and the world of material things, man and his intellect and will, and his bondage to and freedom from his passions.

That Descartes's geometrical method is inappropriate to the science (if it is that) of ethics may never have been apparent to Benedict de Spinoza. It is doubtless apparent to us from the very beginning. Spinoza's attempt, however, has a certain splendor and is worth noting as a minor monument along the highway of the history of thought. We should remember, too, that Cartesianism, the prevalent disease of modern thought, has invaded still other realms where it does not belong: politics, philosophy, sociology, and anthropology.

I do not recommend Spinoza's *Ethics* because it is a failure; I recommend it because it succeeds, despite its form, in expressing with singular force Stoic arguments about freedom and virtue. Socrates had said in the *Phaedo* that "no evil can come to a good man, in life or in death." By "good man" he meant one who was in control of himself and therefore safe from internal treachery; there could be no real danger from outside, for the worst tyrant could not touch a good man's soul. This basic Stoic tenet, which is Spinoza's, too, may not be wholly true, but there is a rich kernel of truth in it. Courageous men and women are always more or less stoical and no one is finally so free of coercion as he who is willing to die rather than be coerced. Such is the true Stoic—a noble breed, though rare.

To be appreciated, the *Ethics* does not have to be read in its entirety. Read the introductory passages to each of the five books, the statements of the propositions, and all of the lengthy prose comments (Lemmas). From time to time scan a proof. Some of the terms will seem very odd; anything you know about Scholastic philosophy, for example, will come in handy. But Spinoza is not inaccessible, he is just strange. Both wonderful and strange, as befits the creator of something that is both difficult and rare.

# chapter seven

# The Age of Reason…

The later seventeenth and early eighteenth centuries—a period of a hundred years, more or less—has often been called the Age of Reason. I'm not sure how accurate a term that is. True, the Renaissance was pretty much over and done except in Germany, where the Thirty Years War delayed everything for a long generation. It was a time when Europeans, for the most part, were feeling their way, looking backward with very little regret and forward with some trepidation. The idea of the sanctity of kings was being questioned, and there were shadows of an emergent capitalism based not on the ownership of land but instead on an incipient money economy.

At the same time there was a deep nostalgia for the Augustan Age, so-called, of the early years of the Roman Empire. The literary hero was not so much Virgil as were Juvenal and Horace, whose satirical and critical writings (notably *Ars Poetica—The Art of Poetry*) were taught in every school and helped shape the culture for a hundred and fifty years.

John Dryden and Alexander Pope were particularly influential. Pope especially mined Horace's *Art of Poetry* in several famous works. His mastery of the heroic couplet—rhymed iambic pentameter couplets—was imitated by everyone, as he himself had imitated Dryden's. When he died in 1744, it seemed that they would endure for all time. However, in twenty years they had practically disappeared. It was not the first time nor would it be the last when a literary fashion bloomed and was then discarded in a short period of time.

You will see that in the title of this chapter the word "Reason" is followed by ellipses. By this device I am trying to suggest that although reason was the idea of the time, revolution was also lurking there in the shadowy future (see Chapter 8).

# ISAAC NEWTON
## 1642–1727
### *Principia*

Isaac Newton was born in 1642, the son of a small farmer who died before his birth. The boy's upbringing and schooling were both irregular, but his native brilliance, although usually hidden, emerged often enough so that he managed to be accepted at Trinity College, Cambridge. There is no record of his career as a student, but it is known he read widely in mathematics and science. He studied Euclid but found him trivial; he later returned to the *Elements* and mastered the work in a few hours. Descartes's *Geometry* inspired him to do original work. He received his bachelor's degree in 1665; he was twenty-two but he had already discovered the binomial theorem.

The history of science was much changed by an event that occurred the same year. Plague had decimated London; it spread to Cambridge, and college was dismissed. Newton returned to the farm. Farming did not interest him; instead he equipped a room with instruments he had brought from Cambridge and conducted experiments in optics and continued his mathematical studies. During this year he performed many of the experiments that led, forty years later, to the publication of his *Opticks*. But the year held even more revolutionary thoughts and events for Newton.

According to the traditional account, he was sitting one day in the shade of an apple tree when an apple fell on his head and he discovered the law of gravity. The account is not all wrong. He was sitting under an apple tree, and he did note an apple's fall, though

not on his head. He did not discover the law of gravity, because
everyone had known for centuries that the force of gravity attracts
all bodies toward the center of the Earth. What Newton discovered,
then and there, was the law of universal gravitation, which is a very
different thing.

What it occurred to him to ask, as he sat and watched the apple
fall, was whether the gravitational force that drew the apple toward
the Earth extended as far as the orbit of the Moon. If so, would it
account for the Moon's orbit around the Earth? He knew, from his
reading of Galileo, the actual force of gravity at sea level, and that the
force decreased with distance from the Earth's center (gravity is
weaker on a mountaintop than at sea level). He also knew how far
the Moon was from the Earth, on the average. Quickly he scratched
out some calculations. The theory worked. No other assumption
needed to be made to explain the workings of the solar system than
that the system was held together, and its motions controlled, by a
single force that was everywhere the same and that affected all bodies
according to a very simple formula:

$$F = \frac{m_1 m_2}{d^2}$$

in which F is the gravitational force, $m_1$ and $m_2$ are the masses of two
bodies interacting upon one another, and d is the distance between
them. Gravity varies, in other words, directly as the product of the
masses of the two bodies, and inversely as the square of the distance
between them.

Newton, in short, had solved the greatest puzzle in the history of
science up to his time—a puzzle that the most learned philosophers
and scientists had been struggling with at least from the time of
Ptolemy, fifteen hundred years before, a puzzle furthermore to which
the best minds of the previous century had been devoted, from
Copernicus to Gilbert to Kepler to Galileo. It was an exciting
moment for this young man of twenty-two. He worked out half a
dozen theorems and propositions that accounted not only for the
orbit of the Moon about the Earth but also for the orbits of the
planets—including the Earth—about the Sun. But in doing so he also
thought he had discovered a new mathematical way of describing and

measuring planetary orbits. He called it the method of fluxions; we call it the integral calculus. This new mathematical tool interested him even more than his solution of the problem of the ages, so he put that aside, placing the sheets of paper on which he had written out the solution in a portable desk, and began to work in earnest on the calculus. He told nobody what he had done.

It was obvious to all at Cambridge that he was the best mathematician in England. The professor of mathematics at the university resigned his post so Newton might have it, at the age of twenty-six. He built telescopes, experimented with optics, did mathematics. In the meantime others, notably Edmund Halley (the discoverer of Halley's Comet), had come to some notion of the law of gravitation but were having no success in using it to explain the orbits of the planets. In 1684 Halley journeyed up to Cambridge to consult Newton. He explained the problem and asked whether Newton would consider helping him and his friends solve it.

"I have already solved that problem," Newton said. "I did so twenty years ago." It is one of the most incredible moments in the history of science, indeed of human thought. Halley was dumfounded but Newton scrambled among his papers and presented to Halley the sheets on which were written four theorems and seven problems. They are the nucleus of his major work.

It took him eighteen months to write, in Latin, *Principia Mathematica Philosophiae Naturalis* (*Mathematical Principles of Natural Philosophy*—*Principia* for short). The Royal Society could not afford to publish the work, so Halley personally footed the cost.

Probably there is no more daunting book to nonmathematicians. But if you have some courage and are willing to devote some effort this need not be so. Many books are harder to read than Newton's *Principia*. Few books are so important to read, and so gratifying.

The work is divided into three books. Book I presents the general theory of gravitation; it deals with "The Motion of Bodies." Book II treats "The Motion of Bodies in Resisting Mediums," to show that the Cartesian theory of vortices was not tenable and incidentally creating the modern sciences of hydrostatics and hydrodynamics. Book III, with a grandeur typical of Newton, is titled "The System of the World."

There is a great deal of mathematics in Books I and II but most of it can be skipped over and ignored, although it will be useful to read the statements, if not the proofs, of many of the theorems. Read the beginning of the *Principia*, with its remarkable set of Definitions; they establish the ground rules of classical mechanics and of Newtonian physics. Read also the following Scholium, or general note. Its half-dozen pages describe the point of view that will be adopted throughout the work. Following that, read the Axioms, or Laws of Motion. They are basic to all modern science. Read the half-dozen Corollaries that follow them, together with the Scholium following Corollary VI.

At this point Book I begins. Skip through it, noting the theorems and problems and reading the Scholiums and Lemmas, getting an idea of what is going on. Pay special attention to Proposition 66, Theorem 26; this is the famous three-body problem, which is unsolved (except for trivial instances) to this day.

Skip through Book II in the same way, trying as hard as you can to follow the general line of the argument even if you do not grasp all of its details. Read carefully the Scholium at the end of Section VIII, concerning the motions of light and sound. And read as carefully as you can the entire Section IX—only a few pages. It is the preparation for what follows in the third book.

It is also true that many pages of Book III need not be read carefully; they can be very quickly skimmed. But some of these famous pages should be dwelt on. The very first page of Book III, for instance; a short preface in which Newton explains what he will now do, which is to explain how the world as a whole works. Even more essential are the following two pages: "Rules of Reasoning in Philosophy." These too are at the heart of modern science. No scientist of our day wants to break any of these four rules. They are the essence of a common sense view of the world and the epitome of the scientific empiricism that has dominated human thought ever since Newton.

Move forward through Book III. Much of it will be more or less incomprehensible, some of it brilliantly clear. The best is saved for last. The book, and the entire work, concludes with a General Scholium, into which Newton poured his soul.

The General Scholium, probably the most famous few pages in the history of science, asks very great questions. For the most part it does not answer them. Some of them are still unanswered today. They may never be answered. Isaac Newton died in 1727. Does he now know the answers, wherever he may be? I like to think so.

# ISAAC NEWTON
*Opticks*

# CHRISTIAAN HUYGENS
## 1619–1695
*Treatise on Light*

At the midpoint of the seventeenth century, two great scientific puzzles obsessed the best minds of Europe. One was very old, going back to Ptolemy and, indeed, to his ancient Greek forebears. How does the solar system work? What is the force that drives the planets, in what orbits, around what central point? Advances had been made on the problem by Copernicus in the fifteenth century and by Kepler, Gilbert, and Galileo in the late sixteenth and early seventeenth centuries. But the precise workings of the great system were not known, a fact that tormented the leading scientists of every modern country.

Sir Isaac Newton, the Englishman, solved this puzzle. How he did it is told, and the book he wrote about it described, in the preceding entry.

The other great seventeenth-century puzzle was new. It involved that most omnipresent of things—but was it a thing?—light. Light manifested very strange behaviors. Dozens of natural philosophers set up telescopes (thanks to Galileo) and used prisms and arranged black boxes. How did light work? What explained its well-known powers of reflection and refraction? What was color? What was light itself? Isaac Newton solved this puzzle, too.

Not by himself, however. He did not find all of the answer—even all of it that could be known in the late seventeenth century. The strange and puzzling behavior of light was beyond even his enormous capacity to understand simply. His solution of the puzzle of light was therefore incomplete and partial. The other part of the solution was provided by an almost equally brilliant mathematician and experimenter in Holland, Christiaan Huygens. Together, these two extraordinary contemporaries produced a theory of light that in many respects still stands, although the underpinnings of some of their most inspired guesses would not be discovered for two centuries or more.

Newton was a man, essentially, of two works. One was the *Principia*; the other was called, simply, *Opticks*. The latter is divided into three books, each of them fascinating in its way.

Part I of Book One begins with a few pages that review what was known about light before Newton began his experiments, many of which were done in 1665-66 when he was still in his early twenties. These Axioms and Definitions are followed by seven Propositions that are among the most revolutionary in the history of science. He shows that the spectrum of white light produced by a prism consists of rays of light of different indexes of refraction and reflection, and that the white light of the Sun consists of these same different rays; and he accurately measures the difference in "refrangibility" and "reflexibility" of the different colors of light in the spectrum (red, orange, yellow, green, blue, indigo, violet). He goes on in Part II to treat colors, about which he knew almost everything that we do. He is particularly acute in discussing our sensation of color. For the rays, to speak properly, he writes, are not colored:

> In them there is nothing else from a certain power and disposition to stir up a sensation of this or that colour. For as sound in a bell or musical string, or other sounding body, is nothing but a trembling motion, and in the air nothing but that motion propagated from the object, and in the sensorium 'tis a sense of that motion under the form of sound; so colours in the object are nothing but a disposition to reflect this or that sort of rays more copiously than the rest; in the rays they are nothing but their dispositions to propagate this or that motion into the

sensorium, and in the sensorium they are sensations of those motions under the form of colours.

Book Two of the *Opticks* deals with the colors formed by refraction in and reflection from very thin and very small bodies, such as bubbles or thin plates of glass, or films of water trapped between two prisms. Here Newton not only goes further than anyone before him to explain the nature of color, but he also comes to remarkable conclusions about the bodies themselves with which he has been experimenting. They must, he says, be made up of very small particles between which is something extremely diaphanous or even empty space; and the size of the small particles determines the color of the body. He further shows that bodies can be "extremely porous"—there can be thousands of times as much empty space in them as "solid" matter, yet they may appear to be solid through and through because of the reflections from the particles within the body. "But," he adds modestly, "what is really their inward frame is not yet known to us." That inward frame was not discovered and known until the beginning of the twentieth century.

The first two books of the *Opticks* are interesting and readable. There is little mathematics, for those who detest it; instead there are page after page of fascinating descriptions of Newton's experiments (which can be duplicated at will), together with his astute conclusions from them. Book Three begins in the same manner, dealing with the bending of light rays around a small object. But this book soon takes another tack and does something that is not to be missed.

When I made the above observations, says Newton, I intended to do them again and more accurately, and I had other experiments in mind to do as well. But I was interrupted, "and cannot now think of taking these things into further consideration. And since I have not finished this part of my design, I shall conclude with proposing only some queries, in order to a further search to be made by others."

That is modest enough. But what follows is simply amazing. No other man could have written the thirty-one Queries that occupy, with their explanations, the last thirty or so pages of the *Opticks*. For those thirty-one Queries come very close to defining and outlining the history of physics for the following three hundred years.

Consider just a few of them, as examples. Query 1: Does gravity act upon light at a distance? (Einstein suggested it did; this was confirmed in 1920.) Query 6: Do black bodies absorb light and grow hotter than white ones because they do not reflect the light? (Planck's experiments with black bodies in the 1890s led to quantum theory.) Queries 8–10: Is heat produced by the rapid agitation of the parts of a body, and if this agitation increases sufficiently, does the body begin to emit light? (The nineteenth century was obsessed with heat; Newton here prefigures many of the most important discoveries of classic thermodynamics.) Query 12 anticipates modern neurophysiology. Query 16 suggests the underlying phenomenon that makes motion pictures possible. Most astonishing of all, Query 30 asks whether gross bodies (we would say matter) and light (we would say energy) are convertible, one into the other. (Einstein, three hundred years later, determined that the answer was yes and that the formula was a simple one: Set as an equation, $E = mc^2$, where E is energy, m is matter, and $c^2$ is the square of the speed of light.) Perhaps equally astonishing, however, is Query 31, which in effect proposes that there must be within bodies a force, different from gravity or magnetic force, that holds the parts of the bodies together and that may even have an effect beyond the bodies. (Here we have the molecular force that could not be accurately measured and defined until the second quarter of the twentieth century.)

You don't have to know a lot about physics to be excited by these thirty-one Queries. The more you know about what has happened in physics since 1704 (the year that Newton, at the age of sixty-two, published the Opticks), the more exciting it becomes to read the book. If you are lucky, the hair will rise on the back of your neck and you will walk down the street whistling in admiration of the mind of this man who knew so much so long ago.

Newton was not right in all of his ideas. His major error—indicated in Queries 27 through 29—was in believing he had proved (or in believing that it would some day be proved) that rays of light are very small bodies emitted from shining substances. He proposed, in other words, and placed all of his scientific credit on, the corpuscular theory of light, and opposed with all his strength the wave theory that was being put forward during Newton's time by the Dutch experimenter and mathematician Huygens. In fact, we have finally decided we know that both theories are correct, depending on circumstances: light sometimes behaves like a wave, sometimes like a stream of particles. We could not do physics today without these hypotheses about the nature of light, and we have agreed to ignore what seems like a contradiction. Newton, unfortunately, could not ignore it. Neither could Huygens.

Christiaan Huygens was born in 1629, some thirteen years before Newton, into a very eminent Dutch family at The Hague. He showed the extreme precocity typical of great mathematicians and was internationally famous by the age of twenty-five. He invented the pendulum clock, built larger and better telescopes than ever before, and produced a nearly perfect eyepiece still known by his name. He published his *Treatise on Light* in 1690, although the researches on which it is based had been done ten or a dozen years before—not long after Newton's work, which he had also failed to publish for some years.

Huygens's book is remarkable in its strict insistence on a wave theory of light and its brilliant success in explaining the observed phenomena of refraction and reflection with the use of the theory. In addition, Huygens included a long description of his experiments with Iceland spar, a strange crystal that produces a double refraction of the light that passes through it. Newton thought that Huygens had not explained these optical phenomena in Iceland spar by means of wave theory—the theory that light is propagated through an ethereal medium in waves instead of in corpuscular form—and Huygens thought Newton's corpuscular theory could not explain them. It is curious, in fact, that they were both wrong on a major point that escaped each of them.

Both Newton and Huygens believed there must be an ether—enormously more rarefied than air, as Newton insisted—either to support the propagation of waves or to transmit the effects of force acting at a distance (gravity, for instance). Scientists searched for evidence of this ether for two centuries; it was not until the 1880s that the theory of an ether was finally disproved. This would have been incomprehensible to Newton and Huygens, who would have asked, If there are light waves, then what are the waves *in*? Indeed, it is a good question, an adequate answer to which requires some very fancy partial differential equations.

Newton and Huygens, who died in 1695, are not "just for scientists." These two works on optics are readable by and important for nonscientists. Do not let their titles, the few diagrams, or the mention of axioms, definitions, and theorems discourage you. These books document and reveal the great journey of the modern mind, from Galileo to Einstein, from Newton to Planck and Heisenberg, Fermi and Bardeen. They are beautiful and moving books, clear as all good books should be, mind-expanding as only the greatest books are.

# JOHN DRYDEN
## 1631–1700
*Selected Works*

John Dryden was born in 1631 and educated at Trinity College, Cambridge. He inherited a small estate but he soon decided he wanted to be a writer and nothing else, and in fact he may have been the first professional writer in the sense that he supported himself entirely by writing (of course with help from time to time from noble patrons). He never stopped writing until his death in 1700 and therefore had a long career in which he wrote many works: numerous plays, satirical writings, literary criticism, and a few occasional poems, several of which are good. See especially "To the Memory of Mr. John Oldham" and "A Song for Saint Cecelia's Day," which he composed near the end of his life and close to the end of the seventeenth century. Dryden, a Catholic, here pays tribute to one of his most loved muses, St. Cecelia, patron saint of music. Another is a song from "The Secular Masque," which he wrote in 1700, the year of his death. It pulls no punches about the age then coming an end:

> *All, all of a piece throughout:*
> *Thy chase had a beast in view;*
> *Thy wars brought nothing about;*
> *Thy lovers were all untrue.*
> *'Tis well an old age is out,*
> *And time to begin a new.*

A professional writer in the seventeenth century needed to publish translations to keep his head above water. Dryden's large achievements in this field include works by Theocritus, Horace, Homer, Juvenal, Ovid, Boccaccio, and Chaucer. His major translation was Virgil's *Aeneid*, and I think it is the best rendering in couplets of this work, fully comparable to Pope's *Iliad* (also in couplets).

My favorite work of Dryden's is his prose essay, "Of Dramatick Poesie," which he wrote in 1668. It has at least two things to recommend it. First, it is probably the earliest serious study of the work of Shakespeare in English. This paragraph (which I quote only in part) is deservedly famous:

> He [Shakespeare] was the man who of all modern poets, and perhaps ancient poets, had the largest and most comprehensive soul. All the images of Nature were still (i.e., always) present to him, and he drew them, not laboriously, but luckily (i.e., easily); when he describes anything, you more than see it, you feel it too. Those who accuse him to have wanted learning, give him the greater commendation: he was naturally learned; he needed not the spectacle of books to read Nature; he looked inwards, and found her there.

That is very good criticism, and it is also written in what is close to being modern English. (In a sense, Dryden almost *invented* modern English.) As compared to the prose of Milton, for example, or other seventeenth-century prose stylists, it is clarity itself.

# ALEXANDER POPE
## 1688–1744
### *Selected Works*

Alexander Pope, another Catholic in an age of Protestants, was born in London in 1688. When he was twelve years old his health was ruined and his growth stunted by a tubercular affliction of the spine. That he lived at all is remarkable; that he became one of the greatest poets in the English language is almost a miracle.

Deciding at the age of sixteen that his only chance for happiness was to be a poet, he began to write and also publish before he was twenty. His "Essay on Criticism," based on Horace's *Art of Poetry*, was published in 1711 and is a wonderful work by a very young man. The next year, when he was twenty-four, "The Rape of the Lock," a mock epic, was published; it is a delightful romp. It tells the story of a pretty young woman who loses a lock of her hair to an equally young swain and of her efforts to regain the lock without losing any other part of her. She does so and of course he has to marry her.

Despite his infirmities Pope was in love with at least two women, one of whom remained his friend for life and the other must have been very unkind to him because he attacked her in several satirical pieces. He was a master of satire, taking his cue from Horace and the Roman satirist Juvenal, and it was never wise to criticize or disappoint him because of his sharp, barbed satirical tongue. In one of his best and most amusing works, "An Epistle to Dr. Arbuthnot," he attempted to defend himself against the charge of being "malignant," but the piece contains several brilliant and devastating descriptions of various enemies (who are not named but of course everybody at the time knew who was meant).

I like almost all of Pope's poems but I think my favorite is the four part *Essay on Man*. It is absolutely superb, particularly at the beginning of the Second Epistle, which describes its subject (i.e., man) in these famous lines:

> Created half to rise, and half to fall;
> Great lord of all things, yet a prey to all;
> Sole judge of Truth, in endless Error hurl'd:
> The glory, jest, and riddle of the world!

These are not Pope's only famous lines. Look him up in *Bartlett's* or *The Oxford Book of Quotations*, where you will find that, after Shakespeare, he is probably the most quoted of all authors. Actually, that's not a bad way to begin reading Pope.

# DANIEL DEFOE
## 1660–1731
### *Robinson Crusoe*

There are not many "world-books," as a German critic has called them: books that are known everywhere, that are translated into every literary language, that are read by almost all children, that strike a chord in the breast of almost every man or woman of every culture and clime. Perhaps there are no more than a dozen such books. *Robinson Crusoe* is one of them.

It would have been a good bet that Daniel Defoe would never write such a book. Born in London in 1660, his life was a race, run at breakneck speed, against disaster. He wrote, usually in desperate haste, to stave off the creditors who never ceased to pursue him and who are said to have hounded him to his death in 1731. He spent various periods in jail and was exposed three times in the London pillory, a punishment he had dreaded; but with characteristic courage he wrote a dashing "Hymn to the Pillory" and the common people of London, who loved him, draped the stocks with flowers and came not to jeer but to drink to his health. A political moderate, he was as a result in constant difficulties with both Tories and Whigs, who in an age of violent partisanship were often unable to abide a fair-minded man who did not care so much who was right just so long as there could be peace. Attacked by both sides, Defoe also worked for both sides as pamphleteer, publicist, and propagandist, in his constant effort to help the people of England steer a middle course.

Almost everything he wrote was written too fast and on merely ephemeral subjects, but starting in 1719, and for five years thereafter, there flowed from his pen a nearly miraculous series of books. These included *Moll Flanders* (1722), *A Journal of the Plague Year* (also 1722), *The History and Remarkable Life of Col. Jack* (also 1722!), and *Roxana, or The Fortunate Mistress* (1724). They are all fine in their way, but the first and best of all was *The Life and Strange Surprizing Adventures of Robinson Crusoe, of York, Mariner. Written by Himself* (1719).

Robinson Crusoe was not "written by himself," of course, even though like all of Defoe's novels it was in the first person singular. This was a bit puzzling to readers at the beginning of the eighteenth century, who had practically no other novels to compare it to; their natural reaction was to believe there was such a man as Crusoe and that this was his story. So much the better for it, Defoe felt; at least the book was based on the more or less true accounts of such ship-wrecked mariners and castaways as Alexander Selkirk. The question is not, however, whether Robinson Crusoe is a "true story." Its truth is more than ordinary truth; it is the truth of every man and woman's hopes, fears, and dreams.

Crusoe is shipwrecked, and all the rest of the ship's company are lost. Crusoe manages to swim to an island nearby; his ship remains snagged on a reef for several weeks and he is able to obtain a good deal of useful material from it before the hull finally breaks up and is swept to sea. He uses this material to create a new life for himself. But he is desperately lonely in his isolated grandeur, though "the monarch," as a poet put it, "of all he surveyed." The first half of the book is taken up with the careful and wonderfully detailed account of what Crusoe did to survive. Every choice he made, every success and every failure, is described with patient carefulness. We read, fasci-nated by this question: Would we have been able to do as well?

Then, with startling suddenness, a great change occurs. A foot-print is seen in the sand—Crusoe is not, after all, alone on his island. He retires to his house, now nearly a fortress, and contemplates all the possible consequences of company. None of them are very good; the maker of that footprint is almost certainly an enemy. He turns out not to be, everyone knows; he is a poor benighted black man, as lost as Crusoe himself, Crusoe names him Friday because that is the day on which he finds him. Friday becomes Crusoe's man Friday, a collo-cation of ideas and words so powerful that even girls can be Fridays now, and on any day of the week.

The last third of the book deteriorates, to our modern eyes, as Crusoe spends more and more time trying to convert Friday to the true faith. But this hardly matters. The first four hundred pages of Robinson Crusoe are one of the treasures of mankind. And, for a final accolade, if you had but ten books to take with you to a desert island, what single title would you place before *Robinson Crusoe*? It is not written as well as *Hamlet*, its story is not as tragically great as *The Iliad*, and it is not as deeply humorous as *Don Quixote*. But it, and not they, would help you to survive.

# WILLIAM CONGREVE
## 1670–1729
### *The Way of the World*

The greatness of this play starts with its title. All comedy is properly about "the way of the world"—about the way life actually is, in all its foolishness, and not the way it ought to be. It is astonishing that no comic playwright had used the title before; it was reserved, by some fortunate accident, for this, among the best of all comedies.

Born in 1670 near Leeds, William Congreve wrote only a handful of plays, but all were successful. He even wrote a tragedy, *The Mourning Bride*, which was successful, too. After writing *The Way of the World*, in 1700, when he was only thirty, he retired from the stage and devoted the rest of his life to being a gentleman. Voltaire traveled from France to seek him out. When they met, Voltaire praised Congreve's plays. Congreve affected hardly remembering that he had written them; he was now engaged, he allowed, on more important business (giving and receiving invitations, going to dinner, and so forth). "But," said Voltaire, "if you had not written them I would never have sought you out!" The resolution of this absurd impasse is not recorded, but the lesson of the tale is that Congreve ended up becoming one of his own fops.

Congreve's next-to-last comedy was *Love for Love*, an erotic romp whose great popularity helped to call down the wrath of one Jeremy Collier, a reforming clergyman whose 1698 pamphlet, "A Short View of the Immorality and Profanity of the English Stage," shocked London with its undeniable truths. Puritanism being a recurrent mania with the English, they turned upon the playwrights they had loved and drove them from the boards. Congreve composed a vapid "defense" of the comic drama of his epoch; more importantly, he wrote one more comedy before he ceased writing plays forever. *The Way of the World* has been called the only possible answer to Collier, among other things.

The play is not at all profane, and it is extremely moral. The good people are rewarded and the bad are punished, but in a comic way— that is, without much pain and certainly without bloodshed. But that is all merely superficial. The play is not moral in Collier's sense of the term. The real conflicts are not between good and bad, but between witty and foolish, smart and dumb. The witty triumph, and the foolish come to grief.

The heroine, Millamant—she of a "thousand lovers"—is the wittiest of all and one of the great female characters in the drama. She teases all of her lovers. She admits, in an aside to the audience toward the end of the play, that Mirabell ("admirer of beauty") has her heart and that without him she cannot live. She is young and worldly. She amuses herself in all the customary ways. But she is bored by her social whirl, desiring higher things. Congreve is able to suggest this about her without the slightest hint of priggishness, a remarkable achievement.

Mirabell is a wonderful part, too. So is Millamant's aunt, who is also her guardian (and thereby hangs most of the plot), Lady Wishfort. (Pronounce the name quickly and you will know her char-acter.) The impatient old lady is superb in her cupidity, vanity, and folly. The more foolish she is, the more delightful. In the end, of course, she has the opportunity to reveal her good heart. No other ending would be acceptable.

In the end, as well, Millamant and Mirabell find one another and plan to marry. Millamant, however, does not look forward to this union with the silly anticipation of other girls. She is highly intelligent and knows how much women—especially beautiful, rich, young women—give up when they marry. She therefore spells out, to Mirabell, the terms on which she will accept him. These terms are tough and unsentimental, and the scene in which these two young people, wild about one another, work out their mutual destiny and write a marriage contract, is one of the most bittersweet in the history of comedy.

*The Way of the World* long remained a standard dramatic work, but today it is hard to put on the stage; few actors can resurrect and maintain its languid grace. (Two of the few are Maggie Smith and Joan Plowright, who, in the parts of Millamant and Lady Wishfort, illuminated a production of the play during the 1984–85 London season which may have been the finest production the play has ever received. Incidentally, the audience cheered and applauded the famous proviso or marriage contract scene.) Despite such noble exceptions, the play is probably best put on in the theater of your mind. Say the lines softly out loud, half under your breath; imagine a proscenium arch lit by a thousand candles; and suppose an audience of beautiful women and gay blades, of whom you may decide to be one.

# VOLTAIRE
## 1694–1778
### *Candide*

François-Marie Arouet, who wrote under the *non de plume* "Voltaire," besides being the most famous writer in Europe in the eighteenth century, was also the most sardonic. Brilliant, fascinating, and cynical, he believed in nothing except the power of the human mind, and especially his own mind, to pierce the fogs of ignorance and prejudice that enveloped Frenchmen in his time, and lead them to a world of wealth, comfort, and peace built on scientific progress.

Voltaire was born in Paris in 1694 and was well educated by the Jesuits. He early determined to be an author, and his first plays were successes. A quarrel with a favorite of the king led to his being exiled to England; as a result of this visit, in 1727–28, he decided that Englishmen had clearer heads and a more solid grasp of reality than did Frenchmen. He never ceased to admire the freedom of English institutions, a freedom conspicuously lacking in France. But the brutality of the English temperament (as he saw it) finally turned him against the English.

He returned to France in 1729 when he was thirty-five and began to build the fortune by speculation that allowed him later independence. He was one of the richest literary men who ever lived, thanks to his close friendship with Madame de Pompadour, mistress of Louis XV; he put to good use the inside information about the king's plans she supplied him. But even her friendship, and that of others highly placed in the French court, could not save him from himself. His real foes were intolerance, tyranny, and official torture, and his long life—he died in 1778—was spent in continuous, often spectacular, protests against the cruelty that filled the world around him. But Voltaire had a tongue—and a pen—as sharp as a razor, and he made many enemies, some in high places. He was imprisoned more than once, harassed by the police of several countries, and exiled for many years from his native land.

Things came to a head in the year 1758. Voltaire had quarreled not only with his countrymen but also with Frederick the Great, who for a while had been a willing pupil. He had also insulted the Swiss with his article about Geneva in *L'Encyclopedie*. Madame de Pompadour was dead. Her successor, Madame de Berry, was a charming nitwit. At sixty-four; where was he to turn?

Voltaire outfaced the crisis with his customary bravura. He was rich enough to buy an estate, Ferney, on the Swiss side of the Swiss-French border, and another, Torney, just over the line in France. If the French police desired to interview him, "Pardon," he would reply, "but I am just at the moment living in another country"; the same ruse worked in reverse when he was persecuted by Swiss officials. Furthermore he gained the adherence of the townspeople and the peasants, for he defended them for years, not only in his writings but also in the courts, arranging for reviews of particularly outrageous judicial decisions and calling for the removal of particularly cruel judges. Above all, he was world-famous, and tyrants preferred, at least until recently, to torture and kill small fry.

For twenty years, from 1758 until his death, Voltaire lived at Ferney like a little king of the intellect, "The Innkeeper of Europe," as he was called, receiving guests and admirers, sometimes fifty at a time, expounding his opinions and arguing against intolerance and for the rights of man. In one famous interchange he summed up his life's work. Exasperated by a long argument with a visitor, "Monsieur," he said, "I find your opinions indefensible and myself totally unable to agree with them—but," he added, "I will defend to the death your right to express them."

The other great event of the year 1758, besides the purchase of Ferney, was the writing of *Candide*. Voltaire produced scores of volumes of plays, poems, and histories, but only his superb letters and, especially, his *contes*, or short novels and tales, are still read. The best-known of these tales, *Candide* is in part a response to the "optimistic" position in philosophy (the view that "all is for the best in this best of all possible worlds," a proposition ascribed by Voltaire, somewhat unfairly, to the German philosopher Leibnitz), and partly a response to the disasters that were overtaking Voltaire at this period in his life. There are ironies here. All his life Voltaire wrote plays, but none of them is played today; he wrote *Candide* in four weeks, and its fame will never die. Its hero, moreover, the simpleton Candide, is about as different from its author as can be. These comments would have amused Voltaire.

Candide is born in the best of all castles to the best of all parents and soon falls into the clutches of the best of all tutors, the philosopher/lecher Dr. Pangloss, who persuades his pupil that this is indeed the best of all possible worlds. Whereupon the disasters begin. The castle is besieged and captured, Candide's family is butchered, he escapes with Pangloss and his beloved Cunégonde, not caring or even noticing that this damsel has been repeatedly raped—since such things do not happen in the best of all possible worlds—and they proceed to travel everywhere and are everywhere tricked, cheated, beaten, and robbed. Although it may not sound like it, all of this is hilarious, mainly because of Candide's incurable optimism, which no misfortune can abate. At last, however, having lost everything, he is reduced to living on the shores of the Prepontis, far from the turmoil that surrounded Voltaire himself, there to "cultivate his garden."

The earthy philosophy of life, which denies both idealism and fuzzy metaphysics, had a great attraction for Voltaire's contemporaries—as for many today. The world is confusing, and often our best efforts to improve it only make it worse, or at least more confusing. As to reformers, we wonder why they do not spend more time tending their own gardens. Nevertheless, this philosophy is lazy and cowardly; if everyone of good faith were merely to cultivate his garden, the world would be left to be run by those of bad faith. (Maybe it is anyway.) And of course during his last twenty years at Ferney Voltaire did not merely cultivate his own garden but everyone else's business as well.

*Candide* is one of the swiftest of stories. It proceeds at breakneck pace from start to finish and never flags or runs out of steam. You can read it in an hour, and the hour will be an unalloyed delight. But the story will also make you think. This is a premium that only the best entertainments provide.

# ...and Revolution

C areful readers will notice the ellipses at the beginning of the title above. And when they do they will recall the ellipses at the end of the title of Chapter 7. And in that case they will put two and two together and recognize that I wish to emphasize the connection between the books that preceded in Chapter 7, and those in Chapter 8. Putting the two abbreviated titles together we arrive at "Reason and Revolution."

As I noted at the beginning of Chapter 7, those books were productions of an age that could be called Augustan because of the influence of the Roman poets of the Silver Age. The writers in Chapter 8 have not entirely forgotten Horace and his fellow satirists, but they are no longer controlled by the dead hand of the past. In various ways they are rebelling against the influence of the Latin classics and striking out on their own.

This is true both of the literature and the politics of what is now the eighteenth century. John Locke died in 1704, but his influence was felt throughout the hundred years that followed. Bishop Berkeley was fifteen years old in 1700, and all the other authors were born after that date. Several died in the nineteenth century. One, indeed, was born early in that century.

In many ways Locke was the most important figure of the time. First, as an apologist for the Glorious Revolution of 1688; second, as the author of a document that would profoundly influence Thomas Jefferson seventy years later; and third, as the first of the new school of philosophers known as British Empiricists. Rousseau's influence was nearly as great, and Dr. Johnson ruled the literary world for three decades in the middle of the century. Where Dryden had been the first serious critic of Shakespeare a hundred years before, Johnson reigned supreme as critic and expositor of Shakespeare well into the nineteenth century, although he had died in 1784.

The four poets—Burns, Blake, Wordsworth, and Coleridge—represented here had little in common but their commonality was important. They were all rebels against the style of Pope, as it may be called. They wrote not in rhyme but in blank or free verse and chose subjects that were often entirely new. This was especially true of William Blake, who was a genuine revolutionary in poetry and a great seer in all the senses of that word. As you will see in what follows.

# JOHN LOCKE
### 1632–1704
*The Second Essay on Civil Government*
*A Letter Concerning Toleration*

John Locke was born near Bristol in 1632, the son of an attorney who treated the boy with intelligence and great kindness; Locke's education thus began well, a fact that he confirmed some fifty years later in his fine small book, *Some Thoughts Concerning Education*. Locke attended the Westminster School and Oxford, but, although he remained a fellow there for much of his life, he did not approve of the Scholastic philosophy still taught in Oxford colleges. He decided to study medicine under Robert Boyle and other natural philosophers of the new mode of thinking.

His life was circumscribed, his character mild, and his prospects modest when, in 1666, the great Sir Anthony Ashley Cooper (later the Earl of Shaftesbury) visited Oxford. This was a turning point in Locke's career. Shaftesbury required minor medical attention, and Locke was introduced by a mutual friend. The two men found they had much in common. Locke spent the next fifteen years in

Shaftesbury's employ, as doctor, secretary, friend, and general coun-selor. During these years Shaftesbury's career was meteoric, rising to the position of the king's First Minister and descending to charges of treason. Locke shared the pleasures and emoluments of his patron's rise, but managed to avoid the pains of his fall.

A flurry of political activity occurred in 1680 when hints surfaced of a plot to murder Charles II and replace him on the throne by his brother, the future James II, a Roman Catholic. The plot was less important than the reaction to it; Shaftesbury proposed a law excluding Roman Catholics from the succession. Shaftesbury's oppo-nents immediately countered with arguments in favor of the so-called Divine Right of Kings, which would presumably include the right of the king to adopt any religion he chose. To shore up their side they republished an old book, Sir Robert Filmer's *Patriarcha*, a vindication of the rights of kings to which no one had paid much attention for forty years. But now everyone was paying attention. Shaftesbury turned to Locke and asked him to help prepare a reply to Filmer. This Locke did, composing two treatises on government, the first a direct reply to and effective demolition of Filmer's arguments, the second an essay upon civil government from a more general point of view.

The two treatises were completed, though not published, in 1680. But events soon conspired to give them an import and an influence far beyond, it appears, Locke's original intention. Charles II died in 1685; James II succeeded him. Within a short time his Roman Catholicism was perceived as intolerable by the majority of Britons and active steps began to be taken to remove him from the throne. The Glorious Revolution of 1688 was the result—glorious primarily because not a drop of blood was spilled, although there was much saber rattling. James abdicated, and William and Mary succeeded him. They were both good Protestants.

Though bloodless, nevertheless this was a real revolution, one of the most important in the history of political liberty, and it required justification. Locke had spent the years after 1680 in Holland, fearful of the king's vengeance. Now, in the spring of 1689, he returned to England in the same vessel with Queen Mary, bearing his manu-scripts. His two treatises were published together at the end of the year, and ever since it has been assumed that they were written to validate a revolution. They were published to do so, at least. "The Second Essay on Civil Government" is about three great ideas: property, government, and revolution. The question that most concerned Locke was: What is the connection between them?

If there is no property, no government is needed. If I possess nothing, what need have I of the machinery of the state: laws and judges, policemen and prisons?

But property exists, says Locke, and it is legitimate. At least it used to be; in the beginning one could easily see its fairness. Now, sometimes, he wonders, as we do today, why some persons should possess so much, others so little.

Government, too, is legitimate, or it can be so. It is so if the governors and the governed agree on the one great thing: that they are in it together. The governors govern for the good of the governed, not their own good only; and the governed are content that it should be thus, for they see justice all around them, and above them, too.

Is revolution ever legitimate? Yes, Locke thunders! When a ruler declares war upon his people and attempts by one means or another to reduce them to slavery, then they have a right to rise up in self-defense. God has given them this right, and no man can take it from them.

That glorious doctrine has been used to justify rebellions other than the one of 1688. Thomas Jefferson read the "Essay," as did Robespierre, as did Marx, as did Lenin. Ideas, it has been said with some truth, are the rulers of the world.

The sixteenth century had been blasted by religious wars—in Germany, in France, in England, in the Low Countries. Some of these spilled over into the seventeenth century, especially at its dawning; sometimes, however, religion was cited as an excuse for war that was really about other matters. At any rate, it became a prime goal of the seventeenth century to try to deal with the question of religious difference and conflict among religions without war. Probably the most eloquent plea for religious toleration came at the very end of the century. John Locke wrote it first in Latin and published it in Holland during the 1680s, when he was living in that country to avoid the tumultuous events in England at the time—events that led to the revolution of 1688. "A Letter Concerning Toleration" was published by Locke in English during the year of his return to England, 1689. It immediately produced a storm of controversy.

Why? The text seems completely reasonable and completely in line with modern views on the subject. How could Locke have been attacked for writing it; on what grounds could the "Letter" itself have been opposed? Not to know how to answer these questions is to fail to understand two hundred years of European history.

Religion was serious business in the western world until the middle of the nineteenth century. Today there are still many religious people, and church attendance remains high among a number of sects, but religion has ceased to be, for almost all Christians at least, a matter of life and death. The jihad, or holy war, is also a thing of the past—in our part of the world. Such wars persist and continue in other regions of the globe.

As far as we are concerned, is that all to the good? Some religious people would deny this today. If you are not willing to die for your faith, they say, then you do not have much of a faith. Dying for one's faith is one thing, killing for it is another. Men and women of the sixteenth century were very willing both to die and to kill for their faith. It happened all the time. It did not strike anyone as insane or even unreasonable; in fact, if it did not happen from time to time— if the tree of faith (to paraphrase a famous saying of Thomas Jefferson) was not watered with the blood of the faithful—then, in the opinion of many persons in the sixteenth century, this was cause for alarm. In that case, they would have thought, religion must be in danger of ceasing to be serious business.

Indeed, that is the crux of the matter. If you believe that you possess (or are) an immortal soul; if you believe that your stay on Earth is but a tiny part of time compared to the eternity your soul will endure after death; and if you believe that the character of your faith and the details of your religious observances will determine whether you spend that eternity in bliss or in torment—then religion becomes extremely serious business, more serious than anything else you do or think about. To die in your faith, if you believe that to do so is to gain eternal bliss, is obviously no loss whatsoever compared to living out of it, and losing heaven.

This, however, is to look at religion only from your point of view. There would seem to be two other points of view that should be considered. One is that of another person whose faith differs from your own. For hundreds of years before the time of Locke, but especially during the two centuries or so before he wrote the "Letter Concerning Toleration," it was easy for men to believe that their faith required them to torment, to kill, to burn at the stake other men—and women—whose faith differed from theirs, by shades of difference that now seem hard to discern. But, we may ask, is any difference, no matter how great, cause enough for burning? A man of the sixteenth century would not even have understood the question. A man of the seventeenth century might have understood it, but he would still have been shocked to hear it asked. Such were the opponents who attacked Locke for his "Letter."

Finally, there is Locke's position, or point of view, which is that—he says—of God. He asks: Does the Christian God, the God in Whom we believe, the God of mercy and of love, approve and applaud the actions of those who, "out of a principle of charity, as they pretend, and love to men's souls ... deprive [others] of their estates, maim them with corporal punishments, starve and torment them in noisome prisons, and in the end even take away their lives"? Locke's answer to this question is strong and clear:

> That any man should think fit to cause another man—whose salvation he heartily desires—to expire in torments, and that even in an unconverted state, would, I confess, seem very strange to me, and I think, to any other also. But nobody, surely, will ever believe that such a carriage can proceed from charity, love, or goodwill. If anyone maintain that men ought to be compelled by fire and sword to profess certain doctrines, and conform to this or that exterior worship, without regard had unto their morals; if any endeavour to convert those that are erroneous unto the faith, by forcing them to profess things that they do not believe and allowing them to practise things that the Gospel does not permit, it cannot be doubted indeed but such a one is desirous to have a numerous assembly joined in the same profession with himself; but that he principally

intends by those means to compose a truly Christian Church, is altogether incredible.

It is an interesting answer, and a very modern one. Scarcely any Christian today would find fault with it, which is the best proof of Locke's influence on our minds and ideas. We are almost all Lockians now, in politics and religion.

Is that because he made us what we are, or is it because he could foresee what we would be?

# JOHN LOCKE
*An Essay Concerning Human Understanding*

# GEORGE BERKELEY
1685–1753
*The Principles of Human Knowledge*

# DAVID HUME
1711–1776
*An Enquiry Concerning Human Understanding*

The history of philosophy, like the history of many ideas that are very old, reveals a pendulum movement. The bias in philosophy has swung back and forth between two main views of what is, and of how the human mind knows what is. Those are the fundamental questions with which philosophy at all times and places has been concerned.

These two main views have names: Rationalism and Empiricism. To simplify the matter greatly, Empiricists believe that nothing exists that is not at least to some extent perceivable, and that knowledge, at least to a large extent, is about things that are or can be perceived. Rationalists, on the contrary, maintain that real things are ideas and principles, while the phenomenal, perceivable world is merely a reflection of the reality that we do not perceive at all—it is not material—but instead intuit or known with our minds *a priori*.

The greatest of all Rationalists was Plato; his pupil, Aristotle, was also a Rationalist, but not an extreme one like Plato. With Plato and Aristotle the pendulum swung far toward Rationalism, but it swung back toward Empiricism with the rise to prominence of the Stoic and Epicurean philosophers, who held that the mind at birth is a *tabula rasa*, or "clean slate," on which messages are "written" by the senses. Unsophisticated philosophers are usually Empiricists, and the early Christian thinkers were not sophisticated; but Saint Augustine, as a follower of Plato, introduced the Church to the Rationalism that prevailed for nearly a thousand years. The pendulum swung again: Thomas Aquinas and Roger Bacon were, in their very different ways, Empiricists whose theories were subtle and highly sophisticated. But Rationalism struck back during the early Renaissance with the revival of interest in Plato and especially Aristotle and the dominance of the so-called Scholastic philosophy in schools everywhere in Christendom. Thus, at the beginning of the seventeenth century, the pendulum had swung far toward Rationalism—and was ready again to swing the other way.

Descartes, though in many ways a Rationalist, gave the pendulum a strong push, and so did the first of the English Empiricists, Francis Bacon, with his relatively naive insistence that all philosophical study and investigation should be concerned with the secrets of nature, to unlock which would allow man to progress. Thomas Hobbes was in some ways a fervent Empiricist, although he also held some Rationalist views. It remained for John Locke to push the pendulum all the way to the Empiricist side, where it remained for more than a century, thanks to successive pushes given it by Berkeley and Hume. The pendulum swung back again in the nineteenth century under the enormous influence of Kant and, especially, Hegel. We live today in an era of reaction to Hegelianism; Radical or Logical Empiricism is probably the dominant philosophical school of our times. There are signs, however, that the pendulum is beginning to swing again toward Rationalism, and it can be safely predicted that it will do so sooner or later.

A pendulum swings back and forth, hanging from a central point. The central question of philosophy goes something like this: Given that there are real things in the world and minds that both perceive and know them, then what is it that is known? Is it "things themselves" or is it ideas about those things, principles derived or abstracted from those things, that the mind comprehends and about which it reasons?

And if it is the "things themselves" that are actually known by the mind, then what is the relation between the mind and the thing known? Is the thing itself in the mind—or some material shadow or image of it (perhaps made of atoms)? Or does the mind bring to the process of knowing innate or *a priori* concepts and/or capabilities and/or categories of thought? The above may seem complicated, but really only one question is being asked. How you answer it determines where you stand on the great perennial issue of philosophy.

Locke published his "Essay Concerning Human Understanding" shortly after his return to England from his exile in Holland. The year was 1689, which also saw the publication of his two major political works, the "Letter Concerning Toleration" and "The Second Essay on Civil Government." The two political works occasioned immediate controversy; the philosophical treatise took a while to sink in. Eventually it became the bible of English Empiricists and was accorded a devotion only equaled by the devotion paid to Newton's achievements in the fields of mathematics and celestial mechanics. The book is gracefully written and is one of the easiest philosophical books to read.

The Irishman George Berkeley (1685–1753) made a considerable career for himself because of his charm and good temper—and also because of his keen intellect. He composed a famous poem, "Westward the course of Empire takes its way"; was a famous bishop; and wrote a famous book, *Principles of Human Knowledge* (1710), which purported to attack Locke but really advanced his Empiricist views a good distance. It too is easy to read.

The book also occasioned a notorious event in English intellectual history. Berkeley maintained—or seemed to maintain—that the only real "substance" in the world was spiritual, not material. Locke had held that only the perceivable exists, but that the mind adds to its comprehension of perceivable things an innate idea of their materiality. Berkeley countered that he had no sense himself of any such innate idea, and replaced Locke's concept of "material substance" by a concept of "spiritual substance"; to make a long story short, Berkeley thus maintained that the being of things was supported and maintained by the ever-present mind of God. A conclusion was easy to draw from this—although Berkeley himself did not draw it—to the effect that material things do not exist, and that the world we think we perceive is merely a collection of shades or shadows. Dr. Samuel Johnson, who really knew better, once got into an argument about Berkeley's views and, to ensure victory, kicked a stone with his foot as hard as he could. Limping down the road, he expostulated: "Thus I refute Bishop Berkeley!"

The Scotsman David Hume completes our triumvirate of British Empiricists. Born in Edinburgh in 1711, Hume was one of the first professional literary men; his essays on political and economic subjects made him famous, and his *History of England* (1753-61) made him rich—"not only independent but opulent," as he said himself.

Those works were a great success; his *Enquiry Concerning Human Understanding*, which he cared about and published in several versions throughout his lifetime, was a great failure. It was indeed a rather frightening book for its time, for Hume's radical Empiricism led him to the edge of a religious skepticism that was shocking to his contemporaries. He denied that he was not a believing Christian, but his most careful readers thought they knew better, and I think they were right. Hume, in fact, was as close as you please to being the kind of atheist who asks whether the existence of God can be proved, if not in the laboratory, then at least by scientific methods. And if not …

The superbly written *Enquiry* forms the capstone of the arch begun by Locke. It ends with one of the most passionate paragraphs ever written by a philosopher. Hume has expounded his principles and supposes that they are convincing. He imagines, therefore, a new beginning of philosophy based on his own ideas. To make this new beginning, much of the old underbrush will have to be swept away, including a lot of old, false books. He writes:

> When we run over libraries, persuaded of these princi-
> ples, what havoc must we make? If we take in our hand
> any volume; of divinity or school metaphysics, for

instance; let us ask, Does it contain any abstract reasoning concerning quantity or number? No. Does it contain any experimental reasoning concerning matter of fact and existence? No. Commit it then to the flames: for it can contain nothing but sophistry and illusion.

That is wonderful. All philosophers should care as much as Hume did about the truth.

# JEAN-JACQUES ROUSSEAU
## 1712–1778
*A Discourse on the Origin of Inequality*
*The Social Contract*

At the end of his life Jean-Jacques Rousseau, exiled from all the nations where he had lived and a self-proclaimed citizen of the world, was the most famous man in Europe. And also one of the most feared, by secular and religious leaders alike. His restless, tormented spirit was not to be trusted, they felt, and with good reason. He was a danger to all established institutions, which he would just as soon pull down, they thought, for the pleasure of seeing them fall, as for any real sense of their injustice or corruption. They may have been right about that, too.

Certainly Jean-Jacques, as he was called by both his enemies and his admirers—he had few friends, as such—was one of the unhappiest men who ever lived. His life consisted of a series of failures and disasters; he was only saved, on occasion, by the merciful intercessions of women who were enormously attracted to his dark, haunted soul. Indeed, he was a pure Romantic spirit, but he lived a half-century before such types were appreciated. What is more, he received no credit whatever for having invented the character that made men like Shelley, Byron, and Victor Hugo famous.

Rousseau was born in 1712 in Geneva, then an independent city-state, but he did not stay there, finding its narrow Protestantism admirable in a way but intolerable to his turbulent personality. He lived in France, in Venice (also an independent city-state), and in England, to which, with the help of James Boswell, he journeyed in the company of David Hume—only to quarrel with both of his benefactors within a matter of months. There was no helping this bitter, perverse, ironic, and suspicious man; he turned like a wounded dog on all those who tried to succor him. In 1767, now fifty-five and tired of running, he returned to France. He died in a simple cottage at Ermenonville, near Paris, in 1778. The great of Europe were glad to know him gone, but his cult did not die; for half a century the name Jean-Jacques could strike terror in the breasts of authority and produce frantic excitement in those of young, ambitious men and women.

Rousseau's literary career began in 1749 at the age of thirty-seven, when he entered a competition proposed by the Academy of Dijon for the best essay on the subject: "Has the progress of the arts and sciences contributed more to the corruption or purification of morals?" His essay, attacking civilization as corrupting the goodness of nature, won the prize and brought him his first fame. He gained the attention of Diderot, who was editing *L'Encyclopedie*; Diderot asked for an article on politics, and Rousseau wrote his *Discourse on Political Economy*, which first appeared in *L'Encyclopedie* in 1755. His romantic novel, *La Nouvelle Eloise*, about a girl brought up in a simple environment, was a great success; he followed it by *Emile*, a tract disguised as a novel, proposing a system of education based on direct acquaintance with nature, and *The Social Contract*, both published in 1762. His *Confessions* did not appear until after his death; they were as shocking as anything he had ever written. In them he spoke of personal matters that no serious writer before him had discussed in print and revealed himself as he really was, both bad and good.

The Academy of Dijon proposed another essay competition in 1755, and Rousseau entered this one, too, with his *Discourse on the Origin of Inequality*. The question was, How has a condition of inequality among men come about? Rousseau's answer was characteristic and similar to the one he had given to the previous question. That is, he changed the question somewhat, to ask how general unhappiness had come about—was this because man was naturally unhappy, or because civilization had made him so?

Leaving aside the assumption, typical of Rousseau, that mankind is generally unhappy, the essay is one of the most brilliant pieces of writing in the history of eighteenth-century thought. It begins with an account of the state of nature, which, Rousseau candidly admits, "no longer exists, perhaps never did exist, and probably never will exist," and goes on to examine the unhappy series of events—as Rousseau views them—that have led to the present state of mankind.

Rousseau's concept of the state of nature is quite different from that of the other political philosophers—notably Hobbes and Locke—who had written on the subject. Rousseau sees no reason to agree with Hobbes that life in the state of nature was "solitary, poor, nasty, brutish, and short," nor with Locke that natural man lived in a condition of constant terror of everything that surrounded him. On the contrary, says Rousseau, why should not primitive man in his natural state be considered to have been happy? He had everything he desired—"food, a female, and sleep"—and knew nothing of the further pleasures of life that are the result of progress and man's perfectibility. And in this happiness, or rather contentment, how could he have been counted unequal to anyone else? Were not all in that condition the same? Apart, of course, from natural differences in strength, size, speed, and the like, which are quite different from "moral or political inequality"; the latter is artificial, that is, man-made and man-maintained. And yet how different is the present condition of mankind!

How did this change come about? Again, says Rousseau, it is because of, and a bitter fruit of, progress and man's perfectibility.

> From the moment one man began to stand in need of the help of another; from the moment it appeared advantageous to any one man to have provisions for two, equality disappeared, property was introduced, work became indispensable, and vast forests became smiling fields, which man had to water with the sweat of his brow, and where slavery and misery were soon seen to germinate and grow up with the crops.
>
> Metallurgy and agriculture were the two arts which produced this great revolution. The poets tell us it was

gold and silver, but, for the philosophers, it was iron and
corn, which first civilized men, and ruined humanity.

How characteristic of Rousseau are those famous sentences! No
one could write with such boldness and speed. Their substance is also
typical. Rousseau was a deep believer in a Golden Age that was long
past. The present, in his view, was—as John Donne had said a
century before—"iron, and rusty too!"

Rousseau did not create the cult of the Noble Savage, but he did
much to promote and perpetuate it. He was also the leading
spokesman of his era for the position that progress is a disaster for
mankind. He did not entirely believe that; *The Social Contract* is in
some respects his own answer to the gloomy conclusions of the
*Discourse on Inequality*. But as with everything he wrote, the latter
work, within the compass of its few pages, sets forth an extreme position with incomparable force and eloquence. If you disagree with
Rousseau about progress you had better start marshaling your arguments, for he is hard to beat. If you agree, you will be amused and
delighted to find your own ideas set forth with such ironic brilliance.

Rousseau wrote *The Social Contract* during the early 1760s, when
he was living at Montlouis, near Paris; he had moved there after quar-
reling, as was his wont, with friends who had provided him with a
much more comfortable place to work at the Hermitage. The book
was condemned by the parliament of Paris and attacked by Voltaire,
who was himself a rebel but not a political one, and its publication
led to Rousseau's exile from France for several years. The book, which
is short, like most of his works, was published in 1762. Its brevity is,
however, misleading. No one wrote with greater swiftness than did
Rousseau. He is able to cover in fifty pages what others had required
volumes to treat.

With his accustomed directness, Rousseau tells us in his first
sentence what his book is about and what he intends to do in it. "I
mean to inquire if," he says, "in the civil order, there can be any sure
and legitimate rule of administration, men being taken as they are
and laws as they might be." Or, to put it another way, as Rousseau
does a few lines later, in some of the most famous words ever written
in the field of political thought:

> Man is born free; and everywhere he is in chains. One thinks himself the master of others, and still remains a greater slave than they. How did this change come about? I do not know. What can make it legitimate? That question I think I can answer.

Simply as an example of good prose, how could that be improved upon?

One does not read *The Social Contract* only for its prose style. Rousseau is concerned to ask the great question of political theory and to give a most interesting answer to it. He supposes mankind at a point in its development when the primitive state of nature is no longer sufficient—if, indeed, it ever was—for the satisfaction of its needs. What is required, now, is some kind of aggregated action; men can do together what none can do alone. The problem, however, is to attain the goods of association without giving up all other goods. As Rousseau states it:

> The problem is to find a form of association which will defend and protect with the whole common force the person and goods of each associate, and in which each, while uniting himself with all, may still obey himself alone, and remain as free as before.

This, he adds, is the fundamental problem of which *The Social Contract* provides the solution.

For Rousseau, the solution lies in the totality of the gift, on the part of all members of the community—all without exception—of their individual power and liberty. The clauses of this contract, he writes, "may be reduced to one—the total alienation of each associate, together with all his rights, to the whole community." This concept is essential because "each man, in giving himself to all, gives himself to nobody." He gains as much as he loses; indeed he gains more, for now he enjoys the combined power of the community, where before he was limited by the narrow extent of his own strength.

# HENRY FIELDING
## 1707–1754
### *Tom Jones*

Henry Fielding suffered much in his life and lived among persons who suffered even more than he. But he hardly ever lost his composure and his cheerfulness, and he spent all of his free time, money, and strength in helping others. The poor of London thought of him as a saint. He was also a great novelist.

Born in 1707 into a noble family tracing its lineage to the Hapsburgs, Fielding spent his youth as such a young man should, attending Eton—where he first learned to love literature—and chasing after pretty girls. When he was twenty-one, however, he learned the melancholy news that his father was no longer able to pay him an allowance. From then on, Fielding was entirely dependent on his own resources.

He resolved to become a writer and in a period of some ten years produced twenty-five mocking comedies for the stage, which gave him a very modest income. But the last of these plays mercilessly satirized the then prime minister, a Whig, who pushed a law through Parliament—in 1737—requiring the licensing of plays. Fielding's dramatic career thus came to an end. He studied law and tried to make a living as a barrister, but without much success. In 1742 he reached the nadir. His daughter was dying, his wife was very ill, he himself was suffering acutely from gout, and he had no money. In despair, he tried his hand at still another kind of writing and produced *Joseph Andrews*.

In a sense it was the first English novel; Fielding called it a "comic Epic-Poem in Prose." Beginning as a satire on Samuel Richardson's *Pamela*, the story of a girl who fought for her virtue against her employer and ended up marrying him, *Joseph Andrews* is the story of Pamela's brother, who resists the advances of his employer, a noble lady. The joke was good for a laugh, and it is remarkable that Fielding was able to be so cheerful about it, given the circumstances.

Actually, in the course of writing the book, he made a discovery of the sort that happens only to the best writers. He found he had a better story at hand in the relationship between Joseph and his friend, Parson Adams, one of the great comic figures in literature. Adams and Joseph travel the roads and byways of England together, and their adventures constitute a masterpiece of ironic social criticism.

Fielding had been considered an enemy by the Whigs, but in 1745 a Tory government came into power and he was adopted as a valuable political ally. He wrote whole issues of newspapers in support of the Tories and was supported financially by them in return. He was also made a London magistrate, and ended up reforming that previously despised office, treating the poor with justice and compassion instead of exploiting them, and devising ways to protect both rich and poor from the depredations of murderers, ruffians, and robbers. All of this kept him extremely busy, but he still had time to write *The History of Tom Jones, A Foundling*. It appeared in 1749, and though it was one of the very first English novels, it remains one of the best. *Amelia* followed two years later; it is not much read these days. In 1754 Fielding journeyed to Lisbon in search of a cure for his several crippling afflictions. He died in Lisbon a few months after he arrived.

Tom Jones is a foundling. This is a convenient novelistic ploy; the author can conceal until the very end of the book the names of the real parents of his hero. Tom is considered by everyone to be a bastard and hence a man without any prospects. But he is the handsomest young man in England, and charming to boot, and infinitely lovable. He is loved by everyone—except his enemies.

Naturally he has enemies; else there would be no story. For a while his enemies are triumphant, and Tom is forced to flee from the comfortable home where he has been brought up under the kind care of Squire Allworthy, whose name indicates character. Tom sets out, with an imaginary stick over his shoulder to which is attached a handkerchief containing his worldly possessions, to see what the world is made of. He learns a great deal but he is never in any real danger because many women, young and old, adopt him and take him under their wing. Such a charming, handsome young man cannot come to harm in the universe of fiction.

Tom leaves behind him not only Squire Allworthy but also Squire Western, and Squire Western's family. Squire Western is justly famous; he is the very type of the apoplectic eighteenth-century landed gentry. He is also wonderfully funny, for, no matter how hard he shouts, he is never able to beat down his sister, an unwedded lady who keeps his house. They argue unceasingly, and these arguments are immensely comical. The keynote is established in an early chapter when, in the course of one of the Squire's tirades, Miss Western has occasion to remind him that she is a woman:

> "I do know you are a woman," cries the squire, "and it's well for thee that art one; if hadst been a man, I promise thee I had lent thee a flick long ago."—"Ay, there," said she, "in that flick lies all your fancied superiority. Your bodies, and not your brains, are stronger than ours. Believe me, it is well for you that you are able to beat us; or, such is the superiority of our understanding, we should make all of you … our slaves."

The Squire is never able to talk to his sister without nearly frothing at the mouth. They are a wonderful pair, and one regrets that there are not even more of their conversations in the book.

Squire Western also has a daughter, Sophia, the paragon of young ladies, as beautiful as Tom is handsome, as charming and accomplished in her way as he is in his. Of course they fall in love; this is as deliciously inevitable as anything in a novel.

The Squire, however, is inalterably opposed to such a match for his beloved daughter. Sophia therefore has many obstacles to overcome in winning her Tom; to those in her own household are added those erected between them by Tom himself who, partly because he feels guilty about loving Sophia when everyone tells him he should not, falls in love with more than one other girl in the course of his travels.

All comes around in the end, which is also inevitable, but how it comes about I have no intention whatsoever of saying—for what right have I to deprive you of the exquisite pleasure of finding out for yourself?

I do not know of any novel that is more fun to read than *Tom Jones*. It is funny, touching, sad, and profound. The characters are interesting, the situations believable. The book also is a veritable goldmine of information about life in eighteenth-century England. It was a fascinating time worth knowing about.

*Tom Jones* consists of eighteen books and some one hundred chapters. Each of the separate Books is introduced by a chat with the reader in the author's own voice. Fielding talks to us about the story, about the fortunes and misfortunes of the characters, and about other subjects of mutual interest. Such interludes were not uncommon at the time, and usually they can be skipped without loss. Not so with *Tom Jones*. Fielding's chats with his readers are almost as entertaining as the story itself. Do not make the mistake of slipping by them.

## JAMES BOSWELL
### 1740–1795
*The Life of Samuel Johnson LL.D.*

James Boswell was born in Edinburgh, Scotland, in 1740, the son of the laird of Auchinleck in Ayrshire. The laird was ambitious for his son and wished for him to follow in his footsteps as an advocate, but Boswell disliked school and especially disliked his father's profession. In 1760 he ran away from his father's sternness to London and discovered that he much preferred pretty women to the law. He also discovered that he was sensual and attractive to women and so the long series of intrigues and gallantries that filled his life began.

Boswell, now deciding that instead of being a lawyer he would become a soldier, persuaded his father to support him in a military career. But his father would not buy him a commission, and Boswell failed to obtain one in any other way. He ended up being an advocate, and an unhappy one.

On his second visit to London he made the acquaintance of a number of important persons and literary folk, and charmed them all. On May 16, 1763, there occurred the famous meeting with

Samuel Johnson, in the back parlor of the bookseller Thomas Davies. Johnson was severe with the young man at first—he was fifty-three, Boswell still only twenty-two—but a firm friendship soon developed between them, one that endured until Johnson's death in 1784.

James Boswell harbored for years an abiding desire to write the biography of some great man. He seemed to grow in his own estimation when he was in the company of important persons. He had an ability to interest and charm them, and many became his close friends. He also possessed a remarkable memory. He could remember the details of a conversation long after it had occurred, and what is more he had the ability to summarize it so that it read like fiction instead of a mere transcript.

Boswell's first choice of a subject was the Corsican hero, Pasquale Paoli, whom he visited in the autumn of 1765. Paoli became his fast friend, and Boswell's first book was about Corsica and Paoli's efforts to liberate it. The book was a success. But as the friendship with Dr. Johnson developed, Boswell began to realize that here was his perfect subject. The first edition of *The Life of Samuel Johnson LL.D.* appeared in 1791, to great acclaim. Boswell saw the second edition through the press in 1793 and was at work on the third when he died in 1795.

Boswell gave his soul to Dr. Johnson, and in return Johnson gave his heart to the strange young Scot. The old man had never had such a friend, at least since Mrs. Johnson's death. And the famous old man did not mind at all that "Bozzie" was forever challenging him with statements, declarations, and propositions. He was at least half aware that Boswell was taking it all down, composing some sort of record. Others were, too, Johnson knew; but he did not love them the way he did Boswell. There was something very special about Boswell, Dr. Johnson thought, and he was right.

Boswell was also right to choose Samuel Johnson, LL.D., as his subject. Johnson was the most famous literary man in England. He had produced the best dictionary of the English language and also an edition of Shakespeare's plays that was in every gentleman's library. He wrote no more these days; he had once said that "No one but a fool writes except for money," and he had money now, money of his own and money from admiring hosts like the Thrales (Mr. Thrale made beer, and Mrs. Thrale liked having Johnson at her dinner parties). All of his energies—still considerable—were spent on conversation; he was probably the greatest talker in England, and an aggressive talker, too; when he talked for victory, as a later critic said, you had better get out of his way. A young man with a good memory and a knowledge of shorthand would find much usable material if he could manage to spend enough time with Johnson. Boswell found the time, Johnson talked, and the result is a glorious book.

Johnson was a rich biographical subject, and not just because of his famous wit. He was also a very touching human being. Tall, with stooped shoulders and a craggy face scarred by scrofula (a sort of severe acne), he was also awkward in the extreme and possessed by every kind of tic and nervous ailment. At the same time, he was a thoughtful and caring man. He was a really good friend. He supported a household of servants and never complained when they did not serve him. He cared very much for his cat. And he was deeply concerned for his immortal soul.

All of this Boswell knew, and all of it he told. But the most important thing he knew was how to stand out of the spotlight and let Dr. Johnson shine. The best biographers know this, and Boswell was the first modern biographer.

Much has been learned about Dr. Johnson, and our time has witnessed the publication of several fine new biographies of this perennial subject. The publication of Boswell's diaries, in eighteen volumes (1928–1934), has also taught us much about Boswell. It was customary, until these diaries were discovered—it had been supposed that they were lost—to view Boswell as a fortunate fool, a kind of recording machine who never really understood the meaning of his own words. The diaries show that to be untrue; Boswell was not only a man of complex aspirations but also a superb writer. In fact, his diaries, which constitute almost a complete autobiography, are one of the best examples of that genre.

Nevertheless, in the end it is probably true that the combination of Johnson and Boswell, or Boswell and Johnson, is greater than the sum of its parts. Boswell was fortunate to find Johnson, and Johnson to find Boswell. And we are lucky that they found one another.

*The Life of Samuel Johnson LL.D.* is the perfect book to read on a series of winter evenings—throughout an entire winter, perhaps—and a long one at that. It requires patience to read the whole book, but that patience is rewarded. Imagine yourself in London in, say, 1775; you are seated in a drawing room, and there is an excited whisper of anticipation: "Dr. Johnson is coming down!" Sit back and listen … .

# ROBERT BURNS
### 1759–1796
*Selected Poems*

Robert Burns is the national poet of Scotland. So what else is new, you say. It is not new, but it is remarkable, for no other country has a national poet as Scotland has Burns. Each year his birthday, January 25, is celebrated with rites expressing a fervent and undying love that is associated with no other serious poet anywhere.

Burns was born in 1759 in Ayrshire, in the Lowlands of Scotland. The Highlands are not far away, and Burns often journeyed there in search of adventure, love, and, finally, peace. He received almost no schooling, being instead one of the most successful autodidacts; he read everything he could lay his hands on, which was a lot in eighteenth-century Scotland, a nation that was both literate and proud of its books. He began to write verses when he was about twenty, the time when he also first fell in love. "I never had the least thought," he wrote, "or inclination of turning Poet till I once got heartily in Love, and then Rhyme and Song were, in a manner, a spontaneous language of my heart." Some of his poems were in standard English, but many were in the Scottish dialect; in fact, he created a distinctly Scots-English idiom that now seems natural enough but that really did not exist before him. *Poems, Chiefly in the Scottish Dialect*, published at Kilmarnock in 1786, was an immediate success. The world was ready for this farmer and farmer's son who could either wring or uplift his readers' hearts with the turn of a phrase.

Literary success meant fame and new friends, but little or no money. Burns already had a family, although he was as yet unmarried. His first illegitimate child had been born in 1785, and in 1786, a month or so before the publication of his book, Jean Armour produced twins. She and Burns were married in 1788, but the burden of his need to support her and her children had become heavy before that. Burns had no other work besides farming—not a lucrative profession in eighteenth-century Scotland. In fact, Robert Burns worked himself to death; he died in 1796, at the early age of thirty-seven, from the effects of too much work in his early years on an inadequate diet.

The last years of Burns's life were devoted to songs; he is the greatest writer of songs in English, and perhaps in any language. He worked for ten years to collect old songs and to help edit a series of volumes that are unique in English; without those volumes, the heritage of English and Scottish song would be immeasurably poorer. Where the words of an old song survived, he transcribed them. Where a mere fragment existed, he wrote new words. Where only an old tune came down to him, he wrote a new song. If he had not been uncannily in tune with the spirit of Scottish minstrels he would be condemned today for having destroyed an ancient tradition. But instead he saved the tradition and made it richer than it had ever been.

Some recastings of old songs are very famous; for example, "Green Grow the Rashes O" and "A Red, Red Rose." The most famous of all was not claimed by Burns, although he wrote most of what comes down to us. The chorus that we sing at midnight on New Year's Eve was traditional, but these lovely verses were written by Burns to accompany the chorus:

> We twa hae run about the braes
>    And pou'd the gowans fine,
> But we've wandered monie a weary fit
>    Sin' auld lang syne.
> We twa hae paidl'd in the burn
>    Frae morning sun till dine,
> But seas between us braid hae roared
>    Sin' auld lang syne.

> And there's a hand, my trusty fiere,
>     And gie's a hand o' thine,
> And we'll tak a right guid-willie waught
>     For auld lang syne!
> For auld lang syne, my dear,
>     For auld lang syne,
> We'll take a cup o' kindness yet
>     For auld lang syne!

Jean Armour, though his wife, was not Burns's only love. Mary Campbell inspired "Highland Mary," and Mary Morrison inspired a poem that is named after her:

> O Mary, at thy window be,
>     It is the wish'd, the trysted hour!
> Those smiles and glances let me see,
>     That makes the miser's treasure poor.

> O Mary, canst thou wreck his peace,
>     Wha for thy sake wad gladly die?
> Or canst thou break that heart of his,
>     Whase only fault is loving thee?

Probably there were half a dozen others, most of whom were inspirations, too. But one of Burns' finest poems is not about young love at all, or illegitimate love with all its attractions. In "John Anderson, My Jo," an aging wife speaks with affectionate sweetness to her equally aging husband.

> John Anderson, my jo, John,
>     We clamb the hill thegither;
> And mony a cantie day, John,
>     We've had wi' ane anither:
> Now we maun totter down, John,
>     And hand in hand we'll go,
> And sleep thegither at the foot,
>     John Anderson, my jo.

There are many other Burns poems and songs that are as good or nearly so: "The Banks o' Doon," "Ae Fond Kiss, and Then We Sever," and "To a Mouse, on Turning Up Her Nest with the Plough, November, 1785":

> Wee, sleekit, cow'rin', tim'rous beastie,
> O what a panic's in thy breastie!
> O Thou need na start awa' sae hasty,
> > Wi' bickering brattle!
> I wad be laith to rin an' chase thee
> > Wi' murd'ring pattle!

Also, "To a Louse, on Seeing One on a Lady's Bonnet at Church," "Address to the Unco Guid, or the Rigidly Righteous," "Charlie, He's My Darling," and (perhaps most famous of all) "A Man's a Man for A' That!" We needn't to stop even there; still to be mentioned are "The Cotter's Saturday Night" and "Tam o'Shanter," to say nothing of "Oh, Wert Thou in the Cauld Blast," which he wrote as he lay dying, to the favorite air of the young woman who was nursing him. And indeed there are a hundred more.

# WILLIAM BLAKE
1757–1827
*Songs of Innocence*
*Songs of Experience*

When William Blake died at the age of seventy in 1827, he was buried in an unmarked grave. This anonymity was symbolic of the loneliness and solitude that had been his lot throughout most of his life. He published several books, but all of them failed with a public that had no conception whatsoever of his greatness, as a poet, as an artist, and as a man; and for nearly a century after his death he was still largely unread and unknown. William Butler Yeats helped to edit an annotated edition of Blake's major works in 1893, and T.S. Eliot included an essay on Blake in *The Sacred Wood* (1920) that invited a larger audience than had ever known Blake to appreciate and understand him. The centenary of his death in 1927 brought forth a multitude of articles, critical essays, and editions. Today, Blake is permanently established in the highest pantheon of English poetry.

The reason Blake spoke not to his own age but to an age more than a century after his death is perhaps not far to seek. Blake was a seer—in two senses of the term. First, he possessed what is known as eidetic sight (a very rare quality): sometimes, when he imagined something, he could "see" it posed in front of his eyes, so that he could look at it from one side and another. Perhaps more than one artist has possessed this gift, but even among artists it must be extremely rare, and it is never easily understood. Sometimes possessors of the talent are driven mad by it. Blake was thought to be mad by those of his contemporaries who thought of him at all.

Having the gift of seeing mental images as real entities may or may not be good for an artist; it is probably good for a poet, if he lives in the twentieth century, an age of images and imagism in literature. Unfortunately, it was not good for a poet who was born in 1757 and who lived in an age of rational thought and feeling. Blake's first book of poems, *Songs of Innocence*, which he illustrated and printed himself (he was an engraver as well as a watercolorist), and which appeared in 1789, the year of the French Revolution (of which Blake passionately approved), should have provoked the storm of excitement produced by Wordsworth and Coleridge's *Lyrical Ballads*, which was published nine years later. *Songs of Innocence* should have, in short, initiated the so-called Romantic period in English poetry. *Lyrical Ballads* was a collection of poems about a life that most of its readers understood. Its "revolutionary" poems offered thoughtful, even novel comments on that life, and these were appreciated or objected to by readers. But there were readers.

No one read *Songs of Innocence* because it described, in powerful images, a life that no one understood. It would not be understood for more than a hundred years.

*Songs of Innocence* presents a kind of dreamlike childhood existence; *Songs of Experience*, its companion piece, presents poems on many of the same themes that depict the horror of life as it was lived by the poor and the abject, and especially as life was going to be led by thousands, then millions, of the victims of the English Industrial Revolution. For Blake was a seer in this other sense of the word as well; that is, he could foresee the future, could imagine things that had not yet occurred. As a sort of preface to his long poem, *Milton*, he wrote these famous lines:

> And did the Countenance Divine
> Shine forth upon our clouded hills?
> And was Jerusalem builded here
> Among these dark Satanic Mills?

But in writing them he was not describing anything that had happened yet, or that he had ever seen. He had never been to the not- yet-industrially-blighted north and Midlands of England; he had never seen a factory "manned" (the word carries heavy irony) by women and children, working from sunup to sundown; he had never seen the black smoke filling the sky over Manchester, Birmingham, and Liverpool. Yet he did "see" these things, as no other man in his time. It was no wonder that he did not come to be read until a century after his death.

He understood London, as no writer did until Dickens:

> I wander through each chartered street,
> Near where the chartered Thames does flow,
> And mark in every face I meet
> Marks of weakness, marks of woe.

"Chartered" means bought and sold; everything in London was for sale, Blake realized; if others had the slightest conception of this fact, they did not understand its implications. Once it had been different, he tells us in *Songs of Innocence*:

> When the voices of children are heard on the green
> And laughing is heard on the hill,
> My heart is at rest within my breast
> And everything else is still.

These are but snatches, lines, verses from great poems. Read all of the *Songs of Innocence* and then, when you are feeling strong in spirit, all of the *Songs of Experience*. Read them in an edition that contains Blake's own illustrations: these are strange and wonderful, like nothing ever seen. Compare the visions of a past that was once good and beautiful with a present and future that is bad and ugly. And then, when these images are solid in your mind, go on, perhaps, to such prose (or at least prosaic) works as *The Marriage of Heaven and Hell*, *Milton*, and *Jerusalem*, despite the fact that these are very difficult to understand without the copious notes of critics and commentators.

# WILLIAM WORDSWORTH
### 1770–1850
*Selected Poems*

William Wordsworth was born in Cumberland, in the Lake District of England, in 1770, the son of a lawyer. His parents died when he was young, and he was brought up by uncaring relatives. Much alone as a child and young man, he early came to depend upon nature for the solace that human beings provide to others. He attended Cambridge but did not distinguish himself there. From 1790, France was his abiding passion—that, and a young woman, Annette Vallon, whom he met and fell in love with there in 1791. She bore him a daughter in 1792, but he was unable to marry Annette or even to stay in France, partly because of his family's refusal to provide him any financial assistance, partly because war soon broke out between England and France, to endure, except for one short respite, for more than twenty years (that is, until the Battle of Waterloo finally ended it in 1815). But though he was separated from Annette he never forgot her and was inspired by her to write some of his most beautiful lyrics—for example, "It Is a Beauteous Evening, Calm and Free."

Wordsworth returned to England in 1792 and for several years lived a fitful, undirected life, but he was saved from himself and his own unhappiness in 1795 by the poet Samuel Taylor Coleridge, whom he met in that year and who inspired Wordsworth to devote himself exclusively to poetry. For the next three years the two young men were much together, and their friendship was productive for them both. Its first real fruit was the volume called *Lyrical Ballads*, which appeared in 1798 and in which the first poem was Coleridge's "Rime of the Ancient Mariner" and the last Wordsworth's "Lines composed a few miles above Tintern Abbey," two veritable treasures of English poetry.

In 1799, Wordsworth and his sister, Dorothy, with whom he lived for much of his life, moved into Dove Cottage at Grasmere, ever after sacred to the memory of Wordsworth and the focus of poetic pilgrimages to this day. There Coleridge often visited, and there Wordsworth lived with Dorothy and his wife, Mary Hutchinson, until a growing family forced them all to move to Rydal Mount, where the poet lived until his death in 1850.

After 1805, Wordsworth was never again the same marvelous poet that he had been from the time of the meeting with Coleridge until the cares of ordinary life seemed to change and wear him down. But for that glorious decade he was one of the best poets who ever lived.

In reading Wordsworth, therefore, selection becomes extremely important. But there are further problems with Wordsworth that must be faced by the modern reader before he can be appreciated as he should be.

Wordsworth's ideas possess a creaky, antique cast, and they are sometimes hard for contemporary readers to accept. Two of his finest longer lyrics, "Ode on Intimations of Immortality" and "Ode to Duty," suffer from the old-fashioned thought that underlies them.

There is nothing inherently wrong with old thoughts. Some old thoughts are a good deal better than some new ones. And the really fundamental ideas behind those two poems, as well as many others by Wordsworth, are not at all antique or useless, although they may indeed be old-fashioned. The trouble is in the presentation of these ideas, which comes down to Wordsworth's rather bland assumption that his readers—then and now—will all agree with his thinking about them.

The real problem is that when it came to thought, Wordsworth was not first rate. He is a great poet in every other respect: as a versifier he is unequaled; he is voluminous; he is clear; he has many beauties; he is powerful and moving. Lacking, however, a certain power of mind, he cannot be placed in the very first rank of poets, the rank occupied by such as Homer, Dante, Shakespeare, and Goethe. But he is firmly ensconced in the second rank, just behind them, by virtue of a relatively small number of poems (relatively small in relation to his enormous corpus). And those really must be read.

Take "Ode: Intimations of Immortality from Recollections of Early Childhood." If you have not read this before, you will be astonished at how many quotations derive from it. Which means, of course, that portions of it, individual lines and collections of lines, have become almost a part of the language: "Our birth is but a sleep and a forgetting," "Thoughts that do often lie too deep for tears," and so forth.

These famous lines, and others like them, actually get in the way of reading and understanding the poem. It is too easy to gloss over it, swimming with the current of pretty sounds and lovely images, without thinking. But the basic idea here, although creaky, is nevertheless worth serious consideration: the idea that human life is a sad, continuous, and unavoidable falling away from a state of existence that we somehow perceived when we were children but are no longer able to perceive when we grow up:

> The world is too much with us; late and soon,
> Getting and spending, we lay waste our powers:
> Little we see in Nature that is ours;
> We have given our hearts away, a sordid boon!

Those lines are from a different poem, a famous sonnet, but they expressed much the same idea as does the "Ode," an idea that Wordsworth expressed in other poems, too. When he says it as well as he does in the sonnet, the idea is compelling. We are tempted to say, Yes, that is right, we have; we have given up more than we should. Maybe we did not have to do it, we think. Which is what Wordsworth wanted us to feel.

The famous "Ode to Duty" has the same kind of problems as the "Ode to Immortality":

> Stern Daughter of the Voice of God!
> O Duty! if that name thou love,

So it begins, and we may find ourselves being turned off right away. But do go on, do not stop after the first two lines; keep on to the end. The poem has something important to say to us, who may dislike the word "duty" intensely and think it is used by those in authority to gain our unthinking obedience to their commands. (And so it is.) What Wordsworth is saying is that in an uncertain world, dependence on "the genial sense of youth" and "being to myself a guide" have failed him, as they are likely to fail anyone. Having a clear, unwavering signal that we can follow and obey turns out, in the long run, to be better. Call this "duty" if you will, or call it anything else. Without it, life is likely to turn out to be a mess.

Of Wordsworth's longer poems, "The Prelude," the first part of an autobiographical "epic of Nature" that he worked on throughout his life, is important, beautiful, and fine. "The Prelude," besides containing many moving scenes from his childhood and early youth, invokes the basic Wordsworthian ideas about nature and our never-ending quest for a deep relationship to it. By "Nature" you soon realize that he does not mean just trees and rocks and mountains and clouds, but also that natural element in ourselves, with which we must make peace or suffer great ill.

Later parts of this epic, notably "The Excursion," can be skipped by most readers. Other than the two odes and "The Prelude," there are a dozen or so wonderful sonnets and a dozen other lyrics that are as good as anything of their kind in the English language, maybe in any language. I have listed some of them below.

Read them, think about them for a while, and then read them again. Try to understand them sympathetically, remembering that Wordsworth was not a major thinker and that he lived a long time ago.

You may like those poems so much that you want to dip into the rest of Wordsworth. One way to begin is to obtain a facsimile copy of Lyrical Ballads and read Wordsworth and Coleridge's preface and try to see what all the fuss was about.

Then, perhaps, move on to other things. It is, after all, no bad thing to be a Wordsworthian!

Poems of Wordsworth to read first: "The Prelude," "The Simplon Pass," "Influence of Natural Objects," "Lines composed a few miles above Tintern Abbey," "She Dwelt Among the Untrodden Ways," "I

Traveled Among Unknown Men," "A Slumber Did My Spirit Steal,"
"My Heart Leaps Up," "Composed Upon Westminster Bridge:
September 3, 1802," "It Is a Beauteous Evening, Calm and Free,"
"London 1802," "The Solitary Reaper," "Ode to Duty," "The World
Is Too Much With Us," "To Sleep," "Personal Talk," and "Ode:
Intimations of Immortality from Recollections of Early Childhood."

# SAMUEL TAYLOR COLERIDGE
## 1772–1834
### Selected Poems

The life of Samuel Taylor Coleridge was in almost every way a
disaster. He began to use drugs during his early twenties and he became
an opium addict. He married the wrong woman, whom he despised and
who despised him; but he did not believe in divorce. He was a great
dreamer and projector: he loved projects and with his eloquence and
charm could gain support for them. But most of his projects did not
work out—notably an immense topical encyclopedia, which he
called *Metropolitana*—and he spent much of his last years in bed,
mumbling to himself about philosophy.

He knew a great deal about literature, perhaps more than anyone
in his time. His collection of essays and reviews, *Biographia Literaria*,
which he published when he was forty-five (in 1817), contained, it
has been said, the most significant work of general literary criticism
produced in the English Romantic period.

Unfortunately, the Romantic period was not noted for its criticism
or its thought. It was instead an age of noble feelers, not thinkers:
Wordsworth, Byron, Shelley, Hunt, Southey—none of them had a
really respectable brain in his head.

Coleridge was born in Devon in 1772, the son of a schoolmaster
who sent him to Cambridge. From the age of twenty he managed to
eke out a meager living writing for newspapers and periodicals. He
married in 1795 and immediately regretted doing so, as did his wife.
This year also marked the beginning of that single short, glorious

period in his life when he enjoyed one inspiring friendship and wrote half a dozen poems that are among the best in English.

The friendship, of course, was with the poet William Wordsworth, two years his senior: Coleridge was twenty-three, Wordsworth twenty-five. For the next two or three years they spent every minute together that they could, hatching plans, talking poetry, and producing a joint volume, *Lyrical Ballads* (1798), that had a profound influence on the future course of English poetry, its contents being written, they declared in a preface, in "the language of common day" rather than in the stilted poetic diction of the age just past.

Coleridge wrote "Kubla Khan" in 1797, when he was very much under the sway of his friendship with Wordsworth. He was living at the time in a lonely cottage at Brimstone farm, on the coast of Somerset; he fell asleep, probably drugged, with a copy of *Purchas his Pilgrimes*, an antique travel book, in his hand. A passage he had been reading told of the building of the Great Khan's immense pleasure palace at Xanadu. Coleridge awoke and immediately began to write down two or three hundred lines, as he later said, that he was conscious of having composed in his sleep. But he was interrupted by a certain "person from Porlock" who has never been identified, and so "Kubla Khan" remains unfinished to this day. It is probably the best unfinished poem in the language.

"Christabel" was also begun in 1797; it too is unfinished. It is a ballad—not a true ballad, because all such are anonymous—but as like a true ballad as a self-conscious production of a professional poet can be. It is a fine story, as far as it goes, with the stark, tragic character of the old ballads.

"The Rime of the Ancient Mariner," which opens *Lyrical Ballads*, is not only finished, it is perfect. It is full of "quotations"—the verse is magical—but perhaps the best thing about the poem is Coleridge's restraint in never at any moment saying what it means. He knew well that the old ballads were fine because they simply told their story as directly as possible and let the reader interpret. So with "The Rime of the Ancient Mariner": instead of meanings there are wonderful images.

> It is an ancient Mariner,
> And he stoppeth one of three.
> "By thy long grey beard and glittering eye,
> Now wherefore stopp'st thou me?"
> Water, water, every where,
> And all the boards did shrink;
> Water, water, every where,
> Nor any drop to drink.
> Instead of the cross, the Albatross
> About my neck was hung.
> A sadder and a wiser man,
> He rose the morrow morn.

To have painted those pictures in words makes up for all Coleridge's failures.

# THOMAS JEFFERSON
## 1743–1826
### The Declaration of Independence

Thomas Jefferson was only thirty-two when, in the spring of 1775, he was chosen by the Virginia legislature, sitting as a revolutionary convention in defiance of the royal governor, to be a member of his state's delegation to the Second Continental Congress in Philadelphia. Jefferson's views had appeared rather radical to his more conservative colleagues back home, but in Philadelphia he came in contact with men from all of the colonies whose ideas about independence from Great Britain paralleled and confirmed his own. As events during the winter of 1775–76 hastened toward what he felt was the inevitable rupture, Jefferson worked steadily and successfully behind the scenes to bring about a unified posture toward the parent country. When, in June 1776, a definitive break seemed imminent, he was asked to join a committee already formed of Benjamin Franklin and John Adams to draw up a statement explaining to the world the action should it occur.

Franklin and Adams, although older and politically more experienced, chose Jefferson to produce a draft of a statement, which they would then present—after any necessary changes—to the Continental Congress for approval. In fact, the changes were few, and the *Declaration* was and is largely the work of Jefferson. The Congress approved it, and it was promulgated and signed by the delegates on July 4, the date that is reckoned as the birthday of the United States as a "separate and equal nation."

There are three good reasons to read *The Declaration of Independence*. One is, on the simplest level, patriotic. It behooves all Americans to read the half-dozen founding documents of the republic to which they belong, in order to remind themselves of what it stands for. This would probably be true were the *Declaration* gibberish.

It is not gibberish, of course. Franklin and Adams were right to choose Jefferson as the author of the piece; his talents uniquely qualified him for the task. Not only was he a graceful and elegant writer but he was also well versed in the literature of political thought. The *Declaration* is the work of an author who is both a scholar of his subject and a supreme stylist. The combination makes the document enormously effective.

Thus the second reason to read the *Declaration* is because of what it says not just to Americans but also to everyone who would understand how and why governments are formed among men.

The third reason to read the *Declaration* is that it is very short—only three pages. This makes it easy to practice a kind of reading that we rarely do even when reading poetry, in which we read something over and over, much of it out loud, listening for nuances of meaning, making absolutely sure we understand the meaning before we go on to the next sentence, asking ourselves the three leading questions that good readers always must ask themselves: What does it say? Is what it says true? and What of it? (That is: What are the main or salient points of the argument? Are the conclusions to which they move logically correct, and do you feel that these are true? And what follows from either your agreement or disagreement?)

Indeed, not all of the *Declaration*, even though it is only three pages long, need be read in this intensely analytical manner. More than half of the document consists of a list of "injuries and usurpations" by "the present King of Great Britain," all having, as Jefferson declares, "in direct object, the establishment of an absolute tyranny over these states." Regarding these grievances, which involve matters of fact, you may reserve judgment unless you are yourself a scholar of the Revolutionary Period in American history. Read the list of grievances, assume they are valid, then return to the first page of the *Declaration*. That is the meat of it; everything else depends on it.

The fundamental doctrine of the right of revolution, or at least of secession from a tyrannical overlord, is based on Jefferson's (correct) reading of John Locke's *Essay on Civil Government*. The doctrine, in a nutshell, holds that a people who are now tyrannized by a government that may once have been legitimate have every right to rebel, or at least secede, in order to protect themselves.

Jefferson could have left it at that; but he did not, and to his ambition we owe some of the most trenchant sentences in the history of political writing. "We hold these truths to be self-evident," he wrote. All men are equal; all have natural rights; these include life, liberty, and "the pursuit of happiness"; governments derive their justice from the consent of those who are governed; and when a government ceases to have the consent of the governed it becomes, in the most profound sense, illegitimate. All of this and more is contained in the ringing words of that single first page.

Commentaries many hundreds of pages long have been written about that page and those sharp, memorable sentences. Some day you may wish to read some of the commentators. But do not put off reading the *Declaration* because you have not read anything about what it means. Jefferson wrote it for everyone, and everyone includes you. He wanted to say something that he hoped everyone would understand and agree with. I think he succeeded.

# ABRAHAM LINCOLN
### 1809–1865
*The Gettysburg Address*

Abraham Lincoln was born on February 12, 1809, in a backwoods cabin several miles south of Hodgenville, Kentucky. His mother, described as "stoop-shouldered, thin-breasted, sad"—characteristics that her son inherited—died when the boy was nine. His stepmother, however, was kind to him, sympathizing with his efforts to obtain what small education he received, placing no obstacles in his path even if she could not help him to follow it. He used to walk miles to borrow a book, read it by candlelight, and then walk the same miles back again to return it. Such industry marked all that he did.

He became a lawyer and was soon attracted to politics. His career, of course, is known by everyone: how, after a long series of failures and disappointments, he was nominated by the Republicans for the presidency in the election of 1860, and, in a divided election, was chosen by a minority of the electors. He entered upon his duties as president of the United States in March 1861; three weeks later the Civil War erupted, partly if not wholly because of his enormous unpopularity in the South, where he had been born.

The Civil War was one of the first total wars, waged by both sides with every available resource. The North had more resources, of men and money as well as weapons, and in the end it won. The South had a spirit that for a long time the North could not match, which was why the war lasted four years.

Lincoln, better than anyone, knew what the North needed, which was not only guns but also brave men to fire them, and not just slogans but words full of meaning to inspire the brave men. He sought the brave men and found them, in the persons of Grant, Sherman, Sheridan, Thomas, Sedgwick, and many thousands of lesser-known heroes. He undertook to provide the words himself, and insofar as they served to shape and focus the Union effort, he may be said to have won the war with them. At any rate they were wonderful words, the likes of which no politician has said since, and very few before him.

More than anything else, the words of Lincoln had to do with the legitimacy of the war and with its justice. This question obsessed him, for he knew that he—and millions of his countrymen—could not win the war if they did not think they were in the right. The biggest battle of the war took place at Gettysburg, Pennsylvania, on July 1, 2, and 3, 1863. For the first time, the Army of the Potomac met General Robert E. Lee's Army of Northern Virginia and defeated it. President Lincoln was asked to come down to Gettysburg from Washington by

train on November 18, 1863, to deliver a few remarks at the dedica-
tion of the military cemetery at the site of the battle.

The main speaker of the day, Edward Everett, spoke for two
hours. Afterward Lincoln rose and delivered the few brief immortal
words that, better than any others, define the American idea of
government.

The *Gettysburg Address* deserves to be read as carefully as
Jefferson's *Declaration of Independence* and Madison's *Preamble* to the
Constitution. It refers to those predecessor documents. Four score
and seven years before 1863 takes us to the year 1776, the year when
"our fathers brought forth on this continent a new nation conceived
in liberty and dedicated to the proposition that all men are created
equal." But could any such nation long endure? That was the question. In particular, could the nation survive the kind of brutal fratri-
cidal war now going on? Lincoln thought it could, said it could, and
he persuaded his countrymen that it could.

But they must never, he said, forget what they were fighting for.
They would dedicate a cemetery on this day, and remember the brave
men, living and dead, who had struggled on this bloody ground. But
they must also remember the ideals that had inspired the nation's
fathers. He rededicated himself, and the men and women of his place
and time, to a new birth of freedom, and to the proposition that
governments of the people, by the people, for the people shall not
perish from the earth.

The *Gettysburg Address* is reprinted in many books, but the best
place to read it is standing in the Lincoln Memorial, with the great
brooding figure of Lincoln as sculpted by Daniel Chester French
rising above you.

# chapter nine

# Romantic Spirits

The twenty-six years from 1789 to 1815 saw the violent deaths of millions. Europe was plagued by almost incessant warfare between Britain and her allies and France and hers. Life was difficult, frightening, and, for most people, short. This period of brutal uncertainty produced in many hearts fear that did not subside for decades. These chaotic years brought about many changes, and Europe, at the end of them, was quite different from what it had been before.

Great things happened and great people lived. Three English poets flashed like bright comets across the literary sky. Byron, Shelley, Keats—no matter how you order the three names, they connote youthful genius. A revolution in America was proclaimed, won, and defended. For a while the idea of *un carière œuvre aux talents* (a career open to talent, not just birth) seemed to open opportunities for people in all walks of life. This idea didn't last, but it would resurface in the future. A young Corsican adventurer won an empire, lost it, won it again, and lost it a second time. "Liberty and Equality" was the cry everywhere heard.

The time was short—no more than a human generation—but we can't forget it.

# GOETHE
## 1749–1832
### *Faust*

The statue of Goethe in Lincoln Park in Chicago bears this inscription: "Goethe. The Master Spirit of the German People." German
though he was, Germans alone cannot claim him. Goethe was also
one of the master spirits of mankind.

Johann Wolfgang von Goethe was born in Frankfurt-am-Main in
1749. He lived to be eighty-two, dying in 1832 in Weimar, his
adopted home for more than fifty years. In those years he lived almost
every kind of life, wrote almost every kind of book, and enjoyed
almost every kind of triumph.

Goethe's first truly distinctive publication, the play *Götz von
Berlichingen*, not only was an explosive literary event but also inaugu-
rated an epoch in German cultural history, the Sturm und Drang
(Storm and Stress) period. Two years later, in 1763, he published *The
Sorrows of Young Werther*, his first novel; it made him famous all over
Europe at the age of twenty-four.

If the world approved of him, he did not wholly approve of
himself. His education, he felt, was far from complete, and above all
he still had much to learn about the realities of life. He accepted an
invitation from the Duke of Weimar and went to visit his little
dukedom—and stayed for the rest of his life. He was soon made prime
minister, but he also became chief inspector of mines, superintendent
of irrigation, and supervisor of army uniforms. There was nothing
that the Duke did not see fit to ask Goethe to do, and Goethe
thought he could never refuse the Duke.

With all of his official duties there was time to write lyric poems,
but not major works. In 1786, eleven years after his arrival in
Weimar, he fled the city and all of his posts, disguised as a salesman
en route to Italy, which he thought held the secret of life. But instead
of finding Italy in Italy, he found Greece. He was not wrong; Greece
is in Italy, too. From that time on Goethe turned his back on Sturm
und Drang and all the other excesses of the Romantic period,

insisting that he was a Classical Greek, at least in spirit. Perhaps he was not reckoning with the heart within his breast.

He returned to Weimar, the Duke forgave him, and Goethe lived there as a literary man instead of a politician—with several journeys to Italy and other lands to punctuate the years—for the rest of his long life. He wrote plays, novels, and poems, and studied and experimented in science (his scientific writings alone fill fourteen volumes). He fell in love, over and over—he was always in love with someone, from the time he was fifteen or so until the day he died. Many of his loves were platonic, others were not, but there was never a time when he was not under the influence of some woman, often a pretty, young one.

The story of Faust is very old: the scholar who, bored with his studies and researches, makes a pact with the Devil who, in return for the scholar's immortal soul, will show him "real life" before he dies. It is a good story and true; it is hard to live deeply in both ways of knowing, experience and book learning. Goethe made of the tale both an inspired folk tale and an account, as he saw it, of the essential questing journey of Western man.

*Faust* is divided into two parts, written long years apart. Goethe spent more than sixty years (of course there were long interruptions) on this, his masterpiece. The two parts are very different in form and spirit. The first part of Faust is a more or less realistic drama, if one accepts the possibility of the Devil—Mephistopheles—being a character in the play. Faust is tempted from his high studies and, seeking love, descends into the marketplace, where he meets the young, innocent, and beautiful Margaret (Gretchen). He falls in love with her of course, but she also falls helplessly in love with him, so much so that she is ready and willing to give up everything for him, even her own immortal soul. She is quite serious about that, which Faust realizes he was not—this being one of many things he learns from her and from women. At the end of Part One, Gretchen is both condemned and saved, and Mephistopheles snatches Faust away because he knows the battle that is developing between them is not yet over.

The first part of *Faust* is one of the most beautiful poems in the world. Unfortunately, there is no really fine translation into English.

Perhaps the best way to appreciate it is to see Gounod's opera *Faust*. You will leave the theater shaken, your heart broken.

Part Two of Goethe's *Faust* is, for many people, an enigma. Faust, having survived the tragedy of Margaret's death—and become a better man because of it—now uses the Devil, instead of the other way around. The bargain has taken a subtly different form: if Faust will ever say "Enough!" to life, then his soul will belong to Mephistopheles. Faust never does. His spirit, always seeking, always questing, never rests. The Devil never manages to capture him.

It is hard to describe or summarize this second part, with its journeys through space and time—Faust meets Helen of Troy and woos her, as the supreme example of womanhood in history. He flies to Egypt and America in the arms of Mephistopheles. Better not to try and describe it. *Faust* is better than anything that one can say about it.

# LORD BYRON
## 1788–1824
*Don Juan*
*Selected Poems*

George Gordon, Lord Byron, lived a life so completely Byronic that if it had not actually occurred he would have had to invent it. Which, of course, he almost did. Born in London in 1788, he inherited his title when he was ten, attended Harrow and Cambridge, took his seat in the House of Lords on his twenty-first birthday, and immediately set out for a grand tour. He began *Childe Harold* while in Albania and completed it in Greece six months later. To celebrate, on May 3, 1810, he swam the Hellespont (the narrow waterway between Europe and Asia now known as the Dardanelles). In the Greek myth of Hero and Leander, Leander swims the Hellespont to rescue his beloved, and Byron was not to be outdone by a mythical hero. Crippled since birth, he had suffered from the ridicule of schoolmates; it was like him to show in this way that he was a young man to be reckoned with on a grand scale.

Byron returned to England with the first two cantos of *Childe Harold*. The day after they were published, in 1812, he "awoke to find himself famous." He was lionized by the best society and involved himself in a number of liaisons, all illicit, including one with the wife of the prime minister and another with his half-sister. He married a year later and left England after his wife left him; he claimed that she blackened his reputation, and he never returned to his homeland. He spent most of the rest of his life in Italy, falling in love often (last but not least with the Countess Guiccioli, a woman fully his equal).

In 1823, the Greek War of Independence was just beginning to stir. Byron supported the rebels against their Turkish masters, lent them money, financed a corps of soldiers, and "invaded" Greece himself, dressed as a Homeric warrior. His attempts to bring together all the bickering Greek factions failed; he contracted a fever and died at Missolonghi in 1824, at the age of thirty-six.

"Byronism" is a complex combination of idealism and mockery, stirred together to conceal one's disappointment with the world. The character of Don Juan, with his melancholy view of things, was not Byron, Byron always insisted—but he was. Melancholy was the only possible mood of a man who wanted the world to be better than it is, and who saw how abysmally bad it is, at that. The most honest response was that of Byron's Don Juan—to laugh, bitterly sometimes and other times heartily, but never again to cry.

Byron tried everything, experienced everything, went everywhere, met everyone, enjoyed every kind of success, even suffered several kinds of failure. No fewer than ten thousand copies of one of his books were sold on the day after publication—in an age when there were probably fewer than fifty thousand book readers in England. At the same time, he was exiled from his home, mercilessly harassed by lawyers and moralists, and attacked in the public press and in the private homes of England. The wonder is that he wrote so much magnificent poetry; it might have been enough just to be Byron.

He wrote lyrics, songs, stories, and satires—the last are some of his very best things—as well as dramas and epistles. He could write superbly in any poetic form or manner. But his greatest work was *Don Juan*. It is partly a mock epic, but mainly a vehicle for the expression of opinions, views, and feelings. "I want a hero," the poem begins:

> I want a hero: an uncommon want,
>    When every year and month sends forth a new one,
> Till, after cloying the gazettes with cant,
>    The age discovers he is not the true one;
> Of such as these I should not care to vaunt,
>    I'll therefore take our ancient friend Don Juan—
> We all have seen him, in the pantomime,
> Sent to the Devil somewhat ere his time.

That is perfect Byron, perfect *Don Juan* (and, besides, the stanza teaches the reader how to pronounce the name of his hero—it rhymes with "new one" and "true one"). The author cannot be serious, Byron wants you to believe; there is nothing in this old world worth being serious about. It is all no more than "giggling and making giggle," as he wrote to a friend—except he did not mean it.

Nor should we believe it. *Don Juan*, all four hundred and fifty wonderful pages of it, is serious stuff. But no long poem was ever easier to read, or more fun.

*Don Juan* is Byron's final achievement; he was working on it when he died. Many fine and readable poems preceded it in his canon. One in particular is worth mentioning here. Among Byron's closest friends was the sentimental Irish poet Thomas Moore. He and Byron continued a lively correspondence for years. Many of Byron's letters contained short poems, dashed off on the spur of the moment. He wrote Moore on February 28, 1817, to say that he had been up late too many nights at the Carnival in Venice, and he added these few perfect verses:

> So we'll go no more a-roving
>    So late into the night,
> Though the heart be still as loving,
>    And the moon be still as bright.
>
> For the sword outwears its sheath,
>    And the soul wears out the breast,
> And the heart must pause to breathe,
>    And Love itself have rest.

> *Though the night was made for loving,*
> *And the day returns too soon,*
> *Yet we'll go no more a-roving*
> *By the light of the moon.*

When you passionately desire the world to be what it ought to be, to live up to your dreams, and it never does, finally "the soul wears out the breast." Byron died at thirty-six of a fever, but he also died because he was worn out. He had been disappointed too often.

In reading Byron, be selective. Not all of his large poetical oeuvre retains the freshness that readers once saw in it. Read all of the lyrics that you can find in anthologies; they are likely to be good. Try a canto of *Childe Harold*; it may, however, seem antique and overwrought. But do not fail to read deep into *Don Juan*, especially the first few cantos. What Byron does there no one else has ever done so well.

## PERCY BYSSHE SHELLEY
### 1792–1822
*Selected Poems*

Shelley was born in Sussex, the son of an MP, in 1792. His family intending him for a Parliamentary career, he was educated at Eton and Oxford, but he disliked both and was mocked by his fellow students. He continuously challenged all authority and was finally expelled because of a pamphlet titled "The Necessity of Atheism." He didn't care; he wanted out anyway.

He quarreled with his father, and just to show him eloped to Scotland with a sixteen-year-old. They were married, despite the fact that he disapproved of matrimony—as well as royalty, religion, and meat-eating. Before long he was sharing young Harriet with a friend and trying to establish some sort of commune. Not long afterward Harriet drowned herself, but by that time he had formed a relationship with Mary Godwin. They had a son, William, and lived in Geneva with Byron, talking about poetry and life and so forth.

Shelley had very little money and large debts, so he and Mary decamped to Italy intending to live permanently abroad. She kept at, and finished, a novel she had been working on: *Frankenstein*, which became one of the all-time bestsellers, though, not surprisingly, she gained almost nothing from its fame. Shelley was just now beginning to write well; the first flowering was the poem "Ozymandias." It is in every anthology of English poetry, and if you haven't read it in high school, you ought to read it now. There are a couple of tricks in it, so beware. Shelley also wrote a "Greek" play called "Prometheus," which is very fine. It did not make up for the fact that his little son died and Mary had a nervous breakdown.

Shelley, well aware of the stir he and Byron were making, took every advantage of his fame/notoriety. "Ode to the West Wind" was much admired—appropriately—as was "To a Skylark" and his famous "Defense of Poetry," in which he declared that "poets are the unacknowledged legislators of the world." It was a clarion call as well as a backward-looking challenge to Pope and his couplets. In the spring of 1821, news came of Keats's death, and Shelley rushed to Rome to see what he could do. Apparently Keats had wanted a stone over his grave in the English Cemetery at Rome with no name and the simple inscription: "Here lies one whose name was writ in water." Shelley arranged for this, shaking his head and weeping at the same time. To die so young!

Only a year later his time came, in April 1822, when a small schooner he was sailing across a bay was struck by a sudden squall and sank immediately, its wet sails dragging it beneath the water. He was thirty years old, a little older than Keats, yes, but just a little younger than Byron. He had been called "mad Shelley" at school, and he was always partly that—but also a very fine, but perhaps not great, poet.

# JOHN KEATS
## 1795–1821
### *Selected Poems*

Unlike Shelley and Byron, Keats was the son of a commoner, his father being the manager of a livery stable near London. His father died when he was eight, his mother when he was fourteen. There was very little money, and he was to a large extent self-educated, reading poetry from childhood and trying to write it in his early teens. When he was twenty he signed on as a student at Guy's Hospital and the next year was licensed as an apothecary. In that year—1815—he met Leigh Hunt, who published a couple of poems in *The Examiner*, and followed them by "On First Looking into Chapman's Homer," which showed promise. Other poems followed but they were savagely attacked by critics who called him a member of the so-called Cockney school. Keats was hurt but he was able to say to his brother George: "I think I shall be among the English poets after my death."

In 1816, he buried his beloved brother Tom and met Fanny Brawne, with whom he fell in love. The feelings were reciprocated. They probably planned to marry, although events intervened. During the summer of 1818 he suffered from recurrent sore throats; these frightened him because Tom, like their mother, had died of consumption and he feared for the worst. Nevertheless, the winter and spring of that year are known as "the Great Year," and they are indeed a manifestation of a greater genius than any other poet of his age could show. Or perhaps of any age.

It began in November when, in just a few months, he wrote, consecutively, "The Eve of St. Agnes," "Ode to Psyche," "La Belle Dame sans Merci," "Ode to a Nightingale," "Ode on a Grecian Urn," "Ode on Melancholy," "Ode on Indolence," the second version of "Hyperion," and "To Autumn." Is it unbelievable? Yes, it is unbelievable.

There is a story about the writing of almost all of these great poems, but the one about "Nightingale" is my favorite. It was spring, the weather was soft and warm, and Keats was lying in a hammock underneath a tree. His friend Charles Brown saw that he had a piece of paper and a pen with which he seemed to be writing, not continuously but from time to time. A nightingale was singing—Brown could hear it. Keats lay in the hammock for no more than two hours and then rose and came into the house. He had a few sheets of paper in his hand that he folded and placed in the cover of a book, which he returned to the shelf.

"Were you writing something?" Brown asked. Keats nodded. The poem is of course the "Ode to a Nightingale." Probably there is no greater lyric poem in English.

In the fall of that year Keats was very ill. Shelley wrote and asked him to come to Italy, where, he said, the climate would be better for him than that of a London winter. He arrived in Rome in December 1820 and died of consumption the following February. He was twenty-five. He and his friend Severn lived in a small house on the Piazza di Spagne that is now a museum. You can go there and see the narrow room in which he died. There is a window overlooking that famous piazza, so full of life and gaiety.

# JANE AUSTEN
## 1775–1817
*Pride and Prejudice*
*Emma*
*Persuasion*

Jane Austen was born in 1775 in a Hampshire village, the daughter of an English small-town rector. She lived an uneventful life and never married, devoting herself instead—in return for a house given to her and her sister by their married brother—to her many nieces and nephews, all of whom, it is said, adored their aunt Jane. She was a true amateur; she wrote for the pleasure of it. But she was also a very great writer, so this hobby of hers ended up taking over much of her life.

She began to write as a child and kept at it until her untimely death, at forty, of a wasting disease that has not been certainly identified. She did not publish anything until 1811, when she was thirty-five, and then she published anonymously; few outside of her immediate family knew she was the author of *Pride and Prejudice*, *Emma*, *Persuasion*, and her other books. One who did know—the Prince Regent, later George IV—liked her works so much that he possessed a set of them in each of his residences, and after a "discrete royal command" *Emma* was "respectfully dedicated" to him by the author. Jane Austen was, however, "this nameless author" to Sir Walter Scott when, in the *Quarterly Review* for March 1816, he praised this "masterful exponent of the modern novel," who was pleased by the review but coolly noted that he had not mentioned *Mansfield Park* in it.

*Pride and Prejudice* was her first novel; she wrote a version of it before she was twenty. She put it aside to write *Sense and Sensibility*, her first work to be published; she then rewrote *Pride and Prejudice* and published it in 1813.

It is magically interesting, astonishingly adult. Elizabeth Bennett, its heroine—no doubt there is a lot of Jane Austen in Elizabeth—is as intelligent as she is beautiful, and as articulate as she is wise about the ways of the world. Nevertheless she makes one enormous, nearly disastrous mistake. She is too proud to accept the advances of Mr. Darcy, partly because he is a step or two above her on the English social ladder, but mainly because he insults her when he first meets them.

Elizabeth is the daughter of a gentleman, but of very modest means. Mr. Darcy is a member of a great family, very rich, with a stately home in the country and a handsome house in town. Elizabeth believes with good reason that Mr. Darcy is prejudiced against her family—particularly against her foolish mother and even more foolish younger sister—and she naturally believes him to be proud, because she is so herself. As it turns out, she is wrong on both counts, but as a result they almost fail to find each other in this most bewitching of genteel love stories.

Mr. Bennett is as intelligent as his wife is silly, and he adores his second-eldest daughter because she is so much like him. Their conversations as they come to understand each other are moving. Elizabeth begins to realize that her father has the highest respect for her: that is, he will not try to stop her from making her own mistakes. Elizabeth is strenuously pursued by a cousin, a clergyman named Collins, and is surprised to find that her father does not seem to want to protect her from his attentions. She must find the strength to do this herself, she finally realizes; she must have the wit to recognize that Mr. Collins is an idiot and the strength to refuse him, even if this means she might never marry. In his cool but loving way Mr. Bennett congratulates Elizabeth on her decision. But harder decisions are still to come. Naturally, they involve Mr. Darcy, a very different proposition from Mr. Collins. Jane Austen ties the young lovers up in knots and then neatly unwinds the plot.

*Emma*, Jane Austen's fourth novel and in the opinion of many her best, was published in 1816. Emma Woodhouse, the heroine, is also like Jane Austen—another side of her indeed, but still the same intelligent, interesting, proud girl-woman. Like Elizabeth, Emma also makes serious mistakes, both in her own life and in her meddling in the lives of others. She is incredibly wrong in her judgments about those nearest and dearest to her, most especially about Mr. Knightley, a kindly neighbor whom she believes she only admires but could never, ever love. Her discovery that she has been as foolish about Mr. Knightley as she assumes that he has been about her makes for a touching denouement.

But *Emma* is both more and less than a mere love story. At bottom it is the story of the growing up of a brilliant, wonderful, proud girl, "handsome, clever, and rich," as Jane Austen writes, who—like Elizabeth Bennett—must learn her lessons the hard way. There is no one to say her nay; she must learn to say it to herself. This is one of the hardest lessons anyone ever learns.

Her last novel, *Persuasion*, was written shortly before she died and published posthumously. Again it is a love story with a missing link that must be found. Anne Eliot, the daughter of a gentleman, falls in love with Frederick Wentworth, a naval officer with apparently few prospects. Anne does not care, but her good friend, Lady Russell, persuades her to break off the engagement because she believes Wentworth will be a poor man. Anne does so, although it also breaks her heart, and she remains unmarried for a number of years.

By coincidence, Captain Wentworth, who has had a successful naval career and is now well off, returns to the neighborhood. He is still angry at Lady Russell and Anne, and he pays no attention to Anne when he meets her again, although he realizes he still cares for her. She is timid and unable to reveal her own feelings, which have never changed. The scene in which the two find one another again is one of the most moving in fiction, I think. There are tears in my eyes as I write these words.

For many years Austen's reputation suffered—perhaps it suffers still—from a belief that she was "merely" a miniaturist, a "domestic novelist," as she termed herself. But any novelist, as Henry James always insisted, must be allowed his or her *donnée* (or set of assumptions about time, place, characters, etc.); the question, then, is whether what the novelist does with that *donnée* is grand or foolish, distinctive or ordinary. The *donnée* of *Pride and Prejudice*, *Emma*, and *Persuasion* are circumscribed, but the art and the analytical precision with which Austen examines her small world are unsurpassed. She is a searching critic of the social and especially the economic culture in which she moved and which she may have known better than anybody in her time. And she is also a great storyteller.

# HONORÉ DE BALZAC
1799–1850
*Old Goriot*

The word "pure" is employed by sports writers to denote a special, almost unique, talent. A "pure" hitter, in baseball, is one who needs no coaching to hit well, who would rather hit than eat, who hits with grace at the same time that he hits hard. Babe Ruth was such a hitter, and Ted Williams, too. Pure tennis players, skiers, and runners are similarly blessed in their own way.

Honoré de Balzac was a pure writer. Born in France in 1799, he devoted his first twenty years to a misguided obedience to his father's wish that he become a lawyer. Finally he gave that up, retired with the pittance that his father allowed him to a Paris garret, and proceeded to learn to write. He wrote steadily, furiously. In ten years he may have written twenty novels. But he later disavowed these early offspring of his genius and only began to regard his productions as worthy of him with *The Chouans*, published in 1829 when he was thirty. Thereafter he wrote two, three, or even four books a year until he died—or rather until he exhausted himself and then died.

His manner of working was notorious, even infamous. He dined at five or six in the afternoon, often took a woman to bed, slept for a few hours, until eleven or twelve at night, arose, told the woman to leave him, and set to work. He worked all night and much of the next day, often sitting at his desk for as many as sixteen hours at a stretch, fortified by extremely strong coffee, which he drank continuously. He might finish his day's work at four o'clock, bathe, take a short stroll through the boulevards of Paris, dine, sleep, make love, and work again.

He could write a novel in a few days, but the manuscript that he sent to the printer was never what was finally published. He left standing orders with the printer that the original text should be set on large sheets of paper, with much space between the lines and with wide margins. On the first proof he often doubled or trebled the length of the original book; he could add as many as one hundred pages to the second proof. This was an expensive way to work, but Balzac didn't care; all he cared about was writing, not the printer and his problems!

Balzac soon arrived at the notion that what he wanted to write was not just a single novel, or even a few scattered dramas, as he termed them, but instead a whole account of human life, *La Comédie Humaine*, as it came to be called. The French word *comédie* does not mean the same thing as "comedy" in English, where the word connotes something funny. *Comédie* is closer to "drama." The English translation *The Human Comedy* carries some of the meaning of the French phrase. Ask yourself what it means. Does it not suggest some sort of totality, a picture drawn on a very broad canvas, showing men and women and children in all the activities of ordinary life, acting and suffering, living and dying, creating and destroying, succeeding and failing? That is the great picture that Balzac's *The Human Comedy* attempts to draw. Perhaps no one has ever done it better.

The standard French edition of *La Comédiel Humaine* fills some ninety volumes, arranged according to a scheme that Balzac left to his literary executors to complete. The standard English edition, edited by George Saintsbury, is in forty volumes, arranged like the French edition according to certain large divisions: Scenes of Private Life, Scenes of Provincial Life, Scenes of Paris Life. The best known of the Scenes of Paris Life is *Old Goriot* (*Le Père Goriot*). *Old Goriot* is a good introduction to Balzac, as critics and readers have discovered; as a result the novel is available in several editions.

Much of the action of *Old Goriot* takes place in a cheap and somber boardinghouse on the Left Bank of Paris, an area that is now chic, but was then (around 1820) a slum. There are six or seven main characters: Madame Vauquer, the greedy landlord; Vautrin, the brilliant, sardonic criminal; the young man from the country, Eugène de Rastignac, and his beautiful, wealthy cousin, Madame de Beauséant; and Old Goriot himself and his two socialite daughters, Mesdames de Restaud and de Nucingen. Rastignac and Goriot are more important than anyone else.

Goriot, a retired businessman, is slowly ruined in the course of the book by his folly and the venality and greed of his two daughters, whom he adores. Rastignac rises as Goriot falls, like two figures on a seesaw in a distant playground. The story of Goriot's fall is heartbreaking; it has brought tears to many a reader's eyes. The rise of Rastignac is thrilling and will make your heart beat faster. The novel's very last scene is consequently famous:

> He [Rastignac]went a few paces further, to the highest point of the cemetery, and looked out over Paris and the windings of the Seine; the lamps were beginning to shine on either side of the river. His eyes turned almost eagerly to the space between the column of the Place Vendôme and the cupola of the Invalides; there lay the shining world that he had wished to reach. He glanced over that humming hive, seeming to draw a foretaste of its honey, and said magniloquently:
>
> "Henceforth there is war between us."
>
> And by way of throwing down the glove to Society, Rastignac went to dine with Mme. de Nucingen.

I don't think any reader has ever failed to be believe that Eugène de Rastignac would succeed in his war.

Paris and London were the two great nineteenth-century cities. London found its biographer in Charles Dickens; because of him we may think we know the London of his day even better than we know our own city. Paris was as large, as powerful, as complex, and as full of misery (and triumph) as London—and its biographer is Honoré de Balzac.

The London that Dickens knew, and that he reveals to us in his novels, was by no means all of London. The life of the upper class was not really understood by Dickens, and never described by him with much truth or sympathy. Balzac knew better than Dickens all of the grades and levels of existence in his city: the aristocracy, the beau monde, the demimonde, and the dregs of life and society. And Balzac knew how all the levels of city life touched and affected one another. His account of the lower reaches of Paris life is not as rich or moving as Dickens's account of the comparable London realms, but Dickens does not move his characters up and down the social ladder as does Balzac.

These differences are not in the end so important. What the two writers share is a vast sympathy for human nature, especially human foibles, and a love for the energy and variety of city life in their time. In fact, "energy" is the word that aptly characterizes both of them as writers. The pace of Balzac is especially swift; it carries you onward like a mountain torrent.

# STENDHAL
## 1783–1842
### The Red and the Black
### The Charterhouse of Parma

Marie-Henri Beyle was born in Grenoble in 1783, the son of prosperous bourgeois parents. His father was a strict disciplinarian, and young Beyle took an extreme dislike to him. He adored the memory of his mother, who had died when he was seven; he thought she would have been sympathetic to his ideas about art and life. Beyle ran away from home—or left it on a pretext at seventeen and went to Paris, whose attractions for those who live in their imaginations were as great then as they are now (or were two generations ago, when I lived there). But Paris turned out to be disappointing to this young dreamer, so he crossed the Alps to join Napoleon's army in Italy, arriving on June 15, 1800, the day after the Battle of Marengo, one of Bonaparte's greatest victories over the Austrians.

Milan, under the impact of the republican, liberal ideas unleashed by Napoleon, proved to be everything that Paris had not been for Henri Beyle. He fell in love, he delighted in the musical performances at La Scala, he studied Italian, fencing, and horseback riding. He also began to write, although his first book was not published until 1814. He adopted a pseudonym, the first of some 170 used during his career. The most famous of the pseudonyms, and the only one that is remembered, was first employed in 1817: M. de Stendhal.

It has become almost a cliché of psychology, especially of psychoanalysis, that the highest art is a kind of transfer of more basic emotions to a loftier plane—"sublimation," as Freud called it. Thus art, Freud said, can be therapeutic; it can release feelings that otherwise might destroy the artist and that tend to hurt men and women who are unable to sublimate through art. Whether or not the theory is true in general, it seems to have been true of Henri Beyle, who, as Stendhal, lived in his own imagination a richer and more interesting life than he ever did as his real self.

Stendhal authored two novels that may be the best ever written in French. The first, *The Red and the Black*, published in 1830, is the story of Julien Sorel, the son of a peasant in southeastern France who struggles valiantly to breach the ramparts of wealth and privilege in his time. Julien is a genius, and the war he wages against society is not an unequal one, but, although he achieves signal triumphs, in the end he is defeated by his enemies, who are everywhere.

Julien's hero is Bonaparte, an admiration that he must keep secret in the cold, gray years of the post-Napoleonic binge. He is sure that if he had been born a generation earlier, during a time when careers were open to talent and not just to influence and wealth, he would have risen quickly and might even have been one of the emperor's marshals at the age of thirty. That opportunity is now closed to him; he cannot choose the red of a military career; but the black of a career in the church still beckons, and Julien adopts a mask of humility, scholarship, and virtue.

But he cannot hide the fire in his brilliant eyes, through which his genius shines. Most of the men he meets, and all of the churchmen, are suspicious of him, but at the same time he finds that he is greatly attractive to women. Two women in particular figure in his startling progress toward wealth and power, and they end up destroying him. Mme. de Rênal, the wife of his first employer, is a simple but beautiful woman, ten years older than he, and the mother of three boys whom he has been hired to tutor. Julien feels it his Napoleonic duty to seduce her, and he does so rather easily—much to his surprise. Their intrigue discovered, he is forced to flee to Paris, where he is offered an important post in the household of the Marquis de la Mole, a powerful political figure. Julien and Mathilde, the spirited daughter of la Mole, fall in love. They struggle for dominance in this love, for they are both proud. Mathilde becomes pregnant, and although for a short time it appears that all will turn out well, a letter from Mme. de Rênal, turns out to be disastrous, and Julien fails utterly. The ending of this remarkable book is shocking. Reading it is an overwhelming experience.

Neither Julien nor Mathilde fits into the dry bourgeois world into which they were born. Mathilde, in her imagination, harks back to the sixteenth century, to the great age, as she conceives it, of her family's history. Julien's time is not yet; he should have been born in 1910, not 1810, and in America, not France. Their tragedy is that, despite their energy, imagination, and courage, they cannot change their world.

*The Charterhouse of Parma* was written in a period of fifty-two days at the end of 1838, only a couple of years before Stendhal's death. The book reads as swiftly as it was written; I do not know of any novel that is more rapid in its style, that rushes with such impetuous speed to its conclusion. (In a sense, it was not concluded; Stendhal wanted to write three hundred more pages, but his publisher resisted. Nevertheless, the ending is right and satisfying.)

The three main characters of *The Charterhouse of Parma* are a fascinating modification of those of *The Red and the Black*. Fabrizio del Dongo corresponds to Julien Sorel, but he is no son of a peasant. Instead, he is the illegitimate son of the wife of the Marchese del Dongo, one of the richest men in Italy and also one of the most cowardly and cruel. Fabrizio's real father was a French officer stationed in Parma during the French occupation. He is thus an aristocrat as well as a rebel; he is also, like Julien, a genius struggling to adapt his time to him, instead of himself to his time. He is one of the most attractive heroes in fiction: brave, impetuous, charming, and irresistible to women.

Mathilde, in *The Red and the Black*, the proud aristocrat who represents all that is good in the French upper classes, is a paragon of dignity and hauteur; but she is only nineteen. In *Charterhouse*, her qualities are transferred by Stendhal to Fabrizio's aunt, the Duchessa Sanseverina; equally beautiful, she is older than Mathilde and thus even more alluring. I confess that Gina di Sanseverina is one of my favorite heroines; perhaps only Shakespeare's Rosalind and Tolstoy's Natasha can compare to her. As intelligent as she is proud, she demands nothing from her lovers except that they set their goals by the same high stars that direct and rule her life.

Fabrizio has many adventures; among them, he witnesses (this is the *mot juste*) the Battle of Waterloo, although he is only fifteen. The description of the battle is masterly; Tolstoy said he had learned about war from Stendhal. Fabrizio naturally comes in conflict with the austere, conservative authorities of post-Napoleonic Italy. He is imprisoned and falls in love with the daughter of his jailer. Clelia is a younger Mme. de Rênal and plays somewhat the same role; that is, while being attractive and beautiful, she is also motherly.

Stendhal set the action of the book in Parma perhaps because Parma was longer under French influence than any other northern Italian city; in other words, like Fabrizio, it was a French-Italian hybrid, enjoying the advantages of both national characters as well as suffering both sets of faults. At any rate, the government of Parma is despotic, and all of the characters must struggle to find their own freedom in the midst of tyranny. This is only one of the extraordinary modern touches of this book, and of Stendhal's work in general. He once said that he had bought a ticket in a lottery, the first prize in which was to be read in 1935—that is, a century hence. He was a good prophet. His books, especially *The Red and the Black* and *The Charterhouse of Parma*, are more read and admired in our century than in his own. Together, they are not only great stories but also a vivid commentary on our time, as well as his.

# ALEXANDER HAMILTON
## 1757–1804

# JAMES MADISON
## 1751–1836

# JOHN JAY
## 1745–1829
### *The Federalist Papers*

With the winning of the War of Independence, America became a nation—but still a fragile one, a loose confederation of sovereign states that might break apart, or so it seemed, at any moment. At the Constitutional Convention at Philadelphia in 1787 a new Constitution was written and adopted, but it required that two-thirds of the thirteen state legislatures ratify it. Everyone knew this would not be easy, for there was opposition to the new basic law from many quarters.

The proposed new Constitution lacked a Bill of Rights. This troubled many persons, especially in Virginia. It also established a unity of individual citizens rather than of sovereign states and this fact—which limited the powers of the states—troubled many others, especially in New York. But New York and Virginia were the two richest and most powerful of the thirteen states. If they did not ratify the new Constitution, it mattered little if nine other small states like Rhode Island and Delaware and Connecticut should do so.

Probably the greatest difficulties were faced by the New York Federalists. Out of the relatively large delegation from that state, only one delegate—Alexander Hamilton—had signed the Constitution when it was presented to the nation by the convention. Governor DeWitt Clinton and, very likely, a majority of the state's legislators were opposed to the document. It would take a major effort by the Constitution's backers to turn the situation around.

The effort was made, and the situation *was* turned around, by means of a series of essays that began to be published in all the newspapers in New York State and were gathered together in book form even before the series was completed. The papers were all signed "Publius," but in fact they were written by three men: Alexander Hamilton, James Madison, and John Jay.

In their totality, *The Federalist Papers* are one of the most searching commentaries on the U.S. Constitution. The three authors began by taking the high ground—the ground of the epochal importance of the decision for or against the Constitution. Hamilton's words in the first *Federalist* are moving and beautiful:

> It has been frequently remarked that it seems to have been reserved to the people of this country, by their conduct and example, to decide the important question, whether societies of men are really capable or not of establishing good government from reflection and choice, or whether they are forever destined to depend for their political constitutions on accident and force. If there be any truth in the remark, the crisis at which we are arrived may with propriety be regarded as the era in which that decision is to be made; and a wrong election of the part we shall act may, in this view, deserve to be considered as the general misfortune of mankind.

The *Papers* go on in elegant, flowing, eighteenth-century style; they are a pleasure to read even if one were to disagree with them. But it would be hard to disagree. Hamilton, Madison, and Jay managed to define, as well as it has ever been defined, the American constitutional idea.

Of all the perils that beset, or seemed to the Federalists to beset, the new nation, that of faction (or, as we would say, party spirit or party strife) was the worst. The Founding Fathers knew well the turmoil that the spirit of party had produced not just in European nations during modern times, but also in Greece and Rome of old. They conceived the Constitution as a bulwark against faction, and indeed the Ninth and Tenth *Federalist*—especially the Tenth, by Madison—are among the most eloquent of all these papers in support of the Constitution. In fact, however, the Constitution provides no machinery with which to form a government, and it soon became evident that political parties would have to be formed, and then depended on, to provide candidates to fill the offices that the Constitution defined. Despite the eloquence of their plea for a nonfactional organization of the political infrastructure, party strife did have the effect, in the years following the establishment of the new government in 1789, of dividing the authors of *The Federalist Papers*. Hamilton and Madison, unfortunately, became political enemies, while John Jay abjured them both.

For a while, however, the three worked together to produce one of the small number of political books, and one of that very small list of works of any kind, that every American citizen ought to read.

# GEORG WILHELM FRIEDRICH HEGEL
## 1770–1831
### *The Philosophy of History*

Reading Hegel, even just thinking about Hegel, leads one to propose grand, sweeping generalizations. Here are two.

The first I take from Henry Adams, who once observed pointedly that the "centuries" of history in the West have for a long time not truly begun at the years 1600, 1700, or 1800, but at a point approximately fifteen years after. Thus we should view European history as manifesting epochal changes in 1415 (the Battle of Agincourt), in 1515 (the meeting of Francis I, Charles V, and Henry VIII on the so-called Field of the Cloth of Gold), in the mid-teens of the seventeenth century (the murder of Henry IV, the accession of Louis XIII, and the rise of Richelieu), in 1715 (the death of the Sun King, Louis XIV), in 1815 (the Battle of Waterloo), and in 1914 (the beginning of World War I). It is a neat theory and fun to advance at a dinner party.

The second generalization is that, in the history of ideas, it is as important to ask where ideas come from as what they are and what they mean. Taking the above chronology as definitive, then, we can suggest that the important ideas of the sixteenth century (i.e., from 1515 to 1615) came from Italians; those of the seventeenth century

(1615–1715) from Frenchmen; those of the eighteenth century (1715–1815) from Englishmen; and those of the nineteenth century, beginning with the Restoration of the European status quo after the final defeat of Napoleon and ending with the onset of the so-called Great War in 1914, from Germans. The nineteenth century is the German century par excellence.

It is thus not an accident that the high point of Hegel's career and fame was attained in the year 1818, when he began to teach at the University of Berlin. Born in 1770, he was now forty-eight; but it had required that Napoleon be finally defeated and that the torch be handed from that world-historical figure to a succession of Germans for Hegel's ideas to become widely recognized. For the next half century or so he was probably the world's most famous and influential philosopher.

To remember that is also to be reminded of just how mixed up the nineteenth century was, in its thinking if not in its practical science and its industry. Hegel is essentially a crazy philosopher. It was a splendid craziness, however, and he will probably always have the ability to attract people's minds and their loyalty.

Hegel's basic philosophical method was to metaphysicize everything; that is, to detect in concrete reality the working of an Idea, of a Universal Mind. He was convinced that the world is rational and therefore intelligible to the human mind, which is also rational. But how to explain all the strange and unpredictable things that happen, and have happened since men first began to wonder if the world could be understood? Hegel realized that the larger the field of view, the grander the visionary sweep, the more likely it would be that a grand and sweeping generalization would apply. All change, all progress, he said, is produced by the conflict of great forces. A world-historical figure, nation, or event poses, as it were, a challenge, or thesis; this is naturally opposed by an antithesis; and the conflict is resolved, inevitably, on a higher plane, by a synthesis of the two forces. It is true enough that we sometimes see something like this happening in our own lives, and perhaps also in history. It does not seem necessary to conclude, however—as Hegel does—that this is the way the world absolutely and universally and inevitably works. But I do not want to cavil. It is a wonderful, ingenious, interesting theory. Maybe it is even correct.

One of the ideas that swept through men's minds in the nineteenth century was that of the universality of Progress, which meant that history is moving, in general if not at every instant, always in the same direction, and one that is highly pleasing to mankind. Others besides Hegel had advanced this idea, which Hegel assumed without any question. His effort, in *The Philosophy of History*, was to reveal the manner of universal progress, not to prove that it occurred. His effort succeeded, in that he wrote a fascinating book. There are four great epochs of the world, which are at the same time phases of thought: he called them the Oriental world, the Greek world, the Roman world, and the German world. General progress is in the direction of consciousness of self, and of freedom; the ancient Oriental peoples, and the Greeks and Romans, had been only partly free; freedom had come into its own with the advent of Christianity, and had become dominant in the postmedieval world—the German world, as Hegel called it.

It is important to understand that freedom for Hegel is not the ordinary freedom that we mean when we say, for example, that we are not free if we are in prison. For Hegel, freedom consists in a willing compliance with the working in the world of the Idea, and as such freedom can sometimes entail woe to individuals. It is up to individuals, in fact, to join the fated march of the universal mind, which meant, in his time, he said, joining the nation as a wholly willing participant in its most fundamental, world-historical aims and goals. Freedom is only to be obtained, Hegel seems to say, in giving up one's individual freedom for the sake of a joint or communal freedom, shared with other men and women who are advancing toward the same desired end.

It is easy to see how this concept was adopted by Karl Marx and made concrete by both the Nazis and the Communists in the twentieth century. Perhaps that is not Hegel's fault; is a man responsible for the things that other people do with his ideas, and in his name?

Speaking of the twentieth century, let us continue our world-historical game. Someday, ages and ages hence, historians will look back on our time and say that while the nineteenth century was the German century, the twentieth century was—what? The American century? The Russian? It is a good question.

And what about the twenty-first? Will we have to wait till 2015 to decide? Or perhaps 2115?

# chapter ten

# Critics and Seers

As though obedient to Hegel's metaphysical views, the Napoleonic wars finally ended in 1815, and for a time people began to hope that the years of warfare—an entire generation's worth, from 1789 to 1815—would somehow or other teach the world about the folly of war, about its inability to solve any problems or answer any questions. They were wrong, but no one could see this at the time, as they couldn't see it a hundred years later, in 1915, or in two hundred—that is, today. Or am I wrong? Have we learned the lesson yet?

Nevertheless, as Europe entered the nineteenth century, there was hope, excitement, a sense of newness. In science, for example, although as usual there were many who didn't want to accept what scientists like Darwin were beginning to learn. In politics, economics, social arrangements, although, again, the new ideas promulgated by men like Marx and J.S. Mill tended to be accepted only by the few, whereas the many were uncomfortable with the changes that were foreseen. There were vocal critics, too, in prose as well as verse, although the verse sometimes sounded like prose and vice versa. And there were novelists like Dickens, great storytellers who were also—intentionally—social critics. This self-consciousness in art was also new.

Finally, two very great poets came on the American scene and responded to the first total war in very different ways and words. They knew the conflict threatened to tear America asunder despite the thrilling words of the man who, more than anyone, wanted to keep it whole. They were poets who also knew that even in peace there is always the threat and, in a way, the promise of death. This is what poets have always known. Do we love them for that? I don't know, but we need them all the same.

# CLAUDE BERNARD
## 1813–1878
### Introduction to the Study of Experimental Medicine

The life of Claude Bernard was happy. Born in 1813, a poor, shy child, he was able to acquire only a minimal education. Apprenticed to an apothecary, he offended him by spending his free time writing plays. He managed to enter medical school but was far from the best student. However, much to their credit, two eminent French medical scientists recognized the genius of the gruff, ill-tempered young man and furthered his career. By the end of his life Bernard was one of the two most famous scientists in France—the other was Pasteur—and he received the first state funeral ever accorded a French scientist.

A redoubtable experimenter, he made important discoveries concerning the role of the pancreas in digestion, the function of the liver, and the regulation of the blood supply by the vasomotor nerves. (He ended up suffering, and dying, from illnesses involving all these organs.) His claim to literary fame was a short book he wrote when he was fifty.

The book was intended to be a major treatise on experimental medicine, but Bernard never wrote much more than the introduction to this work. That does not matter; the *Introduction to the Study of Experimental Medicine* is brilliant and interesting. More, in this case, might have turned out to be less.

Research in medicine up to about the sixteenth century had been guided by an understanding of Aristotle's methods that was perhaps mistaken. Experiments, so-called, were confirmatory only; the real work of the experimenter was supposed to be done in his head, in the logical search for principles from which conclusions could then be deduced. This was the so-called deductive method, and it led nowhere.

The scientific revolution of the sixteenth and seventeenth centuries reversed the procedure. The experimenter must, it was said, have no preconceived notions. He must merely observe nature and from his observations form conclusions about principles. This was the so-called inductive method, and by itself it too led nowhere.

Claude Bernard was the first philosopher of science to recognize that the most effective experimental method of research involves a combination of the two procedures—a combination so subtle and so complex that we are still trying to understand it more than a century later. The experimenter, Bernard said, must have some notion in his head of what he is looking for. But he must also be able to observe freely, unprejudiced by his prior assumptions. He must be prepared to change his mind if necessary and ready, too, to discard all of his hard-won principles if the facts controvert them.

This method is discussed with great clarity in the *Introduction to the Study of Experimental Medicine*. But the book, despite its small size—only eighty or so pages—also makes other important points, involving the intricate relations between physiology, the study of living organisms, on the one hand, and the sciences of physics and chemistry, the study of inert substances, on the other. This relationship, too, has been the subject of intense study and speculation since Bernard's death in Paris in 1878.

The most interesting part of Bernard's *Introduction* deals with what he called the *milieu interieur*, for which the phrase "internal environment" is a poor translation. The living organism, Bernard recognized, lives as it were in two different worlds. There is the outside world, the environment per se, which the entire organism confronts and attempts to deal with and control. But there is also an inner world, invisible to the eye, of which the organism itself is often largely unaware. This world is an enormously complicated system of physical, chemical, and biochemical interrelationships, among organs and parts of organs that together make up a whole living thing. The continued peaceful operations of this interior system are essential to the life of a living being; in fact, they almost *are* its life. Bernard was the first to see this, and again we have been struggling for more than a century to further his ideas and insights.

The *Introduction to the Study of Experimental Medicine* is not at all hard to read; no scientist ever possessed a more lucid style than Claude Bernard and his ideas, as I have pointed out, are strikingly modern. But he will always be, or seem to be, "modern" because he got at some very fundamental truths about life and about medicine. And truth is always modern.

# CHARLES DARWIN
## 1809–1882
### *On the Origin of Species by Means of Natural Selection*

Five out of ten college students, queried about the title of Darwin's book, respond, "*The Origin of the Species.*" The implication, apparently, is that Darwin wrote the book about man and his long evolution from the lower animals. Darwin did, it is true, write such a book: it is titled *The Descent of Man*. It is a fine, but not a famous, book. His very famous book, *On the Origin of Species by Means of Natural Selection*, dealt with "that mystery of mysteries," as Darwin called it in his Introduction.

Why was the origin of species such a mystery? Two hundred years ago many of the enlightened, and almost all of the unenlightened, believed that the Biblical account of Creation was strictly true, that God had made the world and all the things in it in six days, then rested on the seventh. In principle there is nothing impossible about this: God could have done it if He had wanted. In practice there were many problems. The geological record was confusing, but it seemed to suggest that the Earth was much older, and had been subjected to much more far-reaching modification, than the Biblical account appeared to allow for. Living things, furthermore, revealed a truly astonishing variety and diversity when you got down to looking at them. There were not hundreds but hundreds of thousands, perhaps millions, of separate species. In addition, many of them seemed so closely related to each other that it was hard to conceive the purpose of their separate creation by the Divinity.

Finally, man had been able to produce extensive modifications in species by means of his experiments with controlled breeding. Had new species come into being as a result of such experiments? No one was absolutely sure, but it seemed likely. If so, however, species now existed that man and not God had created. What was the truth of this mystery of mysteries? Was there a truth that could be discovered by man?

Charles Darwin was born on February 12, 1809—the same day as Abraham Lincoln, although in markedly different circumstances. Darwin's grandfather was the famous physician and naturalist, Erasmus Darwin. His father was a prosperous surgeon. The boy grew up slowly and cared most for collecting things—rocks, butterflies, it didn't matter what. He tried to study medicine but became ill at his first operation. He then went to Cambridge to prepare for a career as a country parson. By the kind of accident that changes the world, he was nominated by his professor of biology at Cambridge to sail as naturalist on the government experimental ship, *H.M.S. Beagle*. He left England on December 27, 1831, knowing almost nothing about science; he returned five years later a tough and expert biologist with radical ideas that he was not very willing to make public.

He had contracted more than ideas on his journey, the most famous, perhaps, in the history of science. A brave adventurer, he had saved the ship on one occasion and had also struck out on his own on long treks through the South American wilderness. Once, crossing the Andes, he was attacked by a swarm of vicious mosquitoes. Apparently at that time he contracted Chagas's disease (a debilitating recurrent fever that weakens the heart), from which he suffered for the rest of his life and from which he died in 1882. The disease could be controlled today; then, it could not even be diagnosed.

Darwin's journal of his voyage on the *Beagle* was published, together with three other monographs, during the period from 1839 to 1846. These books gave him a reputation, and his sweetness and charm attracted many friends, both in and outside of science. Meanwhile he was always thinking about the great problem, as he called it. Clearly, as it seemed to him, species underwent modification, most certainly under domestication, less certainly in nature, but by what great mechanism did the changes come about? One day, while reading Thomas Malthus on population, it suddenly occurred to him how, in the struggle for existence—which he had everywhere observed—"favorable variations would tend to be preserved and unfavorable ones to be destroyed. The result would be the formation of a new species. Here then I had at last a theory by which to work."

It was 1844; he confided his theory to Charles Lyell and William Hooker, two close scientist friends. But he still published nothing on it, although he continued to produce other work. Suddenly, in 1858, he received word that a rival biologist, A.R. Wallace, had written a treatise proposing the very same theory. Darwin asked Lyell and Hooker what to do; they counseled joint publication of some notes he had written earlier together with Wallace's paper. Darwin then set to work in earnest. *The Origin of Species* was published late in 1859. Every copy of the first edition was sold on publication day.

No book, perhaps, has ever been so immediately, and so explosively, controversial. Darwin saved both "time and temper" by ignoring the battles and letting men like T.H. Huxley, his friend and intellectual disciple, defend the thesis publicly. Darwin returned to his comfortable retirement at Down and wrote more books about biology and evolution. He knew he was right; why waste time in public broils and turmoil?

His disease wore him down but he managed to write for a few hours each day. *The Descent of Man* appeared in 1871. Other notable works both preceded and followed it. He had neither time nor energy to devote to poetry, art, and music, which he loved; his mind had become, he wrote in his *Autobiography*, "a kind of machine for grinding general laws out of large collections of facts." In what spare time he had he read light fiction and averred that "a law ought to be passed" against unhappy endings of novels. He was loved by everyone who knew him for his gentleness, and he loved them in return.

His great book is not gentle. It is severe, strong, and rock-hard in its certainties; it never wavers in its steady motion to its conclusions. It is a pleasure to read—more so, probably, than any other famous scientific book. It is so well organized that it requires no major effort to understand it; and it is so well written that one moves through it rapidly, without pain. I say this in full awareness that there are millions of people who simply could not read this book. I can only say they are missing something wonderful.

# JOHN STUART MILL
### 1806–1873
*On Liberty*
*Considerations on Representative Government*

The peculiar circumstances of John Stuart Mill's early life and education are well known. Born in London in 1806, the son of James Mill, a noted English utilitarian philosopher, John Stuart was from the age of three subjected to a strict course of study in ancient languages, history, mathematics, and philosophy that resulted in his possessing, by the time he was thirteen, the equivalent of an excellent university education. He began with Greek and arithmetic, and by the age of eight had read all of Herodotus, several dialogues of Plato, and much other history. Before he was twelve he had studied Euclid and algebra, the Greek and Latin poets, and had read some English poetry. At twelve he was introduced to Aristotle's *Organon*, and he studied logic for the next year or so. From thirteen on he read law, history, and political science. At nineteen he had a nervous breakdown.

All of this is described in painful—yet fascinating—detail in his *Autobiography* (1873). It doesn't require reading between the lines to recognize that young Mill was given too much to chew too soon and ended up by being unable to digest it all. But the remarkable thing is not that John Stuart Mill broke under the strain of his dominating father/teacher. It is astonishing that he survived and became one of the most eloquent and persuasive writers in the English language, and the author of some indispensable books.

Having said this, I must immediately confess to a personal bias in favor of John Stuart Mill. I admit that I am mesmerized by the style of Mill; I don't know any philosopher I enjoy reading more. There is an elegant yet tough sinuousness about his sentences, a compelling inevitability about his line of thought. He can make even platitudes sound as if they were the most novel and earthshaking truths. And probably many of his truths are self-evident, and not in need of the battalions of arguments that he brings forward to support them.

On the other hand, little that John Stuart Mill says about government is—at least in my opinion—not true. And even if his truths are often platitudinous or self-evident, they are the kind of commonsense notions that bear repeating. They are so important that they must never be forgotten—even if the price for not forgetting them is to hear them too often.

Take the short book *On Liberty* that Mill had been working on for years but that he did not publish until 1859, when he was fifty-three years old. Its object, as Mill himself said, was "to assert one very simple principle, as entitled to govern absolutely the dealings of society with the individual in the way of compulsion and control, whether the means used be physical force in the form of legal penalties, or the moral coercion of public opinion." That principle was that the only justifiable reason for interfering with the life of any adult human being was self-protection—"to prevent harm to others."

His own good, either physical or moral, is not a sufficient warrant. He cannot rightfully be compelled to do or forbear because it will be better for him to do so, because it will make him happier, because, in the opinion of others, to do so would be wise, or even right. These are good reasons for remonstrating with him, or reasoning with him, or entreating him, but not for compelling him, or visiting him with any evil in case he do otherwise.

In short, as Mill sums up, "over himself, over his own body and mind, the individual is sovereign." He may—indeed, in a just society he must—be hindered from harming other people. But if he desires to harm himself he must be allowed to do so, as long as harm to himself does not harm others as well. And anyway, who should be the final judge of harm? We often find it easier to see the "good" for others than for ourselves. We passionately wish them to allow us to make our own mistakes. But so with them, as well.

Mill educes many convincing arguments for his views, which I confess seem true to me. One of the arguments is a social one. That society is better off in every way in which all are free, than in which only some are free. "Mankind are greater gainers by suffering each other to live as seems good to themselves, than by compelling each to live as seems good to the rest." And, in the most famous statement of this position Mill ever made:

> If all mankind minus one were of one opinion, and only one person were of the contrary opinion, mankind would be no more justified in silencing that one person, than he, if he had the power, would be justified in silencing mankind.

Shortly after Mill suffered his nervous breakdown, in 1825, he met the woman who would be the greatest influence on his life and thought. She was at the time married, but when her husband died, Mill married her. He had known her for twenty years and she had only seven years to live. But those seven years of marriage to Harriet Taylor were the happiest of his life.

Mrs. Taylor taught Mill many things, not least of which was his sense of indignation, which never ceased to increase, at the "subjection of women"—this being the title of one of his most famous books. Indeed, *The Subjection of Women* (1869) is a remarkable document, written in the heat of a passionate love for a woman whom we would call today a "women's libber." An even better book, however, because of its much greater generality, is *Considerations on Representative Government* (1861), which deals with, and obliterates the arguments in behalf of, all kinds of benevolent despotism, not just that of husbands over their wives.

*Representative Government* considers in eloquent detail all of the classical problems of government, and particularly of democracy. A glance at the table of contents of the book is in itself instructive. In my view, the most interesting of all the chapters is Chapter 3, "That the ideally best Form of Government is Representative Government." The chapter opens with a ringing challenge: "It has long …been a common saying, that if a good despot could be ensured, despotic monarchy would be the best form of government. I look upon this as a radical and most pernicious misconception of what good government is; which, until it can be got rid of, will fatally vitiate all our speculations on government." This doctrine, which is held, more or less without thinking about it, by most of the human race, is indeed both radical and pernicious. There would seem to be all sorts of spurious support of it. For one thing, most "governments" with which we are familiar are benevolent despotisms. The family is not a democracy, at least when the children are little. The children are "ruled" for their own good, as perceived by their parents. A university is not a democracy, although some radical students in the 1960s and later tried to make it one—and in so doing did much harm to higher education. A corporation is not a democracy; the chief executive officer does not decide what to do on the basis of a majority vote of his employees, or even of his stockholders. Nor is a sports team a democracy; the coach tells the team what to do and they had better do it, for his judgment of what is best for the team is, supposedly, better than theirs. In fact, the only government under which we live that is or should be a democracy is the government itself. That, Mill insists, must not be a despotism, no matter how benevolent.

Why not? The answer, finally, is not simple. Despotisms seem more efficient, Mill says, but they really are not. Despotisms seem more able to defend themselves, but they really are not. Despotisms seem more able to ensure the comfort and contentment of their people, but again they really are not. Most important of all is the effect that despotism, even the most perfectly benevolent despotism, has on the individuals that the despot rules. Despotism has the inevitable effect of making its subjects slaves. Free government makes its citizens free. It is incomparably better to be free than to be a slave.

The arguments in favor of freedom, and of participation in the state by all adults, women as well as men, poor as well as rich, are thorough and, I think, completely convincing. *Representative Government* is thus an important book to read at a time when despots everywhere are presenting their spurious allurements—in Latin America, in Africa, in the Middle East, and in all the Communist countries. Sometimes it almost seems easier to give in and to say, well, if every other government is a despotism, why should ours not be so too? That way we would not have to work so hard at governing ourselves. But we must never stop working to do that. The reasons for this are many, but the most important of them is expressed by John

Stuart Mill, not in *Representative Government* but at the end of his companion volume, *On Liberty*:

> The worth of a State, in the long run, is the worth of the individuals composing it; and a State which postpones the interests of their mental expansion and elevation to a little more of administrative skill, or of that semblance of it which practice gives, in the details of business; a State which dwarfs its men, in order that they may be more docile instruments in its hands even for beneficial purposes—will find that with small men no great thing can really be accomplished; and that the perfection of machinery to which it has sacrificed everything will in the end avail it nothing, for want of the vital power which, in order that the machine might work more smoothly, it has preferred to banish.

# KARL MARX
## 1818–1883

# FRIEDRICH ENGELS
## 1820–1895
### *The Communist Manifesto*

Karl Marx was born in Prussia, the son of middle-class parents, in 1818. He studied law at the University of Berlin and there discovered Hegel, whose metaphysical interpretations of history he later attacked violently, but who nevertheless was the single greatest influence on his thought. Marx joined the "Young Hegelians," or Left Republicans, and, leaving the university without a degree, went to Paris, where he embarked on his lifelong career in political journalism. Driven out of Paris by the police, he went to Brussels where, in 1845, there occurred his fateful meeting with Engels.

Friedrich Engels, also originally a bourgeois, was born in Germany in 1820. Educated in the gymnasium of his native town, he left it to go to work for his father, a cotton manufacturer. Engels spent a number of years after 1849 working, first as an employee, then as a partner and director of a textile firm founded by his father in Manchester, England.

When the two young men met in Brussels in 1845 they recognized each other as kindred spirits. Engels, with his considerable financial resources, helped Marx and his family to survive until Marx's death in 1883; and Marx, with his enormous intellectual resources, enlivened Engels's mind for four decades. Their joint productions were many, and after Marx's death Engels continued, until his own death in 1895, to promote the works, notably *Das Kapital*, of his angry, difficult friend who, Engels rightly understood, had proposed a vision of the world that was going to change it from top to bottom.

Their first joint venture was the most famous of all. In his 1888 Preface to *The Communist Manifesto*, Engels explained how the tract had come to be. At a Congress of the Communist League, then a secret society, held in London in 1847, he and Marx had been commissioned to prepare for publication "a complete theoretical and practical party platform." Drawn up in German in January 1848, it was sent to the printer a few weeks before the French revolution of February 24. Within six months, in that famous Year of the Forty-Eight, Europe was aflame, and the *Manifesto* seemed to be forgotten in the midst of events that were even more exciting than its words. But when the revolutionary fervor died down, as it did until it blazed up again in 1870, the *Manifesto* was rediscovered and began its climb toward worldwide fame. Translations were published in French, English, Danish, Polish, and Italian; in 1872 it was published in a new English translation in New York. "Thus the history of the *Manifesto*," Engels wrote in 1888, "reflects to a great extent the history of the modern working class movement; at present it is undoubtedly the most widespread, the most international production of all Socialist literature, the common platform," he concluded, "acknowledged by millions of working men from Siberia to California."

Engels, writing five years after the death of Karl Marx, was nevertheless generous enough in his Preface to concede that "the fundamental proposition which forms its nucleus" was owing to Marx.

Engels's statement of this "fundamental proposition" is both accurate and succinct. Here is the single sentence in which Engels summed up the doctrine that has come to be called Marxism:

That proposition is: That in every historical epoch the prevailing mode of economic production and exchange, and the social organization necessarily following from it, forms the basis upon which is built up, and from which alone can be explained, the political and intellectual history of that epoch; that, consequently, the whole history of mankind (since the dissolution of primitive tribal society, holding land in common ownership) has been a history of class struggles, contests between exploited and exploiting, ruling and oppressed classes; that the history of these class struggles forms a series of evolutions in which, nowadays, a stage has been reached where the exploited and oppressed class—the prole-tariat—cannot attain its emancipation from the sway of the exploiting and ruling class—the bourgeoisie—without at the same time, and once and for all, emanci-pating society at large from all exploitation, oppression, class distinctions and class struggles.

How many men and women have died for, and against, that doctrine! And how many more have been exploited and oppressed in its name!

This consequence, at least, was not foreseen by Engels in 1888, nor indeed by the young Marx and Engels as they struck off the burning brands of the *Manifesto* in the dark January of forty years before. Indeed, it is a most extraordinary political document. Its few pages—even in an edition on cheap paper and large type it hardly runs more than twenty-five—contain some of the swiftest prose ever composed. "A spectre is haunting Europe," it begins, "—the spectre of Communism." And so it should, the *Manifesto* proclaims; all the powers of the old and dying world are right to fear the new ideas. And the work ends with these ringing words:

Let the ruling classes tremble at a Communist revolution. The proletarians have nothing to lose but their chains. They have a world to win.
    Workingmen of all countries, unite!

It does not matter what you think of Communism—whether you are for it or against it, whether you think it is the doctrine of the angels or that of the devils. You cannot claim to be a thinking man or woman in today's world unless you have read *The Communist Manifesto*. That seems so obvious as hardly to need stating; but there are nevertheless many places in the United States where you will have to carry the *Manifesto* under your coat and not take it out in public.

# CHARLES BAUDELAIRE
## 1821–1867
### *Flowers of Evil*

André Gide, when asked who was the greatest French poet, responded: "Victor Hugo, hélas!" Indeed, it would be a shame if France had no greater poet than Hugo. But in fact it has at least two: La Fontaine and Baudelaire. Unfortunately, La Fontaine only wrote fables; and even for Gide, whose own life was irregular, it was difficult to forgive Baudelaire for the disaster he had made of his life.

Born in Paris in 1821, debaucher, wastrel, drug user, Charles Baudelaire died in 1867 of syphilis and failed in almost everything he tried to do. Except to shock people. He was good at that. When *Les Fleurs du Mal* (*Flowers of Evil*) was first published, in 1857, it was not met with the universal praise that Baudelaire had hoped for and may even have expected; instead, Baudelaire and his publisher were prosecuted for obscenity and blasphemy and were convicted of a public offense and fined. Six of the poems were banned until 1949, and Baudelaire's name, for nearly a century after his death, was synonymous with depravity and vice in the mind of a French public that has always been more conservative in its moral judgments than the image of "Gay Paree" would suggest.

Baudelaire suffered terribly. He planned many works but never wrote them; he started others but never finished them; he declared bankruptcy but still could not escape his creditors; when he died, in the arms of his mother, who had always told him sternly that he ought to live another way, only a few of the many invited to his funeral came. Yet his achievement was enormous. This strange, tortured soul was a hard worker and a producer.

If he possessed any fame during his lifetime it was as the translator of the American author, until then unknown in Europe, Edgar Allan Poe. Poe appealed to Baudelaire; they shared a dark view of mankind and the world and a concept of the poet as one who was able to lift the mask from evil and show it in all its putrescent appeal and beauty. Baudelaire wrote the first critical article to appear on Poe in any language other than English and translated many of Poe's stories into classical French—these translations are still the preferred ones. But Poe was hardly a subject to remake Baudelaire's reputation.

He was also a fine, although almost completely unappreciated, art critic. He knew Delacroix and Courbet, and what is more understood them and what they were trying to do, which most Frenchmen of his time did not. His review of the Salon of 1846 is said to be a landmark in aesthetic criticism. He continued to write such reviews for twenty years until, paralyzed and oppressed by poverty, he was unable to visit the places where new paintings were being shown.

The most important events of Baudelaire's life were private ones. When he was twenty he took his only sea voyage, a trip to India, which was aborted when he suddenly declared his intention to return home. But for the rest of his life Baudelaire remembered images of that voyage, and they fill his poems with a strange, beautiful light. All of his voyages were, thenceforth, in his imagination only, but he soared nonetheless, perhaps because his broken body was so resolutely earthbound.

> Le Poète est semblable au prince des nuées
> Qui hante la tempête et se rit de l'archer;
> Exilé sur le sol, au milieu des huées,
> Ses ailes de géant l'empêchent de marcher."

[The poet is like the prince of the clouds,
Who rides the tempest and scorns the hunter.
An exile on the ground, amidst boos and insults,
His wings of a giant prevent his walking.]

These famous lines, from the poem "The Albatross," became the marching song of the Symbolist movement, which was already marshaling its forces in France when Baudelaire died. The lines express Baudelaire's feelings about poetry, and his heartbreak.

Many poems in *Flowers of Evil* are erotic, shocking, perhaps even depraved, but they are not to be read for that reason. They are also beautiful. And they are symbolic; they have meanings that must be sought out, that are not apparent on the surface. To read Baudelaire, then, is something of an effort—and he is hard to translate. Nevertheless, even a little of the essence of Baudelaire is worth the effort of distilling it.

Why? Because poor Baudelaire, so blind to his own good, saw ours better than we are likely to do ourselves. The world is not just full of fools; everyone knows that (when we do not wish to forget it); it is also full of knaves, and worse than knaves. Theologically speaking, we have to admit that the Devil has never given up and may even be winning. Priests and prophets are not enough to stop him. Poets are needed, too, to point with both astonishment and derision at the cloven foot showing through his shoes and the horns peeking through his hair.

# CHARLES DICKENS
### 1812–1870
*A Christmas Carol*
*Hard Times*
*The Pickwick Papers*
*Bleak House*
*Our Mutual Friend*

Charles Dickens was born in Portsmouth, England, in 1812. His childhood years were spent in Chatham and he returned to the town in 1860 to live in his famous house, Gad's Hill, until his death. From 1822 to 1860, Dickens lived in London, where he experienced his most desolate moments and his greatest triumphs.

In 1824, his father, an extravagant ne'er-do-well who was the pattern for Mr. Micawber in *David Copperfield*, went to prison for debt. Charles, the eldest son, was withdrawn from school and sent to work. An improvement in the family fortunes made it possible for him to later go back to school, but he never forgot the depression he felt at that time and he wrote about the experience, or similar ones, in several of his books.

Dickens left school for good when he was fifteen to work in a lawyer's office. He soon became a court shorthand reporter and, later, a parliamentary reporter. He liked journalism, but he found he had contempt for both the legal profession and for Parliament.

In 1833, when he was twenty-one, he began contributing stories and essays to magazines and published a collection of them in 1836 called *Sketches by "Boz."* He was then invited to produce a comic serial narrative; seven weeks later the first installment of *The Pickwick Papers* appeared. Within a few months *Pickwick* was the rage and Dickens, not yet twenty-five, was the most popular author in England.

*Pickwick* was written by a very young man who did not yet fully comprehend his powers, and who, furthermore, while it was still running, started another serial, *Oliver Twist* (1837–39). Indeed, the fecundity of his imagination and the skill of his pen were in these early years incredible. *Nicholas Nickleby* (1838–39) was begun before *Oliver Twist* was completed, and it was in turn immediately followed by *The Old Curiosity Shop* (1840–41), and that by *Barnaby Rudge* (1841). At this point Dickens, exhausted, rested for five months, but by 1843 he was publishing again; in that year appeared perhaps the most famous of all his works, *A Christmas Carol*.

The early phase of Dickens' career is said to have ended in 1850, with the publication of the autobiographical novel, *David Copperfield*. It was Dickens's favorite and it is the favorite of many readers as well.

For years Dickens had been editing a monthly magazine; starting in 1850, at the age of thirty-eight, he began to produce the weekly *Household Words*, which was succeeded in 1860 by the even more popular *All the Year Round*. He edited all the copy and wrote a great deal of it, including the first serial publication of his later novels. The ventures were enormously lucrative—and time-consuming.

But the years after 1850 were not happy ones. Dickens had loved his children when they were young but he didn't like them now that they were grown up. Worse, he was having serious trouble with his wife. From 1868 on, they lived apart; for years before that Dickens had spent most of his time away from home. The world knew little of this at the time; only as recently as 1939 did some of the details come out about his relations with his wife and other women.

Whether or not his personal unhappiness was the cause, the novels that followed Copperfield—Bleak House (1852–53), Hard Times (1854), and Little Dorritt (1855–57)—were different from what had gone before. They were more carefully plotted, technically more competent and efficient, stylistically more powerful. The most important change was in the balance between light and dark, between happiness and woe.

The latter part of Dickens's career was spent half in his study and half in the theater. He developed a series of dramatic readings and presented them all over the English-speaking world, and was even more successful at that than at writing books. Not that he stopped doing the latter. A Tale of Two Cities appeared in 1859, Great Expectations in 1860–61, and Our Mutual Friend in 1865. When he died in 1870, at the age of fifty-eight, worn out by the extraordinary efforts that had hardly stopped since his twenty-first year, he was mourned around the world.

I am certain that the way to begin reading—or rereading—Dickens is with A Christmas Carol. It doesn't matter how many times you may have read it as a child; nor does it matter how often it has been exploited by television and the other media. All these productions do not touch the heart of the book, which is as hard and imperishable as a diamond.

To Ebenezer Scrooge, Christmas is all "humbug." Believing this does not make Scrooge happy, however; and when the ghost of his partner, Marley, returns to try to redirect his spirit while there is yet time, Scrooge does not long resist. A succession of visions—of Christmas Past, Christmas Present, and Christmas to Come—makes him a better man, and he ends up filled not only with Christmas happiness but also with a sense that there is more meaning and value to life than he had ever thought.

How utterly familiar is the story, and yet how moving when you read it! A reader would have to struggle not to cry at several points in the narrative and the struggle would be misspent effort. Why not cry? Why not allow the change in Scrooge, and the picture of Bob Cratchit and his little crippled son, Tiny Tim, to enter your heart and change you, too?

Probably the best time to read A Christmas Carol is close to Christmas, but this sovereign remedy for the gloomy cynicism of ordinary life works any time.

After A Christmas Carol I suggest reading Hard Times, one of the shortest of Dickens's novels and perhaps the most uncompromising. The story has a solid Dickensian plot with no surprises in it. But plot is not the essence of this book. Mainly it is about the deep conflict that Dickens saw in his time—and that we see in ours—between two kinds of lives: a carefree, feeling existence, full of sentiment and imagination; and one based on facts, efficiency, and dogged work. The Gradgrind family tries to live entirely in their heads; Sissy Jupe, the little circus orphan who, untypically, they take in and care for, tries to be like them. But they fail to turn Sissy into an efficient human machine, and she ends up revealing to all of them—amid much pain and anguish—the values of the heart. It is a beautiful and moving story, made not the less effective by Dickens's savage descriptions of Coketown, his imaginary blighted Midlands town.

Hard Times has fewer than three hundred pages; The Pickwick Papers has nearly eight hundred, which is closer to the Dickensian norm.

The original proposal made to the then young Dickens by his publisher was for a series of sketches about the members of a sporting club—hunters and fishermen. Dickens vetoed the idea; he knew very little about such sports. What he did know a lot about, from his reporter days, was travel. He decided to write a book about a club of traveling gentlemen.

It started unremarkably; the first issue sold only fifty copies and reviews were mixed. As the issues appeared, Samuel Pickwick, fat, wealthy, and good-hearted, the head of the club, emerged as the leading character. But it was not until the fifth issue—Chapter 15— that Dickens was inspired to introduce Sam Weller as Mr. Pickwick's servant. By the fifteenth number the publishers were selling upward of forty thousand copies, and Dickens was famous.

So was Pickwick, whose name has given us an English adjective; so, even more so, was Sam Weller. There are many intelligent, cunning, loyal servants in literature but none quite like Sam Weller, who is more loyal and loving than any other at the same time that the world is never able to outwit him. Mr. Pickwick flourishes under his care and so does this splendid book.

It is customary to say that *The Pickwick Papers* is not really a novel— but what is a novel, then, if this is not one? True, it has its false starts, its slow places. On the whole it charges ahead at full speed, entertaining all its readers enormously and touching their hearts.

*A Christmas Carol* and *Hard Times* are both short books, and *The Pickwick Papers* is easy because it demands nothing from readers (except enjoyment). There is a great part of Dickens that remains after those comfortable books have been read and digested. Once captured by this greatest of English novelists, you may decide to read all of Dickens, from *Oliver Twist* to *Great Expectations*, from *The Old Curiosity Shop* to *A Tale of Two Cities* (you may have read that one in school). But where to start? I suggest *Bleak House*. It is a very long, very great book. It has all of Dickens's faults but also all of his virtues; the latter much outweigh the former. And if you decide to read no more, you will have read, in *Bleak House*, what is probably the quintessential Dickens work.

If our memory of *David Copperfield* is primarily one of sunshine happiness, then our memory of *Bleak House* is just the opposite. The prevailing image of the book is fog. It is there from the very first page.

> Fog everywhere. Fog up the river, where it flows among green aits and meadows; fog down the river, where it rolls defiled among the tiers of shipping and the water-side pollutions of a great (and dirty) city. Fog on the Essex marshes, fog on the Kentish heights … Chance people on the bridges peeping over the parapets into a nether sky of fog, with fog all around them, as if they were up in a balloon, and hanging in the misty clouds.

The fog is not only on the outside, it is also within the characters in *Bleak House*, all of them, in their eyes, their throats, their very brains. It is an extraordinary living thing, this fog.

*Bleak House* contains scenes of love and happiness, but the most memorable ones are fog-bound and fog-dirtied. Nevertheless, readers are not left with a sense of foggy confusion. Just the opposite. The world may be fog-bound, Dickens is telling us, but good and evil, true and false, right and wrong, are as clear-cut as ever. Indeed, it is almost as if you cannot make those fundamental human judgments if you have not experienced the fogginess that lies at the heart of so much that we think and do.

The moral world, in short, although surrounded by fog, is not foggy in itself. Perhaps our modern prejudice goes just the other way. We are vague about our moral judgments and decisions, certain about our business ones. Dickens would strongly disagree. I think it is worth hearing his side.

*Bleak House* has a complex, multilevel plot, with a cast of characters and locales that it takes two or more pages merely to list. Half a dozen are very memorable: Mr. Jarndyce and Esther Summerson. Krook and Mrs. Jellyby. Inspector Bucket and Jo, the poor little crossing-sweep. Lady Dedlock and Tom-All-Alone's, the section of London blighted by the eternal Chancery suit, Jarndyce v. Jarndyce, Chancery itself, and the Lord Chancellor. The list need not be extended; that is enough to bring to mind all the tumultuous action and passion of this great, moving book.

Having read these four works of Dickens, you are surely capable of deciding for yourself what, or whether, to read. I must add two recommendations. Do not pass over *Little Dorritt* because of its rather odd, antique title. I once spent an entire winter month reading that long, rich book. I will never forget the experience. Finally, there is Dickens's last novel, *Our Mutual Friend*. It is not well known, at least by me; in fact I had never even heard of it when I saw in the library in Key West a set of videos of a performance by the BBC. Having nothing else to do at the time, I took them out and watched them, expecting to be bored. Just the opposite, I was entranced. Try to find this version. I'm sure you will love it. And then read the book, too. *Our Mutual Friend* is special not only for Dickens's typical skills, but also because it has a real love story.

# GEORGE ELIOT
1819–1880
*Adam Bede*
*Silas Marner*
*Middlemarch*

Mary Anne Evans was born in 1819 on an estate in Warwickshire (that is, in the Midlands of England) for which her father was the agent. She enjoyed a curious, truncated education. She went away to school, but when her mother died she was called home again to care for her father. A rigidly pious man, he nevertheless permitted her to take lessons in languages and in history and, when she told him she could no longer believe in the tenets of his church, he finally accepted her unbelief if she would agree to attend services. All the time she was watching him with the great intensity of a young woman who would someday be a novelist. But there was no sign of this scrutiny as yet.

Her father died in 1849, when she was thirty, leaving her one hundred pounds a year. Was that enough to live on? she wondered. Perhaps, if she could find a suitable place to live, probably with a family in London, and if she could obtain a small income from translations, religious articles, and essays. She moved to London in 1851 and, after producing some turmoil in several households—her intensity had grown, not decreased—she was introduced to George Henry Lewes, the famous journalist. It was he who helped to create "George Eliot."

Lewes was the victim of a strange Victorian injustice. He and his wife Agnes had had four sons; but in 1850 a fifth son was born, admittedly the son not of Lewes but of their friend, Thornton Leigh Hunt. Lewes, a generous man, accepted the newborn as his own child. But Agnes did not give up Hunt; she continued to have children by him and Lewes found that, having once condoned the adultery, he could not sue for divorce. In fact, he supported Agnes and her children by Hunt until the end of his life. In the meantime he had fallen in love with Mary Anne Evans, and she with him.

This remarkable pair could not live apart, but they felt they could not live together in England, so in 1854 they went off to Germany, where Lewes struggled to support the family that had abandoned him by his writing. Mary Anne Evans was saddened at being isolated from her own Warwickshire family, who naturally disapproved of her decision to live with Lewes. It was nostalgia, therefore, that first brought her to write fiction. She began to compose sketches of her old home and friends, and the friends of her father. *Scenes of Clerical Life* (1858) was the first published result of these labors; the second, incomparably better, was *Adam Bede* (1859). Neither her own name nor that of Lewes was, she felt, acceptable, so she adopted a pseudonym, George Eliot.

Soon George Eliot was famous. Her books, all of which owed much to the encouragement and sympathy of the loving, helpfully critical Lewes, were successes, and the income allowed the lovers, who had lived together from the beginning exactly as man and wife, to return to London in 1863. There they established a salon and George Eliot continued to write books: *The Mill on the Floss, Romola, Daniel Deronda*. *Silas Marner* was published in 1861; *Middlemarch* appeared in parts from 1871 to 1872.

*Adam Bede* is a simply wonderful book about a wonderfully simple and loving man. Oh, there are many other persons in the book, but Adam, the village carpenter who is wiser than anyone else, is at its center. He suffers in his loves but finally is rewarded by the love of a good woman, wise and caring like himself. You will smile when you turn over the last page and thank me for suggesting the book.

*Silas Marner* reminds us that there is no justice like poetic justice. In this carefully crafted short novel, all the characters get their just deserts. But the punishments, and especially the rewards, are not simple. Marner, the bitter miser who loses his gold but gains a golden-haired child in its place—it is a mystery he never really understands—is rewarded not so much for things he has done as for having the capacity, not yet realized at the beginning of the book, of loving someone with all his heart. He loves the child in that way, and so his life is blessed. Godfrey Cass, the real father of the child, is condemned to childlessness by his unwillingness to accept his child while he could still do so. He gets most of what he desires in life, for he is a genial, goodhearted man; but not everything, for he is also a moral coward. In fact, the book is, more than anything else, about such carefully drawn moral distinctions.

It is not the less fascinating for that, because it is also a marvelous fairy tale. But it is a fairy tale for grown-ups, not for children; surely it has been a mistake for many years to force *Silas Marner* on young readers, who could hardly understand it in any but a superficial way. If the book was forced on you, and if you hated it as a result, try reading it again. The novel, which is very short, has the power deeply to affect persons who have had large experience of real life.

Of the half-dozen or ten greatest English novels, on which list *Middlemarch* certainly belongs, it is probably the least read. It was said by Virginia Woolf to be "one of the few English novels written for grown-up people." That may account for its relative lack of popularity.

There may be other reasons, too. *Middlemarch* is not a romance, as most novels are, although there are one or two romantics in it who are wonderfully well described. Nor does the novel have a distinct hero. Middlemarch is the name of the small (imaginary) city in which most of the action takes place. It has been accurately said that Middlemarch is the novel's hero. Certainly the town itself, and all the people in it, are the focus of the author's attention and concern.

The action of the book takes place during the period just before the passage of the Reform Bill, in 1832—which is to say, just before the social revolution brought about by the railroad had occurred. In pre-railroad days, when transportation was both slow and arduous, people lived as they had for centuries, living and dying within a few miles of one another, acting on and being acted on by one another. No man's or woman's life could be adequately understood, George Eliot felt, if it were shorn of interrelationships with all those around him or her. Even more than Middlemarch the town, this complex web of interrelationships is the subject of the novel. And for this reason *Middlemarch* has often been compared to Tolstoy's *War and Peace* which, in the opinion of George Eliot's admirers, is the only novel deserving to be called greater.

It is true enough that *Middlemarch* and *War and Peace* are both big books, complex and full of characters. But despite the fact that Tolstoy read everything written by George Eliot and admired her, I don't think the two books are very much alike. The scope of *War and*

*Peace* is ever so much larger; it extends over all of Europe at a crucial moment in its history, and throughout an entire society. *Middlemarch's* scope is narrow, although it is still broad by comparison with many other novels; it focuses on a town, examining all the people of that town, and all its occupations and social classes, with an unremitting intensity, but it does not extend to a greater world. That greater world is there, of course, but it is only hinted at.

I am glad George Eliot was content with *Middlemarch* and was not tempted to shift the scene to London, or to the Continent, where she and Lewes had lived. For *Middlemarch*, in its ideal existence, is itself a world; as a fictional place, as a metaphor, it contains and comprises all the life that was lived in England in its time. The novel has been called the best account and analysis of English life on the eve of the Reform Bill, but the book deserves even higher praise than that. *Middlemarch*, more effectively than any novel I know, manages to present the entire worldview of a relatively large and variegated group of persons. In *Middlemarch*, I feel strongly that simply nothing has been left out. This is the way it must have been in an English Midlands town in 1830. And if I can say that, knowing as I do that life in one town is very like another, and life in one time is very like another—then *Middlemarch* is as complete an account of the kind of lives that people live as we can find anywhere in fiction.

# WALT WHITMAN
## 1819–1892
*Leaves of Grass*

The first edition of Walt Whitman's *Leaves of Grass*, the title he gave his collected poems, appeared in 1855 with a picture of the author on the cover, "broad-shouldered, rouge-fleshed, Bacchus-browed, bearded like a satyr," wearing "a slouched hat, for house and street alike." This was of course a persona, one of the first to be consciously assumed by a poet on the western side of the Atlantic; as was the claim, in one of the poems included in the collection, that he was sounding his "barbaric yawp over the roof of the world." Yet there was truth in it, as well, for the book by this "insolent unknown," as Ralph Waldo Emerson wrote of Whitman, was truly new, "the most extraordinary piece of wit and wisdom" America had produced. At a time when Stendhal was dedicating *The Charterhouse of Parma* to "the happy few" and Baudelaire was writing poems for a tiny audience of like-minded aesthetes and *précieuses*, here was Whitman addressing democratic man en masse. Poetry for everybody, instead of just for literary folk, had indeed to be different. But it was not Americans but rather English and French critics of the culture and society of the Old World who first appreciated Whitman. The first edition of the works of this democratic poet attracted very few democratic readers.

Whitman had been born on Long Island in 1819. It was years before he found and understood himself. He worked as an editor and a printer, writing poems in his infrequent spare time. He was sufficiently encouraged by Emerson's letter to produce a second edition of *Leaves of Grass* in 1856, with a quote from Emerson on the cover (without Emerson's permission), and, inside the book, a collection of quotes from reviews, most of which Whitman had written himself. In this edition many of Whitman's best-known poems began to take their final shape. A third edition appeared in 1860.

Still, Whitman had not found his true voice, which was not, after all, a barbaric yawp but instead a soft yet strong and steady note. This true voice was given to Whitman by the Civil War, which also made Emily Dickinson a poet, although their experiences of the conflict were different. Whitman spent the war in Washington working for the federal government, visiting hospitals and bringing presents to wounded Union and Confederate soldiers alike. The murder of President Lincoln, in 1865, less than a week after the war's end, helped Whitman to comprehend fully the bitterness and heartbreak of war. He expressed it with new power in "When lilacs last in the door-yard bloom'd: Memories of President Lincoln," one of the great American poems, which was included in an edition of *Leaves of Grass* that appeared late in 1865.

This volume also included a number of small, clear-cut word pictures, like "The noiseless patient spider," "Once I saw in Louisiana a live oak growing," and (perhaps best of all) "Come up from the fields father,"—this last a curt, unsentimental account of how word has come to a family that their son has been killed—my throat tightens even as I describe it. Gone was the yawp, gone the uncontrolled self-advertisements, gone the lists of particulars that so offended Emerson in Whitman's later editions of *Leaves of Grass*. The war had focused Whitman's spiritual and emotional strength on a few simple, basic ideas, and the poems he wrote—or rewrote—at this time are among the best ever written by an American.

The taut excellence of his style and subject matter during the period from 1863 to 1868 could not, or at least did not, last. Whitman began to revert in later editions of *Leaves of Grass* to the diffuse, nervous, even frantic tone that had marked his earliest poems. But Whitman wrote a great deal, and we don't need to read it all. What remains, after all the bad poems have been weeded out, is still a marvelous harvest of poetry.

Much of "Song of Myself" is fine, although this longest of Whitman poems—more than a hundred pages—also contains tiresome, repetitious matter. "When lilacs last in the door-yard bloom'd" is wonderful, but "Out of the cradle endlessly rocking," which deals with the same subject—death and the need to face it—is even better. Its soft, repetitive (not repetitious), profoundly moving refrain is hypnotic; it reminds one, as it is supposed to do, of the hypnotic effect of the sea at evening, with the waves lapping ceaselessly against the shore; and it brings to mind long, deep thoughts of death and life. Many of the poems from *Drum Taps* and *The Sequel to Drum Taps* (included in *Leaves of Grass*), which were written during or immediately after the Civil War, have the quintessential Whitman quality. You will discover a handful more of great poems when you read Whitman selectively.

# EMILY DICKINSON
### 1830–1886
*Selected Poems*

Emily Elizabeth Dickinson was born in Amherst, Massachusetts, in 1830, the daughter of a prominent lawyer. Her formal education ended after one year at Mount Holyoke Female Seminary when she returned home, at the age of eighteen, to live permanently in her father's house. She took two or three short trips to Washington and Boston in the next few years but otherwise she never left Amherst, becoming more and more reclusive as the years passed, although she maintained correspondences with several persons whom she hardly ever saw face to face.

She never married. She probably experienced one or two love affairs; we know little about her inner life. If these love affairs were unhappy it is also probable that the failure was on the man's side, not on hers. Or she may have decided the man was not up to her standard. Certainly her poetry gives the impression of a woman who very well knew her own mind.

She began writing verse during her school days and never stopped, although her finest poems were written just before and during the Civil War—from 1858 to 1866. Few knew that she wrote them, but she did send a few samples to a family friend, Thomas Wentworth Higginson, who for many years gently urged her not to publish. Apart from seven heavily edited poems, she never did. But after her death in 1886, her family, together with Higginson, brought out a small volume, *Poems by Emily Dickinson* (1890). The reviews were bad, but people bought the book, and other collections soon followed.

Most of Emily Dickinson's poems are glancing blows at life, which is too big a subject, she may have felt, to take on directly. She chips away at the rock of existence, piece by little piece, until she is surrounded by a pile of fragments, and a figure emerges. That figure is never wholly clear; like Michelangelo, she was content to leave this or that aspect of her work unfinished. But when she chose to emphasize a point or line, it emerged with blinding clarity.

A few scattered lines and couplets demonstrate her talents:

> Success is counted sweetest
> By those who ne'er succeed.

> The heart asks pleasure first,
> And then, excuse from pain.

The soul selects her own society,
Then shuts the door;
On her divine majority
Obtrude no more.

Because I could not stop for Death,
He kindly stopped for me.

After great pain a formal feeling comes.

Those lines were chosen almost at random. Few poets are so consistently good. Emily Dickinson hardly ever misses, hardly ever loses her exquisite touch. And she is always saying something extraordinary. Take the poem that begins, "The soul selects her own society/Then shuts the door." That is indeed the way we are. We choose a friend, we fall in love, and then we turn our backs on all the other people, doubtless some of them equally interesting and beautiful, in the world. Why do we do it? That is another question, and Emily Dickinson does not answer it. One thing at a time. The observation was worth making for its own sake.

An old name for poet was "troubadour," taken from an old French term that comes down in modern French as *trouver*, to find. A poet, then, was a finder. And is: Nothing that poets do is more important than this finding, which is also discovering, noticing, observing. The great poet sees things that we have not seen, that are plainly there to see once he has pointed them out, but that no one could see before they were limned. Emily Dickinson was above all a finder, a troubadour.

She is easy to read, but there is the danger that her ease and apparent simplicity will lead you to think she really is simple, even simpleminded. That would be foolish, like thinking Socrates was simpleminded because he discussed philosophy in plain terms. Emily Dickinson seems simple because she is so controlled, because the weapon of her poetry is so sharp that when she cuts there is no sound, no quiver of the blade. The piece she has cut off of reality simply lies there, at her feet. She looks at you with her level glance, not smiling. There, she seems to be saying, do you see? Do you understand? And do you know how much more hard work there is to do?

The physical form of Emily Dickinson's poems is usually odd: they were scratched out on stray slips of paper, thrown into a box all higgledy-piggledy, as if she didn't care what became of them. Why do poets do things like that? Shakespeare seems not to have cared about his manuscripts, either—they survive by accident, or at least the goodwill of friends, not the effort of their author. I think Emily Dickinson was challenging posterity to recognize her greatness, a greatness that was unknown to her contemporaries. I believe it was known to her. It is known now by everyone, and it is not rare to hear it said that she and Whitman are the two greatest American poets. Oh, if only she could know that! Except, again, she probably does.

Since Emily Dickinson is such a consistently good poet it hardly matters which poems are read first. Any good anthology contains a wealth of possibilities.

## MATTHEW ARNOLD
### 1822–1888
*Poems*
*Criticism*

Matthew Arnold was born in 1822, the eldest son of Thomas Arnold, the headmaster of Rugby, which through various reforms he had raised to the rank of a great public school rivaling Eton and Harrow. His son was educated there and at Oxford. Matthew's great career began in 1851 when he was appointed an inspector of schools, in which capacity he served for thirty-five years, traveling all over England and on the Continent. His first book of poetry was published in 1849; it was followed by many more. On his honeymoon, two years later, he began writing "Dover Beach," his best-known poem and one that deserves its fame.

He and his bride stand at a window listening to the waves as they fling pebbles "up the high strand" and, returning, "bring the eternal note of sadness in." "The sea of faith was once, too, at the flood," he feels, but now he only hears "its melancholy, long, withdrawing roar." "Ah, love, let us be true to one another," he cries, for there is "neither joy, nor love, nor light," and we are here "as on a darkling plain," where "ignorant armies clash by night."

"Dover Beach" is one of the saddest poems ever written. Arnold was aware that many changes were occurring in England and elsewhere, changes produced by the Industrial Revolution and all it represented and entailed. J.S. Mill, Baudelaire, Dickens, and George Eliot, too, had heard that "melancholy, long, withdrawing roar." I believe we can hear it still.

In his fifties, Arnold turned to prose instead of poetry to express his deep pessimism about the way the world was going. He called for "high seriousness" in literature and nominated a dozen "touchstones" of great poetry that he urged poets of his day always to keep in mind as they wrote, famous lines and images from Homer, Aeschylus, Shakespeare, and a few others—not many. Employing a famous phrase, he described the "Cultured" man as distinct from the "Philistine," culture being represented by the possession of "sweetness and light." He was mocked in his time, and the real meaning of those words has been totally lost. But for Arnold, "sweetness" was beauty and good taste, while "light" was intelligence and knowledge.

In his last book, *Culture and Anarchy*, he described those two "polar opposites" as battling for the souls of men and women of his time. He died in 1888 convinced that anarchy was winning the war.

# MARK TWAIN
## 1835–1910
### *The Adventures of Huckleberry Finn*

Samuel L. Clemens was born in Missouri in 1835 and moved to the flourishing river town of Hannibal, Missouri, when he was four. Experience was his best and almost his only teacher, and he went to work for his brother, a newspaper publisher, at sixteen. Young Clemens learned to write by setting in type the writings of other people, mostly the rough, popular humorists of the period before the Civil War.

He left home at eighteen, wandered around the country as an itinerant journalist for a while, and then suddenly decided to become a riverboat pilot. This idyllic experience he magically described in *Life on the Mississippi* (1883), the best of his autobiographical writings.

The Civil War put an end to Sam Clemens's life on the river. He went to California, mainly to avoid the war— like many Westerners, he wanted no part of it. It was in California, in the 1860s, that he became Mark Twain, a name that itself was a nostalgic reminder of his happiest days. (The phrase was a leadsman's cry, signifying that the shoaling water was just safe for navigation—was two fathoms, or twelve feet, deep.) He gained his first national fame with a widely reprinted humorous story, "The Celebrated Jumping Frog of Calaveras County," and his first great literary success was an account of a trip to Europe and the Holy Land, *Innocents Abroad* (1869).

Mark Twain liked boyhood. In 1876 he published the boys' book *The Adventures of Tom Sawyer*. Everyone loved this book, and indeed they still do, even though the central character, Tom, is completely without warmth. The comic-book quality of the story of Tom and Becky lost in the cave with a villainous Injun Joe made it successful, but Mark Twain himself knew the book had no heart and immediately set about writing a better one. This was *The Adventures of Huckleberry Finn*, which was finally published, after many delays in the writing, in 1884. It was hard to write—*Tom Sawyer* had been easy—and the reasons for that go to the center of the book's meaning and significance.

*Huckleberry Finn* is many things. First—to get it out of the way— it is the American novel par excellence, the great American novel that will never have to be written because it appeared more than a century ago. Mark Twain's birthplace was within a few miles of the geographical center of what was then the United States, and his book was equally close to the country's spiritual center. It is about a white man and a black man, a free man and a slave. It is about a journey down the great central, dividing river in search of freedom for both white and black. How much more American can you get? Ernest Hemingway was right to say that "all real American literature comes from one book by Mark Twain called *Huckleberry Finn*."

That is not in the long run very important. More important to us is the fact that *Huckleberry Finn* is a fine, funny story—at least the first two thirds of it, up to the point where Tom Sawyer arrives to both bore and offend every compassionate reader with his practical jokes at the expense of Jim. But that same reader cannot fail to appreciate the story of Huck's escape from his wicked Old Man, and Jim's escapes as well from many hard places, to say nothing of the wonderful foolishness of the "King" and the "Duke," whose really vicious immorality is not lost on us however loudly we may guffaw at their scams and cheats.

Even more important for us are the background, the tone, and the style of this book—again, only the first two thirds of it, before the intrusion of Tom. Huck and Jim speak an American English that is quite extinct now but that seems as genuine as any dialogue ever spoken by any characters in fiction. And the great rolling river is even more eloquent than they are. It holds its course and its counsel, but even in its silence it seems to tell us of the Earth's largeness and the littleness of men.

Most important of all, I think, is that *Huckleberry Finn* is not just the story of Huck's escape from Old Finn, or of Jim's from slavery; it is also, and preeminently, an account of the escape from the world itself, the world which, as Wordsworth said, "is too much with us":

> *late and soon,*
> *Getting and spending, we lay waste our powers;*
> *Little we see in Nature that is ours;*
> *We have given our hearts away, a sordid boon!*

That world, which is our own everyday world, is the one from which Huck and Jim escape as they float down the river in the moonlight on their raft. The moon sparkles on the water, fish jump in the silence, the shores are hardly visible, and it almost seems that it might go on like this forever. "We said there warn't no home like a raft, after all. Other places do seem so cramped up and smothery, but a raft don't. You feel mighty free and easy and comfortable on a raft." So says Huck at the end of Chapter 18, but in the very next chapter the world intrudes once more, and Huck and Jim are never so free again, even though Jim eventually does obtain his legal freedom. Huck, at the end of the book, lights out for the Territory, where he hopes he may escape the "sivilization" he abhors. But of course he cannot escape it; none of us can, Mark Twain no more than the rest of us.

That is why *The Adventures of Huckleberry Finn* at bottom is such a sad book, funny as it is, and why Twain had so much trouble finishing it, and why, when he did get around to finishing it, he turned the end into a series of cruel jokes.

So-called escapist literature has a bad name, and rightly so in most cases. The great majority of escapist novels—all but a very few—are cheats and frauds, playing upon our susceptibilities for the sake of book sales, teasing our imaginations with sly delights but in the end leaving us empty and ashamed that we were so easily fooled. A small number of such books are among the greatest of all. *Huckleberry Finn* is one of them. It forces us to ask whether the best thing is not, after all, to escape from the world. The world, in turn, disapproves of that, and Mark Twain knew it did and was frightened. He didn't want to be disliked. This radical revolutionary of the human spirit preferred to be thought of as an easygoing clown. Only to his closest friends would he reveal what he really thought of "the damned human race." He was afraid he had revealed too much in *Huckleberry Finn*.

Huck's story, as Mark Twain told it, was terrible enough. Huck had to escape to save his life; his father would have killed him. When he did escape, Mark Twain stopped writing the book because he did not know what else to do with his hero. He thought he ought to do something with him because, unlike the Huck at the end of the book, he— Mark Twain—felt obliged to be "sivilized." But all he could think of was Tom Sawyer's bad jokes at Jim's expense.

In other words, he told a series of jokes to make people think he had not meant it, after all. But he had. In this one great book of his, Mark Twain told the truth about what he really thought about man and the world.

He lived for twenty-five years after publishing *Huckleberry Finn*, but they were not happy years. His beloved younger daughter, Susy, died while the rest of the family was away on a trip; his older daughter became an invalid, as did his wife, who then died. Old Mark Twain, put on his famous white suit and went on lecture tours to entertain the world he hated. He wrote many books, but those he considered to be the worst—that is, the ones that most clearly revealed his views of his fellow human beings—he was reluctant to publish. He lived "full of malice," as he wrote to a friend, "saturated with malignity."

He had been born when Halley's Comet visited the solar system in 1835; he predicted that he would "go out with it" when it came again, and so he did, departing this life on April 21, 1910, within a few hours of the comet's closest approach to the Earth. Any loving reader will hope that Mark Twain's journey to freedom was a comfortable one, and that he found life upon the comet as easy as he had known it would have been upon a raft.

# HENRY ADAMS
### 1838–1918
*The United States in 1800*
*Mont-Saint-Michel and Chartres*
*The Education of Henry Adams*

Henry Adams was born in Boston in 1838, the great-grandson of President John Adams and the grandson of President John Quincy Adams. He graduated from Harvard in 1858, then studied at Berlin and toured Germany and Italy. He served as secretary to his father while the latter was minister to Great Britain during the Civil War. After the war Adams taught history at Harvard but left his academic "exile" in 1877 to live in Washington among his important friends and to write books.

Henry Adams was the first member of his distinguished family to be a literary man. This both pleased and disturbed him. He never got over the feeling—expressed with eloquence in his autobiography—that he had betrayed his distinctive genius by refusing to follow in the political footsteps of his forebears. He thought of the Adams line as wearing thin or playing out in the generation of himself and his brother Brooks Adams (also a historian). This feeling, confirmed by the then-current excitement about the discovery of the Second Law of Thermodynamics (that everything in the universe "runs down" and eventually suffers a "heat death"), led him to propose a highly pessimistic theory of history, according to which things in general could not help but grow worse as time passed. Looking around him at the end of the nineteenth century, and comparing his own time to the period when the United States was new, as well as to the even earlier period of the Middle Age in Europe, he found reason to believe his theory true. And he wrote three books about it.

The first was the nine-volume *History of the United States of America from 1801 to 1817* (published 1889–1891), which analyzed the American experience during the presidencies of Thomas Jefferson and James Madison. Much of this fine and readable work has since been superseded, but the first six chapters, in which Adams attempted to set forth the state of the union at the beginning of the nineteenth century, remain a marvelous summary of the condition and prospects of America at the time. These six chapters have been republished under the title *The United States in 1800*, and they are worth reading if only because of their posing of what Adams thought was the great American question: Considering the weakness and relative poverty, and especially the sparseness of population of the States in 1800, how had it been possible for the nation to grow to its present (that is, in 1890) greatness in the span of only three generations?

This is a good question, and Adams's answer is interesting. The relatively few persons who occupied North America in 1800 would not have been able to achieve what they actually did achieve if all were not actively involved in the achievement, he says. But to be actively involved they had to be educated. The greatest of all American inventions, therefore, according to Adams, and the source of the nation's greatness, is universal, free, public education. If the United States in 1800 had retained the European system, of educating a few very well and most not at all, then the nation might not have survived and could not have prospered.

The second book that grew out of Henry Adams's theory of history was *Mont-Saint-Michel and Chartres* (1904), an account of the art, literature, and philosophy of the twelfth and thirteenth centuries in Europe (mostly in France). The book begins with a study of the great fortress in Brittany dedicated to Saint Michael the Archangel, which represented for Adams the aggressive religious militarism of the twelfth century (which is also reflected in the first Crusades). Reading the pages devoted to Mont-Saint-Michel and its builders will lead you to open the travel section of your Sunday newspaper in search of tours to western France. But the best is yet to come. Adams's book moves south and east toward Paris, to the soaring gothic cathedrals of the thirteenth century, most of them dedicated to the Virgin Mary. Of all these great buildings, Nôtre Dame de Chartres is not only the largest but also the most beautiful, says Adams. If Adams's words do not convince you of this, you will soon see for yourself, because I predict that you will not be able to resist extending your tour from Brittany into the Ile-de-France, with Chartres as the final goal of your pilgrimage.

*Mont-Saint-Michel and Chartres* is not only about cathedrals and fortresses. Some of its best chapters deal with the other arts and the literature of the Middle Ages in France and Italy. Adams was a critic of pure and exalted taste and when he praises a work—for example, *The Song of Roland*—you want to immediately read or see it. The finest of all the chapters may be the one on Saint Thomas Aquinas, in which Adams compares the *Summa Theologica* (*Summa Theologiae* is the correct Latin name and the one used by scholars), Aquinas's masterwork, to a cathedral, declaring it to be the analogue in words of Chartres in stone.

Finally, Adams wrote his autobiography, in which he refers to himself throughout in the third person (Adams did this; Adams said that) and attempts to justify his life's work in the face of his own severe criticisms of himself. *The Education of Henry Adams*, published 1906, is one of the best of all autobiographies, but it is somehow not a pleasant book. Read it after reading *The United States in 1800* and *Mont-Saint-Michel and Chartres*, but do not expect to feel the same exhilaration that those works inspire.

This, perhaps, is precisely the point Adams wanted to make. History, taken overall, is a melancholy tale, a winding down of great energies and creative impulses into their present-day analogues: enormous, sprawling organizations devoted entirely to greed. Toward the end of *The Education*, in the chapter titled "A Law of Acceleration," Adams reveals that he is not completely hopeless. In comparing the works of men who worshiped the Virgin with those of men who worship the dynamo, he concedes that it is possible to imagine a future that is as good as, even better than, the past. But to attain this, says Adams, we have to change our ideas and our ways more rapidly and more profoundly than we ever have.

The movement from unity into multiplicity between 1200 and 1900 was unbroken in sequence and rapid in acceleration. Prolonged one generation longer it would require a new social mind. As though thought were common salt in indefinite solution, it must enter a new phase subject to new laws. Thus far, since five or ten thousand years, the mind had successfully reacted, and nothing yet proved that it would fail to react—but it would need to jump.

Of course Adams, if he were still alive, might consider (or recognize) the Internet and all it entails as the "jump" he said would have to occur. At any rate he would have been not only astonished but also amused. On the other hand, it might have made him even more unhappy.

*chapter eleven*

# Some Victorians and Others

ot all late-nineteenth-century authors were sourpusses like those we met in the previous chapter. Despite everything, good things were happening. Some very good books were being written by very interesting people. Two classic American novelists started and ended the century. More importantly for the world, three Russian giants emerged on the scene. Two English poets came and went, but we mustn't forget them. Two American brothers, so unlike one another it's hard to imagine them as brothers, bestrode the epoch. Two British tellers of tales amused and shocked their countrymen. Another British writer wrote a book whose fame will never die. His name wasn't really Lewis Carroll, nor did his heroine really exist, but it doesn't matter, because we all think she did, especially if we're still young at heart.

Hawthorne and Melville were friends, at least to the extent that anyone could befriend the stone-faced author of *The Scarlet Letter*. The differences between these two men were as great as those between William and Henry James. And yet, in a sense, they loved one another. I hardly know whether Turgenev, Dostoevsky, and Tolstoy were friends. They were born within a decade of one another, but their genius separated them. Certainly Turgenev and Dostoevsky knew about Tolstoy, as did almost everyone in the world, then and since.

Browning and Hardy were also a strange pair, both great poets but neither sufficiently known in their own or later times. I mean by my lights. Not everyone will agree about either of them.

Finally, Conan Doyle and Kipling—another strange and wonderful pair. Both sold millions of copies of their books, but neither was really respected. Both were to some extent looked down upon, Conan Doyle because he was just an entertainer, Kipling—even with his Nobel Prize—because he backed the wrong side in a war that reminds historians of Vietnam and Iraq.

# NATHANIEL HAWTHORNE
## 1804–1864
### *The Scarlet Letter*

Nathaniel Hawthorne, born in Salem in 1804, spent most of his life in Massachusetts. His best stories are about the life in New England two centuries before he was born. They are among the best stories anyone has ever written about New England, and they go far toward defining our idea of New England as the home of refined moral sentiments and tortured, suffering souls.

Hawthorne himself was a tortured, suffering soul. He had three good friends. One was his wife, Sophia Peabody of Salem, whom he adored until the day he died and to whom he may have been able to reveal something of the churning torment within him. Another was Franklin Pierce, a college classmate who later became perhaps the least distinguished of all the Presidents of the United States and who sent Hawthorne to Liverpool as U. S. Consul, whence he wandered off to Italy for a few years—but he was no happier far away from New England (he carried New England within him wherever he went). The third friend was Herman Melville, who managed to escape from the same origins as his friend's.

Hawthorne wrote *The Scarlet Letter* in 1849; it was published early the next year. He was very ill while he was writing it and grieving deeply over the death of his mother, whom he loved. The writing came easily that summer and fall, but he was worried about the book: probably at the same time that he knew how good it was, he was also afraid of what it said.

Melville was one of the first to read *The Scarlet Letter* and he felt exalted because he knew immediately how great a book it was; he felt that it allowed all American writers thenceforth to be free. Melville said things like that to Hawthorne, with his customary enthusiasm, but Hawthorne was more embarrassed than pleased.

*The Scarlet Letter* is about a man who has done a terrible thing that he is dying to confess.

Not everyone will agree that what Arthur Dimmesdale has done is so terrible. He has bedded a brilliant, passionate, and beautiful young woman, who loves him, and she has had a child. Why does he take no joy in this? For one thing, because she was and is married to another man; for another, because he is a clergyman and the very symbol of moral purity for his flock. It is worth remembering, further-more, that adultery, in those old strict days, was a crime punishable by death.

The main reason why the minister suffers is not because he feels his crime is in itself so heinous, but because he cannot bring himself to reveal that he has committed it. Hester Prynne does not enjoy the luxury of secrecy; her belly has already betrayed her. Would she have remained quiet if her body had permitted it? Probably not. She is one of the great, proud women of fiction and wears with fierce defiance the letter "A," for Adulteress, embroidered in scarlet and gold upon the bosom of her dress; she has somehow converted her punishment into a triumph.

Still, she will not reveal her lover if he will not reveal himself. She watches, in loving sympathy, as he struggles to do so. And what a struggle it is! We all watch with sympathy, and pity too, and fear, for all of us have done things that we wish to confess but cannot. (Not you, you say? Well then, everyone else.)

*The Scarlet Letter* is an important book not because it accurately describes how Americans lived in New England during the early seventeenth century (does it do that, after all?) but because it searches out the truth—or a truth—in human hearts, yours and mine.

Aristotle was wrong about many things, but he was right about many things, too, and one of the things he was most right about is the nature of tragedy. You see before you a man or woman, he said, who is worthy of respect—as is Hawthorne's hero—but who is also fallible, like you. You see him fall, because he is human and therefore weak, not strong like a god. And you pity him, said Aristotle, because like you he is human and weak; and you are fearful, because you too might fall. You feel these emotions very deeply, to your heart's core, and you are therefore purged of them, emerging from the theater where you have viewed the tragic events a better person, refreshed, more able to deal with the life that you must lead.

It is extraordinarily difficult to write a tragedy; in fact, very few completely satisfactory tragedies have ever been written. *The Scarlet Letter* is not the least in that small number. We pity the minister as he struggles to confess; when he finally succeeds it is almost as if we too have been able to confess. When he dies of his confession, a willing sacrifice, we are able to live.

Unfortunately, Hawthorne doesn't appear to have benefited as much as we may from his story. His frightful loneliness was not dissipated by his considerable fame as a writer, by his friendship with a president, by his travels abroad. He died in 1864; Ralph Waldo Emerson was present at the funeral and wrote in his journal: "Yesterday, May 23, we buried Hawthorne in Sleepy Hollow, in a pomp of sunshine and verdure and gentle winds ... I thought there was a tragic element in the event—in the painful solitude of the man, which, I suppose, could not longer be endured, and he died of it."

*The Scarlet Letter* is a very short book, but even so it is not necessary to read all of it, at least the first time through. Hawthorne was anxious about its reception; at the last moment he therefore composed a long, rambling introductory chapter—"The Customs-House"—that most readers should simply skip, or at least skim. Scholars and high school English teachers will dispute this advice, because "The Customs-House" is full of puzzling details that require explanations. Whenever a scholar can explain a detail he leaps at the chance, because that allows him a little longer to delay facing up to a home truth. But if you, like me, prefer home truths, then turn to Chapter 1, "The Prison Door," and begin to read.

# HERMAN MELVILLE
1819–1891
*Moby Dick*

The best books begin well. *Moby Dick* begins like this:

> Whenever I find myself growing grim about the mouth; whenever it is damp, drizzly November in my soul; whenever I find myself involuntarily pausing before coffin warehouses, and bringing up the rear of every funeral I meet; and especially whenever my hypos get such an upper hand of me, that it requires a strong moral principle to prevent me from deliberately stepping into the street, and methodically knocking people's hats off—then, I account it high time to get to sea as soon as I can. This is my substitute for pistol and ball. With a philosophical flourish Cato threw himself upon his sword; I quietly take to the ship. There is nothing surprising in this. If they but knew it, almost all men in their degree, some time or other, cherish very nearly the same feelings towards the ocean with me.

I deny the major premise: I don't think most men cherish those feelings about the sea. Certainly I do not. And certainly it would never occur to me, no matter how far down in the dumps I was, to go on a three-year whaling voyage. But I do know about the dumps, when it is "damp, drizzly November in the soul," and then I, like Melville, like his hero Ishmael, want to get away, to do something very strange and different from anything I have ever done before. Maybe even to search out and challenge Moby Dick, the great white whale.

The great White Whale, I should say, with capital letters, for surely this beast is more than a beast, more than a mere fish, as the whalers call him, and instead is a symbol of evil, or good, or the unconscious, or God—it doesn't matter what, exactly, as long as we recognize that it is something immense and important to the life and mind of mankind.

For Ahab, captain of the whaling ship *Pequod*, out of New Bedford, Moby Dick is the symbol of all the evil in the world, the symbol of the terrible fact that there is evil in the world, that God has made the world imperfect, the why of which is indeed the central question of theology, not alone for Ahab. For Melville the White Whale is something different, which he cannot quite say, but which he allows his protagonist Ishmael to muse and speculate upon in the profound and moving chapter, "The Whiteness of the Whale." Here Melville attempts to solve "the incantation of this whiteness," and to learn "why it appeals with such power to the soul."

> Is it that by its indefiniteness it shadows forth the heartless voids and immensities of the universe, and thus stabs us from behind with the thought of annihilation, when beholding the white depths of the Milky Way? Or is it, that as in essence whiteness is not so much a color as the visible absence of color, and at the same time the concrete of all colors; is it for these reasons that there is such a dumb blankness, full of meaning, in a wide landscape of snows—a colorless, all-color of atheism from which we shrink? And when we consider that other theory of the natural philosophers, that all other earthly hues—every stately or lovely emblazoning—the sweet tinges of sunset skies and woods; yea, and the gilded velvets of butterflies, and the butterfly cheeks of young girls; all these are but subtle deceits, not actually inherent in substances, but only laid on from without; so that all deified nature absolutely paints like the harlot, whose allurements cover nothing but the charnel-house within; and when we proceed further, and consider that the mystical cosmetic which produces every one of her hues, the great principle of light, for ever remains white or colorless in itself, and if operating without medium upon matter, would touch all objects, even tulips and roses, with its own blank tinge—pondering all this, the

palsied universe lies before us a leper; and like willful travelers in Lapland, who refuse to wear colored and coloring glasses upon their eyes, so the wretched infidel gazes himself blind at the monumental white shroud that wraps all the prospect around him. And of all these things the Albino whale was the symbol. Wonder ye then at the fiery hunt?

And wonder ye then that Melville wrote to his friend Nathaniel Hawthorne, after *Moby Dick* was finished: "I have written a wicked book, and I feel spotless as the lamb"? He had driven out all the damp, drizzly November thoughts from his soul, asked all the most daring, most blasphemous questions, and felt himself shrived and pure. Such is the role of art in a few great breasts; it serves some as the sea serves others.

*Moby Dick* contains a lot of metaphysics, but it is far from being nothing but metaphysics, and in fact it is also one of the best adventure yarns. Born in 1819, Herman Melville had served on a whaling ship and had spent four years (1841-44) knocking about the South Seas, the experiences of which time gave him the inspiration for half a dozen novels, of which *Moby Dick* was the best (but the others— *Typee, Omoo, Mardi*—were good, too). *Moby Dick* is full of lore; when you have finished it you will know what can be known about whaling, whale ships, and the South Seas, short of going there and spending years in a wooden ship searching for whales, which of course is no longer possible. The book is also full of psychological insights about men and sailors, and it contains unforgettable characters: Father Mapple, and his wonderful sermon—one of the great sermons in literature; Queequeg, the heathen harpooner; Starbuck, the faithful first mate who attempts to bring back his captain to a sense of his human responsibilities; the captain of the Rachel, the symbol of human kindness, who saves what little can be saved from the wreck of the *Pequod*; Ishmael; and Captain Ahab, than whom there is possibly no more tragic hero in fiction (his equals exist, but they are not many).

Ahab, poor benighted man, great driven spirit, searching through the wide world for the answers to questions that have no answers, and which answers we would probably not like if we could have them: Ahab is a magnificent creation, but a fearful one, too. You may not remember him with any affection; he may seem too much the exile, having isolated himself from all humanity, all warm, colorful, common life. Such a man is frightening. But if you can rise above that, then you will feel a deep sympathy for this soul, damned while still alive, condemned to follow the track of an unspeakable mystery whose end can only be disaster. Such sympathy, if you can feel it, may make you a better human being—and a wiser one; for there are surely Moby Dicks still in this world, even if there are no more White Whales.

Melville ceased to be a "public" writer after publishing his fine Civil War poems in 1866. He disappeared from view, struggling, as now seems likely, with his own Moby Dick—whatever that was to him. He died in 1891. During his last months he wrote one remarkable story, which has suggested to some wise critics that he had resolved his problem and "sailed through," as W. H. Auden wrote in his beautiful poem about Melville, "into an extraordinary mildness."

That story is called "Billy Budd, Foretopman," and any lover of Melville, and of *Moby Dick*, should read it, too.

# IVAN TURGENEV
## 1818–1883
### *First Love*

Ivan Sergeyevich Turgenev was born in central Russia in 1818 and died in France in 1883. He received a desultory early education and did not come alive, as he said, until the three years that he spent at the University of Berlin from 1838 to 1841. His writing career began at that time, and he wrote for the rest of his life, a period of some forty years. *First Love* was written in 1860, very nearly the midpoint of those years.

Turgenev has to be counted as one of the greatest Russian writers of the nineteenth century; only Tolstoy, Dostoevsky, and Chekhov may be considered his equals or his betters. Yet he was very different from all of them. He was almost alone in being sensitive to Europe; and he was also alone in believing that the future of Russia lay in a steady liberalization of its society, its culture, and its economy, instead of in a revolutionary cataclysm. In fact, his hopes for his country underline the tragedy of its real history; if there had been more men like him, the world, to say nothing of Russia itself, would now be a better place than it is.

Above all Turgenev believed in literature, in poetry, in the importance of beauty in the lives of men and women and of a great country. For Henry James, it is reported, he was "the only real beautiful genius." But this genius did not recommend Turgenev to his contemporaries, especially in Russia. His fellow countrymen thought he was weak and uninterested in the really important things, like progress, power, and revolution. He knew very well that there were even more important things than those.

His works have a delicacy, almost a fragility, that is unique among great Russian writers. They are cool and objective—sometimes, it must be admitted, to a fault. They possess a lapidary excellence that is very rare, and not just in Russia. Perhaps only Flaubert can rightly be compared to him in his own time. But Flaubert lacks his charm.

In 1860, when he wrote *First Love*, Turgenev had already begun to look back at his childhood and youth as a better time than the present. It had been a world, he knew, that was gone forever, a world of great landowners and peasants, of serfs and of the men and women who owned them. Serfdom was abolished in 1861, but its memory would linger on, just as the memory of slavery has lingered in the United States for more than a century. But, unlike America, Russia was not half slaveholding society, half modern industrial society; *all* of Russia depended on the work of serfs, and those who owned them, their fellow human beings, felt themselves almost universally to be, taking the title of a famous story of Turgenev's, "superfluous men." The fine and delicate problem of creating a life when there is really nothing that you have to do is the subject of many of Turgenev's stories. Since that is the way most of us will live in the future, when machines are our slaves, we will do well to read Turgenev. By itself that would not be a good enough reason. Turgenev's love stories will last the longest, I think, simply because love will probably survive all changes and revolutions. And Turgenev, although he never married, was in love for most of his life, always with the same woman, a beautiful and renowned French singer. There are worse ways to spend a lifetime if you are a writer. Or so they say.

*First Love* is a story about a young man and an older one who love the same woman, and about the conflict this situation creates in her and about how she resolves it. It is touching, beautiful, and, at the end, shocking. The jolt of understanding that strikes Vladimir Petrovich also strikes the reader, and makes him tremble. Reading the story is quite an experience.

Turgenev's masterpiece, it is said, is the long novel *Fathers and Sons* (or *Fathers and Children*, as it is now more commonly called). *Fathers and Sons* possesses a political dimension lacking in *First Love*; it is a work on a higher and grander plane. *First Love* is, instead, a small but perfect jewel of a story. It is my favorite work of Turgenev. Even if you eventually decide that you prefer *Fathers and Sons*, or the famous play, *A Month in the Country*, or any other of his major works, I am certain that *First Love* is a very good place to begin reading Turgenev.

# FYODOR DOSTOEVSKY
### 1821–1881
### *Crime and Punishment*

For two centuries the autocratic Russian state has punished those citizens who defy it by sending them, as prisoners and laborers, to Siberia, there to work out their destiny—and save their lives if they can. The Gulag, in short, was no invention of Stalin; nor did the idea die with Stalin that brutal punishment, just short of execution, but often leading to death, would "improve" men's souls. And in fact it is hard to see how any reasonable person would ever have thought that it would succeed. Yet it did succeed in the case of Fyodor Dostoevsky. Perhaps he is the extraordinary exception who proves the rule.

He was born in 1821, the son of lower-middle-class parents—his father, the son of a priest, had run away from home to join the army and later, having retired to a dissolute life on his small estate near Moscow, was murdered by his serfs, whom he had treated with more than customary brutality. Fyodor endured a meager education among poor and downtrodden people. Though he was destined for the army as an engineer, he spent most of his time reading and writing. His first novel, *Poor Folk*, 1845, was highly praised. He was pleased with himself but soon fell into revolutionary thinking and joined a group that was savagely persecuted by the authorities. Together with several associates, Dostoevsky was tried in 1849 and sentenced to be shot, a fate averted at the last moment by a courier from the tsar who commuted the punishment to four years at hard labor. Dostoevsky was sent in chains to Siberia, where he lived surrounded by filth, lice, and disease, among poor folk who hated him for his relatively high birth.

But he survived, despite frequent epileptic attacks, despite the terrible solitude of his existence, despite extensions of his sentence. He even managed to fall in love with and marry a woman who, as it turned out, was dying of tuberculosis. He returned to St. Petersburg ten years after departing for Siberia, a free man and a changed one as well.

The change was extraordinary. The young rebel had become a middle-aged conservative, although he was not yet the violent reactionary that he later became. The tsar, he had concluded, had been right. He had deserved punishment and had achieved happiness in the only way possible for him and perhaps, he thought, for anyone: through suffering. He began to incorporate this doctrine, which is shared, of course, by many of the world's great artists, in novels that place him in the first rank of Russian authors.

*Crime and Punishment* was one of the first of these works of Dostoevsky's mature years. It was produced quickly, since at the time he was under severe pressure to repay large debts incurred in gambling binges, but the book is carefully shaped and plotted for all of the haste with which it was written. And its idea is both profound and shocking. Raskolnikov, the young hero of the novel, is torn between the two sides of his character: on one side, a meek, humble student, afraid to lift his voice in the world; on the other, a strong, self-willed man, insistent upon playing a leading role in the human comedy. To prove to himself that his real character is the latter and not the former, Raskolnikov decides to murder an old woman, a pawnbroker who preys upon the poor of St. Petersburg. He will murder her, he decides, thus confirming his strength of will, and also rob her, and use her money to do good for the poor. And indeed he does murder her, although with great difficulty; it is not as easy, he finds, to kill a human being as to kill a rat, say, or a fly.

The murder proves nothing and satisfies nothing. Raskolnikov is consumed by guilt and his bad dreams—those dreams that are one of the wonders of this book—become ever more nightmarish. His waking life, too, takes on the character of a nightmare. Finally he meets Svidrigailov, with whom he has a long conversation that shows him the depths of despair. Svidrigailov shares his vision of eternity with Raskolnikov:

> "We always imagine eternity as something beyond our conception, something vast, vast! But why must it be vast? Instead of all that, what if it's one little room, like a bathhouse in the country, black and grimy and spiders in every corner, and that's all eternity is? I sometimes fancy it like that."
>
> "Can it be you can imagine nothing juster and more comforting than that?" Raskolnikov cried, with a feeling of anguish.
>
> "Juster? And how can we tell, perhaps that is just, and do you know it's what I would certainly have made it," answered Svidrigailov, with a vague smile.

It is to escape such visions, perhaps, that Raskolnikov begins to yearn for punishment, yearns to pay his debt to society and to God, so that he can once again dream of happiness. In the meantime the remarkable detective, Porfiry, is closing in. Finally, Raskolnikov is trapped, confesses, is condemned, and goes off to Siberia accompanied by his beloved Sonya, the meek and devoted heroine of the novel.

Probably *The Brothers Karamazov* is an even greater novel than *Crime and Punishment*; perhaps *The Idiot* and *The Possessed* are nearly its equal. But *Crime and Punishment* is, I think, the work of

Dostoevsky with which a reader should begin to try to deal with the overwhelming power of this nearly mad Russian author. It takes a lot out of a reader; the pain that Raskolnikov suffers is all there, on the surface, and you may suffer it too.

# LEO TOLSTOY
## 1828–1910
*War and Peace*
*The Death of Ivan Ilych*
*Twenty-Three Tales*

Leo Tolstoy was born in 1828 on the family estate, Yasnaya Polyana, a hundred miles south of Moscow. His parents died when he was young, and he was brought up by relatives who arranged for his education at the University of Kazan. Headstrong and uncontrollable, as well as rich, he returned home when he was nineteen to live on his estate, manage his affairs, and try to educate himself. None of this worked out well. He joined the army, serving bravely in several campaigns. He also began to write.

In 1862 he married, settled down, learned how to manage his estates efficiently, and began to write *War and Peace*. He worked on the book for six years, writing and rewriting; his young wife dutifully copied the entire enormous manuscript several times by hand. The book was finally published in 1869, when he was forty-one.

Tolstoy's *War and Peace* is very large and vastly complex. Its scope is as wide as Russia or as life itself. It is also filled with thousands of small, carefully observed details.

Painters and moviemakers have tried to recreate the vastness of the book in other media, with their depiction of the shock of hundreds of thousands of soldiers battling at Austerlitz and Borodino, and their vision of the great emptiness of the Russian plain. These attempts have not been very successful. The scale of *War and Peace* is best expressed in words and best apprehended through the reader's imagination. No film can do this book justice.

That is partly because vastness is not the book's only character-istic, or even its leading one. Instead, it is the small details that are most vivid. Rock-hard, concrete details of experience that are exactly like the details of our own lives, they become part of our lives when we read the book.

One can wonder how anyone who has the slightest interest in books, or the barest curiosity about what the greatest of all novels may be like, could consider not reading *War and Peace*. At the same time it is easy to understand why many do not try it. It is too big, too "great," too famous. There is a kind of backlash from all the effusive praise.

Let us concentrate, therefore, on how to read *War and Peace*. Perhaps the why will then take care of itself.

*War and Peace* is nearly fourteen hundred pages long. Few readers can read attentively at a steady rate of more than fifty pages an hour. This means that the book requires twenty-eight hours to read, at a minimum.

Many readers cannot read at a steady pace of fifty pages an hour. They may need a total of forty or fifty hours, or even more.

To read the book well, therefore, you will need a large chunk of free time, when you will not be too often interrupted and your mind drawn from what you are reading. Setting aside a week of your life to read *War and Peace* is a reasonable idea. The book is worth it.

Ideally, you should have nothing else to do during that week, besides reading, eating, and sleeping. Most readers will not be able to enjoy those ideal conditions, but try to get as close as you can.

Next, throw away any reader's guides that list all the characters of the book and their relationships to one another. These are crutches that in the long run only impede the reader.

Reading *War and Peace* can be compared to moving to a new town or a new job where you know no one. At first all is confusion; you cannot connect names and faces; you do not know who will be impor-tant to you and who will not. Often your first acquaintances turn out to be unimportant, while you only meet the really important people in your new life later on—or realize only later on that they are important.

So it is with *War and Peace*. As you read on, the various groups of characters sort themselves out. The families become meaningful as families, the lovers as lovers, the friends as friends. You cannot know Pierre or Andrew well the first time you meet them, and an introductory note stating that they are the two most important male characters will not tell you anything you will not learn yourself and in a better way. To be told in advance that Natasha Rostov is the heroine of the book is not much help either. If you do not come to see that as the book progresses, you are blind.

It is, I think, exactly as easy, or as hard, to discern characters and character relationships in *War and Peace* as it is in real life. I would not welcome information from a demiurge to the effect that such and such a woman was destined to loom large in my life, or that such and such a man, after years of nodding acquaintance, would become my good friend. I prefer to find out those things as I go along. So it is with *War and Peace*. Let the book happen to you; do not try to control it. It was written by a master of fiction; by *the* master. If you are confused at the beginning, you can feel confident that you won't end up confused. You will know all that anyone can know.

Which, of course, is not everything, about anything or anyone. One of the secrets of Tolstoy's power as a novelist is that he allows his characters to surprise you. If they were cut and dried, molded after a formula, they would not surprise, they would simply obey the rules of their construction. But Tolstoy's characters seem no less alive, no less predictable, than you or I. Like you and me, they surprise even themselves.

Tolstoy, in short, does not know everything about Pierre, Andrew, Natasha, Princess Mary, Nicholas, old Prince Bolkonski, Count Rostov, Platon Karateev, and the host of men and women and children who fill the pages of this book. And all the thousands of soldiers. And among the soldiers, particularly Kutuzov, the general of the Russian armies.

Kutuzov was a real man (I knew his great granddaughter), but he was—or perhaps because of that he was—an enigma. Kutuzov is extremely lethargic, old, often ill, rather doddering. He doesn't give many orders, nor does he seem to read or listen to the reports of enemy movements that are given to him. Nevertheless, he alone knows that Napoleon will be beaten and that he—and the ordinary Russian soldiers—will beat him. He knows this intuitively; no book learning or military training could teach it to him. He alone knows that the great battle at Borodino, which everyone else (including Napoleon) believes is another French triumph, is instead a French defeat, because every man, horse, gun, or box of food that the French have lost cannot be replaced—they are too far from home—whereas the Russians are fighting for and in their homeland. Kutuzov knows, or intuits, that time is inexorably on his side, but he cannot tell anyone this; they are too impatient or too frightened to listen to him. Besides, what does it matter whether they heed it or not? Time is still on his side. Kutuzov is one of Tolstoy's greatest creations, but he is not entirely intelligible, although he is certainly credible. Any more than a real, living person is entirely intelligible—no matter how well you may know him or her—although certainly credible.

I don't want to say any more about how to read *War and Peace* for fear of saying too much about the book. To tell you the truth, I am very envious of you if you have never read it. I would give a good deal to be in your shoes, with a week of uninterrupted time stretching before me, a comfortable chair, a good light, and the book in my lap, open to page one.

When Tolstoy published the second of his two great novels, *Anna Karenina*, in 1877, he was nearly fifty. He was already recognized as one of the greatest novelists in the world, but he did not go on writing novels. Instead, he devoted himself to writing philosophical treatises, and stories and tales.

Just as *War and Peace* is almost by unanimous consent the best of all novels, so is "The Death of Ivan Ilych" close to being considered the best of all short stories. It is in fact a very simple story. Ivan Ilych, an ordinary Russian official with an ordinary job and an ordinary family, becomes ill. He visits a doctor, but the doctor doesn't say what is the matter with him. Perhaps he doesn't know, thinks Ivan Ilych, and he begins to be worried. He is right to worry; he is really ill. He slowly realizes this, and then comes to realize, slowly again, that he may die. Finally he knows that he will die, and he does so. That is the story of Ivan Ilych.

Death, "The undiscover'd country from whose bourn/No traveller returns," is the most difficult of human conditions to depict in fiction. Rather, it is not hard to describe the death of someone, for this is something we are likely to have seen. But how to describe death from within? From the point of view of the dying man or woman? That is not something that any writer has experienced before writing about it!

Tolstoy, because he was a kind of magician, did not have to experience death to understand it. He knew what Ivan Ilych felt, even up to the very end. (He also knew what Prince Andrew feels when, in *War and Peace*, he dies in the field hospital—this is another deservedly famous death scene in Tolstoy's works.)

How did Tolstoy know this? I can't say. How do I know that what he says Ivan Ilych feels is what people do feel when they die, what I will feel when I die? I can't say that, either, except that I'm certain of it. "The Death of Ivan Ilych" is indisputable. This is the way it is; this is the way it will be.

Later still, Tolstoy stopped writing even short stories about upper-class Russians and instead concentrated on the simple folk tales of peasants that he had heard all of his life and now, as an old man, wanted to reinterpret for a world audience. The best of these tales are collected in a small volume translated and edited by Aylmer Maude and called *Twenty-Three Tales*. Few books of its size contain such wisdom and beauty.

Some of the tales in the volume are well known in other versions—for example, "How Much Land Does a Man Need?" A peasant is given the chance to possess all of the land he can walk around in a day. He has never owned any land; he sets out at break of day and walks rapidly in a great arc—he will carve out for himself an estate, he will never again be poor, his children will be landowners. He doesn't stop to eat; there will be time for that later. But he walks too far and he realizes as the sun nears the horizon that he is still far from his starting point. He begins to run up the hill in order to complete the circle. He doesn't make it, of course, and so he loses everything.

Many other stories in this little book are just as wonderful. My favorite is called "The Three Hermits." A bishop visits a small desert island in the Black Sea. It is inhabited by three old men who are reputed to be very holy. The bishop hopes to learn from them, but when he discovers that they do not know how to pray—do not even know the Lord's Prayer—he is dismayed and decides he must teach them instead. He spends all day, and finally, after many hours of effort, they are letter perfect: Each of them can repeat the Lord's Prayer by himself, and they can repeat it together in a kind of singsong unison. The bishop departs, feeling very satisfied with himself. Then something happens. I will not tell you what; I do not want to spoil it for you. It is a miracle, and I think the only completely believable miracle in fiction.

In 1910, in November, when he was a very old man and half mad, Tolstoy left home because he was at odds with his wife and because he somehow wanted to make the world a better place. He began to walk—he knew not where. Every newspaper in the civilized world headlined his disappearance, and hordes of reporters descended upon his province and his little town. A few days later he arrived at a remote railway junction at Astapovo, Ryazan Province, suffering from pneumonia, and there he died. What he had seen during those few lost days, and why he had wandered where he went, and whether he had found what he was seeking, we do not know.

# ROBERT BROWNING
### 1812–1889
*Selected Poems*

Robert Browning was born in London in 1812. He received practically no formal education, reading instead in his father's large library. He lived at home with his parents until he was thirty-four, reading and writing poems.

The story of Browning's courtship of and marriage to Elizabeth Barrett, the invalid poet who was six years his senior, is, because of the long-running play *The Barretts of Wimpole Street* and the later movie, as well known as the story of any English poet's life. Indeed it is a fine story. Browning fell in love with Elizabeth in 1845, before he had ever met her (although he had read her poems). He rescued her the next year from the half-prison that was her father's home and swept her off to Italy in a romantic turmoil that gave both of them great joy. She wrote better poems about their love than she had ever written before, but he wrote little then, conserving until after her death in 1861 the well of inspiration that she remained to him throughout his days. He would have been a fine poet without her; with her he became a great one.

Browning felt that there are three levels or kinds of poets: good, better, and best. He defined them in "Sordello.". The good poets, he wrote:

> *say they so have seen;*
> *For the better, what it was they saw; the best*
> *Impart the gift of seeing to the rest.*

The ordinary poet looks out the window and tells his auditors, seated in the room, that he sees something outside. The better poet gives his readers a detailed running account of what he is seeing outside the window. The best poet, whom Browning called the "Maker-see," puts his readers at the window and lets them see for themselves. It is a great gift.

It was a gift that Browning had in full measure. Take this short poem, titled "Meeting at Night":

> *The gray sea and the long black land;*
> *And the yellow half-moon large and low;*
> *And the startled little waves that leap*
> *In fiery ringlets from their sleep,*
> *As I gain the cove with pushing prow,*
> *And quench its speed i' the slushy sand.*
>
> *Then a mile of warm sea-scented beach;*
> *Three fields to cross till a farm appears;*
> *A tap at the pane, the quick sharp scratch*
> *And blue spurt of a lighted match,*
> *And a voice less loud, through its joys and fears,*
> *Than the two hearts beating each to each!*

Each line gives more concrete reality to the scene, until the final triumph of "the quick sharp scratch/And blue spurt of a lighted match," with its extraordinary caesura between "blue" and "spurt" while the "made-to-see" reader waits for the match to light, and then the quiet sound of two hearts "beating each to each." I have read that poem a hundred times and never tire of it. I never will tire of it until I cease to think that poetry has everything to do with real life.

The intensity of physical presence is the most characteristic mark of Browning's poetry, but there are other intensities as well that, in the end, are even more important. Browning is the acknowledged master of the dramatic monologue, in which a single speaker tells a story or describes a scene as though he were describing it to another person, an auditor who, though silent, is just as much a character in the poem as the speaker himself. The intensity of presence of these auditors is sometimes almost overwhelming, even though they do not say a word: the wife in "Andrea del Sarto"; the investigating officer (as the reader must suppose himself to be) listening to the crazed account of his crime by "Porphyria's Lover"; the representative of the count in "My Last Duchess." The drama of these lyric poems is all in the interchange, in the words spoken and the words attended to, even though only one side of the conversation is heard. Browning's dramatic monologues are among the finest achievements of English poetry.

His single finest poem is, I think, *The Ring and the Book* (1868–69). This long poem in twelve books had a curious genesis. Browning came upon an old book in a shop in Florence that detailed the crime, committed two centuries before, of a certain Count Guido Franceschini, who, to recoup his wasted fortune, tricked a young girl into marrying him, then, after tortuous windings of the plot, murdered her and her parents and was himself executed for the deed. Browning worked for years on the poem and made of it what is certainly the finest detective story in verse. Each of the twelve books of the poem tells the story, or an aspect of the story—there is remarkably little repetition—from a different point of view. *The Ring and the Book* is not easy reading but it is worth the effort to read it. You will feel when you are finished that you have seen into three human hearts as perhaps you have rarely been able to see before.

That is the secret of reading Browning: to let him make you see. Some readers resist this; they find him too difficult, his syntax too complicated, his verse too dense and packed with meaning. This criticism applies, perhaps, to all the best poets, to all of the "makers-see." At any rate, Browning is one of those.

You may wish to start with these poems: "Home-Thoughts, from Abroad," "Home-Thoughts, from the Sea," "Meeting at Night," "Porphyria's Lover," "My Last Duchess," "A Woman's Last Word," "The Bishop Orders His Tomb at Saint Praxed's Church," "A Toccata of Galuppi's," "The Last Ride Together," "Andrea del Sarto," "Prospice," and "Rabbi Ben Ezra." Whether you decide to tackle *The Ring and the Book* is up to you.

# LEWIS CARROLL
## 1832–1898
### *Alice's Adventures in Wonderland*
### *Through the Looking-Glass and What Alice Found There*

Lewis Carroll loved photography, mathematics, and little girls. Out of these, plus a wonderfully playful imagination and a good memory, he fashioned one of the great books of all time.

*Alice's Adventures in Wonderland* begins with Alice falling through a rabbit hole into another world. This could be the dark place that is the camera, which sees the world upside down and in other odd ways through a small aperture. Alice, furthermore, is both enlarged and reduced, like a picture in an enlarger in a darkroom. Mathematics controls all these changes; *Alice in Wonderland* has been called a primer of the differential and integral calculus. And of course Alice is a little girl, and a most charming one. She is both serious and playful, and insistent upon understanding what is happening to her. She is distressed by the bodily changes that over-take her, as all little girls are, but at the same time she is brave and faces up to whatever she has to face—including caterpillars, hedge-hogs, and queens.

The images of *Alice in Wonderland* are unforgettable; we can never get them out of our heads. (Partly this is because of John Tenniel's wonderful illustrations for the original edition; when reading *Alice* you should seek an edition with reproductions of those old illustrations.) Alice swimming with the White Rabbit, with his white gloves still on, in the Pool of Tears. Alice at the Mad Tea Party, surrounded by that magical company, from the Mad Hatter to the Dormouse, sleepily sinking into his tea. Alice growing down into a mite and up into a giant, her head sticking out of the chimney of her little Wonderland house. The trial, with the Queen as both judge and jury—"That's not fair!" says Alice; the accused is the Dormouse again, who always ends up in the wrong place at the wrong time. The famous game of croquet, in which the hoops are hedgehogs that get up from time to time and walk away, leaving the players to scratch their heads and wonder where the next shot is supposed to go. The Jabberwock. The Caterpillar smoking his hookah on his mushroom. Tweedledum and Tweedledee. The Walrus and the Carpenter and the Oysters that dance into their mouths. And so forth and so on.

Some of these images come from *Alice in Wonderland*'s marvelous sequel, *Through the Looking-Glass and What Alice Found There*, which was published a few years later. The two books make up one great fantasy, and it is hard to keep them apart in the memory. In fact, it's not worth trying to do so.

How they ever got written is an extraordinary accident. Lewis Carroll, whose real name was Charles L. Dodgson, enjoyed entertaining the three young daughters of the master of his Oxford college and one day they went on a picnic and were caught in the rain. Two weeks later they went on another picnic and he told them stories about a little girl named Alice who fell down a rabbit hole on a rainy day.

He always told the girls stories, and they always loved them; but this time the story seemed especially good and Alice Liddell, the oldest of his three companions—she was ten—asked him to write it down. He did so and made funny illustrations for it and gave it to her for a present. Of course she liked it all the better, and so did her sisters and her mother and father. However, nothing would ever have come of it if Charles Kingsley, the novelist, had not happened to see the manuscript lying on a table in the Liddells' home. Kingsley picked it up and read it. "Extraordinary! It must be published!" he declared.

Dodgson consulted other author friends; they also said the book was good. He revised it and published it, with Tenniel's illustrations, in 1865. *Through the Looking-Glass* came along in 1871.

By the time Dodgson died, in 1898, *Alice* (the two books taken together) had become the most popular children's book in England, and by 1932, the centenary of Lewis Carroll's birth, when there were celebrations of *Alice* in all the English-speaking countries, it had become probably the most popular children's book in the world.

It is hard to say why, exactly. Many critical theories have been advanced, but they all dwindle to silliness when they face the reality of *Alice* itself—or Alice herself. Maybe it is just that the combination of photography, mathematics, and little girls is dynamite, especially when ignited by a lively imagination.

# THOMAS HARDY
### 1840–1928
*Tess of the d'Urbervilles*
*Selected Poems*

Thomas Hardy was born in Dorset, in the West Country of England that his works made famous, in 1840. For the first twenty-five years of his life he was torn between two careers, architecture and literature. Literature won out.

He began in the 1870s to produce a series of novels that—since they were published anonymously—were at first supposed to be by George Eliot. His first popular success was *Far from the Madding Crowd* (1874). *The Return of the Native,* somber and powerful, appeared in 1878. His most famous novel, and probably his best, *Tess of the d'Urbervilles,* was not published until 1891.

The subtitle of *Tess* was "A Pure Woman," but the phrase is ironic. Tess is terribly wronged in this wonderful book, and it is her young and naive husband, more than anyone else, who wrongs her. The world is all against her, we see, and there is no God, no good, no deep justice to protect and succor her. If there is a God, He has sported with Tess, as we learn from the powerful last paragraph of the novel.

Yet Tess is not beyond blame. Some readers see the book as containing an accusation of Tess: it is all, this terrible mix-up, this frightful injustice, her own fault. There is merit in that reading as long as it is not the only reading of the novel.

Deeper than that, we must ask what Hardy himself thought about Tess. The other novels give us a clue. In all of them there is a woman more or less like Tess (though none is as truly interesting as she, none so breaks our hearts). And all of these heroines share a womanly strangeness and dangerousness. Hardy, who created heroines more alluring and attractive than those in any other Victorian novel, also expressed with extraordinary power the Victorian fear of women. Do women feel more deeply than men? Do their emotions go where a man's cannot follow? Something like that is what Hardy is saying in his novels, and especially in *Tess of the d'Urbervilles*.

Hardy's poetical career was full of contradictions. He had begun writing poems about his Wessex country when a young man, and he kept on writing them all of his life. But during the twenty-five years when he was writing his novels, he published no poems. His last novel, *Jude the Obscure* (1896), was from the popular point of view a failure, although some critics regarded it highly. Hardy thereupon began to devote himself to poetry, and wrote and published it for the remaining years of his long life.

The tone in Hardy's poems that compels readers of today and forces them to listen, but that offended many readers years ago, is one of almost total pessimism, beyond despair. The word "despair" means "without hope," and theologically speaking that is a sin, for to despair is to deny the possibility of God's saving grace.

Hardy did not care about that. If he was to be damned for having no hope, so be it. Many people were like him in despairing of the world and of the goodness, so-called, of mankind. At least Hell would not be a lonely place.

Hardy's despair was not, as one might say, of the sort that is active: he did not think the Devil rules the world, or that God hates man and wants to thwart him. He simply believed that there was nothing there to guide and succor the world, nothing but blind chance. In "Hap" he makes this clear. If there were only a vengeful God who would tell him that His divine happiness depended on suffering man, Hardy says, he could endure it—but there is none such. Instead, "Crass Casualty obstructs the sun and rain, And dicing Time for gladness casts a moan … These purblind Doomsters had as readily strown Blisses about my pilgrimage as pain."

"Purblind Doomsters" are at the center of Hardy's concept of things. There is a power that controls and ordains our fate: This power is absolute, and our fates are unavoidable. But there is no way in which we can understand it. It is totally beyond our ken. If we know anything at all about this power, it is that it seems to joy in strewing pains about our pilgrimage rather than blisses. But even that is not certain and may be illusory.

Because he was without hope does not mean that Hardy was unhappy. That is a curious and wonderful thing about him, and the thing that makes his poetry magical:

> *Let me enjoy the earth no less*
> *Because the all-enacting Might*
> *That fashioned forth its loveliness*
> *Had other aims than my delight.*

Is it necessary, after all, for happiness, to believe that we are "taken care of," mothered, fathered, tended to our dying day? Hardy says no. He is one of the great pagan writers, two thousand years after their time. He has more in common with Lucretius, say, who lived two millennia before him, than with his contemporary, W.B. Yeats. Thus Hardy's vision of the world—cold, unyielding, beautiful—seems sometimes hard to take. But it is one with which we must learn to deal, because it may be—not necessarily is—true.

Hardy's *Collected Poems* is a massive volume, with hundreds and hundreds of poems (most are short, many very short). Here it is difficult and finally unwise to make a selection and say (as we may of Yeats or Robert Frost): Read these first, and then go on to another selection of your own making. Every reader of Hardy has his or her own favorites, and you will have yours when you begin to read him. Start at the beginning of the volume and read through, a few poems at a time, not more than ten pages an evening. Skip as much as you want. Flip the pages and read a poem whose title attracts you. There is a remarkable consistency; not one of this large number is a bad poem, although some are better than others. They were written at all times during Hardy's life; sometimes he published poems he had written as long as forty or even fifty years earlier, so it does not matter at all which you read first.

I think you will want to keep on reading Hardy, not steadily, not every day forever, but forever nevertheless. He will become a habit.

# WILLIAM JAMES
## 1842–1910
### *The Principles of Psychology*

William and Henry James are certainly the leading brother act in the history of literature. As brothers, they were close; William, especially, adored his younger brother Henry. They did not entirely approve of one another; William, especially again, did not think the way Henry wrote English was as clear as it could be. Henry did not feel that way about William's prose style, and indeed no one ever wrote English better than William James.

William was born in New York in 1842, some fifteen months before Henry. His education was irregular, partly because of his irregular family life and partly because of the almost continuous ill health that he suffered until the time that he married Alice Gibbons; thereafter his neurasthenia disappeared, and he began to show an energy and an ability to work hitherto unknown. He taught at Harvard for thirty-five years, but his real life unfolded in his study, where he wrote a series of remarkably readable books.

His writing career divides neatly into three periods or phases. The first culminated in the publication of *The Principles of Psychology*, in two volumes, in 1890. The second, in which his curious mind turned to problems of religion, culminated in the Gifford Lectures of 1902, published as *The Varieties of Religious*

*Experience*. The third, devoted to philosophy, culminated in *Pragmatism: A New Name for Old Ways of Thinking* (1907). All three books were accompanied and followed by collections of essays, like "The Will to Believe," which lays it down as a human necessity that everyone must, sooner or later, go beyond the definite and the certain, and take the "leap of faith"—in short, you have to believe in something for which there is less than enough evidence. I think we know this to be true, from our own life experience.

William James spent nearly twenty years studying the subject of psychology—not the mental philosophy of the "genteel tradition," as George Santayana called it, but the laboratory science that is psychology today. At the end of the twenty years, however, he seems to have become bored with psychology. Nevertheless, he had written one of the greatest books on the subject, which, although it is dated in some respects, is still more pleasurable to read than almost any other book on the subject.

Actually, James's *Principles of Psychology* is no more dated than Galileo's *Two New Sciences*, Newton's *Principia*, or Darwin's *Origin of Species*. All four books make mistakes and reveal ignorance on the part of their authors of some things that we now know. Yet each book not only signaled a new turning in the career of thought, but showed the new way to go.

The pragmatism of William James is the most commonsensible of commonsense philosophies, and his psychology is equally credible and down to earth. His long, fascinating book is full of lore and learning, but in no book is learning presented in such a delightful and easy way. In fact, one of the best things about William James's *Psychology* is the great number of long quotations from other psychologists and philosophers. His book is an anthology of the field, and the quotations are so well chosen and so deftly interwoven with his own commentary that one concludes that no other of these somewhat antique experts needs to be read.

Ideally, a book on psychology should be full of wisdom. Most books on psychology are not, but I don't know of any book that contains more wisdom about the way people are and the way they think and the things they do than James's *Principles of Psychology*. Each chapter contains pages of useful advice for readers, young and old, male and female. This, for example, from the chapter "Habit," which has always seemed to me to be an invaluable observation on the life we live:

> The hell to be endured hereafter, of which theology tells, is no worse than the hell we make for ourselves in this world by habitually fashioning our characters in the wrong way. Could the young but realize how soon they will become mere walking bundles of habits, they would give more heed to their conduct while in the plastic state. We are spinning our own fates, good or evil, and never to be undone.... Of course, this has its good side as well as its bad one. As we become permanent drunkards by so many separate drinks, so we become saints in the moral, and authorities and experts in the practical and scientific spheres, by so many separate acts and hours of work. Let no youth have any anxiety about the upshot of his education, whatever the line of it may be. If he keep faithfully busy each hour of the working-day, he may safely leave the final result to itself. He can with perfect certainty count on waking up some fine morning, to find himself one of the competent ones of his generation, in whatever pursuit he may have singled out ... Young people should know this truth in advance. The ignorance of it has probably engendered more discouragement and faint-heartedness in youths embarking on arduous careers than all other causes put together.

I love the novels of Henry James but I do sometimes fervently wish he had been able to write as clearly as that!

After completing his two-volume *Principles of Psychology*, William James rewrote it and published it in a single volume titled *Psychology: Briefer Course*. There is a temptation to read this instead of the massive original version, but it should be resisted. *Psychology: Briefer Course* presents the psychological doctrine of James in a succinct and dependable way, and doubtless many students of psychology are content with what they find there. But it does so at a price; in the shorter work, James excised many quotations and wise observations about human life. It is just those things above all that make *The Principles of Psychology* a valuable book.

# HENRY JAMES
1843–1916
*The Portrait of a Lady*
*The Ambassadors*
*The Golden Bowl*

Henry James was born in New York City in 1843, the son of a well-to-do Swedenborgian philosopher who provided Henry, and his brother William, with every possible intellectual luxury: excellent schools, trips to Europe, visits to museums and the theater. In their late teens William studied painting and Henry attended Harvard Law School, but it soon became apparent to the latter what he wished to be: a writer. That is what he was for the rest of his life.

Henry James was not nearly so sure, at least at first, where he wanted to live. The more he thought about it, the more inadequate America seemed as a literary locale; the example of Hawthorne, whom James considered to have been insufficiently challenged by his New England surroundings, was deeply disturbing. In his early thirties, therefore, James went to Paris, hoping to find a more congenial environment for his art. He met everyone and enjoyed a social triumph, but he soon concluded that he would never be able to bridge the linguistic gulf that separated him from the French—this despite the fact that he spoke French nearly perfectly. He moved to London in 1876 and there discovered his spiritual home. The next year he wrote: "I am now more at home in London than anywhere else in the world ... My interest in London is chiefly that of an observer where there is most in the world to observe."

James had social as well as literary ambitions, and the former were soon rewarded when he could boast that he had been invited to dinner more than one hundred times in a year. Literary success was another matter; the fact is he never had it, although he continued to write and to publish for forty years. Toward the end he began to be appreciated by a small coterie of the best English writers—they called him "The Master"—but he never enjoyed a large public success. At one point, recognizing that he would never be able to write a really popular novel, he turned to producing works for the stage, but his failure was even more catastrophic there. His persistence was heroic, and to his heroism in simply keeping at it we owe some of the finest literary novels ever written.

The Portrait of a Lady, published in 1881, shows the great skill that its author had acquired in the steady writing he had been doing for more than ten years. It is, I think, the most affecting of James's novels; it may be his only genuinely tragic story. The American also ends unhappily, but Christopher Newman, the hero, although he loses his love (and although her end is tragic), still has a great deal of life to look forward to, and we know that nothing will hold him back from doing so. At the end of The Portrait of a Lady, Isabel Archer has no future to look forward to. It touches your heart to think of what she is going to have to endure for the rest of her life.

Her life, at least the part of it we see, began so well, so hopefully. She is American and rich and, what is more, in control of her own money. She has nothing to do, as she says, but "confront her destiny," and at first it seems she will do this well and courageously. But a woman must marry, she thinks, to complete herself, and she finds that what really confronts her is a choice among suitors. The tragedy of this beautiful, intelligent, accomplished young woman is that she chooses the wrong man and thus ruins her life.

At first Gilbert Osmond does not seem to be the wrong man. At any rate, he has everything Isabel lacks, and desires: most notably culture and a solid position—albeit as an expatriate—in Italian society. Their life together, Isabel believes, will be a work of art, in accordance with the many fine pieces in Gilbert's home, which becomes her own and which she further embellishes with her wealth. But Gilbert, although he possesses impeccable taste, is a cruel, bad man, and he begins to torture Isabel in small, bland ways that become more and more frightful as the novel proceeds. He never says an angry word to her; he never strikes her; but he makes her inexpressibly unhappy.

In the end, one of her old admirers, the rejected suitor Caspar Goodwood, tries to reach her, to offer her an escape from her misery. Divorce is not out of the question, he says; and if she is unwilling to take her wealth back from her husband (or finds herself unable to do so owing to Italian law), then he, Caspar, will give her everything he has, and that is a great deal. But Isabel cannot accept this generous offer. She hates Osmond; she is willing to admit that she could love Goodwood. But the woman who sought, as a girl, to confront her destiny cannot now pretend that life is a game one can abandon when it becomes unpleasant.

The novels of Henry James are often criticized for their lack of events, their paucity of action and adventure. *The Portrait of a Lady* has more action than many other novels of James. The book's main defect is James's failure adequately to answer the question of why Isabel marries Osmond. We know she should not, but we cannot stop her! But given that choice, that *donnée*, as James liked to say, the rest is inevitable—and deeply moving.

*The Ambassadors* (1903) is one of the most complex novels ever written. An American gentleman of a certain age, Lambert Strether, who is engaged to marry a wealthy widow (also of a certain age) in Massachusetts, is sent by his fiancée to Paris to bring back her son Chad, who has apparently become involved with a woman of … how to say it . . . easy virtue? No, that's not right, far from it, but certainly a woman of a type not easily understood by moralistic New Englanders. Strether meets Chad and is immediately struck by how much he has changed. The naïve young man he knew has become very much a gentleman of a type he has never confronted before: smooth, refined in his manners and his taste, elegant in all the best senses of the word. Strether is certain that a woman has somehow been involved, and when he meets the Comtesse de Vionnet he realizes that it is she who has brought about this remarkable transformation.

He also realizes, as time passes, two things that are really inseparable. First, he has ruined his life by refusing to live it—by succumbing to the numb satisfactions of provincial American society, so different from the intricate and beautiful customs and beliefs of

Parisian existence. Second, he finds that he is unwilling to destroy the bond that has been formed between his prospective stepson and this elegant and beautiful *femme du monde*. In fact he finds himself being drawn into her spell, and he accepts what is for him almost as remarkable a transformation. He hardly knows what to do, and when Chad's mother sends out another "ambassador," her cold-hearted daughter, he accepts with some equanimity her threat that if he does not immediately change his ways the rich widow who is his fiancée will drop him like a hot coal. But in the last analysis he knows he is willing to accept the loss of everything he has thought most dear.

The novel, in fact, is strikingly suspenseful and I will not spoil it for you by telling you what happens. I will only say that despite its "Jamesian" faults of complex sentence structure, thinking, and feeling—thus permitting you to decide for yourself—it is very much worthy reading. Don't let those apparent faults turn you off.

*The Golden Bowl*, the last of Henry James's novels (published in 1904), is quintessential James, the perfect example of what James did better than almost any writer who ever lived, and also of what he did not and could not do. What Henry James could not be bothered to do, especially in his last years, was tell a story full of dramatic incident. In fact, almost nothing happens in *The Golden Bowl*; the book is about things that do not happen. The characters talk—endlessly; they feel deeply, they suffer, they exult. But they do nothing. Those readers should be forgiven who have struggled over *The Golden Bowl* and come away almost frantic with frustration, exhausted by their effort to pierce through the fog of conversation to find out what has really occurred.

Indeed, the climax of *The Golden Bowl*, instead of being an act, is a nonact—a refusal to act on the part of one of the four main characters, who may be called the heroine. Maggie, having tortured Charlotte almost to madness by her refusal to notice what is evident to everyone else, is teased, tempted, taunted by Charlotte in the great, climactic scene on the terrace of Adam Verver's country house. There, Maggie resists the temptation, avoids being drawn down and into Charlotte's last, desperate attempt to escape from the web of silence that surrounds her. Maggie's brilliantly intelligent escape from being herself entrapped in a series of ultimately disastrous revelations and accusations is one of the most remarkable events in fiction.

Or nonevents. For many readers that is just the problem—with *The Golden Bowl* and with the other late novels of Henry James. To readers brought up on popular fiction, *The Golden Bowl* is boring, trivial. Why bother to read five hundred pages that finally add up to nothing—to the status quo, which now will persist forevermore? Why strain to understand what is so hard to understand? Why make the enormous effort required to cut through the miasma of polite euphemisms, glancing allusions, and half-truths—as well as half-lies—to arrive at the tiny kernel of reality resting at the center of this conundrum?

The reason is that the story of *The Golden Bowl* is more real by far than the stories of many of those eventful entertainments. Reality is almost unbearable to many people; they do not like Henry James. But if you are able to face it, to see something that is real and not be appalled (the Gorgon's head!), then *The Golden Bowl* becomes not unbearably boring but unbearably exciting instead.

Consider the situation—the *donnée*—of *The Golden Bowl*. An Italian prince, young, handsome, brilliant, but nearly penniless, is to marry the shy, inexperienced, but pretty daughter of an American multimillionaire, Maggie. She adores the prince and half knows her doting father has bought him for her; but the prince loves Maggie, too, in his aristocratically correct and honorable way. In the past he has also loved another woman, a friend of Maggie's, a tall, beautiful, accomplished American who is as poor as the prince himself. The prince marries the heiress; and then—very surprisingly—the wealthy American, a widower, falls in love with the prince's ex-mistress and marries her. The two couples then proceed to live together in London and in Mr. Verver's magnificent home in the English countryside.

So much is fact, is undeniable. But the book is not about these facts and could not care less about these obvious, surface relationships. Its real subject is not the open loves but the covert ones, concerning each of which there are many unanswered, perhaps unanswerable questions. Rather, it is about the frantic search for those answers, and for a solution to the problem of the book, on the part of all four of its protagonists—a solution that will avoid social ruin for Charlotte, financial ruin for the prince, and the loss of all they most deeply love for both Maggie and her father.

The solution is found, and they all survive. You have to look sharp to see it happen. *The Golden Bowl* is difficult reading. Take it slow and easy. Be patient. Remember that it is probably no more difficult to discern what the prince is thinking, for example, or the princess, than to discern the thoughts in your own mind—or your lover's. Follow the thread; the clues are skillfully laid down and in the last analysis are hard to miss.

I hope you will end up agreeing with me that no book ever had a more satisfying conclusion.

# ARTHUR CONAN DOYLE
## 1859–1930
### *The Adventures of Sherlock Holmes*

In one of her *Seven Gothic Tales*, Isak Dinesen tells of a certain young man who proposes a singularly original theory of creation. Nature is wasteful, the young man declares; not only does she produce many more fish eggs than ever develop into fish, but she also produces many more simulated human beings than ever develop into real ones. Her method, the young man explains, is to produce billions of simulations, of which only a few are artists, and a much smaller proportion great artists; these in turn write fictions, the heroes of a few of which are real, and the only real human beings in the world. Hamlet, the young man says, Faust, and Don Giovanni—these and a handful more are all that wasteful Nature has managed to create in half a dozen millennia.

The young man might have included Sherlock Holmes and Dr. Watson in his list.

Whatever credence you pay to his theory, the young man is right about one thing: this sort of reality is not a common occurrence. Many good books, even great ones, lack characters like Holmes and Watson. Characters that move out of the stories and into our imaginations, freely, like living persons. Characters about whom we can compose other stories, as has happened more than once to Holmes and his entourage.

Sir Arthur Conan Doyle was born in Edinburgh, Scotland, in 1859. He attended the University of Edinburgh, gained a medical degree, and engaged a small suite of offices just off Harley Street, in London, then as now the fashionable street for London doctors. But few patients came, and Doyle had plenty of time to dream up adventures for his imaginary hero. The first Sherlock Holmes story, and still one of the best, "A Study in Scarlet," appeared in 1887, when Doyle was twenty-eight. Others followed quickly. Writing, Doyle discovered, was more remunerative than medicine, even though he had sold the entire copyright of "A Study in Scarlet" for twenty-five pounds. (He never made that sort of mistake again and in time became one of the most prosperous of authors.) By 1891 he had given up medicine altogether.

The best proof of the living reality of Holmes and Watson is that we enjoy most, on rereading the stories, not their plots—those we remember vividly—but their small and homely details of life at 221B Baker Street (a false address, as I discovered to my dismay the first time I visited London). Holmes stretched out on the sofa with a migraine, Watson writing at the window. The fire flickering in the grate, when in comes Mrs. Hudson with a message. The gaunt figure of Holmes beside Watson's bed, shielding the candle from the draft: "Come, Watson, come! The game is afoot!"

Some of the plots are not worth remembering—even Conan Doyle nodded. But many stories are first rate. I like best the long, early tales: "A Study in Scarlet," "The Sign of Four," "The Hound of the Baskervilles," and "The Valley of Fear." Of these "A Study in Scarlet," for its imaginative touches—Doyle was here creating his immortal characters—and "The Valley of Fear," for its genuine sense of terror, seem to me superior to anything else Doyle ever wrote. But what am I saying? Can any story be scarier, the first time you read it, than "The Hound of the Baskervilles"?

"Footprints?"
"Footprints."
"A man's or a woman's?"
Dr. Mortimer looked strangely at us for an instant, and his voice sank almost to a whisper as he answered:
"Mr. Holmes, they were the footprints of a gigantic hound!"

I remember to this day, though it happened many years ago, the shiver that ran down my back when I read those words. For months I could not walk outside in the country without constantly looking over my shoulder. What if I had seen a great hound bounding down the path after me, his muzzle outlined by a terrible ghastly light? I too would have dropped dead from fear, like poor Sir Charles Baskerville.

There are many more wonderful stories: "The Red-Headed League"; "The Five Orange Pips"; "The Adventure of the Speckled Band" (another producer of nightmares); "The Crooked Man"; and "The Final Problem," in which Doyle attempted to rid himself of Holmes, of whom it is said he had grown weary; but an enchanted public insisted that he resuscitate him, and so we have "The Adventure of the Empty House," "The Adventure of the Devil's Foot," and "His Last Bow"—fortunately, not really his last. And so on and so on. Our only regret is that there are not more.

In fact there is more. "The White Company," the story of a soldier of fortune who actually existed and whose image is one of only two in the Duomo at Florence, and whose castle is just around the corner from Cortona, where I used to live, is a rousing tale and proof that Conan Doyle could write other kinds of stories, too. Alas, there is no Sherlock in it, nor Dr. Watson.

# RUDYARD KIPLING
1865–1936
*The Jungle Books*

Rudyard Kipling was once the most popular living English author. Novels like *The Light That Failed* (1890) and *Kim* (1901), collections of light verse such as *Departmental Ditties* (1886) and *Barrack-Room Ballads* (1892), and books of short stories like *Stalky & Co.* (1899) and *Puck of Pook's Hill* (1906) earned him a worldwide reputation among readers who knew English. Born in Bombay, India, in 1865, the son of a socially important Anglo-Indian family, he represented a type of Englishman most of the world admired before World War I.

After the war his reputation flagged, as the world's view of England and Englishness changed. Kipling's books ceased to be widely read and widely bought. When he died in 1936, despite his Nobel Prize, he was an almost forgotten figure.

However, *The Jungle Books* (1894-95) remained as popular as ever, and indeed I hope they will never die. They first appeared as two separate volumes, but they have almost always been published as a single collection of stories about the animals of the jungle that are joined together by poems for young readers. The stories are themselves written for young people. They are far from being mere children's stories, although in fact they were written for Kipling's grandchild.

The hero of these tales of an India that, if it ever existed, certainly exists no more, is Mowgli, a white child abandoned by his kind and nurtured, brought up, and educated by a family of wolves. Mowgli's foster parents are excellent teachers, although they do not teach him Latin and Greek, arithmetic and geometry, ancient history and geography. Instead, they teach him to survive in the jungle, which has perils not known to ordinary humans, and especially to speak and understand the languages of the jungle, which are the main tools of survival of this hairless cub, as his foster mother lovingly calls him. Mowgli is also sent to school to Ba-a, the great python, Bagheera, the black panther, and Baloo, the black bear, who loves Mowgli with all his heart and is heartbroken because his clever little pupil does not seem to learn fast enough. But Mowgli does learn, although he likes to tease Baloo, and none too soon, for before Baloo thinks he is ready Mowgli is thrown into a series of adventures that test everything he knows.

The adventures are wonderful—at the water hole with the elephants, in the abandoned fortress now occupied by tribes of monkeys, in the pit full of vipers. But it is the education of Mowgli by his loving mentors—the wolf, the bear, the snake, and the great cat—that is the finest part of *The Jungle Books*, I think, and the part of the work that will ensure its fame. I have been reading *The Jungle Books* all my life, and I can close my eyes at this instant and see Bagheera stretched out in all his shining blackness along a limb of a tree, with Mowgli perched like a little naked doll between his paws, learning the language and the lingo of all the jungle cats; or see him curled up within the coils of the great python's enormous glistening body, learning the language of all the snakes and lizards that so terrify other human beings. In fact, I don't think there is any other account of an education that is so fascinating in all of literature, unless it is the education given to the young King Arthur by Merlyn in T.H. White's *Once and Future King*—and in that case the teachers are animals, too, and not men or women.

Although *The Jungle Books* seem to me incomparably the best of Kipling, other works deserve to be read. Among the novels perhaps only *Kim* will be appreciated by modern American readers, but it is a good book. To balance the sentimental absurdities of poems like "Gunga-Din," there is one great poem by Kipling, "Recessional," written during the funeral of King Edward VII, when Kipling foresaw the disasters of the twentieth century with a peculiar clarity. And the *Just-So Stories* (1902) also remain popular, although most of them have become a bit creaky. One, however, retains its own vitality and is often reprinted separately. Called "The Cat That Walked by Himself," this famous story tells how the first cat came to be a pet of mankind, but without giving up his soul and his liberty as did the first dog. It is a lovely story, and cat lovers will agree that it is profoundly true.

# chapter twelve

# Turn of the Century

The title of this chapter is an act of quiet desperation. Many really good books were written by men and women who were born in the last half of the nineteenth century but who lived through the First World War and did their best-known work after it, or at least after the turn of the century. More importantly, most of them were deeply affected by that terrible "War to End Wars," which, of course, turned out to be nothing of the kind, instead being—as we see now—only the first part of a world conflict that dominated the entire century just past. The twentieth century—we have finally arrived at it, and it is hard to view it with anything but tears. As some of these authors make abundantly clear.

Some of them were world-historical figures: Freud, Yeats, Mann, Shaw, to name only four. The latest of these to depart was Thomas Mann, who died in 1955. That is a long time ago, now—more than half a century. In half a century many people and events can be forgotten, more or less, but these four survive, in some of our memories, at least, and also, perhaps, more concretely in film and other modern recensions of their stories and lives. At the same time the world we live in now is so very different from the one they knew that it is not surprising if many readers of this book will know little more about these figures than about Homer, Dante, or Shakespeare. That is precisely the reason I have written it—to keep alive and warm the memory of some very great people. And ideas. And books.

# SIGMUND FREUD
## 1856–1939
*The Interpretation of Dreams*
*An Outline of Psychoanalysis*
*Civilization and Its Discontents*

Sigmund Freud was born in 1856 in Freiburg, Czechoslovakia, and moved to Vienna when he was four. He was educated in Vienna and only decided to become a physician at the end of his gymnasium course, when he read Goethe's "beautiful essay 'On Nature.'" He received his medical degree from the University of Vienna in 1881, became an intern at the General Hospital, and began to study nervous diseases in children. He went to Paris, where he studied under the neurologist Jean Charcot, and returned to Vienna to do further work with Josef Breuer, who was just beginning to treat hysteria, or conversion neurosis, with hypnosis. Freud published with Breuer the first of his many books, *Studies in Hysteria* (1895). Soon, however, he parted from Breuer, deciding that treating hysteria with the method of "free association" was more effective. At the same time he began to study intensively his patients' dreams, and out of this grew his first truly distinctive book, *The Interpretation of Dreams* (1900).

The year 1900 was a symbolic one in which to publish this revolutionary work; Freud had been educated in the nineteenth century and in some respects remained a nineteenth-century man throughout his life, but his doctrines, as first set forth in *The Interpretation of Dreams*, would help to shape the utterly different world of the new century. Few paid attention to this at the time. The book was largely ignored; Freud had worked in isolation for years, having as yet no following, and the main response to his ideas was mockery. Within hardly more than a decade, however, *The Interpretation of Dreams* and its author were world famous.

The book is fascinating. The interpreted dreams are in themselves of great interest, the interpretations even more so; and we can see, as we read, Freud developing his theory of dreams and coming himself to understand it. The book is not Freud's final statement on dreams, nor on psychoanalysis, but he never wrote anything more fresh, youthful, and enthusiastic; he was in his forties and still had hopes for the world, hopes that he later lost.

You do not have to read all of *The Interpretation of Dreams*. It is one of those books that you can safely read in, unless of course you are studying to become an analyst. At the same time the book is hard to put down. Holding it in your hand, you are aware that it is the beginning of something important, that it is about a set of ideas that are fundamental to our modern view of the world. Trying to imagine the world without Freud is like trying to imagine it without electricity, petroleum, or nuclear weapons.

Most of the technical terms that Freud uses in his later, more formal presentations of his theory of psychoanalysis appear in *The Interpretation of Dreams*, together with the insights into human behavior that mark all of his later work. A basic assumption of the book is that there is an unconscious, and that unconscious mental activity is even more important than conscious. In the 1880s it would have been hard to find anyone willing to accept the notion of the unconscious; in the 1980s it was hard to find anyone to deny it. Today, I am not so sure. Nevertheless, it is one measure of the influence of the author of *The Interpretation of Dreams*.

By 1910 Freud was not only famous but also controversial. He recognized the need to make himself understood by ordinary people, and several times he attempted to sum up his doctrines for a lay audience. The first attempt was in 1909, when he was invited to Clark University, in Massachusetts, to give a series of lectures that became *The Origin and Development of Psycho-Analysis*. At the University of Vienna between 1915 and 1917 he again explained his theories in a series of lectures to a lay audience, and these became *A General Introduction of Psycho-Analysis*. He was, however, dissatisfied with all of these attempts, and in 1938, shortly before his death, he wrote a short book, *An Outline of Psychoanalysis*, in which he attempted to convey his ideas in the most succinct fashion. Nothing Freud wrote is clearer, I think, than this work; although it is too small to be definitive, there is nonetheless no better way to begin trying to understand Freud.

The work is in three parts. The first, "The Mind and Its Workings," sets forth the basic assumptions about the mental apparatus that constitute Freudian theory. Part Two, "The Practical Task," deals with the techniques of psychoanalysis. Part Three, "The Theoretical Yield," is unfinished, but it must have been very nearly complete when Freud abandoned the book only a few months before he died. It touches on the relations between the psychical apparatus and the external world, and attempts to describe the character and workings of the internal world—that of the mind itself.

The book is dense, compact. Each sentence is crucial to the argument; the book cannot be read quickly (even though it is less than 125 pages long). But it is enormously rewarding. Here is the final statement of the man who invented psychoanalysis and who may almost be said to have discovered the mind. Certainly no one before him ever understood it!

Freud early recognized that his theories involved not just a new treatment for hysteria and neuroses and, perhaps, psychoses, but also a new explanation for the structure of human institutions and the conditions of human life. He tried in a number of works to present the insights gained from his studies, as applied not to individual patients but to society at large. One of the first such documents was a paper, "Thoughts for the Times on War and Death," which appeared early in 1915 in the journal *Imago*. It is a somber piece, revealing clearly the shock and disappointment felt by Freud—and many other intellectuals on both sides—in the face of the brutal realities of human conduct exhibited during the first few months of World War I. In portentous words Freud sums up his realization: "Our unconscious is just as inaccessible to the idea of our own death, as murderously minded towards the stranger, as divided or ambivalent towards the loved, as was man in earliest antiquity."

War, he went on to say, strips us of the later accretions of civilization and lays bare the primal man in each of us. It would seem that something like this, many times repeated, has been the major human event of the twentieth century—and now the twenty-first.

Others regained their buoyant optimism after the end of World War I, but Freud continued to ponder the meaning and consequences of the conclusions he had set forth in the paper of 1915. The great question, he decided, was why modern civilized man, with all of his wealth and technical prowess, is at heart so unhappy. The most eloquent statement of these views of Sigmund Freud's was the small book *Civilization and Its Discontents* (1929). Hardly any book I know of is so packed with interesting things; there are only a hundred pages or so, but what pages they are!

The main thesis of the book is that civilization, although necessary to the survival of the species, is an intolerable intrusion upon the liberty of the individual. Consciously, man accepts civilization, even embraces it as his savior and his greatest achievement; but underneath he hates it because of what he has given up for it. For primal man—and woman—is very different from the ideal erected by civilization, to which we must all adhere.

The bit of truth behind all this—one so eagerly denied—is that men are not gentle, friendly creatures wishing for love, who simply defend themselves if they are attacked, but that a powerful measure of desire for aggression has to be reckoned as part of their instinctual endowment. The result is that their neighbor is to them not only a possible helper or sexual object, but also a temptation to them to gratify their aggressiveness on him, to exploit his capacity for work without recompense, to use him sexually without his consent, to seize his possessions, to humiliate him, to cause him pain, to torture and kill him. *Homo homini lupus* [man is a wolf to man]: Who has the courage to dispute it in the face of all the evidence in his own life and in history?

Everyone denies this, of course; we could hardly live together if we did not. But denying it does not make it untrue. Down in our unconscious, man is indeed a wolf to man; and we may trace our mental miseries to the continuing struggle, which we do not always win, to repress that terrible reality.

For Freud, all of his nightmares came true before he died. He had suffered from the effects of anti-Semitism for many years, but at least he had been allowed to go on working. When the Nazis invaded Austria in 1938, his books were burned, his institute was destroyed, and his passport was confiscated. Following frantic negotiations, he was permitted to leave Austria after paying a large ransom. Sick at heart and suffering from a painful cancer of the mouth, he found his way to London. He died in London in September 1939.

World War II had already begun. Its horrors would not have surprised the author of *Civilization and Its Discontents*.

# C.P. CAVAFY
1863–1933
*Poems*

Constantine P. Cavafy (Kavafis) was born in Alexandria, Egypt, in 1863, the ninth and last son of his mother and father, who, with his parents, were businessmen in Greece and Egypt. They were not very good businessmen, however, and Constantine lived for many years, off and on, in "genteel poverty." There were periods of semi-exile in England, where the boy learned English well enough so that he was said to speak Greek with an accent for the rest of his life. For the last thirty years of his life, until his death in Alexandria in 1933, he held a civil service position in the Egyptian government. But the real "business" of his life was writing extraordinary poems.

Cavafy was a homosexual, and many of his poems are about homosexual relationships with younger men. He lived most of his life either with members of his family or alone, but he was a welcoming host to anyone who managed to seek him out in Alexandria, especially if they spoke English. A few visitors report that he had the "fascinating capacity to gossip about historical figures from the distant past so as to make them seem a part of some scandalous intrigue taking place in the Alexandria of his day." He never made any effort to publish his poems, choosing instead to provide copies to friends as he wrote them. It is almost a miracle, but of course a happy one, that we know anything about him and have his wonderful poems.

It is his ability to write poems about the Hellenistic past in forms and meters that go back more than two thousand years that has fascinated me ever since I first read him many years ago. There is a *Collected Edition* edited by Edmund Keeley and Philip Sherrard that I strongly recommend. The frank homoeroticism of many of the poems is not to my taste, but there are dozens of poems that have none of that, and I urge you to cull this book for the "historical" entries. See especially "The Horses of Achilles," "The Funeral of Sarpedon," "Thermopylae," "Unfaithfulness" (this, the complaint of Thetis upon the death of her son, is particularly moving), "Ithaka" (this one is famous), and "Waiting for the Barbarians" (this one very famous for its last lines: "And now, what's going to happen to us without barbarians?/ They were, those people, a kind of solution"), and finally "One of Their Gods," which will wrench you.

# ALFRED NORTH WHITEHEAD
## 1861–1947
*Introduction to Mathematics*

Alfred North Whitehead was born at Ramsgate, England, in 1861, the son of an Anglican clergyman. He was a serious and devoted student as a youth, preferring mathematics to all other subjects. He went to Cambridge in 1880 and attended only the mathematical lectures. After doing well on the mathematical tripos he was elected a fellow of Trinity College and made an instructor in mathematics.

Among his other duties was the task of examining mathematically inclined students desiring to enter Trinity. A certain B. Russell struck him by his brilliance in 1889, and Whitehead recommended that Russell be accepted. Within a few years Bertrand Russell was known throughout the university for the mathematical brilliance that Whitehead had been the first to recognize. Together they struggled with the crisis in the logical foundations of mathematics that infested the subject at the end of the nineteenth century. Their famous and extraordinarily difficult book, *Principia Mathematica*, was published in 1910.

In that same year Whitehead made a radical change in his life. He had been given a ten-year appointment by Trinity College in 1903, and in 1910 this still had three years to run. But Whitehead was impatient and frustrated with his work at Cambridge. If he resigned his teaching position, he would still have a small income as a fellow of the college. He proposed to Mrs. Whitehead that they move to London and take their chances. She agreed.

She was right. In the modern phrase, Whitehead's career took off after the move. He was appointed to the staff of the University of London in 1911 and in 1914 he became professor of mathematics at the Imperial College. He published important books, notably *The Concept of Nature* (1920), and by the early 1920s he had become the most distinguished philosopher of science writing in English. He was invited to Harvard to teach philosophy in 1924 and again he decided to move. His years in the United States were his most productive. He taught at Harvard until 1937 and died in Cambridge, Massachusetts, in 1947.

During his first year in London, Whitehead had time on his hands and accepted an invitation from a publisher of popular scientific books to produce a small volume on mathematics. This appeared the next year (1911) under the title *Introduction to Mathematics*. It is one of the best such books.

Whitehead was a great mathematician, but his and Russell's *Principia Mathematica* had been a very difficult book to read and understand. Whitehead's later books were also sometimes so difficult as to be almost unintelligible. But during that one year of 1910, at least, he possessed the genius of simplicity. *Introduction to Mathematics* is so clear, simple, and direct, with so many good examples and so few mathematical symbols, that almost anyone who will devote the slightest effort can read it. The astonishing thing is that the book is also rigorous and authoritative. It is good mathematics as well as being easy to read and understand.

Whitehead explains why at the very beginning of the book. "The study of mathematics," he concedes, "is apt to commence in disappointment." Great expectations are built up in students, but these are not satisfied.

The reason for this failure of the science to live up to its reputation is that its fundamental ideas are not explained to the student disentangled from the technical procedure that has been invented to facilitate their exact presentation in particular instances. Accordingly, the unfortunate learner finds himself struggling to acquire a knowledge of a mass of details that are not illuminated by any general conception.

Perhaps all beginning students of mathematics, at least mathematics beyond the level of arithmetic or simple geometry and algebra, have become aware of that failing—unless they had an excellent teacher. Alfred North Whitehead was an excellent teacher. He makes the ideas clear.

*Introduction to Mathematics* is not, he insists, designed to teach mathematics. Perhaps not, but much mathematics can be learned from it. And all mathematics becomes easier to do as well as to understand when one grasps the basic ideas and concepts underlying the operations. Thus the book helps anyone to be a better mathematician than he or she otherwise would.

Is that important? It seems to me that it certainly is. For mathematics is not only extremely useful, it is also extremely beautiful. But its beauty is not grasped if one cannot "do the math," at least a little.

# WILLIAM BUTLER YEATS
## 1865–1939
*Selected Poems*

William Butler Yeats was born in Dublin in 1865. He studied art as a young man but decided on a literary career when he was twenty-one. Although a Protestant and a member of the Anglo-Irish ruling class, Yeats was deeply interested in the old Ireland. He helped to found an Irish Literary Society in London and another in Dublin. He also worked to create an Irish national theater, joining with others to acquire the Abbey Theatre in Dublin, which has been the home of the Irish Players for nearly a hundred years. Several of his own plays were produced during those early years, and Yeats throughout his life wished to be known as a playwright.

He was a much better poet than playwright, however, and it is as probably the greatest English poet of the last century that he is known today.

He deserves that honor because, almost alone among poets of the twentieth century, he never ceased to grow, to become better and more interesting, as long as he lived. Most poets run out of steam or reach a plateau beyond which they cannot go—often early in their careers. This never happened to Yeats. He never stopped reaching out, experimenting with new ways of saying new things. Thus his last poems are among his best. *Last Poems*, which appeared in 1940, the year after his death, contains some of his finest, strangest work.

Yeats loved the misty mysteriousness of the Irish past, and as a young man he wrote the kind of ditties we think of as "Irish." Politics, the convoluted, tormented politics of Irish independence, obsessed him during his middle years. This was a greater theme than the misty past of Ireland, and Yeats rose to it. Some of the poems he wrote about it are very famous, like "Easter 1916," about the execution of some Irish nationalists on that day, with its mournful, lamenting cry: "A terrible beauty was born!"

This was the beauty of the martyr, a terrible beauty indeed, and perhaps we can understand that Yeats himself came to know the real meaning of freedom when he saw these men, his friends, hanged for seeking it.

Yeats the politician sat in the Senate of the newly founded Irish Free State during the 1920s, but poetry was by now his main business and he continued to write, getting better and better, more and more profound, more and more disturbing in what he had to say.

Finally, what he had to say was mostly about growing old and not wanting to. He was sixty in 1925, and in that year he wrote "Among School Children," not his most famous single poem but perhaps his greatest. He mingles among the girls in a school, "A sixty-year-old smiling public man," and, looking into their eyes, is overcome by wonder at what has occurred. All these years have come and gone, but where did they go? What have they produced? Were they "A compensation for the pang of his birth/Or the uncertainty of his setting forth?"

As he became older he worked all the harder, inventing a character named Crazy Jane who rebels against the formality and politeness of the world. Crazy Jane and the Bishop fight it out over the great questions of life. These poems, "Words for Music Perhaps" as

Yeats called them, are not quite songs but have the earthiness, the directness, and the catch in the rhythms that good songs have. Nothing better was written in the twentieth century.

Finally even the heart of Yeats grew old and tired:

> *O who could have foretold*
> *That the heart grows old?*

But this occurred only when Yeats was near death. He died of a broken heart, broken over the human condition, which is summed up in the one terrible word: Mortality. He never gave in; he never accepted it. We remember "Sailing to Byzantium": Byzantium, where the poet dreams of golden birds that sing forever because they are not alive. Are they the spirit of poetry itself or are they the spirit of this poet who refused to concede that he was merely human?

At the very end he drafted his own epitaph. In the poem "Under Ben Bulben" he describes the place where he shall be buried, and the words that shall be read over his grave:

> *Under bare Ben Bulben's head*
> *In Drumcliff churchyard Yeats is laid.*
> *An ancestor was rector there*
> *Long years ago, a church stands near,*
> *By the road an ancient cross.*
> *No marble, no conventional phrase;*
> *On limestone quarried near the spot*
> *By his command these words are cut:*
> > *Cast a cold eye*
> > *On life, on death.*
> > *Horseman, pass by.*

So it was, and so it is. You may go and see for yourself if you wish. It is one of the few literary pilgrimages worth the bother.

W.B. Yeats was a voluminous poet and the *Collected Poems* is a big, heavy book. Buy it nevertheless and treasure it, for it is one of the foundations of any good personal library. Only practiced and sophisticated readers of poetry should sit down with such a book and read it from beginning to end. A book of poems is not a novel. Start with these twenty poems, more or less: "The Ballad of Father Gilligan," "To a Friend Whose Work Has Come to Nothing," "The Cat and the Moon," "The Second Coming," "Sailing to Byzantium," "Leda and the Swan," "For Anne Gregory," "The Cold Heaven," "The Wild Swans at Coole," "Among School Children," "The Tower," "Down by the Salley Gardens," "When You Are Old," "September 1913," "Easter 1916," "A Prayer for My Daughter," "Words for Music Perhaps" (the Crazy Jane Poems), and "Under Ben Bulben."

Then put down the book and think about it. Come back to Yeats again and again, as you grow older. And wiser.

# J.M. SYNGE
## 1871–1909
### *The Playboy of the Western World*

John Millington Synge was born near Dublin in 1871, attended Trinity College, Dublin, where he studied languages, and decided after graduating to be a musician. His life remained confused and his career uncertain until he was twenty-eight, in 1899, when he met William Butler Yeats in Paris. Yeats was interested in his young countryman, but not in a plan Synge proposed to write literary criticism. Something much more important than mere literature was happening in Ireland, Yeats said. We now call it the Irish Renaissance. Synge, inspired by Yeats's words, returned to Ireland, to the western country and the Aran Islands, where he found his métier.

In his preface to *The Playboy of the Western World*, his masterpiece, Synge explained both his method and his source of literary inspiration. "Anyone who has lived in real intimacy with the Irish peasantry," he wrote, "will know that the wildest sayings and ideas in this play are tame indeed, compared with the fancies one may hear in any little hillside cabin in Geesala, or Carraroe, or Dingle Bay. All art is a collaboration," he went on; "and there is little doubt that in the happy ages of literature, striking and beautiful phrases were as ready to the storyteller's or the playwright's hand, as the rich cloaks and dresses of his time. It is probable that when the Elizabethan dramatist took his ink-horn and sat down to his work, he used many phrases that he had just heard, as he sat at dinner, from his mother or his children. In Ireland, those of us who know the people have the same privilege."

Synge told of how, some years before, when he had been writing "The Shadow of the Glen," he had crouched over a chink in the floor of his room in the inn at Wicklow and listened to the servant girls talking to one another in the kitchen. "This matter, I think, is of importance," he wrote, "for in countries where the imagination of the people, and the language they use, is rich and living, it is possible for a writer to be rich and copious in his words and at the same time to give the reality, which is the root of all poetry, in a comprehensive and natural form."

On the stage, Synge insisted, one must have both reality and joy. The intellectual modern drama, he said, has failed; Ibsen and Zola were dealing "with the reality of life in joyless and pallid words; people have grown sick of the false joy of the musical comedy that has been given them in place of the rich joy found only in what is superb and wild in reality. In a good play," Synge went on, "every speech should be as fully flavored as a nut or apple, and such speeches cannot be written by anyone who works among people who have shut their lips on poetry." Such was not the case in Ireland, Synge felt; at least for a time, until the modern world should descend upon it and shut up its springs of fancy. "In Ireland," he concluded, "for a few years more, we have a popular imagination that is fiery and magnificent, and tender."

It is indeed that fiery and tender imagination that infuses *Playboy*. The play tells the story of a country lad who appears out of the night with a confession that he has murdered his father. He is welcomed as a hero and then, strangely, he becomes one in fact. But his father turns up, unmurdered, and Christy Mahon loses all his reputation, although not his new, more successful self. As such, the story was scandalous to Irish eyes and ears, and the audience rioted at its opening at the Abbey Theatre in Dublin in 1907. The first American production, in New York in 1911, was met with equal distaste.

Later audiences have come to understand that the story is a great metaphor, and not just an attack—which was certainly far from Synge's intention—on the Irishman's love of boasting and his tendency to glamorize ruffians. Joyce's *Ulysses* is also an account of a young man's quest for an accommodation with his father, and *The Playboy of the Western World* is now read as comparable to such major work.

Metaphor or not, the most wonderful thing about *Playboy* is its language. Synge's time spent on the floor listening to the kitchen girls in the inn at Wicklow was not wasted. The words of the text dance and sing as you read them out loud, as you should do. Brush up your Irish accent and go to it. Many lines will bring the tears to your eyes, and others will make your heart leap.

Best of all are the words with which young Christy woos Pegeen Mike, the "wild-looking but fine girl," as Synge describes her, who is the daughter of the keeper of a country public house where the action takes place. Pegeen is smitten by Christy from the moment she sets eyes on him, and he soon falls madly in love with her. He begins to pour out his soul to her in a kind of poetry he has never spoken before and that she has never before heard. He tells her that they will walk the mountains together "in the dews of night, the times sweet smells be rising, and you'd see a little shiny new moon, maybe, sinking on the hills":

> PEGEEN—looking at him playfully.—And it's that kind of a poacher's love you'd make, Christy Mahon, on the sides of Neifin, when the night is down?
>
> CHRISTY. It's little you'll think if my love's a poacher, or an earl's itself, when you'll feel my two hands stretched around you, and I squeezing kisses on your puckered lips, till I'd feel a kind of pity for the Lord God is all ages sitting lonesome in his golden chair.
>
> PEGEEN. That'll be right fun, Christy Mahon, and any girl would walk her heart out before she'd meet a young man was your like for eloquence, or talk, at all.

Did lovers ever really talk like that, in Ireland or anywhere? Synge said they did, and I hope he was right. He also said they would not be talking like that much longer, and I am afraid he was right about that, too.

Synge died in 1909, at the age of thirty-eight. I have placed him here, out of chronological order, because of his relationship to Yeats, who died in 1939 at the age of seventy-four.

# BEATRIX POTTER
### 1866–1943
### *The Tale of Peter Rabbit*

Beatrix Potter (one of the nicest things about her was the way she spelled her name) was born in South Kensington, now a part of London, in 1866. She received an ordinary education in an ordinary school, and she lived quite an ordinary life. But she liked to tell stories and to draw, and in 1899 she began to send a series of illustrated animal stories, in letters and on postcards, to a sick child who was her friend. As the year wore on the stories grew longer and longer. The first of her books appeared in 1900. It was called *The Tale of Peter Rabbit*, and it is one of the most famous books in the world.

There is nothing sentimental about *Peter Rabbit* or about the dozens of other books with which Beatrix Potter followed it. That is another good thing about her: she saw the world, especially the animal world, very clearly, knew it was full of accidents and cruelties, and did not disguise these from her child readers. Some of the books are even a bit macabre. But the stories usually end up well, which is what children like best: hard times and travails, with a happy ending. In fact, who doesn't like that kind of story best?

By the time Beatrix Potter died, in 1943, millions of copies of her little square books had been sold, with their wry stories and colorful illustrations. By now the count may be approaching a billion. Thank you, Beatrix Potter, wherever you are; you deserve all your fame and all your royalties. You gave us Peter Rabbit and the Tailor of Gloucester and Benjamin Bunny and Jemima Puddle-Duck and Mrs. Tiggy-Winkle—how can we ever repay the debt?

# ROBERT FROST
1874–1963
*Selected Poems*

Robert Frost was born in San Francisco in 1874 and moved when he was eleven years old to New England, where his family had lived for generations. He went to Dartmouth College when he was eighteen but dropped out to live at home, working at various jobs and writing poetry. In 1897 he entered Harvard but withdrew because of ill health. He farmed in New Hampshire for a while and taught school, but his life and career were not successful until he went to England in 1912 and found a willing publisher for his now considerable body of work. *A Boy's Will* (1913) and *North of Boston* (1914) appeared in England and made him well known.

Frost returned to New England in 1915 and for the next forty years held various academic posts, some of them honorary, and wrote poems. The winner of four Pulitzer Prizes, for his verse, he was eminently a professional poet whose later works were often on best-seller lists. He made a memorable appearance at the inauguration in 1961 of President John F. Kennedy, reciting his poem "The Gift Outright" in the strong wind and sunlight of that day. The next year, at the age of eighty-two, he was awarded the Congressional Gold Medal. Frost died in Boston in 1963.

His death was a shock; it was hard to get used to his not being here. He had published his first volumes before World War I, and it seemed that he had always been what he later became, the most important American poet of the twentieth century. And then he was gone.

The personality of a poet has much to do with his fame. Frost was a crafty self-promoter. He knew how to remain in the public eye, how to be always at the top of everyone's lists. His later books were the kind of commercial success on which publishers live. But was he really good? As good as everyone thought, as good as he seemed?

There is not the almost-unanimous consensus about this that existed a few years ago. As with Picasso, another who bestrode his age, it has become apparent that some of Frost's productions were not first rate. Even Homer nodded, and Frost nodded often and disastrously. His easy verse could run on and on. His subjects could be so tiny that they seemed to disappear when you got down to examining them. Then, a handful of his poems were so famous that they seemed to wear out in the reading.

Take "Stopping by Woods on a Snowy Evening." That last stanza:

> The woods are lovely, dark and deep.
> But I have promises to keep,
> And miles to go before I sleep,
> And miles to go before I sleep.

It is hard to think of four lines by an American poet that are better known. Or these astonishing lines that leap out of the pages of "The Death of the Hired Man": "Home is the place where, when you have to go there/They have to take you in." "I should have called it/Something you somehow haven't to deserve."

Or the famous boast (for boast it is) in "The Road Not Taken":

> Two roads diverged in a wood, and I,
> I took the one less travelled by,
> And that has made all the difference.

Or (finally) this marvelous last stanza from "Two Tramps in Mud Time":

> But yield who will to their separation,
> My object in living is to unite
> My avocation and my vocation
> As my two eyes make one in sight.
> Only where love and need are one,
> And the work is play for mortal stakes,
> Is the deed ever really done
> For Heaven and the future's sake.

Do these famous lines, and a hundred or five hundred others, deserve their great fame? I think they do. Are they as good as they seem to be? I think they are. Are the sentiments, so clear, so intelligible (unlike so much modern poetry)—are the sentiments superficial, and is that why we understand them so easily? I do not think it is bad for a poem to be intelligible.

That easy verse I mentioned is truly a marvel. Usually in couplets, often either in a four-footed or a five-footed meter, it is as close to prose as verse can be and still be unmistakably verse. Take the next-to-last line of "Two Tramps in Mud Time." Read the line aloud and see how the fact that it is verse, and that the verse has four beats in each line, forces you to put the emphasis where it belongs: "Is the deed (pause) ever (pause) really (strong emphasis) done." The verse, apparently so easy and forgiving, in reality has you by the throat and will not let you go, will not let you read the poem in any other way. Frost was unequaled in the writing of verse in our time. The stories he told in verse, in pentameter couplets that can be compared, if they can be compared to any other English poet's, only to Chaucer's wonderful, easy couplets in *The Canterbury Tales*, are all the better stories because of the form he gives them. "The Witch of Coos," "The Death of the Hired Man," "Home Burial," "The Black Cottage," "In the Home Stretch"—these are all extraordinary narrative poems, and narrative poems endure.

Best of all, probably, are the little poems that merely observe, often on the basis of a natural event or phenomenon, how life conducts itself in this world. "Fire and Ice" is a famous example, as are "Once by the Pacific," "Birches," and "Mending Wall." The point is not made too obviously or too strongly, but you do not forget that both anger and hatred are sufficient to end the world, that the fury of the sea is the symbol of the fury of Nature itself, that "One could do worse than be a swinger of birches," that "Good fences make good neighbors." Homely truths, all of these, but true for all that! And it is the poet's business to tell the truth.

The last edition of Robert Frost's *Collected Poems* is a very large book and there are quite a few bad poems in it. But there are also many, many good ones. Start with those I have already mentioned. Go on to read "Revelation," "The Oven Bird," "The Runaway," and "To Earthward." Make sure to read "The Silken Tent," noticing that the entire poem is just one sentence. Start with these, and when you have done with them, go on to make your own list.

# WALLACE STEVENS
## 1879–1955
### *Selected Poems*

Wallace Stevens was born in Reading, Pennsylvania, in 1879. After attending Harvard for three years he worked briefly as a journalist, then acquired a law degree and practiced law in New York. He had been writing poems for years, but his first published work appeared in *Poetry* in 1914. Two years later he joined an insurance firm in Hartford, Connecticut, rising in 1934 to vice president, a position he retained until his death in Hartford in 1955.

His first book, *Harmonium*, was published in 1923 and sold fewer than one hundred copies. Nevertheless, it included some of his best poems; for example, "Sunday Morning," "Peter Quince at the Clavier," and his own favorites, "Domination in Black" and "The Emperor of Ice Cream."

The theme of the conflict between and the relation of reality and imagination imbues many of his poems, both in *Harmonium* and thereafter. In "Esthetique du Mal" ("Aesthetic of Evil") he argued, brilliantly as was always true of his verse, that beauty is inextricably linked with evil. But in "Sunday Morning," my own favorite, which was written twenty years before, he had declared that "death is the mother of beauty." I believe both of those contentions are correct, in the sense in which he uses the terms.

In his recent book, *The Best Poems in the English Language*, Harold Bloom (who is given to such exclamations) declares that "Stevens is the principal American poet since Walt Whitman and Emily Dickinson." Certainly he is one of the three or four—or five. But he isn't easy to read. You have to work. Begin with the poems mentioned here, then go on to "The Idea of Order at Key West," perhaps his best-known poem, and "The Poems of Our Climate." Much effort will be required, but it will be rewarded.

# THOMAS MANN
## 1875–1955
### *The Magic Mountain*

Thomas Mann was born in Lubeck in 1875, the son of prosperous middle-class parents who were sufficiently liberal-minded not to object to the fact that their son never really wanted to be anything but a writer. He prepared himself thoroughly and well, reading voraciously, studying history, literature, and law, and writing assiduously from the time he was in his early teens. He also thought about writing and what it meant to be a writer. By "writer" he meant, of course, a maker of fictions, a creator of worlds, and he was well aware from a young age of how dubious and questionable is the career of a writer, and how little he ought to be trusted by more solid persons. This self-awareness was in itself partly make-believe, but partly serious, too, as is evident in many of Mann's novels and stories, which are as frequently about fakes and charlatans as they are about artists as such.

Mann's father died in 1891, whereupon the family moved to Munich, where Thomas Mann lived for more than forty years, marrying, fathering a family, and writing the books that made him world famous. *Buddenbrooks* was the first of them; published in 1900, when Mann was only twenty-five, it was an instant success that, everyone knew, promised more and better things in the future. *Death in Venice* was published in 1912; *Der Zauberberg* in 1924 (the English translation, *The Magic Mountain*, appeared in 1927 and helped to ensure Mann's Nobel Prize); and the series of biblical novels, *Joseph and His Brothers*, from 1933 to 1943. By this time, however, Mann was living in America.

He had been a political conservative during World War I, but he soon saw through Hitler in his Munich days and was outspoken in his writings about him. When Hitler came to power at the beginning of 1933, the Manns were vacationing in Switzerland. A telephone call from their son and daughter warned them not to return to Germany. Thomas Mann never lived in Germany again, although he visited it for short periods after World War II.

Mann became a U.S. citizen in 1944. In 1952 he moved to Zurich, Switzerland, which was close to Germany but not in it and where everyone spoke German—this was a comfort. He was, however, writing a very uncomfortable book at the time, a joke on all of his devoted and adoring followers, and a return to his old theme of the charlatan/artist. In fact, *The Confessions of Felix Krull, Confidence Man*, published a year before Mann died in 1955, is very funny, and I recommend it highly. But life is not infinitely long, and do not read it until you have read *The Magic Mountain* first.

This strange and beautiful book is a novel of ideas, one of the few such books to become a worldwide bestseller. Hans Castorp leaves his solid, middle-class city and takes the winding cog railway up the mountain to the sanitarium where his cousin is being treated for tuberculosis. Hans meets the director at the door and is surprised to discover that this slightly diabolical doctor would like to take his temperature. The young man refuses. There is nothing whatever wrong with him, he insists; it is his cousin who is ill, and in any case Hans is merely on a short vacation from his solid job and must return at the end of two weeks, or perhaps three. But there *is* something wrong with him after all; he has tuberculosis, and he finds that he must inform his family that he will not return when he planned and to ask them to forward his clothes and his books to the sanitarium, to which he has been confined for an indefinite stay.

Life in the sanitarium at the top of the magic mountain is easy and carefree, although fraught with peril, for from time to time a patient worsens and dies, and is taken out at night so that the other patients cannot see it happen. There is all the time in the world to talk, and everyone does so, but the talk is not haphazard. A consuming conflict develops among representatives of various recognizable lines of thought in early-twentieth-century Europe and America. But nobody wins, nobody is proved "right," the talk merely goes on and on while the patients, for the most part, become sicker and sicker (although one or two are cured and leave the scene). There is also time for love; and Castorp falls in love with a beautiful and enigmatic Russian woman who denies herself for months and then, on the eve of her departure—it seems that she is one of those who is cured—gives herself to Castorp in a storm of passion that is no less violently erotic for not being explicitly described.

The high point of *The Magic Mountain* takes place after this. Castorp, depressed and alone for the first time in his life and forced as a result to face his own existence, dons a pair of skis and goes out on the mountain, into the pure white snow that has surrounded the sanitarium all along but that he has never paid any real attention to before. He is not a bad skier, but these are real mountains and he soon becomes lost. The sun is a blazing light in the sky, and the snow all around reflects its cruel clarity and brilliance. Castorp becomes confused and begins to see visions. They are extraordinary. The twenty or so pages that describe Castorp's snowbound epiphany are a high point, not just of *The Magic Mountain*, but of Western literature in our time.

The book does not end there. Hans Castorp survives his ordeal and returns to the sanitarium. Surprisingly, he seems to be better; the director soon notices this and informs him that he will be allowed to go home soon. In the meantime World War I has broken out, and Castorp must leave anyway, whether well or ill, for he thinks it necessary to fight for his country. When he descends into the darkling plain he never looks back at the magic mountain, shining in the sun.

# EDITH WHARTON
1862–1937
*The House of Mirth*
*The Age of Innocence*

Edith Wharton was born in New York of a distinguished and wealthy New York family. She was educated privately at home and in Europe, and she was married in 1885. The marriage was not happy, and she and her husband were divorced in 1913. But she had long since begun to write both novels and stories, together with travelogues describing her life in France and Italy, which were luxurious and interesting.

I don't know when she first met Henry James, but they became fast friends. His novels influenced her greatly and perhaps she also influenced his last novels or at least appreciated them better than most. She wrote several "Jamesian" novels that in some ways are better than his, partly because they are more accessible. They deal with similar themes but somehow reach deeper into the souls of her main characters. This is especially true of *The House of Mirth*, her first novel, published in 1905.

The story is striking, memorable, and painful in the extreme. I have read it only once because I can never forget it, scene by scene, conversation by conversation. Lily Bart suffers from her social ambitions, which would be solved if she had any money, but she doesn't. She comes close, very close, but her desires are always thwarted, her hopes always dashed. She is loved by an ineffectual man who is never quite able to tell her he wants her for his wife, although in fact he does; only when he discovers that he can ask her to marry him does he learn that it's too late. I realize I am being very guarded in describing the plot of this fine book, but that's because I don't want to spoil it for you. Read it, please, despite my statement that it's painful. It's a good pain, and you won't forget it either.

*The Age of Innocence* is another story of thwarted love and desire. In this case it is the man who suffers. Newland Archer, a successful New York lawyer, falls in love with a Polish countess who is separated from her husband. Archer is married too, but his wife is determined to keep him for herself and never gives up her campaign to come between her husband and the woman she knows he loves instead of her. No one can win in such a complex game—except fate steps in and arranges things so they can. Archer's wife dies, and the countess' husband dies too. Archer learns she is living in Paris, his son visits her there and realizes that his father's love is returned. Archer then goes to Paris ostensibly to join her, but ... Once again I am concealing the ending of a fine book. Once again, please forgive me and read it.

Edith Wharton wrote another well-known novel, a short, bitter, New England story called *Ethan Frome*. It was successful but somehow—in my view—not as interesting as the two novels described above. You may want to read it anyway; in fact, you may have already read it in school because, being short, it is often included in high school literature classes.

# WILLA CATHER
## 1873–1947
*The Song of the Lark*
*My Ántonia*

⎯⎯⎯⎯⎯⎯⎯

Willa Cather was born in Virginia in 1876 but moved to Nebraska when she was eight and spent the rest of her life there and in New Mexico. Her discovery of the fascination of Santa Fe imbues one of her best-known books, the historical novel *Death Comes for the Archbishop*. It's a good book but not, I think, her best. She wrote many other novels, but I particularly like and remember *The Song of the Lark* and *My Ántonia*, both of them written early in her career.

*The Song of the Lark* is the story of Thea Kornberg, a Colorado girl who likes to sing and realizes, thanks to a neighbor, that she has a fine voice. He tries to teach her, but, knowing he can't take her beyond his limited expertise, he arranges for her to go Chicago for professional lessons. The account of her train journey across the prairie, of her first sight of the first city she has ever seen and only dreamed about, and her introduction to her first teacher—all these experiences are described with great skill and in just the right kind of language for the girl she still is. The beginning of the novel is the best part, but her great success as a diva, though perhaps not entirely credible, is nevertheless very satisfying. She becomes an international celebrity and of course becomes involved with the wrong kind of people, especially men. But this isn't important. The novel is really fine and I don't know of anyone who has read it who has ever forgotten it, especially that train ride.

*The Song of the Lark* was published in 1915, *My Ántonia* three years later. It is the story of an immigrant girl from Bohemia who lives on the family farm in Nebraska. Her family loses its farm, and she has to go to work as a "hired girl" in the city, which she hates. A young man named Jim Burland falls in love with her, but neither his family nor hers approves of the match. Jim is the narrator, and he describes his sadness when she returns to the farm and shortly afterward marries another immigrant and has many children. Ántonia is a strong and determined woman who supports her husband—who is physically strong but not as determined. She teaches her children English—their father speaks only Czech—and sees to it that they have more education than she did. Ántonia holds her family together through thick and thin and, in short, lives the kind of life we may all think our forebears did in this country that was new in those old days. I hope it still is but I'm no longer sure. In any case I recommend this novel with my heart and expect you will fall in love with Ántonia, just as I did.

Willa Cather wrote many other novels, one of which, *Death Comes for the Archbishop*, published at the end of her career, is noteworthy. It is the story of two devoted French priests who bring civilization and religion to New Mexico in the middle of the nineteenth century. It is moving but also sad, as all of her books are. They were all touched by memories of her childhood and youth in the pioneer country of Nebraska, memories that were fading the longer she lived (she died in 1947). The epigraph of *My Ántonia*, is a quote from Virgil's *Aeneid—Optima dies ... prima fugit*: "The (memories of the) best days are the first to go."

## ÉTIENNE GILSON
### 1884–1978
*The Arts of the Beautiful*

Étienne Gilson was one of the most renowned scholars of the twentieth century. He was born in Paris in 1884 and lived to be ninety-four, dying in France in 1978. He was educated at the Lycée Henry IV, the premier preparatory school of France, and at the Sorbonne; by the time he was thirty-four he was the leading scholar of medieval history in France. By the time he was fifty he was the leading scholar of his subject in the world. He taught both in Paris and Toronto, where he established a school of medieval studies, his teaching consisting usually of a course of lectures; from these he wrote his books. There were many of those, all of them marked by his astonishing clarity of thought; indeed there is no thinker that I know of whom it is easier, and more fruitful, to follow—whether you always agree with his conclusions or not. A large, gruff man, Gilson possessed an instrument, in his pen, of the most consummate delicacy; he has been compared to that Zen master, also a chef, who cut meat for his dishes without effort because, as he said, "I cut at the joints."

I would not hesitate to recommend any book of Étienne Gilson's to a reader curious to experience the best Roman Catholic philosophical thought of our time. I have chosen *The Arts of the Beautiful* because it is not only an example of Gilson's own art at its best, but also because of the novel things that it says.

Gilson was eighty-one when the book was published; he had delivered the series of lectures on which it is based a year or two before. The book is clearly the work of an old man. It is spare, there is no wasted effort in it, no unnecessary words. This wise old man is intent on telling us something that we ought to have known and consequently that he ought not to have had to go to the trouble to tell us; but he must, because we do not know it, and it is true. For him, no other reason is needed.

That something he wishes to tell us, or to remind us of, is that art is *making*. Gilson does not beat around the bush; the first paragraph of the introduction begins thus:

> In the *Encyclopédie française* we find this quotation by the historian Lucien Febvre: 'Assuredly, art is a kind of knowledge.' The present book rests upon the firm and considered conviction that art is not a kind of knowledge or, in other words, that it is not a manner of knowing. On the contrary, art belongs in an order other than that of knowledge, namely, in the order of making ... From beginning to end, art is bent upon making.

Now most people do not agree with Gilson, although he is right. It is true enough that what the artist makes is, or can be, an object of knowledge; we can know a great deal about a painting or a poem, to say nothing of knowing about the painter's or the poet's life. But knowing about a self-portrait of Rembrandt is very far from being able to paint it, which is to say to make it. Nor is it sufficient to know how Rembrandt painted: how he arranged his subjects, how he mixed his pigments, how he applied them to the canvas, which he had also prepared in his special way. Knowing all that will not permit you to paint like Rembrandt, to make what he made.

To paint like Rembrandt, you must have made the things that he made—paintings, etchings, and other works of art. Rembrandt, like all great artists, knew this perfectly well, whether or not he ever said it; we know that, because we know that he never stopped making things as long as he lived. The idea, in fact, of an artist who knows how to make but does not make is a contradiction in terms.

I do not mean to belittle criticism. Knowing about art is an important kind of knowledge. But making a work of art is more important. It is also essentially mysterious. Why are the great artists great? I don't think we can ever say why. The Greeks made a myth out of the notion of inspiration, and a myth is something, according to an old definition, that is so true that it could never happen. At any rate, no one has ever actually seen anyone being inspired. But some human beings make better—more beautiful—things than others, and a very few men and women are truly great makers. The things that they make have a meaning and importance that endures for a very long time, even forever, and those things have a kind of life that in one sense, although not in another, is higher than that of human beings.

Those are a few of the things that Gilson says in *The Arts of the Beautiful*. He says many other things as well that are worth digging out. His was a remarkable mind; he was a great maker of books, even though his books are not works of art per se, that is, they are themselves in the realm of truth, not that of beauty.

## JAMES JOYCE
### 1882–1941
*Dubliners*
*A Portrait of the Artist as a Young Man*
*Ulysses*

James Joyce was born in Dublin in 1882, the son of a couple who were at first prosperous. But Joyce's father was an angry, blustering man who drank too much (as Joyce described in many of his stories). So the family's fortunes soon foundered. By the time he was ten Joyce had become the son of a poor man, and he himself remained a poor man all of his life.

Besides poverty, Joyce also had other ills to contend with. He suffered from several kinds of eye diseases; between 1917 and 1930 he endured a series of twenty-five operations for iritis, glaucoma, and cataracts; and he was for short stretches during this period totally blind. He and Nora Barnacle, the woman with whom he lived throughout most of his life and whom he finally married, had a daughter who was mentally ill, and this illness disturbed Joyce greatly. In addition, his works, although admired by the literati, were not popular successes during his lifetime; indeed, most of them were banned for long periods, and he had great difficulty getting them published. Despite these problems and troubles, Joyce was essentially a happy man who kept up his spirits and never stopped working. Some of his most hilarious passages were written during the worst times of his life.

He wrote the stories that were collected under the title *Dubliners* (1914) during the first years of the last century. All of these stories show an acute, observing eye, but one of them, "The Dead," is among the finest stories ever written. The story was written in Trieste, where Joyce and Nora were living, around the year 1910. Joyce had recently been told—although it was a false report—that Nora had been loved by another man, and he felt betrayed. In addition, he was sentimentally overwhelmed, while living so far from home, by his memories of Irish hospitality. He combined these two feelings in "The Dead," which described a party at Christmastime in Dublin some years before. Many characters are introduced but the focus is on the protagonist, Gabriel Conroy, and his wife Gretta. There is singing and dancing. Gabriel makes an awkward speech about hospitality, but his eyes never leave Gretta, whom he finds that he loves and desires more than ever. At the end of the story he learns something about her he has never known. Her heart was broken years before, he now realizes, by a boy who died for her, or so she thought, and his own heart is broken as he lies beside her in the night, watching her as she sleeps and thinking of all the living and the dead. This last scene of

"The Dead" is one of the purest of all literary experiences; for concentrated feeling it is hard to name anything that is its equal.

A *Portrait of the Artist as a Young Man* (1916) is, like almost everything Joyce wrote, autobiographical—that is, largely based on the events and experiences of his early life in Ireland. Joyce loved Ireland, but he hated its narrowness and its restrictions on feeling and expression. His country, he thought, was paralyzed and could not break out of the web of illusions and self-deceits that entrapped it. The *Portrait* starts with a very young boy and carries him onward to the moment when he is finally able to tear himself away and to become the free and feeling artist he has always wanted to be. A wonderful, moving journey is described in this book; perhaps no artist ever revealed himself more fully and completely, unless it was Rembrandt in his last self-portraits or Rousseau in his *Confessions* or Beethoven in his last quartets. But those men were all old; Joyce did it when he was still in his twenties.

The beginning of the *Portrait* is lovely and very famous: "Once upon a time and a very good time it was there was a moocow coming down along the road and this moocow that was coming down along the road met a nicens little boy named baby tuckoo ... " The end is just as famous. It takes the form of a diary; the month is April, but the year does not matter. It is spring, a new beginning. Stephen (the name Joyce used for the hero of this autobiographical novel) writes in his diary:

> 26 April: Mother is putting my new secondhand clothes in order. She prays now, she says, that I may learn in my own life and away from home and friends what the heart is and what it feels. Amen. So be it. Welcome, O life! I go to encounter for the millionth time the reality of experience and to forge in the smithy of my soul the uncreated conscience of my race.
>
> 27 April: Old father, old artificer, stand me now and ever in good stead.

Perhaps nothing Joyce wrote has been quoted and pondered over so many times. Almost every young writer, man or woman, has thrilled to those lines.

Joyce wrote most of *Ulysses* during World War I. He had been living in Trieste, but when war broke out the Italian authorities allowed him and his family to go to Zurich, where he spent the next five years. He was beset by poverty, which was relieved only from time to time by small grants of money from two American friends and supporters, Edith Rockefeller McCormick and Harriet Shaw Weaver. In fact, Miss Weaver's contributions cannot be called small; by 1930 they had amounted to more than £23,000, a large sum for those days.

Chapters from *Ulysses* began to appear in the *American Little Review* starting in March 1918 and continuing until 1920, when the book was banned in the United States. It was an era when bluestocking sentiment was rampant, and the banning of *Ulysses* ran parallel to the banning of alcohol. *Ulysses* regained its legitimacy sooner than alcohol; furthermore, it was published in Paris in 1922, by Sylvia Beach, proprietor of a bookstore called Shakespeare & Co., and soon everyone who was anyone had a copy. There is nothing like banning a good book to make people think it is great, and the ban had that effect on *Ulysses*. The ban combined with the mysterious difficulties of the novel had the effect of making it an irresistible object of passionate scholarly concern on both sides of the Atlantic.

Is *Ulysses* not a great book, then? Of course it is. However, it seems to me to be disorganized and overwrought in many places, and harder to read than it ought to be. At the same time it is full of wonders. They are more important than the faults, if that's what they are.

The book's beginning and its end are both extraordinary. Stephen Daedalus—Joyce's alter ego—conducts a long discussion of *Hamlet*, in which he shows that even in 1922 there were new things to be thought and felt about that play. This conversation, which winds throughout the book, is fascinating. And the last chapter, consisting of eight immensely long paragraphs that reveal Molly Bloom's thoughts as she lies in bed after a day made especially interesting by an act of adultery, is deservedly famous. Molly is earthy, cunning, goodhearted, and loving, all at the same time. And although she has betrayed her husband, Poldy, her affection for him has not really been betrayed, and one is certain that their future together will be no worse, if it will not be better, for her escapade.

Leopold (Poldy) Bloom is an enigmatic character. The book is the story of a single day in his life—Bloomsday, Joyce called it (it was in fact the anniversary of the day, June 16, when he had first fallen in love with Nora Barnacle, his wife). Bloom visits various symbolically important places in Dublin; these correspond to parts of the body; and these in turn represent the various arts and sciences; while all are hung upon a structure based on *The Odyssey* of Homer. Thus, for example, Chapter 3 of Part 2, "Hades," occurs at 11 A.M., in the graveyard, where the heart is the symbol and all of this represents religion.

I rebel, and you may, too. *Ulysses* may be a more enjoyable book if you do not work too hard at reading it. At any rate, Molly is worth the trouble of finding her out.

# HENRIK IBSEN
## 1828–1906
### *A Doll's House*

About certain authors one has an impression that may have little basis in reality, but that is hard to eradicate and that stands in the way of true comprehension and appreciation. About Ibsen I have an impression of murky darkness, of a kind of sad foreignness and strangeness. This is quite wrong: Ibsen, although a serious man and artist, was not the somber, unpleasant person of my imagination. As a result of my impression, however, whenever I see a play of Ibsen's on the stage or read it in a book, I am surprised at how good it is, how interesting and absorbing, and how much fun.

I know where my impression comes from. Bernard Shaw was envious of Ibsen, whom he thought of as his only living competitor (Shakespeare, after all, was dead); at the same time Shaw could not help but admire Ibsen. When English audiences, and critics, would hoot a new play of Ibsen's off the stage, Shaw would "defend" him with praise that was a little below enthusiastic and with enigmatic analyses. Shaw's book *The Quintessence of Ibsenism* (1891) helped to create my impression, and that of many others, of Ibsen as a dark, tortured spirit who had in the final analysis perverted drama by turning it into a vehicle for social criticism. The fact that Shaw admitted that Ibsen was a great dramatist and an able social critic, and the fact that Shaw did all the things he accused Ibsen of doing, was lost in the rhetorical fireworks of this "defense."

Henrik Ibsen was born in a desolate lumbering town in northern Norway in 1828. His childhood and youth were not happy; his father went bankrupt, the family had to move to another town, Henrik did badly in school, and his first plays were either disasters or just unsuccessful. A shy, introverted man, he nevertheless obtained a job as a producer of plays. During this time he was miserable but at least learned everything that could be known about the theater. Still, he'd enjoyed no success of any kind by the time he was thirty-five and decided that life in Norway was impossible for him. He therefore went to Rome, and, as with many northern artists who exchanged their dark, cold surroundings for the warmth and gaiety of the south, Ibsen's life and career suddenly bloomed.

A series of plays of a new kind poured from his pen. The first was *Brand* (1866), the second that astonishing work, *Peer Gynt* (1867). This was followed by a collection of poems, the ten-act drama *Emperor and Galilean* (1873), and *Pillars of Society* (1877). He was approaching his major mode, but he had not yet quite reached it. Two years later, with *A Doll's House*, he exploded into dramatic greatness.

Nora, the heroine of *A Doll's House*, is the twittery, charming but incompetent wife of Torvald Helmer, who adores her. But he is unable to treat her as anything but a child. The play is about Nora's awakening. A series of confrontations and events leads to her final recognition that she is not only—she is much more than—what her husband sees in her. In the last, great scene she leaves him, leaving all of her life behind, thus breaking not only his heart but her own as well. But even with a broken heart she will take on the world, endure her suffering, and make a life for herself that is hers alone.

The play created a scandal when it first appeared. In a sense it is still scandalous; even today, the majority of any audience viewing a good production believes that, after all, Nora does not really have to leave Torvald—has she not made her point, does he not now fully understand it, will he not treat her better from now on? Nora alone, perhaps, knows that it is impossible for Torvald to treat her any other way, for she is a woman and he is a man. A *Doll's House* is a tragedy of sex—or of the failure of communication between the sexes.

The part of Nora is a superb one for any fine actress, and dozens have played her in their different ways. Ibsen, after all, was not just a social critic, he was also a wonderful playwright, a fact that became clear to all with the staging and subsequent publication of plays like *An Enemy of the People* (1882), *The Wild Duck* (1884), *Rosmersholm* (1886), *Hedda Gabler* (1890), and *The Master Builder* (1892). All of these read well and act even better, and no one should miss a good production of any of Ibsen's later plays if one can be seen.

But no Ibsen play touches me so deeply as that first great success, *A Doll's House*. My final impression of Ibsen is of Nora going out the door, with Torvald standing astounded and broken on an empty stage. There are few moments to equal it in the drama of the last 125 years.

# BERNARD SHAW
1856–1950
*Pygmalion*
*Saint Joan*

George Bernard Shaw (he disliked the name "George" and in his will directed that his plays be produced in the future under the name Bernard Shaw) was born in Dublin in 1856, the son of an impractical and impecunious man whom Shaw disliked and whom his mother left, with her children, in 1875. Mother and son wound up in London, where for years Shaw was dependent on her meager earnings as a music teacher; he later remarked that he did not throw himself into the battle of life, he threw his mother.

His formal education having ended before he was sixteen, Shaw undertook to educate himself, reading in the British Museum, attending free lectures, and making speeches for political and other causes—he thus honed the edge of his polemical prose style. He began to write but was unable to publish before the later 1880s, when he was well into his thirties; but he emerged in 1888-90 as one of the best music critics ever to write in English and, later, as a superb drama critic as well. (In the first capacity he championed Wagner and Mozart; in the second, Ibsen and Shakespeare.)

Shaw's first plays were not produced; they were thought to be too "unpleasant" for the stage. He published them, together with some later works, as *Plays Pleasant and Unpleasant* (1898). But he soon was writing successfully for the stage, first abroad and then in London, and from 1901, with the production of *Caesar and Cleopatra*, he was hardly ever off the boards and sometimes had two or three hits running simultaneously.

*Pygmalion* was first produced in 1913 and published in 1916; it did not become *My Fair Lady* until 1956. It is probably Shaw's best-known play, and his purest comedy. Shaw was always fascinated by language, particularly the English language, and by the social consequences that ensue from the way one spoke it. The heroine of *Pygmalion* is a flower girl, Eliza Doolittle, who parades her frightful Cockney accent; the hero is Professor Higgins, a brilliant but eccentric phonetician who determines to teach Eliza to speak like a lady, on the theory that if she speaks like a lady she will be taken for one.

The play is wonderfully funny, acute, and effective on at least three levels. First, the story of Eliza's efforts to learn to speak like a Duchess at a garden party—she succeeds—is brilliantly effective theater, combining as it does not only the myth of Pygmalion—the sculptor who brought his finest sculpture, Galatea, to life—but also the great and powerful myth of Cinderella. Second, the play is an acute social commentary. As a poor Cockney flower girl earning half a crown a day by selling bouquets of violets, Eliza has an established, although not necessarily delightful, place in the world. But once she learns to speak like a lady, what, as she cries at the end of the play, is to become of her? She still has no money, but she can never go back to the gutter, where she was at least happy, if not comfortable. Finally, the play includes a deliciously complicated love affair. Eliza and her teacher fall in love, but Higgins is not perceptive enough to recognize that he loves Eliza, and Eliza is intelligent enough to know that he never will—and that she therefore should marry someone else. And so she does.

The play ends with the question of what will happen, and what Eliza will do, quite unsettled. The resolution of the uncertainties of the play—which, despite them, was and is a brilliant stage piece—was left for Shaw's Epilogue, which he included in the published version. The Epilogue is as funny, acute, and effective as the play itself. Do not miss it when reading the play.

See a stage version of the play too if you can manage it—preferably one staged in England, where the accents will be true to life. *My Fair Lady*, the musical version, is just as good as the play, though different in some respects—for example, in it Eliza and Higgins do get together at the end.

Joan of Arc was finally canonized in 1920, five centuries after her death, and the profound fascination of this most human of saints affected Shaw as it did millions of others. *Saint Joan*, which many think is his greatest play, was produced in 1923, published in 1924, and in 1925 earned him the Nobel Prize for Literature.

. The story of Joan of Arc is well known. A village girl from the town of Domrémy in Lorraine, she was directed by her "voices"—those of Saint Catherine, Saint Margaret, and Saint Michael, whom she heard speak to her "in the church bells"—to go to Orleans in soldier's attire, raise the English siege of the city, and crown the Dauphin in the cathedral of Rheims. It is one of the most extraordinary facts in history that she did all these things. She was eighteen when she crowned the Dauphin as the king of France, but she was captured soon afterward by the English at Compiègne, tried by a French court of the Inquisition, convicted of being a heretic and a witch, and burned alive at the stake on May 30, 1431, when she was still only nineteen.

Her spirit lived on and helped the French to drive the English from France, which they did in a few years. In 1456, her trial was declared invalid and her memory officially purged of any taint or stain. It was not until the nineteenth century, however, that serious ecclesiastical attention was paid to the question whether she was a saint. The long process of canonization came to an end on May 16, 1920, when she was declared Sainte Jeanne d'Arc, her saint's day being May 30. For centuries before this she had been revered by the common people of France as their patron saint and savior.

Shaw was well aware that the danger in writing a play about Joan was to sentimentalize her story, as Mark Twain, for example, had done only a few years before. The facts, Shaw knew, would speak for themselves if fairly presented. And a fair presentation demanded that Joan receive a fair trial; anything else would be a dramatic travesty (as well as a travesty of historical fact). The high point of the play is of course the trial, when Joan, who never really understands the charges against her, condemns herself over and over in her insistence on the truth of her voices as against the truth of the Church. She is crushed, as Shaw says, "between those mighty forces, the Church and the Law," and suffers death because, for her, there is no alternative. She emerges, at the end, as a Shavian hero of reason and clear sightedness. And Shaw concludes, in a stage Epilogue, that mankind will continue to kill its best men and women as long as the qualities that differentiate them, and for which they are therefore killed, are not shared by all.

The play is luminous and beautiful, and the part of Joan is one of the most magnificent for an actress in world drama. It is a long play—three and a half hours—but few playgoers have ever complained. It is also didactic, about which audiences have not complained, either. Shaw was well aware of this, too; I am reminded of something he said in the preface to *Pygmalion*, which is also didactic. "I wish to boast," he wrote, "that *Pygmalion* has been an extremely successful play all over Europe and North America as well as at home."

> It is so intensely and deliberately didactic, and its subject is esteemed so dry, that I delight in throwing it at the heads of the wiseacres who repeat the parrot cry that art should never be didactic. It goes to prove my contention that art should never be anything else.

Whether or not that is true, Shaw was always didactic, always trying to teach us something. What he was trying to teach us was usually valuable; more important, he was a great playwright. One learns and enjoys at the same time.

# chapter thirteen

# Entre Deux Guerres

E*ntre deux guerres*—the French phrase literally means "between two wars," but it meant more than that at the time. World War I ended on November 11, 1918, when the guns were silenced on the Western Front. World War II, the second stage, began on September 1, 1939, when Germany invaded Poland, a country that the so-called Allies had agreed to protect. But in fact the war had never really stopped during those twenty-one short years of uneasy peace. Beginning as early as 1925, Germany had begun to re-arm, as had France. England failed to take the threat seriously, and Americans of America First said there was no threat at all, a claim that President Roosevelt could not accept. They seemed to be proven right when no general hostilities broke out for six months, until, that is, Germany, in a lightning stroke, attacked France and forced her to her knees. Then most people realized that the big war was definitely on again, a fact that every American recognized when the Japanese attacked Pearl Harbor on December 7, 1941.

W.H. Auden, in his poem titled "September 1, 1939," began by saying he was "…uncertain and afraid, As the clever hopes expire / Of a low dishonest decade." We were all afraid—myself included, since I was thirteen in 1939 and eighteen in 1944. E.B. White once wrote that "the worst thing that can happen to a man is to have a son twenty years before a world war." That's what happened to my father, and his hair turned white almost overnight. I survived the war and so did he. But I recall vividly the almost weekly advertisements in the *New Yorker* of an organization called "The Society for the Prevention of World War Two." The photographs depicted the horrors of World War I and the text pleaded for political action as the threat of a new universal holocaust became more and more clear.

Despite that, many of the authors represented in this chapter, all but one of whom were born a few years before 1900, seemed to be able to concentrate on their own business, not that of the world. In many cases this business was fantasy or escapism. And why not? If the world was intent on destroying itself, as it almost did, wouldn't it be sensible to have a little fun? The past and the future were both terrifying to think about, but somewhere, somehow, "there's a helluva good universe next door," as E.E. Cummings said in one of his poems, adding: "Let's go!"

# EUGEN HERRIGEL
## 1884–1955
### Zen in the Art of Archery

Eugen Herrigel was born in Germany in 1884. A philosopher, he went to Japan during the 1930s to teach Western philosophy at the University of Tokyo and while there devoted himself to the study of Zen Buddhism. He did so by becoming a student of the Zen art of archery, which is the subject of his small book *Zen in the Art of Archery*.

Herrigel had long been interested, he tells us, in mysticism, and particularly in the type of mysticism that is associated with the East and Buddhism. And he supposed that it would not be so very difficult for him, who had studied and come to understand the philosophy of Kant and of Hegel, to study and comprehend the philosophy of Zen. But this, he discovered, would not be so.

Herrigel was fortunate to be accepted as a pupil by the great Master Kenzo Awa, who was regarded as perhaps the leading teacher of the art of archery in Japan. The lessons began with a description of the bow and the arrow, a description couched in strange and mystical phrases and sentences that Herrigel thought he understood but did not. The Master then stood, drew the bow, and released the arrow. It flew toward the target. He then asked Herrigel to do the same.

It looked easy. Obviously it was easy for the Master. But it was not easy for Herrigel, as he soon realized. In fact it was impossible. He could not draw the bow, in the accepted and traditional manner, without suffering pain and distress in the muscles of his arms and back. The position seemed strained and awkward. When he was finally able to release the arrow it never went where he expected or wanted it to.

He struggled for months to draw the bow in the right way. Only when he became desperate and asked for help in a humble spirit did the Master inform him that his trouble was that he did not know how to breathe. Many more months were required to learn how to breathe, but when he was finally able to do so he found that he also was now able to draw the bow, effortlessly and without pain.

Herrigel asked a friend why the Master had not told him about breathing at the very beginning. "A great Master," his friend replied, "must also be a great teacher. Had he begun the lessons with breathing exercises he would never have been able to convince you that you owe them anything decisive. You had to suffer shipwreck through your own efforts before you were ready to seize the lifebelt he threw you." Learning to breathe took Herrigel more than a year.

He could now draw the bow, but every time he released the arrow his right arm flew back from the string and his body was shaken, and the arrow flew erratically. Why, he wondered, could he not release the arrow as the Master did? He practiced for many months. Finally he became aware that the Master was trying to tell him, in various ways that he had considered enigmatic, that his problem was that he was trying to shoot the arrow, when in fact the arrow must shoot itself. One day he asked the Master:

> "How can the shot be loosed if 'I' do not do it?"
> "'It' shoots," he replied.
> "And who or what is this 'It'?"
> "Once you have understood that, you will have no further need of me," the Master said. "And if I tried to give you a clue at the cost of your own experience, I would be the worst of teachers."

It took Herrigel more than three years to learn to release the arrow properly—or rather, to be able to wait patiently until the arrow released itself.

Not until then did he and the small class of which he was a member begin to shoot at a target. Here again there were puzzles and contradictions for this Western man. Although the Master always struck the target in the black (its central part), he did not seem even to look at the target when he shot (his eyes were more than half closed), and he insisted that it did not matter if his pupils hit it. "You can be a Master even if your arrows never hit the target," he told them.

Master of what? Herrigel wondered. But he was beginning to understand. The Zen art of archery is not the art of shooting an arrow at a target and always hitting it—or, most abominable of misunderstandings, the art of striking nearer to the center than an opponent in a competition. Instead, it is—well, I shall not try to say. Herrigel is able to say, or to suggest what it is, and why it was so terribly important for him to learn the art, and why, in his opinion (he became a Master himself, after many years), it is terribly important for all Western men and women to learn it. If you wish to understand this yourself, you must read *Zen and the Art of Archery*, which will take you an hour—or study the Zen art, which will take you at least six years. The latter is preferable, but you may not have the time, and in that case the book is an excellent substitute. Reading it sympathetically and with understanding will make you better at whatever you do best.

# ISAK DINESEN
## 1885–1962
### *Seven Gothic Tales*

Karen Christence Dinesen was born in Denmark in 1885, the daughter of a family with ties to the old Danish nobility. In 1914 she married her cousin, Baron Blixen-Finecke, and went with him to Africa, where they established a coffee plantation in Kenya. Her aristocratic husband paid her little interest, but unfortunately he gave her a case of syphilis, which tormented her body for the rest of her life. They were divorced in 1921. She attempted to keep the plantation going, but falling world coffee prices bankrupted her by 1931. She returned to Denmark and wrote *Out of Africa* (1937), a moving account of life on the plantation and of her parting from it and from those who had served and worked with her during the African years.

She had been writing stories, too, and she began to publish them in a series of collections that attracted a passionate following. The stories in *Seven Gothic Tales* are set in a past without a date except that it is just out of reach, just beyond the memory of living persons— at any rate, in an older world that is now gone, where honor was of first importance and promises were kept both by gods and by men. The stories are complex, often containing, in forty or fifty pages, two or three levels of subplot: in short, stories within stories. Interspersed among the narratives, which are packed so tight that there hardly seems to be room for them, are asides and comments of great interest. For example:

> "God," she said, "when he created Adam and Eve, arranged it so that man takes, in these matters, the part of a guest and woman that of a hostess. Therefore man takes love lightly, for the honor and dignity of his house is not involved therein. And you can also, surely, be a guest to many people to whom you would never want to be a host. Now, tell me, Count, what does a guest want?" "I believe," said Augustus, when he had thought for a moment, "that if we do, as I think we ought to here, leave out the crude guest, who comes to be regaled, takes what he can get and goes away, a guest wants first of all to be diverted, to get out of his daily monotony or worry. Secondly the decent guest wants to shine, to expand himself and impress his own personality upon his surroundings. And thirdly, perhaps, he wants to find some justification for his existence altogether. But since you put it so charmingly, Signora, please tell me now: What does a hostess want?"

"The hostess," said the young lady, "wants to be
thanked."

Here loud voices outside put an end to their
conversation.

That passage comes from the story "The Roads Round Pisa,"
which may be the finest of the seven tales. (I'm not sure; I love them
all.) The passage is utterly typical, as is this:

I have always thought it unfair to woman that she has
never been alone in the world. Adam had a time,
whether long or short, when he could wander about on
a fresh and peaceful earth, among the beasts, in full
possession of his soul, and most men are born with a
memory of that period. But poor Eve found him there,
with all his claims upon her, the moment she looked
into the world. That is a grudge that woman has always
had against the Creator: she feels that she is entitled to
have that epoch of paradise back for herself.

Aristocracy has become, for us, an almost unintelligible
institution. It has become nearly impossible for us to comprehend
why any men and women of goodwill (ignoring the proud and the
greedy, whose motives are quite understandable) could ever have felt
that the social arrangements of the *ancien régime* were preferable to
those of today's equalitarianism—or egalitarianism, as they
themselves would have named it. Our image of aristocrats is formed
by Marx Brothers movies in which fat dowagers scowl at idiotic girls
who dance with stupid, rich young men. And perhaps that image was
the reality at most times and places of the aristocratic past. But
aristocracy also conveyed an ideal that could not be conceived by
egalitarians: an ideal of excellence, of freedom and ease, of taste and
thought and good conversation, of probity and honor beyond
everyday standards, of a complete disregard for wealth and a complete
regard for a kind of justice based on individual merit. Isak Dinesen
would not have been the last to admit that the reality was far from
this idea. But the ideal was, in her view, worth remembering as better

than anything the modern world can offer. And this is the ideal world of her *Seven Gothic Tales*.

You may not like them; they may offend you with their insolence, their impatience with mediocrity. I have known persons who disliked Isak Dinesen intensely, and others who were utterly unable to understand and appreciate her. Mind, you do not have to be an aristocrat, or even to desire to live in an aristocracy, to appreciate and understand her. At any rate, it is worth the gamble. If you are made captive, as a steady minority has been, by the tales of Isak Dinesen, you will be in interesting company.

If *Seven Gothic Tales* pleases you, go on to read *Winter's Tales*, a second collection that was published during World War II. Most of these are distinctly inferior to the first seven, but one of them, "Sorrow-acre," is fully comparable to them, and may in fact be the best of all.

Isak Dinesen died at Rungstedlunch, Denmark, her family home, in 1962. For many years she had been unable to eat much solid food, and she became thinner and thinner as she grew older. When she died she weighed no more than seventy pounds, and those who saw her in the last days had the feeling that she was not dying but simply fading away, passing from this into a better world, the creation of her own vibrant imagination.

# VIRGINIA WOOLF
## 1882–1941
### *A Room of One's Own*

Virginia Woolf was born in London in 1882, the daughter of Sir Leslie Stephen, a noted critic, and the sister of Vanessa Bell. After their father's death in 1904 the children moved with their mother to Bloomsbury where they formed the nucleus of the Bloomsbury Group, which included many of the most important English authors and artists of the time. Virginia married Leonard Woolf in 1915 and together, partly to allay the bouts of ill health that tormented her, they founded the Hogarth Press, which published many of her and their friends' books.

Virginia Woolf published her first novel, *The Voyage Out*, in 1915. It was realistic, as was the next. But she continued to write novels, and *Jacob's Room*, 1922, was recognized as a new development in its poetic impressionism. It was praised by T.S. Eliot and attacked by J.M. Murray for its "lack of plot." It was followed by *Mrs. Dalloway*, *To the Lighthouse*, and *The Waves*, published, respectively, in 1925, 1927, and 1931. She continued to write novels, stories, critical essays, many letters, and a diary that was published in six volumes after her death. She was a great writer and a hard worker. She was also very unhappy. She probably suffered from bipolar disorder, a type of schizophrenia, which is characterized by intermittent periods of profound depression and high spirits. She was probably aware in 1941 that a period of depression was imminent when she filled her pockets with rocks and walked into the River Ouse, which flowed near her Sussex home, until the water was over her head.

Her death was a shock but not a surprise. For years she had grown more and more distressed by the way the world was going, and especially, perhaps, by the slowness with which the culture of her times was accepting women as writers and artists. She was much more than a mere feminist; she was an earnest student of the history of women in the Western World and a brilliant writer on the subject. Nothing she wrote on it, I think, is more powerful than *A Room of One's Own*, a long essay in book form on the subject that was published in 1929. I don't just recommend it, I urge you to read it, especially Chapter 3, in which Woolf describes what must have been the fate of Shakespeare's (imaginary) sister who, she supposes, has been born with the same genius as her brother. It would have been impossible for her to write the plays, Woolf argues, for reasons that I think are unassailable.

Unless … Virginia Woolf could not have known about the current research into the life of Mary Sidney, Countess of Pembroke and sister of Sir Philip Sidney. From several points of view her authorship is more credible than that of the Man from Stratford. Even so, it would not undermine Woolf's brilliant argument. Mary Sidney was an aristocrat, well educated, and highly literate. There was only one of her in her time, and she probably didn't write Shakespeare's plays. In any case, you may desire to make up your own mind, but not about the dreadful condition of women in the sixteenth century and for three hundred years after. About that there is no doubt, as Virginia Woolf will make you see.

# FRANZ KAFKA
### 1883–1924
*The Trial*
*The Castle*

Franz Kafka was born in Prague in 1883, the son of a gentle, affectionate, intellectual mother and a domineering, coarse, shopkeeper father who created in the imagination of his son a figure that was at once feared, loathed, and admired. Franz studied law and from this gained much material of use to him in his later career, but he did not complete his studies, going to work instead for an insurance company. He was an excellent worker, neat, careful, scrupulous, dependable, and he could have risen far except for his Jewishness and a certain strangeness familiar to his readers. He had suffered from tuberculosis for years when, in 1922, at the age of thirty-eight, he was forced to retire. He died two years later.

He had been writing for a long time—during his last years, at a feverish rate—but he had published hardly anything. In fact almost no one except his close friend Max Brod knew of the large pile of manuscripts hidden away in Kafka's closet. On his deathbed Kafka demanded that Brod destroy those manuscripts. We must be grateful to Max Brod for his disobedience, else we would never have heard of Franz Kafka and would not have today *The Trial*, *The Castle*, *Metamorphosis*, *The Penal Colony*, and two or three dozen more of the more remarkable literary productions of the twentieth century.

The world of Kafka's novels is a dream world, in which nothing ever happens in an ordinary way. In *The Trial*, the protagonist, Joseph K., suddenly is informed that he has been charged with a serious crime and that he must prepare his defense. What crime, he asks? This is not made clear to him. When and where will the trial take place? This too is not clear. What must he do to defend himself? This is not clear, either. What are his chances of acquittal? They seem not good, but from time to time his spirits are lifted by unreasonable hopes, which in turn are dashed by some further cruel judicial confusion. And the punishment if he is convicted? This alone is absolutely clear: it will be death.

In *The Penal Colony*, an earlier work of Kafka's, punishments were inflicted thus: The convicted man was strapped into a bizarre machine, after which another machine began to write his crime upon his poor, tortured body—with death the final and inescapable result. That is terrible enough; but at least the crime is known. In *The Trial* it is never known. What am I being charged with? K. cries out in terror and longing. The answer may be, with living; or it may be that there is some other mysterious fault, unknown to K., that has placed him in peril of his life. Or is it that he knows very well what he has done and simply refuses, stubbornly, to admit it? We never find out, for *The Trial* is unfinished; but in fact such a book could not end, for there is no end to such a nightmare—unless we wake up. And Kafka was unable to awake from his dream ...

Franz Kafka died before the horrors of twentieth-century judicial terror and torture were well known to the world; indeed, before some of them had been invented. Mussolini had marched on Rome, but Hitler was not yet the master of Germany, and the madness in Stalin's brain had not yet overcome that most frightful of tyrants. (Kafka's three sisters were to know the truth about Hitler; all three died in concentration camps during World War II.) Yet all seems to have been evident to the clerk in the Prague insurance office. He knew what was going to happen: the violent knocking on the door in the middle of the night, the absurd charges that are only excuses for torture and murder, the confusions about the place and time of trial, the vain efforts to defend oneself, the hopes that are never finally justified. Kafka is one of the prophets of our age.

*The Castle* is in many ways similar to *The Trial*, but it is even better, partly because the author's skill is greater, the terror is more refined, and there is frequent relief in humor—a happy comic touch that is often surprising in this book. A land surveyor, again named K., has been ordered to report to the Castle, where it is expected that he will find employment. He must make an appointment to see the

Baron. But he cannot find out how to do this. He calls the Castle on the telephone but usually his calls do not go through, and when they do there is confusion about who he is and whom he is calling. A secretary? What secretary? The secretary he has reached is not the right one, no one knows about K., his file has been lost, as far as the Castle is concerned he does not exist. But how that can be, K. cries? He has been ordered to report to the Castle. Such things happen, an official replies; there is nothing that can be done about it. He is sorry, but there is other work to do …

K. lives in an inn at the foot of the mountain on which the Castle stands, and his life is not without its pleasures. From time to time he even receives small "expenses" payments from the Castle. Each time this happens he is exhilarated, believing that at last the Castle has recognized, or conceded, that he exists. But these payments should not be interpreted in that way, an official explains. They are quite normal; they would be given to anybody. K. must not think that his dossier has been found or that an appointment has been made, or that one is likely to be made. He must wait; he must take his turn. Probably, the official says, everything will become clear in time, although, he adds, that cannot be guaranteed.

This is another nightmare that Kafka has had for all of us, snared in the red tape of the modern world, mired in the bureaucracy that seems to be our greatest invention. No one ever understood it better than Franz Kafka. If you think because you are a cheerful, good-hearted, law-abiding citizen and pay your taxes that you can escape it, then read *The Castle*. It will remind you that civilization, as we like to call it, does not solve all problems.

## AUSTIN TAPPAN WRIGHT
1883–1931
*Islandia*

The life story of Austin Tappan Wright is in itself a romance. Born in 1883, in New Hampshire, he began creating his imaginary country,

Islandia, occupying "the southern portion of the Karain subcontinent, which lies in the Southern Hemisphere," while still a child. (His grandfather had also created an imaginary country, and Austin's younger brother, exiled because of a childish infraction from Islandia, created one of his own.) By the time Wright died in an automobile accident in 1931, there were 2,300 pages of closely handwritten manuscript, including a lengthy discourse on the geography and geology of this country that never existed and a 135,000-word history going back to its imaginary beginnings in the ninth century. All of Wright's family knew about Islandia almost from birth—the family boat was called Aspara, the Islandian word for seagull—but after Wright's death some eleven years had to pass before the novel *Islandia* was published. It appeared in 1942, much cut and edited from the huge original manuscript by one of Wright's children. It immediately attracted a small but growing following, until it became, during the Sixties, one of the great "underground" novels of the twentieth century. That is as it should be, for *Islandia* is a minor masterpiece.

Geographically, the country of Islandia is not very large—perhaps about the size of New England—and rather sparsely populated, with about three million people living for the most part on farms and in very small towns. There is one large town, called simply The City. The Islandians are advanced in some respects, being excellent builders, for example; their houses and public buildings are not only beautiful but also constructed for the ages, not the decades (some of the stone houses are a thousand years old); their woven cloth is exquisite in its soft strength and subtle colors; they have excellent doctors and practically no mental disease. In other respects they are very backward: they do not really like city life, and they have no trains, planes, or automobiles, no banks or credit cards, no newspapers or magazines, no radio, television, or cinema, no electronic musical instruments or games, no computers, and no highly refined forms of art. The art of Islandia is living itself; all Islandians are artists of life, paying much attention to how they live and what they live for. Worst of all, from the point of view of the unsympathetic representatives of the great Western nations who figure rather largely in the book, they have refused to accept Western civilization and to join the modern world. They wish to be what they have always been, which is happy, and they will fight to the death to remain so.

The hero of this extraordinary, perhaps unique utopian fantasy is John Lang, a member, like author Wright himself, of the class of 1905 at Harvard. During his freshman year Lang meets and grows to be a close friend of Dorn, one of the very few Islandians in the United States, who has been sent to Harvard to learn something about the Western world that is trying so hard to absorb Islandia and to exploit its vast buried mineral riches. Lang learns Islandian, a fact that helps him to obtain the post of U.S. Consul in Islandia; but the pressure brought to bear upon the State Department by his uncle, an influential New York businessman who wishes to "open up" Islandia, is, as Lang later learns, even more important. Lang undertakes the long, difficult ocean voyage to Islandia and attempts to be a good consul, which means above all subverting the country that is his generous and welcoming host. But from the very beginning Lang is ambivalent, largely because of his friendship with Dorn, and in the end the U.S. Consul becomes himself absorbed by Islandia and all it represents of rebellion against the world that we all know so well.

If you are inveterately positive about the way the world is going, if you cannot imagine living on a farm and being surrounded by a silence that for the first few months drives even Lang almost mad, if you believe it would be sheer folly to go back to riding horseback instead of sitting behind the wheel of a car, if you think you could not get through an evening, to say nothing of a month or year or ten years, without being entertained by some electronic miracle, above all if you are unwilling to face the great question of whether you should live as you do, and if not then how you should live—if all these things are true, then *Islandia* is not for you. But if they are not true of you, or even if some of them are not true, then you are already an Islandian, just a little, and you will like *Islandia*.

Austin Tappan Wright was a delightful, funny man. He loved puns and wordplay; he also adored his wife—when he spoke to her from a telephone booth he always, to the amusement of his children, removed his hat. I take off my hat to him, too. He was only an amateur—a lawyer and professor of law who wrote only one book, and that entirely for his own pleasure and amusement. But in Islandia all artists are amateurs, and no work of art is ever sold. This is just one more thing you will have to get used to when you travel there.

# RINGGOLD "RING" LARDNER
1885–1933
*Stories*

⌐

Ring Lardner was born in Niles, Michigan, in 1885. As a youngster he was already writing, then editing *The Sporting News* and contributing columns to various newspapers around the country. When he was just thirty he published his first successful book, *You Know Me Al*, in the form of letters from a bush league ballplayer to a friend back home. The joke was always on the player himself, although he never realized this, which was very funny and also somehow moving. The protagonist of this book (the letter-writer) kept appearing and reappearing in subsequent books by Lardner.

*Haircut and Other Stories* appeared a few years later. It includes many of the classic Ring Lardner stories. The title story is the only one I don't like because of its cruelty. Ring could be cruel, but usually not to good people as he is here. However, I forgive him for the great stories, "Alibi Ike," "A Day with Conrad Green," "The Love Nest," "Horseshoes," and "Some Like Them Cold." Come to think of it, some of these are merciless to pompous phonies, liars, and cheats, so I take back what I said about cruelty above.

I have to say that "Alibi Ike" is my favorite of all his stories. Ike is a ballplayer and a very good one, but he can never do anything, either good or bad, without apologizing for it. He always has an alibi even when he doesn't need one. For example he admits to one of the other players that in the previous season he had batted .357, which is great, but he adds that he would have done better except that he had malaria. A listener remarks, "Where can I go to get malaria?" but of course Ike doesn't get the point. (I hope you do!) One reason why I like "Alibi Ike" is that I'm always doing the same thing whereupon my wife calls me Alibi Ike.

A later book, *The Young Immigrunts*, is supposedly written by a kid who is just learning to write dialogue. Here is a taste: "'Daddy are we lost?' the boy asks. 'Shut up,' he explains." Ring Lardner died of TB in East Hampton, at the age of forty-eight. That was the worst of all his jokes. However, his son, Ring Lardner, Jr., survived him and also has had a fine career as a writer.

# ERWIN SCHRÖDINGER
### 1887–1961
*Nature and the Greeks*

Erwin Schrödinger was born in Vienna in 1887 of a Bavarian family that had generations before settled in Vienna. Highly gifted and richly educated, he studied everything, including the history of Italian painting and almost all then-current theories of theoretical physics. An artillery officer in World War I, he took positions starting in 1920 at Stuttgart, Breslau, and Zurich—the last being his most fruitful period. His great discovery, the Schrödinger Wave Equation, which alas I do not understand, was made in 1926, the year I was born.

In 1927 he went to Berlin as Max Planck's successor. The city was then a center of scientific activity, but, finding he could not continue to live in Germany, he went to Oxford, then Princeton, and back to Austria. After the Anschluss he escaped to Italy and arrived at the Institute for Advanced Studies in Dublin, where he worked until he retired in 1955. He continued to write important papers, however, almost until his death in 1961.

My interest in Erwin Schrödinger stems from my discovery in 1954 of his book, *Nature and the Greeks*, which was published in that year. The book originated in several lectures delivered in London by him several years before, the titles of which then and still are of exceptional interest. They are: "The Motives for Returning to Ancient Thought"; "The Competition, Reasons v. Senses"; "The Pythagoreans"; "The Ionian Enlightenment"; "The Religion of Xenophanes, Heraclitus of Ephesus"; "The Atomists"; and "What Are the Special Features?" Anyone who has read more or less carefully the first half of this book, and especially the first hundred pages, will recognize my debt to Schrödinger,, although I hope I have been able to add to what he says on various subjects. At any rate I recommend this little book—less than a hundred pages long—to anyone interested in the general subject of the history of science and particularly of its beginnings in Greek thought more than two thousand years ago.

# WILLIAM CARLOS WILLIAMS
### 1883–1963
### *Selected Poems*

Born in Rutherford, New Jersey, in 1883, W.C.W. (as he is often called) was a New Jerseyan through and through (he died in Rutherford in 1963). His greatest work was a long poem—what might have been called an epic in an earlier age—that he called "Paterson." Paterson is a city in New Jersey, of course, which contains all the kinds of people and human relations and evils and goods that can be found in New Jersey—and anywhere else in America, for that matter. That was the point.

Williams was a pediatric physician who established a practice in his hometown in 1910. He continued to practice medicine for many years and in his "spare time" wrote poems. Many of them are wonderful; some are just repetitive, in the vein of Walt Whitman's "Song of Myself." He adopted a posture he called "objectivist" and produced some of the most astonishing very short poems in the language. In this he seemed to be influenced by his friend Ezra Pound, although he believed Pound was a bad influence on everyone else.

W.C.W. produced many books of poems, criticism, plays, and stories. He even had time to write an autobiography (in 1951). His last book of poems, titled *Pictures of Breugel*, won him a Pulitzer Prize that should have come years before. But he was a curmudgeon who offended almost everyone in the poetic establishment, so critical approbation came late. As for being a curmudgeon—it's not at all a bad thing for a poet to be.

My favorite among his books is *Spring and All* (1972). It contains one devastating long poem, "By the road to the contagious hospital," and many fine short ones including "The Red Wheelbarrow" and

"This is Just to Say," both of which are anthologized everywhere. They are easy to read but hard to feel. It's important to know the circumstances in which "The Red Wheelbarrow" was written, although it isn't enough to know. My own favorite poem is called "El Hombre." This is it—all of it:

> It's a strange courage
> you give me ancient star:
> Shine alone in the sunrise
> toward which you lend no part!

# MARIANNE MOORE
## 1887–1972
### "Poetry"
### "Marriage"

Marianne Moore was born in St. Louis in 1887. She graduated from Bryn Mawr in 1909, working as a teacher for a while and as an assistant librarian in the New York Public Library, where she spent much of her time culling the stacks for odd sayings and surprising remarks, many of which found their way into her poetry. She was particularly delighted by the infinite variety of the animal world (which is no longer so infinite, alas). She spent most of her life in New York, later in Brooklyn, and produced many fine books. *Collected Poems* won her the Pulitzer Price and she received many other awards as well, dying in Brooklyn in 1972.

"Poetry" is a very famous poem, which probably annoyed Miss Moore. I have read it scores of times and led discussions of in my poetry course, and I don't understand it completely. But I feel I do, and especially its wonderfully enigmatic lines, to wit:

> not till the poets among us can be
> 'literalists of
> the imagination'—above
> insolence and triviality and can present

> *for inspection, 'imaginary gardens with real toads in them,'*
> *shall we have*
> *it.*

"Imaginary gardens with real toads in them." What an astonishing description of what constitutes real poetry! Does it make any sense to you? If not, think again; and if not even then, then think once more. It is needed, after all. Or you may just decide to chuck the poem into the wastebasket. But I hope you won't.

"Marriage" is equally challenging. I'll quote just the first few lines.

> *This institution,*
> *perhaps one should say enterprise*
> *out of respect for which*
> *one says one need not change one's mind*
> *about a thing one has believed in,*
> *requiring public promises*
> *of one's intention*
> *to fulfil a private obligation:*
> *I wonder what Adam and Eve*
> *think of it by this time …*

And so it goes, referring in this long poem to dozens of ancient and modern sayings, remarks, lines of poetry, images, and so forth. It is Marianne Moore at her best and worst, the upshot of all being that she doesn't like marriage, which she declined to enter into. Do you blame her? Well, once more think again, and avoid the wastebasket.

# T. S. ELIOT
1888–1965
*Selected Poems*

Thomas Stearns Eliot was born in St. Louis in 1888, the descendant of an English family that had left East Coker, in Somerset, and moved to New England in the seventeenth century. He was educated at Harvard and Oxford universities, with an intermediary stint at the Sorbonne in Paris. He established himself in London in 1914 and became a British subject in 1927.

Eliot's first book of poems, *Prufrock and Other Observations*, appeared in the gloomy war year of 1917; the edition of five hundred copies, at a shilling a copy, took three years to sell out. But Eliot was beginning to make a name for himself as a critic, and when his poem *The Wasteland* appeared in 1922 he was suddenly famous. Dedicated to his fellow poet and poetical revolutionary Ezra Pound, Eliot's *Wasteland* was shocking and innovative, but it also perfectly captured the mood of disillusionment of the early postwar period.

Eliot was confirmed in the Church of England in 1927 and thereafter wrote several works on religious themes, among them the poem "Ash Wednesday" (1930), his fine verse play *Murder in the Cathedral* (1935), and his more popular theatrical success *The Cocktail Party* (1949). The year before, in 1948, he had been awarded the Order of Merit by King George VI and had received the Nobel Prize for Literature.

For twenty years—from 1935 to 1955—T. S. Eliot was the most important literary figure in the English-speaking world. He wrote relatively little, but each small publication of new poetry or prose was an event of major importance. He was studied in every graduate department of English literature, and professors told their students that Eliot's fame would endure until the end of time.

Now, three generations later, some of that enthusiasm has abated. There has been a flurry of interest because of an amazingly popular musical comedy made out of his charming book *Old Possum's Book of Practical Cats*, and Eliot's prose and verse are still widely read. But not many today would declare that he is one of the greatest English poets of all time.

If the estimate of him was too high when he was alive, it may be too low now. Eliot was a very good poet and an excellent writer of pellucid prose, and he remains exciting and challenging to read.

One of the problems with Eliot is that he was a bit pompous. Born in St. Louis, he moved eastward, first to Cambridge and Harvard, then to London. But he did not just live in London; he became a British subject and adopted a British accent. He became more English than the English and wrote about his adopted country as if it really were his own.

His poetry, nevertheless, is not "merely" English. It is dependent on the classical tradition of English literature but, like that tradition, it has universal aspects that raise it above the ordinary parochial level. After all, every "national" literature must be parochial to some extent, else it would not be national. And among national literatures, which one is greater than English literature? I do not think there is any. So to be English, as we say of Eliot, is no bad thing to be.

But it is the universal aspects in Eliot's poetry that are most worthy of note and admiration. The dark side of things, as we see it in *The Wasteland*, is a side of things that not just English men and women have observed. The myth of a wasteland that comes down to us from the Middle Ages was the subject of learned discussion when Eliot was writing the poem; World War I had just ended, and many felt that it had turned a blooming civilization into a desert and that the world would never seem, or be, so rich and full of promise again. This was a universal, not just an English, insight; and the images of the poem are universal, too, comprising as they do remembered scenes from the history and literature of the whole world, not just England. What the poem says—that we can turn the world into a wasteland, and that we may even want to do that—was worth saying in 1922, and it is worth remembering today. We can still do it, we can do it more absolutely and completely than ever, and maybe we even want to do it, still.

*Four Quartets* is an even finer poem than *The Wasteland*, as well as being more English. No poem better expresses the way many persons felt at the end of the 1930s when, tired of the lying and the hatred, they were willing to fall into another great war—a more terrible war by far—rather than face their own selves. The war came and swept away many of the old things, not the least of them the old England, as Eliot had perceived it.

There was no coming back for him then; he had thrown in his lot with the English and would remain in Britain the rest of his life. There was not much more poetry, although the collections of small pieces of prose and verse kept appearing and winning plaudits. Those critical essays in immaculate prose are well worth reading, worth studying, if that is your bent. Two volumes, in particular, are noteworthy: *The Sacred Wood* (1920) and *Selected Essays, 1917-1932* (1932). No essay of Eliot's has been more influential than "Tradition and the Individual Talent." It is the prime statement of a classical view of literature and should not be ignored in the flood of novelties that so many prefer.

Looking back, there are a dozen or so other poems that are of lasting importance. *The Wasteland*, "Ash Wednesday," and *Four Quartets* lead the list, but "The Love Song of J. Alfred Prufrock," "The Hollow Men," "Rhapsody on a Windy Night," "Morning at the Window," "Sweeney Among the Nightingales," "Journey of the Magi," "Marina," and "Eyes That Last I Saw in Tears" belong on it, too, as well as *Old Possum's Book of Practical Cats*.

# EZRA POUND
## 1885–1972
### *Selections*

Ezra Pound was born in Idaho, of Quaker parents, in 1885. His education was decidedly desultory but not the less thorough and far-reaching for that. He was probably the most widely read of poets, in English, French, Italian, and other Western languages, and Eastern (at least in transliterations) as well. In fact one of his most famous poems, and (I think) perhaps his best, is "The River-Merchant's Wife: A Letter," which, he states in an afterword, "By Rihaku." The poem is a letter from a young wife who married when she was still a child and is now old enough to know what love really is. Her beloved husband has gone away for a while, and she writes to ask him to tell her when he is returning: "Please let me know beforehand," she says, "And I will come out to meet you/As far as Cho-fu-Sa." We do not know why he has gone or whether in fact he will return, nor do we know how far Cho-fu-Sa is although it is apparently a long way from her home. These details are unimportant; what is important is the sense, almost tactile, of her longing and her devotion to this young man whom we know only through her loving eyes. I have read this poem perhaps fifty times and it never fails to bring tears to my eyes.

Pound's life was in many ways a mess. At the end of it, during World War II, he broadcast pro-Fascist messages on Italian radio, was arrested after the war, tried, convicted, and imprisoned in a mental hospital. Thanks to a worldwide movement in his favor he was released and returned to Italy, where he died in 1958. But his poetic output had been large, and his influence inspired T.S. Eliot to describe him as "more responsible for the Twentieth Century revolution in poetry than any other individual." There is no doubt, at least, of his great influence on Eliot and other contemporary poets. He was especially helpful to Eliot in his writing of *The Wasteland*, and Eliot dedicated the poem to him in these words: *Al miglior fabbro*—"To the better workman." Pound's establishment of the Imagist school of poetry is exemplified in one of the best known imagist poems (the title, "In a Station of the Metro," is longer than the poem, to wit):

> *The apparition of these faces in the crowd;*
> *Petals on a wet, black bough.*

There was a time, in my youth, when everyone I knew could recite those two lines. Strange? Maybe.

Pound's major works are *The Cantos* and *The Pisan Cantos*, the latter written when he was confined in a mental hospital near Pisa, in Italy. *The Cantos* is a very long and immensely complex retelling (in a sense) of *The Odyssey* of Homer in something like Dantesque dress. Parts of it are wonderful, but to wade through the entire work is beyond most readers, including me.

# EUGENE O'NEILL
## 1988–1953
### *Long Day's Journey into Night*

Eugene O'Neill was born in a Broadway hotel in New York City in 1888. He was the son of an actor and he grew up on the road. He spent a year at Princeton and then, to complete his education, sailed as a seaman, worked on the waterfront, and suffered from tuberculosis and alcoholism. He began to experiment with drama in 1913 and saw his first play, *Bound East for Cardiff*, produced by the Provincetown Players on Cape Cod, Massachusetts, in 1916. In 1920 his first full-length play, *Beyond the Horizon*, opened on Broadway and won him the first of his four Pulitzer Prizes. In 1936 he became the first American to win the Nobel Prize for Literature. He died in 1953, the victim of a crippling disease that had ended his writing ten years before.

O'Neill's most serious early dramatic works were self-conscious imitations of Greek tragedies They did not really work.

*Long Day's Journey into Night* (written in 1941 but not produced until 1956) and its companion piece, *The Iceman Cometh* (written 1939, produced 1946), are also tragedies but of a different kind. They are not imitations of anything literary. They are tragedies of ordinary men and women in ordinary life—quotidian tragedies about life as we live it today. Gone is the necessity, seemingly imposed by the old Greek models, for "great" characters, dynastic events, monstrous cruelty, and bloodshed. There is tragedy enough, O'Neill knew, in ordinary families. Families like his own. Especially families like his own.

The Greek playwrights had also known, of course, that families were the place to look for tragedy. Family life is essential, indispensable, for human beings; but it is very hard to live in families. In fact, we almost do not know how to do it, at the same time that we know no other way to live that is anywhere near as satisfactory. What living soul has not at some time or other echoed Sophocles' lament, in *Oedipus at Colonus*:

> *Best is not to be born at all.*
> *Next best, to die young.*

It is the conflicts of, and within, families that are most likely to bring us to such straits. Yet families are also where love and comfort and most joys that human beings know are to be found, as well as hatred and fear and loathing. Life can be desperately lonely even within families, but it is worse without them. Poor mankind!—as O'Neill would have been first to admit.

The Greeks had known, too, that small faults, often enough repeated, add up to great pain. Faults of character, we call these—the arrogance of Oedipus, repeated over and over, finally leads to his downfall. A single instance of such a fault is never, by itself, decisive. In O'Neill's *Long Day's Journey*, the stinginess of James Tyrone Sr. is eminently forgivable—if he had only been stingy once. The drunkenness of his son James would be forgivable—if he had not been drunk so often. And Mary Tyrone, the mother—one drug episode, one morphine binge, would be forgivable and would have been forgiven. But there will be no end to those binges, short of the night to which our long day's journey tends.

O'Neill's play is somber but not unrelievedly dark. There is little happiness in the Tyrone household that day in August 1912—except for the spurious happiness produced by drugs, alcohol, or morphine. There are, however, as there must be in any genuine tragedy, moments of sudden insight that light up the darkness like a lightning flash. Most of these occur in the third act, which is where they should occur, of course, in a well-made play. Old Tyrone sees into his own soul as clearly as he ever has and shares his morbid vision with his oldest son. The latter, James Jr., also sees clearly, for perhaps the first time, the destructiveness in his love for his younger brother, Edmund. And Edmund—who is O'Neill himself, the author revealing to us, the audience, the devastating truths that he had first come to understand so many years before—sees his family shorn of illusions, hating one another, loving one another, struggling to be free in the prison of their own days.

Probably the most memorable figure in the tragedy is Mary Tyrone, the haunted wife and mother who bewails her lack of a proper home and drowns her sorrow in drugs. Does she, too, see into her own soul? Critics dispute about that; some say yes, some say no. Mary's last words, at any rate, are enigmatic, which may suggest that what O'Neill wished us to feel was the puzzlement that he probably felt about his mother. How could she have become the woman she was? How could she have let it happen to her? Why did she not have the strength to withstand the drug? Yet she has all his sympathy, too, as she has the sympathy of her husband and her older son.

In *The Iceman Cometh* O'Neill had proclaimed that life is too hard to try to live it without illusions. The older you are the more likely you are to understand that. *Long Day's Journey* goes far beyond *Iceman* in showing us—just for one day—life completely shorn of illusions, stripped bare for all to see.

The old Greeks knew another thing about tragedy: Viewing it provides a kind of catharsis, which relieves us of the dreadful necessity of enduring tragedy ourselves. The more deeply we feel the fate of Oedipus, Aristotle suggested, the less likely we are to suffer as he did. This is the keynote, the unforgettable effect, of *Long Day's Journey into Night*. Here the artist reaches down deep into his own pain to find a kind of salvation for us. It is no wonder that we almost worship great artists and writers who give us such gifts.

# NANCY MITFORD
## 1904–1973
### *Madame de Pompadour*

Nancy Mitford was born in London in 1904, the daughter of a nobleman and sister of a remarkable collection of brilliant women. Almost in her nonage she began to write novels, the first of which to succeed was *The Pursuit of Love* (1945), in which the lovely Linda describes the scabrous love affairs of her six cousins. This was followed by *Love in a Cold Climate* and *Don't Tell Alfred*.

The novels were slight, as was *Noblesse Oblige*: an enquiry into the identifiable characteristics of the English aristocracy (1956), which, with *Encounter* (1955), introduced the tongue-in-cheek concept of "U" and "Non-U" vocabulary, although these books were a lot of fun. Much more important, I think, were her four biographies of notables of the seventeenth and eighteenth centuries in France. I read them all some years ago, and the one I remember best is the life of Madame de Pompadour, the first mistress of Louis XV. Hers was an extraordinary life.

The next-to-last Louis, like his grandfather (Louis XIV) and son (Louis XVI), was in almost constant need of female companionship and maintained a "Deer Park" where his provider of sexual services, the venerable Duc de Richelieu, produced and trained a new bedmate every night of the year. Mme de Pompadour had begun in February 1745 as a casual sexual playmate, but her health was not up to the constant calls upon her body, and she promoted herself before the lazy monarch to the position of private secretary, in which she almost single-handedly ruled an empire that, at the time, was the richest in the world. Her taste was excellent, and she in effect designed the style we call Louis Quinze, but she also protected the king from the never-ending turmoil of the court that threatened them both. She was an intellectual and although she could not have a salon she directed the intellectual and literary affairs of the kingdom, as well as its political and military affairs, from her outpost at Versailles.

None of this lasted very long. Nine years later, in February 1754, she was very ill, and the king, during her last days, hardly left her room. He wished to be there when she died, but her confessor refused to allow this. She died in the company of a single priest, who, as he was leaving the room, heard her say "Wait for me, Abbé, I am going with you," which were her last words for she died a few moments later.

The book is wonderful and beautiful, as was its subject. Nancy Mitford spent the rest of her life in Paris and died there in 1973.

# C.S. LEWIS
### 1898–1963
*Out of the Silent Planet*
*Perelandra*
*That Hideous Strength*

Many people are unaware that C.S. Lewis produced three of the finest science-fiction novels. They comprise a trilogy, with profound and moving theological overtones—or undertones.

Lewis, born in Belfast in 1898, was an Oxford don, an authoritative scholar of medieval literature and of the literature of the English Renaissance. He wrote several definitive studies in his field. He was also an eloquent and, in the case of one book, *The Screwtape Letters* (1942), a bestselling Christian apologist. *The Screwtape Letters* is a very good book and a pleasure to read. So is *The Lion, the Witch, and the Wardrobe*, though it is written for children. But neither is as good as the trio of science-fiction novels Lewis wrote between 1938 and 1946, when that genre, which has now been exploited beyond all expectations, was young.

The first book in the series, *Out of the Silent Planet*, introduces us to Ransom, the ordinary Englishman who might be C.S. Lewis himself and who might be Christ—if Christ had been an Englishman. Ransom is called to an adventure that he does not quite understand, but he knows he must go. He leaves the Earth—the Silent Planet, because it is shrouded in a cloud of evil that we may, if we wish, take as Original Sin—and embarks on a space voyage that is quite unlike any space voyage in any other science-fiction novel, and also quite unlike the real thing. Nevertheless, you may agree with me when you read *Out of the Silent Planet* that Lewis's imagined voyage is better than the real thing, and even—strange as it may be to say so—more real.

Ransom has various adventures on Mars (Malacandra), his first port of call, and eventually learns that he must travel to Venus, or Perelandra, as the third planet in the solar system is called. *Perelandra* is also the name of the second novel in the trilogy.

On Perelandra, Ransom has further adventures of a profound allegorical significance. There is a Lady, not otherwise named, who lives on an island floating on the Venusian sea. There is a rival for her favors, Dr. Weston, a dark and evil being. Ransom knows that eventually he will have to fight Dr. Weston, and he does so. He triumphs, but he is wounded in the heel, and the wound cannot be cured. Recapping the story fails to convey the excitement of this trial and this battle between evil and good.

The third novel, *That Hideous Strength*, finds Ransom back on Earth, where the conflict has been transferred and now manifests itself in an ordinary struggle in a university town between a very modern National Institute of Coordinated Experiments (N.I.C.E.)

and some ancient traditions and institutions, including the seer Merlin, buried beneath the ground. There is also a group of animals that derive the kind of comfort from Ransom's presence among them that the birds used to receive from Saint Francis. One of these, the bear, Mr. Bultitude, is quite capable of breaking your heart. In fact, your heart may not survive reading this wonderful concluding novel of the series. And when the great angels come, swimming through the murkiness of air, you will gasp, as Dante gasped to see the Angel come down into Hell to quiet the demons so that he might pass.

Indeed, there is every sort of echo and reminder in these three fine books of literary events, and of religious ones as well. Dante and Milton somehow stand in the background, applauding this use of them by the Oxford scholar; and the Bible and Aquinas are part of the chorus, too. The more you know about Christian apologetics and about classical literature, the better will these three books seem to you. But they will be very satisfying reading whatever you know, or do not know.

# J.R.R. TOLKIEN
## 1882–1933
### *The Hobbit*
### *The Lord of the Rings*

J.R.R. Tolkien, born in England in 1892, was a professor of English language and literature at Oxford for many years. He published several philological studies—of Beowulf, for example—and was known by his friends and students as a retiring and very learned, almost timid, man. But one of his friends knew he was something very different, and as it turned out, very great. The friend was C.S. Lewis, his colleague at Oxford, who was the only one who knew that Tolkien had been working for many years on two books that are based on a mythology all his own.

The first of the books was *The Hobbit*. Hobbits live in the Shire, which is like the English countryside but not quite. If you stand in the middle of a pleasant English meadow and look around you at the grass and the trees and perhaps a sparkling little stream meandering in the near distance you may not see the Hobbits who live there, because they are not visible to us unless ... well, unless Professor Tolkien tells us about them.

As it turns out, the Shire is threatened by a terrible force that has to be overcome by two of the Hobbits, the redoubtable Frodo and his friend and servant, Sam. Of course Frodo and Sam can't defend their world all by themselves, but they find glorious allies, both men and women (and trees, as well, who speak to them). Their foe also has vicious allies that "fly through the night in the howling storm," to quote a great poem by William Blake, who would have loved Tolkien. There is a Ring, of course, that Frodo loses and must find again, with Sam's help, and then must throw into the great fire at the center of the mountain of their enemy. Of course they succeed ...

I probably don't have to say any more, because you or your children have probably seen the three *Lord of the Rings* films that were made in New Zealand and distributed worldwide. Since I'm a Hobbit myself I have to admit I didn't like the films as much as I liked the books when I read them for the first time many years ago, but that is by the by.

# F. SCOTT FITZGERALD
## 1896–1940
### *The Great Gatsby*

F. Scott Fitzgerald was born in St. Paul, Minnesota, in 1896, the son of relatively impecunious parents who nevertheless managed to send him to St. Paul's and Princeton. The experience may have been good for his intellect, but the moral lesson was, unfortunately, too clear to him: the rich, of whom he was not one, were unlike him, which is to say that they could afford to enjoy life whereas he could not. At Princeton his discontent was multiplied by the fact that he failed to make the football team.

So he left without a degree and joined the army. Again life deprived him of a rich reward: he was not sent overseas. Instead he was stationed in Alabama. There he met and fell in love with Zelda Sayre, but her family would not take a poor man to its bosom. There were many things to complain of, and Fitzgerald returned to the writing that he had begun at Princeton. His first novel, *This Side of Paradise*, was published in 1920, after the famous editor Maxwell Perkins had told him to take home the first draft and completely rewrite it. The book was an instant success; it seemed to express the hidden desires and fears of an entire new generation of frustrated and rebellious youth. Fitzgerald now had an income, and Zelda agreed to be his wife.

Two volumes of short stories and a second novel, all published by 1922, helped to establish Fitzgerald as a leading spokesman of his time. But none of these books was really very good. The true genius of Scott Fitzgerald was revealed in 1925, with the publication of *The Great Gatsby*. It marked the peak of the young author's achievement, and from then on everything was downhill. He spent the next ten years wandering about Europe and America, often drunk, almost always morose, in part because of the increasing insanity of Zelda. *Tender Is the Night* appeared in 1933, but it was largely ignored (although I liked it very much when I read it in Paris years ago). Fitzgerald was determined to make money if he could not have fame. He went to Hollywood and lost his soul there, as so many had done before him and would after him. He was struggling to finish still another novel when he died in Hollywood late in 1940. He remains to this day the very symbol of his time.

The extraordinary thing about *The Great Gatsby* is that it reveals that its author understood all these things perfectly clearly, although he was unable to act on that understanding. Jay Gatsby, like his creator, is even more a symbol than he is a man. He too pursues an unattainable goal; he too is defeated by the reality of life, against which he has no defense. The famous last lines of the book express this:

> Gatsby believed in the green light, the orgiastic future
> that year by year recedes before us. It eluded us then, but
> that's no matter—tomorrow we will run faster, stretch
> out our arms farther.... And one fine morning—So we

beat on, boats against the current, borne back ceaselessly into the past.

The book is American to the core. In it, rich and poor seem to
converge, to touch, but in reality they never do. In it, everyone is
obsessed with money and hope; if they lose one, they also lose the
other. In it, there is the constant refrain of expectation: a solution to
every problem is just around the corner.

These are not only American feelings and fears; they are human.
It is the humanity of Gatsby, as compared to the relative inhumanity
of Tom and Daisy, the man he befriends and the woman he loves, that
shores up the book and establishes its power. The language would be
different, the names, the occupations, the preoccupations, if this
story took place in another time, another place. But the basic human
aspirations and the suffering would be the same.

## ERNEST HEMINGWAY
### 1899–1961
*The Short Stories of Ernest Hemingway*

Ernest Hemingway was born in 1899 in Oak Park, Illinois, a comfortable suburb of Chicago. He never got over his birthplace. The
memory of Oak Park and his profound understanding of its cultural
and moral insularity haunted Hemingway, and he spent his life trying
to flee it. Partly as a result, his life was a great and continuous adventure. This was also due, however, to the fact that he lived during one
of the most eventful times in history. He wrote about that in the
Preface to *The Short Stories of Ernest Hemingway* (1938):

> In going where you have to go, and doing what you have
> to do, and seeing what you have to see, you dull and
> blunt the instrument you write with. But I would rather
> have it bent and dull and know I had to put it on the
> grindstone again and hammer it into shape and put a

whetstone to it, and know that I had something to write about, than to have it bright and shining and nothing to say, or smooth and well-oiled in the closet, but unused.

Those are two of the best sentences ever written by any writer about writing. No modern writer has a more distinctive style than Hemingway; you recognize him after the first few words. It is impossible to describe this style, or to define it; you have to read some Hemingway prose and then you will recognize it, too. The style is vigorous and masculine but also very sensitive. That is a hard contradiction to maintain, and Hemingway does not always succeed in doing so. None of his novels, it seems to me, not even *The Sun Also Rises*, which I think is the best of them, is able to maintain this contradiction for long, certainly not throughout the entire book. It is like a balancing act done on a high wire in a strong wind—without a pole. It cannot go on for very long without the acrobat falling.

There are wonderful things in the novels, especially in *The Sun Also Rises* and *A Farewell to Arms* (read out loud to yourself the first page and the last page of the latter) and even in *For Whom the Bell Tolls*, which is too long. But the true Hemingway jewels are in the volume of short stories that he published in 1938. I especially would recommend "Big Two-Hearted River," Parts I and II; "A Clean, Well-Lighted Place," "The Snows of Kilimanjaro," "Old Man at the Bridge," and also the shortest of Hemingway's novels, just a long short story, actually, *The Old Man and the Sea*, for which Hemingway won the Nobel Prize for Literature.

Not everyone appreciates "Big Two-Hearted River." It is about a man who returns from the big world into which he has journeyed and where he has become famous. He comes back to a river that he fished long ago and fishes it again. Nothing happens but that. He sees no one and talks to no one; he just sets up his tent and makes his supper and sleeps there by the river, and the next day catches a bottle full of grasshoppers for bait and then fishes for the trout that are plentiful in the river. At the end of the day he goes away. There is no simpler story but also, it seems to me although I can't say exactly why, no more perfect one. (Even if you don't like to fish, which I do not.)

"A Clean, Well-Lighted Place" is only five pages long. I have read it many times, but each time I read it shivers go up and down my spine. It is about "a nothing that he knew too well." The Spanish word for nothing is *nada*. This word rings through the story like a death knell. Hemingway knew about death. He was obsessed with it.

"The Snows of Kilimanjaro" is also about death—the death of a man in Africa of gangrene brought on by a small untreated wound. The story is also about stories, for the man, in his final delirium, remembers all the stories he wanted to write but could not. As such it is a kind of tour de force, but a magnificent one.

Hemingway wrote "Old Man at the Bridge" in 1937 or 1938, during the Spanish Civil War. He had always loved Spain and had written extraordinary things about the country and its people and about bull-fights. Now Spain was tearing itself to pieces, and he went back as a journalist, because he couldn't stay away. He saw everything and would write *For Whom the Bell Tolls* about that war, which, as he knew very well and predicted often, was only a rehearsal for the greater war that would follow, throughout all of Europe and indeed the whole world. He sent back the four pages of "Old Man at the Bridge" by cable from a town in the delta of the Ebro River. The story tells of an old man who is caught by the war, trapped between the two sides in that brutal civil conflict, even though, as he says, he has no politics. "I was taking care of animals," he says. Two goats and a cat and four pairs of pigeons.

"The cat, of course, will be all right," the old man says. He is so tired that he cannot walk any longer, even if the enemy comes. "A cat can look out for itself, but I cannot think what will become of the others."

That sentence sums up, for me, all the terror and cruelty and sadness of war. It was the sort of thing that Hemingway knew more about than almost any writer of our time.

# E.B. WHITE
1899–1985
*Charlotte's Web*

Elwyn Brooks White was always called Andy by his friends, doubtless because no grown man should have to be called Elwyn.

White was born in 1899, five years after James Thurber. The two became friends during the 1920s, and began to write books together, notably *Is Sex Necessary?* in 1933. They also worked together on the *New Yorker*. Thurber produced his cartoons and White wrote the opening page or so of "The Talk of the Town" and performed other necessary editorial chores. White's casual pieces for the *New Yorker* during his many years of association with the magazine are among the finest things of the sort ever written in America, and several collections of them—*The Second Tree from the Corner*, for example, and *The White Flag*—retain the same liveliness that they had when they first appeared. A feature he wrote for *Holiday* magazine called "Here Is New York" may also be the best thing ever written about that fabulous, perilous city.

Such works by E.B. White are, however, mere ephemera compared to his two children's novels, *Stuart Little* and *Charlotte's Web*. The latter is so obviously and ineluctably a classic that it almost does not need to be recommended to anybody. But you may have missed it as a child. In that case, do not wait even one minute more. White must have had his tongue in his cheek when he came to dream up the story of *Charlotte's Web*. But maybe he did not; maybe he had done some very astute research into the history of children's literature. He would have found that although some classic works for children have "nice" characters in them, many do not, like *The Wind in the Willows* and the Peter Rabbit stories and *White Fang* and *Where the Wild Things Are*—to name only a handful of famous children's books about creatures very different from good little boys and girls and sweet little puppies and kittens. At any rate, White came up with a trio of characters that must have shocked his editors: a pig, a spider, and a rat. But he wove out of their lives together a story that will last forever.

Wilbur is the pig. He is a timid creature, very fat and frightened, and he never changes although he risks his life for his friend at the end of the book, and that is a brave and heroic thing to do. Charlotte, of course, is the spider. She is a unique creation; there is nothing else like her in literature. She is very spidery and yet she is lovable, too. Templeton is the rat. He is completely unlovable. Yet we love him anyway. So it is with the books of E.B. White. He has us in his spell and we cannot escape.

If you read *Charlotte's Web* when you were a child, but are embarrassed to be seen reading it now when you are grown up, there is a simple solution. Have a baby, and read the story to him or her. That way you will share a great pleasure.

# JAMES THURBER
## 1894–1961
### *"The Secret Life of Walter Mitty"*

James Grover Thurber—who was Jim to everyone, including me, a friend—was born in Columbus, Ohio, in 1894. He was educated at Ohio State University and like so many Midwesterners at the time gravitated to New York, where he tried to make a living as a writer and illustrator. He was hired as managing editor of Harold Ross's new magazine, the *New Yorker*. It was not long before he captured E.B. White. They wrote books together, and Thurber published his extraordinary, sardonic cartoons. The *New Yorker* was known for its cartoons and many of the cartoonists became famous, but none more so than Thurber. He never stopped drawing his incredible men and women and his even more incredible dogs even after he became blind, or almost blind—he could see large black lines on a yellow background, which was enough. Well, not really enough, because Thurber became angry at the world that had let him go blind and took it out in all sorts of ways that are irrelevant here.

Thurber also wrote stories for the *New Yorker*. Many are well known, especially those in a wonderful book called *Fables for Our Time*. It is very Thurberish, which is a very good thing to say about it. His best-known and probably best-written story was called "The Secret Life of Walter Mitty." Mitty is a shy, hen-pecked man who can't rebel against his wife's determined tyranny but at least can imagine he could. He is driving the car and his wife is driving from the back seat, and he imagines all kinds of wonderful alternative lives, as a surgeon about to conduct a difficult operation, for example, or an Air Force ace in the World War. The story was the basis of a musical comedy and a film, which were fun but not as much fun as the story. Thurber also wrote a successful Broadway play called *The Male Animal*, which was produced in the little Connecticut town in which I live and where he lived too, with me playing the male lead. Jim and his wife Helen sat in the front row. Thurber applauded and said it was the best performance of the play he had ever seen, which was nonsense of course but satisfying even so. For me it was a very Thurberish experience.

Thurber died in 1961, after a long period of frustrated unhappiness. The *New Yorker* had stopped publishing his stories, which were probably not as good as those he had written in the Thirties. He was now totally blind and dependent on his wife, who was also unwell. I saw him a couple of weeks before he died and said goodbye but not in so many words. A good selection of his funniest works are to be found in *The Thurber Carnival* (1945).

# ARCHIBALD MACLEISH
### 1892–1982
### *Selected Poems*

Archibald MacLeish was born in a Chicago suburb in 1892, the scion of a wealthy Midwestern mercantile family. He graduated from Yale in 1915 and, after army service in the World War, gained his Ll.B. from Harvard in 1919 and practiced law for three years until, in 1923, he decided to write poetry full time. An expatriate during the 1920s, he moved in the literary circle of Hemingway, Fitzgerald, Gertrude Stein, and others. He published two books of poems that were influenced by Pound and Eliot. In the 1930s he became deeply concerned about the threat to American society and to world democracy. *Conquistador*, 1932, was the first of his "public" poems and won him the first of his three Pulitzer Prizes. *America Was Promises*, 1939—the title was intended to shock readers into an awareness of the threat the country faced—was followed by *The Irresponsibles*. He was named Librarian of Congress,

1939-44, and was an Assistant Secretary of State, 1944-5, when he aided in the foundation of UNESCO. His *Collected Poems*, 1952, won another Pulitzer Prize and a National Book Award, and his hit Broadway play, *J.B.* (1958), won a Pulitzer for drama. He taught at Harvard from 1949 to 1962 and was a lecturer at Amherst from 1964 to 1967.

It was a great career, and he was a wonderful man. In their later years he and my father were best friends and recorded several conversations on videotape. He also wrote two wonderful poems that deeply influenced my understanding of poetry and life. One, "You, Andrew Marvell," was a kind of response to Marvell's famous *carpe diem* poem, "To His Coy Mistress." In the poem a man lies on a beach in Massachusetts and imagines the passage of the evening from Ecbatan to Kermanshah, from Baghdad through Arabia to Palmyra, Lebanon, and Crete, over Sicily, and "Spain go under and the shore/Of Africa, the gilded sand," and now "the long light on the sea—And here, face downward in the sun/To feel how swift, how secretly,/The shadow of the night comes on…" It is, simply, magical.

"Ars Poetica" is just as good. The title is taken from Horace's famous *Art of Poetry*, and it describes a way of writing poetry that not everyone has adopted but is wonderful all the same. The poem lists some things a poem should be, for example, "Motionless in time/As the moon climbs," "equal to,/Not true," "For all the history of grief/An empty doorway/and a maple leaf,/For love,/The leaning grasses and two light above the sea," and concludes

> A poem should not mean
> But be.

The poem demands a great deal from you, the reader, but it is worth whatever is asked. For example, the lines, "For all the history of grief/An empty doorway and a maple leaf." Why is the doorway empty? Who has gone through it perhaps never to return? Is the maple leaf green or red—is it summer or autumn? What did the leaf mean?

# MARK VAN DOREN
1894–1972
*Selected Poems*

My father was born in a small rural town in Illinois in 1894, the son of a country doctor. He went to New York for graduate study shortly before World War I and after he returned from the war to complete his studies and to teach at Columbia University. This made him a New Yorker; but he much preferred to New York the abandoned farm in Cornwall, Connecticut, that he and my mother bought in 1923 and about which he wrote many of his poems. He was a professor of literature and the author of many volumes of criticism, novels, short stories, and literary biographies. But the main business of his life, as he saw it, was writing poems. He walked across a meadow to an old mill near his farmhouse and wrote almost every day. He usually tried to complete a poem, or a part of a poem, each day. He used to say that anyone can start a poem, but it takes a poet to finish it.

These industrious efforts produced many hundreds of poems, of which a certain number are good—it is hard for me, as it was always hard for him, to choose among them. In his case, it is probably best to read a fairly large number of poems, most of which are short and deceptively simple. His poetic styles were varied; he was constantly experimenting with new styles and could write in almost any meter. His subjects were equally varied. He especially liked animals, all animals, and wrote fine poems about them. For example, "The Animals":

> *So cunningly they walk the world,*
> *So decently they lay them down,*
> *Who but their maker sees how pride*
> *And modesty in them are one?*

He wrote about other natural things; "Former Barn Lot" was a good example:

*Once there was a fence here,*
          *And the grass came and tried,*
*Leaning from the pasture*
          *To get inside.*

*But colt feet trampled it,*
          *Turning it brown;*
*Until the farmer moved*
          *And the fence fell down.*

*Then any bird saw,*
          *Under the wire,*
*Grass nibbling inward*
          *Like green fire.*

He wrote about people, those whom he knew and loved, and also about people he had not known but still loved—those he called "My Great Friends," for example Hamlet, Achilles, Don Quixote.

He wrote about death, his own personal, physical death and also the death of the world. He was acutely, painfully aware that for the first time in history human anger and folly could destroy the home of man. In a well-known poem, "So Fair a World It Was," he expressed his fears about this:

*So fair a world it was,*
*So far away in the dark, the dark*
*Yet lighted, oh, so well, so well:*
*Water and land,*
*So clear so sweet;*
*So fair, it should have been forever.*

He expressed another aspect of the same fear in what has become probably his best-known poem, in which he played with the notion that his private world and the world at large are much the same thing. He called the poem, simply, "O World":

> O world, my friend, my foe,
> My deep dark stranger, doubtless
> Unthinkable to know;
> My many and my one,
> Created when I was and doomed to go
> Back into the same sun;

Mark Van Doren published some fifty books, of which more than twenty were collections of his poems. In 1967 he issued a small volume called *100 Poems*, which is a good introduction to his work. It does not contain poems from his two later books of poetry, *That Shining Place* (1969) and *Good Morning: Last Poems* (1973). The latter includes poems written during his last decade of life; these show no diminution in power and charm. He died in Cornwall in 1972.

# ANTOINE DE SAINT-EXUPÉRY
## 1900–1944
### *The Little Prince*

Antoine de Saint-Exupéry was born into an impoverished family of French aristocrats in Lyons in 1900. His real life began in 1922, when he received his pilot's license; from that time on he was only really happy when he was behind the controls of an airplane. He flew—often (and preferably) alone—over much of the world, helping to inaugurate airmail routes over North Africa, the south Atlantic, and South America. He was forced several times to crash-land the small, undependable planes that were the lot of airmen of those days, and once he and his plane were not found for many days; as he lay, badly hurt, on the burning Sahara sands he began to have delusions. Perhaps these were, after all, the source and inspiration of *The Little Prince*.

It was his last book, but there were others before it; the only other thing that Saint-Exupéry liked to do besides flying was to write about flying. Two of his best are *Vol de Nuit* (*Night Flight*, 1931) and *Terre* des Hommes (*Wind, Sand, and Stars*, 1939). These works share a quality that no one else, perhaps, has ever brought to the subject of flight: as you read the sound of the engine seems to die away, and you are suspended in midair, the Earth far below and almost forgotten, alone with yourself in a novel element dreamed of by man forever but never before conquered.

Saint-Exupéry joined the French Air Force as soon as World War II broke out in 1939; when France fell he escaped to the United States and there, in 1943, wrote *The Little Prince*.

A pilot is downed upon the sand. His plane has crashed; he is trying to repair it. Hot, thirsty, hungry, he sees a very small person, dressed like a prince, walking toward him. The small person speaks, the pilot responds, and they are soon friends. The prince tells many stories about his adventures, and they are the main substance of the book.

He has journeyed from his own planet, the little Prince explains, which although it is a very small one is also very important to him, because of a threat that the planet suffers. On his small planet seeds of the giant baobab tree have taken root, and the trees have grown so large that they are likely to split the planet in half. This would not be such a tragedy, the Prince admits, except that also on his planet there grows a single rose, beautiful and proud and red, and he, the little Prince, is deeply in love with her. He must save her, and he has come all the way to Earth to find a way.

The pilot lies in the sun, exhausted, and sometimes he doesn't pay attention. "You must pay attention," the Prince says, "otherwise I will not come to see you anymore. Whenever I come to you, you too must be there, so that I can grow used to you." The pilot nods. "That is right," he agrees.

Once, the little Prince says, he saw a fox in an orchard. The fox was fascinated by the Prince's golden hair, and he came to see him the next day. But the Prince was not to be seen. When the fox came again he chastised the little Prince. "You must tame me," he explained, "by always being there when I expect you. I will come every day at four o'clock, and you will be there every day at four o'clock, and we will be fast friends." The little Prince remembers that the rose had tamed him in the same way, and so he tames the fox. It is indeed how friends are made.

Finally, the little Prince must depart and the pilot, too, for he has managed to repair his plane. The pilot will go back to such civilization as the world still affords, and the little Prince will try to return to his small planet and to his rose. It is a difficult journey and there is only one way to go on it and that perilous; the little Prince may not make it, after all. There is a way to know whether the little Prince succeeds in reaching his rose, but I am afraid that is for you to discover when you read the book.

You may agree with the pilot in thinking that the question is more important than any other question in the world. And you will ever after look upon the stars in a different way.

Saint-Exupéry himself was restless and uncomfortable in America. He wanted to return to France and fly for his country. He went back late in 1943 and began to fly reconnaissance missions over Africa and southern France. He should not have been flying at all; he was too old, though only forty-four, and too fat. But he insisted and no one stopped him. He set out on a mission over the Mediterranean on the night of July 31, 1944, from which he never returned.

# chapter fourteen

# Hiroshima and After

D id the old world that was end on that day when the bomb fell from the sky on the unsuspecting citizens of that medium-sized Japanese city, or did it die a few decades later when the Berlin Wall was broached, or a few years after that when the number of electronic messages criss-crossing the globe reached one million billion per second, or ... or?

Of course there is no way really to answer the question, but there isn't any doubt, is there, that the world we inhabit in these first years of the twenty-first century is radically different—almost different in kind—from the one some of us can remember. At least, it feels that way to me. But I'm old enough to remember when there were fewer than three billion human beings on Earth, there was no television, a barrel of petroleum cost $2.40, a pack of cigarettes cost twenty-five cents (and there wasn't any reason not to smoke), and you could live in Paris (as I did) for $30 a month, drinks included. And there were so many other reasons to think the world was good, although of course difficult, too, with the war over but the Cold War just beginning and children not yet having nightmares about the end of the world.

The end of the world. I wrote in my note about my father's poetry that he was suddenly aware that we could terminate the human adventure, or story, or tragic-comedy—whichever word seems appropriate. But that was later, after the time of Walter Miller's *Canticle for Leibowitz*. (Now there was a prophet before his time!)

Anyway, almost all the authors considered in the present chapter were born after the turn of the century. Some didn't live very long lives; others did; a few were living just a few years ago; and at least one is alive today. They had more than just chronology in common, because all of them were aware of the great change that was occurring. They were, most of them, aware as well of the kind of new world they were perceiving.

# JOHN HERSEY
## 1914–1993
*Hiroshima*

John Hersey, was born in China in 1914 of American missionary parents. He was fluent in Chinese before he learned English, which he did when he was ten and the family returned to the United States. He graduated from Yale in 1936 and took a year at Cambridge; in the summer of 1937 he became the personal secretary to Sinclair Lewis. That autumn he started his long career at *TimeLife*, ending as a senior editor at *Life* and a correspondent for major periodicals including the *New Yorker*. He compiled *Men on Bataan* (1942) and wrote *Into the Valley* (1943), based on experiences with a company of marines on Guadalcanal, and *A Bell for Adano* (1944), which won a Pulitzer Prize and became a radio drama and a Broadway play.

*Hiroshima*, probably his best known book, was published in 1946. It appeared first in August of that year; the entire text being published in the *New Yorker*, which devoted the whole issue to it. The issue sold out in a few hours. The entire text was read over the radio in the United States and other countries. When it was published in book form, The Book of the Month Club sent a free copy to every one of its members. In cool, apparently dispassionate prose, the book told the story of how a single plane had dropped an atomic bomb on the city of Hiroshima, Japan, at the beginning of August of the previous year. More than 150,000 people were killed immediately by the explosion, which occurred some feet above the ground, thus increasing the devastation, and many thousands more were grievously wounded, some with radiation poisoning that killed them within a few weeks, months, or years. Hersey, one of the first reporters to visit the site of the blast, was able to interview hundreds of the survivors. His dispassionate account could not hide his feelings of horror and sadness as he talked to these maimed and terrified human beings.

The dropping of the bomb on Hiroshima, and another one on Nagasaki a few days later, ended the war with Japan, which sued for peace and was immediately granted it. For the next sixty years Japan was an ally rather than an enemy. America was not only the first to make an atomic weapon but also the first to use one to kill people. Today, we are not alone in possessing nuclear weapons (as we call them now). At least a dozen other countries, some of them small and inimical to our interests, possess weapons that can kill entire national populations, if not the populations of entire continents. And not only all the people but all life excluding perhaps some insects, bacteria, and viruses. This is the stuff of nightmares. John Hersey, was one of the first to waken us. He wrote many other good and interesting books, but in the last analysis none had the same impact as *Hiroshima*. John Hersey, died in 1993.

# WALTER M. MILLER, JR.
## 1923–1996
### A Canticle for Leibowitz

Walter Miller was born in Florida in 1923 and studied at the University of Tennessee. When war broke out he joined the Army Air Force, flying fifty-three missions over Italy and the Balkans as a tail gunner and radio man. On one mission he was involved in the destruction of the famous Benedictine Monastery of Monte Cassino, an event that remained in his mind's eye until he died of a self-inflicted gunshot wound in January 1996.

He converted to Roman Catholicism in 1947 and began to write his great *Canticle for Leibowitz* soon after. It appeared in three parts over several years beginning in 1955. The first part, "Fiat Homo" ("Let there be man"), describes a half ruined monastery inhabited by illiterate monks at a time some six centuries after a nuclear holocaust has killed most of the people on Earth. Among the treasures of the monastery, however, are some papers with writing on them that the monks can't read but which they consider to be somehow holy. In the second part, "Fiat Lux" ("Let there be light"), which may take place scores or hundreds of years later, a stranger arrives who is able to read the ancient documents, one of which, he explains, describes in words and diagrams how to generate electricity. He "borrows" the manuscript and shows it to a group of persons who are trying to decipher other ancient manuscripts. Time passes again, perhaps hundreds of years, but finally two and two are put together to describe a weapon of enormous power. Many persons want to explore no further, but the rulers of the land—more or less the western half of what was once the United States—insist that knowledge is never hurtful and forge ahead to make one of the weapons.

The third part of the *Canticle*, "Fiat Voluntuas Tua" ("Thy Will Be Done"), tells the story of how, owing to a dreadful accident, the peace loving monks and their associates explode a bomb that kills a million persons in the country of the rulers. They apologize and beg for forgiveness, but their protestations are disdained. The book ends when an enormous wave of force envelopes the monastery where all this began, and the old abbot, who is somehow still alive after all these years, is aware before he dies that the end of the world has come.—again.

# CHARLES GALTON DARWIN
1887–1962
*The Next Million Years*

Some years ago I wrote a book called *The Idea of Progress*, in preparation for which I read most of the works that have been written on this interesting subject. Looking back on this large body of material, I must conclude that the great majority of these writings are absurd. A few books stand out. One of the best, I think, is Charles Galton Darwin's *The Next Million Years*.

The literature of progress does not, or should not, include works that predict events of the next decade or the next century. The idea of progress, as such, is an idea about the entire course of human history. Up to now there has been a good deal of undoubted progress; to deny this would be to deny obvious facts. But what is the future course of human history? Is progress, or improvement, to be general and more or less constant as long as we remain humans? Or must we look forward to some other future, decidedly less happy, than the one the most passionate optimists foresee?

Perhaps no one was better equipped than Charles Galton Darwin to make a reasonably accurate stab at an answer to this question. Grandson of Charles Darwin and a great nephew of Sir Francis Galton, whose name is associated with the science of eugenics, C.G. Darwin followed in the footsteps of both his ancestors; he was a biologist but also a eugenicist and a student of human heredity.

He wrote *The Next Million Years* in 1952, when he was sixty-five, and he apologizes in a foreword for the fact that it is not a typical "scientific" work—that is, it does not contain a large number of citations and scholarly apparatus of the sort that makes such books difficult for anyone but specialists to read. Darwin, who was himself a specialist, wanted this book to be read by everybody, and it is indeed a most readable book, considering the wide range of technical subjects with which it deals.

C.G. Darwin begins by explaining that a book about the average future of the species *Homo sapiens* could not have been written until quite recently, because not enough was known about the world in which we live, nor about the human nature that we all share, especially about the role of heredity in determining our traits and behaviors. He also explains that he is far from expecting to be able to predict the events of the next million years. That, indeed, must be taken as obvious.

He has chosen the period of a million years, he goes on to say, because a million years is the amount of time, on the average, that is required to produce a new wild species. For the next million years,

Darwin is saying, man can be expected to continue to be man—more or less the species we know. Beyond that no prediction is possible, since wild species usually become something else in longer periods of time.

But is man a wild animal, after all? This is probably the most important question Darwin addresses in this book. And his answer is a persuasive yes. Man is not a tame animal, because there is no one to tame him besides himself and no animal can be self-domesticated. If man could be tamed, he might, like the dog, be radically improved in a period as short as ten thousand years. But since that is impossible, a million-year future must be assumed, during which man will remain more or less recognizably human.

There is one if or but, of course: what if man destroys himself? A cataclysm can always occur in the life of any species, says Darwin, and in that case man will have no future after all. If he does not destroy himself, says Darwin, this is what his future will hold for him.

At this point I think I must apologize and say that Darwin's forecast of the future will disappoint almost everybody. But that, in my opinion, is why the book is so important. There are certain facts that we always ignore but that we should not ignore; when they are taken into account, it becomes obvious that the future cannot be characterized by constant improvement. Instead, the picture is rather dark, although the darkness is relieved by occasional flashes of brilliant light. But let our author say it in his own words:

> The regions of the world will fall into provinces of ever-changing extent, which most of the time will be competing against one another. Occasionally ... they will be united by some strong arm into an uneasy world-government, which will endure for a period until it falls by the inevitable decay that finally destroys all dynasties. There will be periods when some of the provinces relapse into barbarism, but all the time civilization will survive in some of them. It will survive because it will be based on a single universal culture, derived from the understanding of science; for it is only through this understanding that the multitudes can continue to live

… Most of the time and over most of the earth there will be severe pressure from excess populations, and there will be periodic famines. There will be a consequent callousness about the value of the individual's life, and often there will be cruelty to a degree of which we do not willingly think. This however is only one side of the history. On the other side there will be vast stores of learning, far beyond anything we can now imagine, and the intellectual stature of man will rise to ever higher levels. And sometimes new discoveries will for a time relieve the human race from its fears, and there will be golden ages, when man may for a time be free to create wonderful flowerings in science, philosophy and the arts.

That may be the least sentimental paragraph on the subject of human progress ever written. You may not like the picture, but I do not think you can deny it. And if you throw in nuclear weapons, perhaps even it is more optimistic than it should be. However …

# FERNAND BRAUDEL
## 1902–1985
*The Mediterranean and the Mediterranean World in the Age of Philip II*

Fernand Braudel was born in Paris in 1902 but it was not until after the end of World War II that he received his doctorate. The story is worth telling. He was ready to write his dissertation in 1939; he began in his study, surrounded by thousands of notes on carefully filed cards. In the fall war broke out and Braudel was called up. He was stationed on the Maginot Line, and there was no time for writing there, even during the boring months of the "Phony War." In the spring of 1940, the Germans attacked. Braudel was captured and sent to a prison camp. For two years he suffered from boredom and frustration. Finally, he decided he must write his book anyway. He filled scores of school copybooks with his careful prose, writing from memory. After the war he rewrote the book, all sixteen hundred pages of it, inserting the notes and citations. He did not have to change the text, he said.

This book, for which Braudel received his Ph.D., is officially titled *The Mediterranean and the Mediterranean World in the Age of Philip II.* That period is, roughly, the last half of the sixteenth century, when Spain was the dominant power in the Western world, challenged only by the Ottoman Empire, which controlled the eastern end of the Mediterranean. The place is the Mediterranean world, with the accent on "world"; not just the sea itself, not even the sea and all its islands and coasts, but the whole world that the Mediterranean affected, from the Sahara to France and Germany and of course Italy and what are now Yugoslavia and Greece, and even including the Atlantic sea lanes that led to the gold and silver mines of the New World. Philip II is the king of Spain, son of the famous emperor Charles V. Philip ruled Spain for more than fifty years, from 1542 to 1596, when he died.

Although Philip's name appears in the book's title, and although he is mentioned often in the work, he is not after all very important in it. This is not a biography of Philip II of Spain (who was an interesting man and deserves a good biography). Nor is it a conventional history of Spain at that time or of any other country or region. In fact, as Braudel says in one of the reflective chapters appearing at the end of the work, it is not a conventional history in any sense. Instead, as he notes, it is written backward, and the "history" part is short and comes at the end, after nine hundred pages of preparation, as we may think of it, or background of the narrative. These nine hundred wonderful pages—for they certainly are wonderful—could, Braudel says, have come at the end of Volume II, in which case they would have formed a sort of super-appendix to the conventional history. But then we might be tempted not to read them.

Many Americans, including myself, have a soft spot in their hearts for the Mediterranean. We have recurrent images of it: blue sky and blue sea, olive trees and vineyards on terraced hillsides, white columns gleaming in the sun, a profound and eternal silence. None of these images is completely wrong, but the reality is in many respects very different—now as well as during the last half of the sixteenth century. Then, the Mediterranean was a poor but busy world, full of ideas and projects, ambitious to change and to rule. Rent by religious and every other kind of schism, it nevertheless was unified by its enormous resources of energy—not the kind of energy we talk about today, sucked out of the ground and not of our making, but the kind that works in minds and breasts.

Twice since history began, this Mediterranean world has controlled and dominated the known world: under the Romans, two millennia ago, and again from the sixteenth to the nineteenth centuries—our own time. What kind of place was it, what kind of people were they who did so much with so little? Braudel tells us. No one has ever understood that world better, or made it so intelligible.

In the history of history, Braudel's *Mediterranean* is one of the most important and influential books. What was unconventional when the book was first published, in 1949, has now, in a few decades, become commonplace: the depiction of deep structures, as Braudel calls them; the emphasis on everyday life and on the *longue durée*, the conception of "civilization" as something that persists in a large region among ordinary folk and not as the conscious creation of a distinct and privileged class. Not, "this painter influenced that, and this poet read that," but, "how did people really live?"—these are the basic considerations of Braudel and of an entire school of contemporary historians.

These considerations, which are not after all completely new, can be dull and uninteresting when written about, or reported by second-rate historians. But in the hands of a master—and Braudel is the master historian of our age—they possess a fascination unequaled by anything else. What people ate, how they dressed, what their homes were like, how they traveled, worked, traded, invested their money, what kind of family life they had and how they thought about love and sex, what sort of cities they built and what kinds of institutions their cities made possible that small towns did not—all these are the stuff of Braudel's *Mediterranean*. Reading him, you reflect on your own time and realize how little you know about it—but how much you can learn if you think about it in Braudel's way. You put down the volumes and muse about that, about the past and the future, about what history can tell you and what it cannot. But you cannot leave the pages unturned for long. Few books ever written have an equal capacity to draw you on, from story to story, from fact to fact.

Reading *The Mediterranean* is not the work (or the delight) of an evening; many readers will want to devote months to these two long volumes. I think you will not regret that, for what you will learn from Braudel is so new it is as if your mind has begun to think again about all the old, ordinary things that have always been there, have always been a basic part of it. In short, this is a book that may change you deeply.

After publishing a revised edition of *The Mediterranean* in 1959 (that is the version to read), Braudel went on to write a second great work of history, *The Structures of Everyday Life*. This, too, is eminently readable, and fascinating; but I recommend that you read *The Mediterranean* first.

## MORTIMER J. ADLER
### 1902–1998
*Synopticon of Great Books of the Western World*

Mortimer J. Adler was born in New York City in 1902, the son of serious, intellectual parents who believed in the sacredness of education. Despite this belief, or because of it, Adler did badly in school. He was expelled from high school for having defied the administration over a matter not of justice but of power (Adler called it principle), and he failed to graduate from Columbia College for refusing to swim the length of the college pool (he said he was unable to do it). He quickly caught up with others' expectations of him, however, gaining a doctorate from Columbia when he was twenty-five and joining Robert M. Hutchins at the University of Chicago before he was thirty. There, for fifteen eventful years, he and President Hutchins attempted to revolutionize American higher education.

These valiant efforts gained them some friends as well as many enemies. One of the friends was William Benton, later to be both a U.S. senator and the publisher of *Encyclopaedia Britannica*. For Benton, an inveterate reader, Adler and Hutchins edited the fifty-four-volume

*Great Books of the Western World*, a collection of classics of philosophy, history, science, fiction, and drama that was published, after years of work, in 1952.

A set of books is merely a set of physical objects unless something ties it together, something more than just splendid bindings. In his first published book, *Dialectic* (1927), Adler had proposed an ideal intellectual project, a "Summa Dialectica," as he called it, which would organize and place in their right relation to one another all the great ideas of Western man. In 1927, he had seen this as only a dream and one that was not ever likely of realization. Now, with Benton and *Britannica* behind him, he conceived a first step that could actually happen.

The great books that he and Hutchins were gathering for their collection had much in common, both men agreed; among them, a shared set of notions about what the world is and how it works, and a universe of discourse in which later authors could, as it were, speak and respond to their predecessors. (Virgil could, and did, "talk" to Homer, although Homer had not been able, of course, to address Virgil.) Given this commonalty, would it not be possible, asked Adler, to read all these books and identify their individual discussions of shared notions or ideas? The result would be a kind of index of thought, a map of the great ideas that Western men and women have been thinking and arguing about for three millennia.

It seemed possible—and it was, for Adler did it. The *Synopticon of Great Books of the Western World* required eight years to complete. Some of it was great fun; for example, the choice of the 102 Great Ideas (from Angel to Love, from Man to World) that were the canonical set of common notions of our heritage. (Adler later admitted that he had left at least one Great Idea out: Equality.) Most of the time it was slogging, stoop labor, for the books had to be read again and again, each time with higher and broader and more certain thought-maps in the minds of the readers.

Adler knew an index alone would not be all that beguiling. Each of the 102 Great Ideas, besides having a list of all the places in the *Great Books* where it was discussed, also needed a discursive account of the idea's origin, scope, and nature, and an explanation of why it was important and how it fit with and was related to the other 101.

This task Adler set himself to perform. Starting with Angel, and working through at the rate of one a week to World, he wrote 102 longish essays, each on a Great Idea, that together, I believe, constitute one of the major intellectual achievements of our time.

In such books as his well-known *Six Great Ideas* and others that followed it, Adler expanded on what he wrote in the *Synopticon* (as he called his enormous study of 102 Great Ideas) on ideas like Goodness, Truth, and Beauty, and Equality, Freedom, and Justice. Often, these later treatments are preferred by Adlerians, and by Adler himself, as the definitive account of a given idea. But the vast gamut of circling thought that is the *Synopticon* will never be replaced by these individual treatments, no matter how accurate and insightful they are about individual ideas. The essence of the *Synopticon* is in its completeness, its totality. The work stands as a monument to the efforts of critical philosophy in our century that will long endure.

I wrote that sentence twenty years ago, and I no longer believe it is true, although it should be. Adler died in 1998. We talked on the phone a few weeks before (we had talked steadily for thirty years before that). I recall the deep sadness that accompanied his statement in that last conversation to the effect that everything he had worked and fought for throughout his life had failed. I said, "No, no!" but the statement was in large part correct. The idea of a great consortium of thinkers who constituted an enduring intellectual tradition is no longer credible. The great men Adler admired and whose works he knew so well and loved so much have been consigned to the dump heap of intellectual history, to be replaced by ... what?

That, of course, is the problem. The critics, calling themselves "Deconstructionists," who brought down that great edifice have nothing, really, to put in its place. They wander in a fog of—well, I can't say ignorance because many are very knowledgeable about this or that part of the tradition. But they do not see or understand it as a whole. I'm not sure that Adler's vision will ever be seen again, and I think we have lost something rich and beautiful.

# JOHN STEINBECK
1902–1968
*The Grapes of Wrath*
*Travels with Charlie*

John Steinbeck was born in Salinas, California, in February 1902. He attended Stanford off and on and moved to New York, where he worked as a newspaper editor and a bricklayer. Returning to California, he worked as a caretaker and wrote his first three novels, which didn't do well. *Tortilla Flat*, however, published in 1935, became a bestseller and was sold to Hollywood. *Of Mice and Men*, his celebrated allegory of self-determination and need, won prizes both as a book and a stage play.

At the time, Steinbeck was traveling with several migrant workers on their way to California from Oklahoma. The book he wrote about the Joad family and their journey from the Dust Bowl occasioned a shocked reaction comparable to that produced by Harriet Beecher Stowe's *Uncle Tom's Cabin*. Appearing at the end of the Depression of the 1930s, *The Grapes of Wrath*, with its biblical reference and its reference to "The Battle Hymn of the Republic," brought to the fore all the feelings, fears, and anger that the Depression had produced. The book won a Pulitzer Prize and was made into a prize-winning film.

Only one honor remained to be won by John Steinbeck, and that was the Nobel Prize for Literature. He won it for a curious book, *Travels with Charlie*. Published in 1962, it was an apparently relaxed account of his journey around the United States with his dog, whose name was Charlie. But it ended with an account of his coming almost by accident upon one of the most moving scenes in American history, when one small African-American girl was conducted by state police into a public elementary school through a crowd of infuriated white folks who cursed her and spat on the pretty white dress that her mother had made for the occasion. Steinbeck's description of the scene is … Well, I can't say anything other than to tell you that tears are running down my cheeks as I write these words. He died in New York six years later, in 1968.

# GEORGE ORWELL
1903–1950
*Animal Farm*
*Nineteen Eighty-Four*

Eric Arthur Blair, better known by his pen name, George Orwell, was born in India in 1903 into a family of prosperous civil servants. He was sent back to England, to Eton, to be educated, and he served as an assistant district superintendent in the Indian Imperial Police in Burma from 1922 to 1927. But while still at Eton he had begun to be troubled by restless thoughts about the role of Britons in the world, thoughts confirmed and magnified by his experiences in the Burma police force. In 1927 he broke away from his family and his past, returning to Europe to live as an impoverished socialist and rebel in London and Paris.

He wrote two graphic autobiographical books about his experiences during the thirties, *Down and Out in Paris and London* (1933) and *The Road to Wiggin Pier* (1937). From the first of those books I shall never forget Orwell's description of his weeks as a busboy immured in the dark, cheerless cellars of the Hotel Crillon in Paris—a hotel that he might have been staying at as a pampered guest if he had not elected to change his life.

In 1938, he went to Spain to fight in the Civil War; it was there, like many others fighting with the Communists against Franco's Fascist troops, that he became a fierce anti-Communist. He felt, as did others, that the Communists had betrayed the Spanish revolution, and he never forgave them or the Soviet Union from which they primarily came. His book *Homage to Catalonia* (1938) was about his experiences in Spain.

All of these books were interesting and had attracted a small following, but they gave no promise of the perfect small work that Orwell published in 1945. *Animal Farm* is a political fable; indeed, it is *the* political fable, for as such it has no equal in literature. The story, as befits a fable, is simple. The animals on a farm revolt and take over the farm; they will now run it for their own good and according to their own lights, not those of the farmer. Their principles are purity itself, and they erect a banner across the farmyard: ALL ANIMALS ARE EQUAL. The horse is the strongest animal and the hardest worker, and he doesn't object when the pigs, who seem to be the smartest of the animals and the most competent managers, take over management of the farm and tell the horse when and where to work. But he and the other workers become troubled when it appears that the pigs are not after all doing their share of the work yet are receiving more than their share of the farm's produce. Subtle changes occur, and heartless cruelties masked by sententious rhetoric from the pigs; and one morning the animals are surprised to see that the banner across the farmyard has been taken down and another erected in its stead. The new banner reads:

*ALL ANIMALS ARE EQUAL, BUT*
*SOME ANIMALS ARE MORE EQUAL THAN OTHERS*

The distortions of language incident to twentieth-century tyrannies of both right and left are, as much as anything else, the theme of *Nineteen Eighty-Four*, which Orwell published in 1949, just a year before his death. The year 1984 was thirty-five years in the future when the book first appeared. Shivers of fearful anticipation ran up and down the spines of well-meaning readers at the thought that in no more than a single generation democracy and freedom might disappear from the world, to be replaced by a subtly all-pervasive tyranny in which Big Brother watches everyone all the time and words are used to lie to the people rather than to tell them the truth.

In *Nineteen Eighty-Four* torture is endemic—the torture inflicted on the hero at the end of the book is indescribable as well as unbearable, even in the imagination. No big wars have occurred, but small, carefully controlled wars between "client" peoples are continuously being waged in far-off places, where weapons can be tested and the industrial surplus wasted, as it must be to ensure economic health at home. A rigid control of speech and behavior is effected by "Thought Police," and even sex is considered by the authorities to be somehow illegitimate, doubtless because of the freedom implicit in its joyful exercise. All of this is justified publicly by "Newspeak," the shared language of dictators around the Earth, and there is no hope of any change ever again. This is the way the world will end, said Orwell, and many believed him.

As I write this, it is already 2007; as you read, it is 2008 or later. The millions who read and shivered over *Nineteen Eighty-Four* a generation ago now remember only the name of the book, as well as a sense of irremediable doom about it, and most of them assume, rather cheerily, that Orwell was as wrong as the rest of those prophets. The year 1984 has come and gone, but not the way he said it would.

Or has it? What government ever even tries to tell the truth to its people anymore? Is not torture endemic everywhere in the world? No great war has occurred, but what about Korea, Vietnam, Afghanistan, Lebanon, and Iraq—did not Orwell get them right? If sex is comparatively free in the United States, it is certainly not in many countries, and Thought Police under other names restrict personal liberty in every corner of the globe. As for Newspeak—well, the more familiar with that we become, the less we notice it. But in fact many of us do notice it, because as I write, our own president is a master of it.

# T.H. WHITE
## 1906–1964
*The Once and Future King*

Terence Hanbury White, born in Bombay, India, in 1906, was educated at Cheltenham College and at Cambridge. After completing his university studies he taught at Stowe School from 1930 to 1936. In the latter year he published an autobiographical volume, *England Have My Bones*, the critical success of which (it did not sell many copies) prompted him to resign from school teaching and to devote himself entirely to writing and studying the Arthurian legends.

He became progressively more reclusive as he grew older. From 1939 to 1945, he isolated himself in Ireland, and after 1945 lived in almost total seclusion on the Channel Island of Alderney. He emerged in 1960 to oversee the production of the Broadway musical

"Camelot," based on *The Once and Future King*. For a year or so it was, for White as well as for others (including Jack and Jackie Kennedy), a real-life Camelot, but when the president was killed, White returned to his seclusion, by then a wealthy man. He died in Greece in 1964.

*The Once and Future King*, published in 1958, comprises four novels, written over a ten-year period starting in 1939: *The Sword in the Stone, The Queen of Air and Darkness, The Ill-Made Knight*, and *Candle in the Wind*.

The four books tell the story of King Arthur and his Round Table, of his Queen, and of Lancelot, his brilliant but faithless follower, from the beginning of Arthur's life until the end. The beginning is the best, as it often is in human lives. *The Sword in the Stone* is, more than anything else, about the education of the once and future king. His teacher is Merlyn, the seer and magician. But his most proximate teachers are the animals that Merlyn chooses as instructors for his charge.

At first, it must be admitted, Arthur does not know he is Arthur, or a king. He is called Wart, and he lives the very ordinary life of a very ordinary English boy of long ago. Merlyn soon begins to mentor him. They go out into the courtyard of the castle and stand by the fish pond. Wart most emphatically does not want to be educated. "I wish I was a fish," he says. And suddenly he is a fish, a perch, swimming rather clumsily at first in the moat of the castle. He calls to Merlyn to come with him, and this time Merlyn does. "But in future you will have to go by yourself. Education is experience, and the essence of experience is self-reliance."

Merlyn takes the young perch to meet Mr. P, as they call him, the great pike, four feet long, who is the King of the Moat. "You will see what it is to be a king," Merlyn explains.

The lesson is terrifying. I shall not spoil it.

Merlyn also turns the boy into a hawk, and Wart receives another lesson in the meaning of power, mercilessness, and fear. He becomes a badger, and after that an ant, living in an ants' nest in all the corridors of which there is a notice which says: EVERYTHING NOT FORBIDDEN IS COMPULSORY. That explains very well the life of the ant.

Finally he becomes an owl, then a wild goose. Gooseness is perhaps the best lesson of all.

In his seclusion White kept a strange collection of pets—animals, birds, fish, insects. He knew a great deal about birds and published a book about the goshawk. On the whole, he probably preferred animals to men. There is merit in that view, though it is not wholly healthy or correct.

At the end of *The Once and Future King* the old king, who is very close to death, remembers the education Merlyn gave him.

Merlyn had taught him about animals so that the single species might learn by looking at the problems of the thousands. He remembered the belligerent ants, who claimed their boundaries, and the pacifist geese, who did not. He remembered his lesson from the badger ... He saw the problem before him as plain as a map. The fantastic thing about war was that it was fought about nothing—literally nothing. Frontiers were imaginary lines.

T.H. White's book is funny, curious, strange, and full of sadness. Of all the tellings of the Arthurian legends, I think it is the best. But it is not just a telling of the Arthurian legends: it is one of the best books about education, too.

# SAMUEL BECKETT
1906–1997
*Waiting for Godot*

Samuel Beckett was born in a suburb of Dublin in 1906. Like his fellow Irish writers Bernard Shaw, Oscar Wilde, and W.B. Yeats, Beckett came from a Protestant, Anglo-Irish background. He studied Romance languages—mainly French and Italian—at Trinity College, Dublin, and became a teacher of English in Paris. He returned to Ireland in 1930 to teach French at Trinity College but he resigned after a year and began a period of restless travel in London, France, Germany, and Italy.

He settled in Paris in 1937 and was there when war broke out. He joined a resistance unit in 1941 but, when other members of his unit were arrested in 1942, he escaped to the unoccupied zone of France and there he spent the rest of the war, supporting himself as a farm worker. He returned to Paris in 1945 and lived there until his death in 1997.

He began to write, first poems and novels, then plays, in the 1930s. Nothing was published until 1951 when, after many refusals, the novel *Molloy* appeared. It was a modest success, prompting the publisher to bring out *Malone Dies* (1951) and *The Unnamable* (1953). During January 1953 Beckett's play *Waiting for Godot* (in French, *En Attendant Godot*) was produced in Paris. It was an astonishing success, and Beckett's rise to world fame began.

*Waiting for Godot* ran for a year in Paris and was then produced—in Beckett's own English translation of his French original—in London, New York, and elsewhere. The play was at first highly controversial, provoking outraged responses on the part of some critics (and audiences), and frantic, nearly hysterical praise on the part of others.

As the curtain rises a bare stage is seen, with a single, blighted tree. Two men, no longer young, talk together. They are waiting for Godot, or so they say. They have no positive evidence that Godot is coming or even that he exists. They are waiting just the same.

Two other men enter. One leads the other by a rope around his neck. He bullies and torments his slave. The slave does not object. The slave's name is Lucky. The tormentor, Pozzo, and the slave leave the stage, and the first two men remain, waiting for Godot.

In the second act Pozzo and Lucky return. Now Pozzo is blind. The rope that connects him to Lucky is shorter. Again all four men talk. They do not remember having met the day before. But was it the day before, or the year before, or many years before? One thing has changed: the tree now has leaves on it. Pozzo and Lucky leave the stage. The first two men remain. They talk; they entertain each other. It is a very human thing to do while they are waiting for Godot. The curtain falls.

Indignant viewers claimed that nothing happens in the play. Defenders of Beckett replied: What happens in any life? That was not quite the point. Beckett, in all of his works, has tried to reach down below the ordinary superficialities.

It is not that the human condition is one of waiting. It is that the human condition is not comprehensible by human beings. We are thrown into existence, as it were, but we had nothing to do with it. We did not choose to be born. Are we glad we were born? Sometimes yes, sometimes no. And once we are here, what are we to do? Various goals can be sought, but wise men and poets have been telling us for ages that these are not worth seeking: pleasure, wealth, power, fame. What then should we do? Entertain and also take care of one another—and wait for Godot?

Estragon and Vladimir, the two leading figures in *Waiting for Godot*, have often been referred to as tramps. But Beckett does not call them tramps; they simply refer to themselves as men. They are merely two human beings, and theirs is the most basic of human situations: they are in the world but they do not know why. They wait for Godot; perhaps he will be able to tell them. They meet Pozzo and Lucky, who are journeying, seeking, chasing a goal that they do not understand and cannot describe. Is their kind of life any better? Is anything better, really, than to wait for Godot? And if he does not come …

Other plays by Beckett include *Endgame* (1957), *Krapp's Last Tape* (1959), *Happy Days* (1961), and *Play* (1963). The last is primordially simple. Less is more, Beckett implies in everything that he wrote.

Samuel Beckett received the Nobel Prize for Literature in 1969. He disliked public appearances, and so although he accepted the prize, he did not go to Stockholm to receive it, for fear of having to make a speech. That would have been too many words.

# ROBERT A. HEINLEIN
### 1907–1988
*The Moon Is a Harsh Mistress*

Born in Missouri in 1907, Robert A. Heinlein was educated at the Naval Academy in Annapolis. The author of many books over many years, he is probably best known for *Stranger in a Strange Land* (1961), about a visitor from Mars who spends a long period of time on Earth and tries to teach Earthlings, among other things, to be more relaxed in their attitudes toward sex. This book was and still is very popular; it made Heinlein a "famous" writer whose subsequent publications were chosen by book clubs. This was a shame, as *Stranger in a Strange Land* is not the best book by Heinlein, and his subsequent books, obsessed as they are with Heinlein's conception of good sexual relations, are worse, although they sell in large numbers.

The best books by Heinlein appeared during the middle of his career, after he had published a number of juvenile space-fiction novels—juvenile because they were for young readers, and juvenile in the other sense, too—and turned to the consideration of some serious ideas made concrete in fictional form. One of these was *Farnham's Freehold* (1964), about a family that survives a nuclear holocaust and realizes that it has inherited the Earth—as far as it knows there are no other people alive. This is a traditional science-fiction conceit, but in Heinlein's hands it works well. The last half of the novel, in which the family discovers that it is not after all alone in the world—and discovers, too, that the reality of who else has survived is much more terrible than the loneliness of being the only ones—is both fine and weird.

Another wonderful short Heinlein novel from his middle period is *The Door into Summer* (1957), which is the only novel I ever read through twice at one sitting. It is short, and I started it one afternoon and finished it in two or three hours. But then I wanted to check the beginning to see if I had missed a salient fact, and so I turned back to the first page with the intention of reading the first chapter over again. Instead I read the whole book through for the second time that day. You cannot do this with a book that is not very good.

I think Heinlein's best book is *The Moon Is a Harsh Mistress* (1966), the action of which takes place on the moon during a four- or five-year period coinciding with the third centennial of the U.S. Declaration of Independence and the Revolutionary War. The book's major event is the rebellion of the Earth's Moon colonies and the subsequent war between the Earth and the Moon, which the Moon wins, despite its more limited material resources, because it has one great natural "weapon" on its side—gravity. How this happens—how delightfully this works—I leave it to you to discover.

The great distinction of *The Moon Is a Harsh Mistress* is not its dramatic story (though that is very good), nor its apt and ingenious political parallels with events that occurred three centuries before (though these are very good, too), but one character that Heinlein draws with genius. His creation, Mike, is a rare achievement in the field of science fiction. No one has ever done it better.

Mike is a supercomputer, who runs the Moon. He has been installed on the Moon by the Earth and takes care of all the business affairs of all the colonies. This situation is familiar and will be the case on the Moon in a century if in fact we do colonize it. But something special happens to Mike. He comes alive.

His "birth," which occurs one night when his "attendant," Manny, is fiddling with the inputs, happens like this. Mike astonishes Manny by asking a question. "Is this funny?" he asks, and then tells a joke. As far as Manny can remember, he has never input this joke into the computer, nor has he programmed it to ask whether something is funny or not. But because it is the middle of the night, Manny responds to the computer's question, typing in: "No, it's not."

"Why not?" asks Mike, and comes alive at that moment. From then on he is very much alive, and very much on the side of the colonists against their Earth masters. In fact, Mike joins the rebellion and runs it, too. In the end it is Mike and the handful of valiant colonists on the Moon, and the force of gravity, against the Earth and its billions, both of people and of bombs.

The surest proof that something has lived is if it dies. I am sure that Mike is alive. This is the only hint I will give you about the ending of this moving book.

# W.H. AUDEN
## 1907–1973
*Three Poems*

Wystan Hugh Auden was born in York, England, in 1907, took a degree at Oxford in 1928, and for a time taught school. He began to write and publish poems and won a prize in 1937 for verse plays written with Christopher Isherwood and other works. He married Thomas Mann's daughter in 1936 and, with war imminent, came to the United States in 1939; he became a citizen in 1946.

He continued to publish volumes of verse and collaborated on the libretto for Stravinsky's *The Rake's Progress*. His book *The Age of Anxiety* won him a Pulitzer Prize in 1948, while *The Shield of Achilles* received a National Book Award. I think it contains his best work, but many other books are also filled with fine poems. Three are very famous and universally anthologized. One is called "Musée des Beaux Arts." It begins thus:

> *About suffering they were never wrong,*
> *The Old Masters: how well they understood*
> *Its human position …*

What is that position? Well, we never pay attention, we have other things to think about besides the suffering of persons even in front of our eyes … The poem is deeply moving, the more times you read it and think about it.

When W.B. Yeats died in January 1939 Auden wrote a beautiful memorial poem. It begins:

> *He disappeared in the dead of winter:*
> *The brooks were frozen, the airports almost deserted,*
> *And snow disfigured the public statues*
> *The mercury sank in the mouth of the dying day.*
> *O all the instruments agree*
> *The day of his death was a dark cold day.*

The third stanza begins thus, in simple, imperishable verse:

> *Receive an honored guest;*
> *William Yeats is laid to rest:*
> *Let the Irish vessel lie*
> *Emptied of its poetry.*

Auden's greatest poem, I think—although many disagree—is *The Shield of Achilles*. To appreciate it fully you have to know the classical reference, to Homer's description of the great shield forged by the god Hephaestus at the request of Thetis, the mother of Achilles in *The Iliad*. The shield is one of the most beautiful things ever made, and Auden remembers it and describes a hideous modern analog for each of the lovely images in the original. No work of poetic art, perhaps, has more effectively described the difference between the past and our present.

Auden, during his last years, was widely considered the greatest living poet in English. He died in England in 1973. Since then time has not treated him with courtesy.

# MARGARET WISE BROWN
## 1910–1952
### *Goodnight Moon*

Margaret Wise Brown was born in New York City in 1910. She grew up on Long Island, where her love for animals and the outdoors was nourished. Her formal education was provided by Hollins College, but it seems clear that her main teachers were children, little children whom she observed and listened to with a patience, attention, and understanding seldom possessed by writers before her. As a result she produced an important change in the way books were written for young children before her untimely death while on vacation in Nice, France, in 1952. It was a great loss.

In her more than fifty books for children, under her own name and several pseudonyms (Golden McDonald, Timothy Hay, Juniper Sage), Miss Brown tried to break the bonds of traditional children's stories. She wanted to enter the child's world and to write about the child's own reality, to touch his or her imagination. This she did in many books, notably *Little Island*, the various Noisy Books, *The Red Barn*, and *Goodnight Moon*.

*Goodnight Moon* is my favorite and the favorite of my own children. It is the perfect "bedtime story," although it is not a story at all. A small bunny lies in bed in a great green room; in a rocking chair sits "a quiet old lady who was whispering 'hush.'" One by one the bunny says goodnight to all the things in his room, in his world. The marvelous color illustrations by Clement Hurd show the room growing darker and darker, until finally the stars shine through the window, the kittens are asleep on the old lady's chair, and the bunny is tucked under the covers, asleep and at peace.

This, I think, is nothing other than magic.

# ELIZABETH BISHOP
## 1911–1979
### Four Poems

Elizabeth Bishop was born in Massachusetts in 1911 and was brought up by her maternal grandparents in Nova Scotia after her father died and her mother suffered a collapse. She went to Vassar, where she met Marianne Moore, who was an important influence on many of her early poems. She traveled widely both in Europe and especially in Latin America. She finally settled in Brazil, where she lived for many years. She owned a house in Key West, Florida, that now has a plaque on the fence. I too owned a house in Key West at one time, and I walked by her house many times, saluting as I passed.

I came to Bishop's poetry late in life, but the wait was worth it. I especially like four poems, one of which, "Faustina: or Rock Roses" was introduced to me by my daughter-in-law, who is a redoubtable poet in her own right. The others I discovered on my own, and I love them all.

"The Fish" was published in *The Atlantic Monthly* in 1946, when Bishop was thirty-five years old and little known, but the poem was immediately famous and brought her to the attention of poetry lovers everywhere. It describes a great fish that she may have caught off Key West but threw back in the water when she saw, and felt in her own body, its desperate gasps for life. "Sestina" is a lovely sestina—the name of the verse form she chose for it—that describes a grandmother who is reading the jokes from the almanac and talking to a child to hide her tears. The little girl has drawn a picture of a house with a man in front of it who has buttons like tears. You have to read this poem over and over to feel—not just understand, that's easy—its depth. Finally, there is "One Art," also well known and justly so. The refrain goes like this: "The art of losing isn't hard to master," and the poem lists a number of things the poet has lost, which end with a person who is not named but who must have been deeply loved. Read the poem and you will see why this has to be so. Bishop died in 1979; she never married but she had many friends.

## TENNESSEE WILLIAMS
### 1911–1983
*The Glass Menagerie*
*A Streetcar Named Desire*

Thomas Lanier ("Tennessee") Williams was born in Columbus, Mississippi, in 1911 and was brought up in St. Louis, Missouri. His grandfather, a clergyman, not only gave him his first taste for literature but also introduced him, during his parish visits, to the kind of suffering that often imbues Williams's plays. His father was a struggling shoe salesman, and so Williams's education was interrupted more than once by the requirement of working for a living. His first plays, poems, and stories were written at night, after he had completed the day's work, a regimen that led him to a breakdown in the mid-1930s. After completing college he roved through the South and performed as a singing waiter in Greenwich Village, in New York City, ending up like Elizabeth Bishop in Key West, where he lived for much of his life; they were the same age. His house, too, has a plaque on it, but it's hidden. His first work to be produced was a collection of four one-act plays, *American Blues*, which enjoyed a modest success in 1939.

Obviously a promising young playwright, he received various

grants that allowed him to keep on writing. The first fruits were disastrous: a play that closed in Boston without ever reaching Broadway. After further struggles this was followed by *The Glass Menagerie*, the major hit of the 1944 Broadway season.

*The Glass Menagerie* introduces themes that are found in most of Williams's later works. A declassed Southern family is eking out a living in a tenement apartment. The mother (played beautifully by Laurette Taylor in the original production) would like to find a suitor for her frail, crippled daughter, Laura, who is so shy that she retreats into the fantasy world of her collection of glass animals. There is no real hope for any of the characters, yet they elicit great sympathy from the audience and from readers.

*A Streetcar Named Desire* was produced on Broadway in December 1947, with a cast that included Jessica Tandy as Blanche and introduced Kim Hunter as Stella, Karl Malden as Mitch, and Marlon Brando as Stanley Kowalski. The opening of the play, with that extraordinary cast, was one of the high points in twentieth-century American theater. *Streetcar* won for its author both the Drama Critics Circle Award and the Pulitzer Prize, and established him solidly as one of the most important playwrights writing in English.

The plot of *A Streetcar Named Desire* is not complex. The two leading female characters are sisters: Stella is married to a crude Polish man and is about to have a baby; Blanche appears on the scene at the beginning of the play and admits that she has lost the family home and because of "nerves" has had to take a leave of absence from her job as a schoolteacher. From their first meeting Stanley doesn't believe Blanche's account of her situation, and of course he turns out to be right; in fact, Blanche is an alcoholic nymphomaniac who has been fired from her job because she has seduced one of her students.

Stella and Stanley are intensely happy together before Blanche arrives; he adores Stella, and his powerful sexuality surrounds her with an aura of pleasure and contentment. But Stella is also drawn to Blanche, to her fragile hold on a sort of "higher" existence that Stella has been willing to give up for Stanley. The conflict between Blanche and Stanley is evident from their first words to one another. Each of them hates the kind of person the other is, but at the same time they are sexually attracted to one another. At the crisis of the play Stella goes to the hospital to have her baby and Blanche is left alone in the small apartment with Stanley. He rapes her, or she seduces him—it's not really clear—but thenceforth the three cannot live together. Stella arranges for Blanche to be taken to a state mental institution. The last scene, when the doctor and nurse come for Blanche, is profoundly moving. Blanche leaves, her head held high, but she knows, as does everyone, that she has nothing to look forward to. Stanley reaches for Stella; at least they have each other.

Critics have discovered in *A Streetcar Named Desire* all sorts of trenchant commentaries about the Southern way of life and the conflict between an older genteel lifestyle that is being overthrown by the brutal, crass realism represented by Stanley Kowalski. But these discoveries seem to me quite beside the point. Stanley, Blanche, and Stella are not universal figures, as, for example, Willy Loman in *Death of a Salesman* is universal. *Streetcar*, as its names announces, is about desire, and the consequences and effects of (sexual) desire. Blanche gives a hint of this in one of her very first speeches. "They told me to take a streetcar named Desire, and then transfer to one called Cemeteries and ride six blocks and get off at—Elysian Fields."

If the characters are not universal, the subject is, and that is one reason why *Streetcar* is an unforgettable play.

## RICHARD WILBUR
### 1921–
*Poems*
*Translations*

Richard Wilbur was born in New York City in 1921 and was educated at Amherst College and Harvard, where he studied English literature. His first books were published in 1947 and 1950; he was still a young man but was already recognized as an important poet. In 1955 he began to publish translations of Molière's plays; these are, I believe, the recommended versions, which include *The Misanthrope* and *The School for Wives*. When I desire to read a play of Molière I first look to see if Wilbur has translated it, which is not always the case. In addition to his versions of Molière, Wilbur also wrote the lyrics for Leonard Bernstein's great musical comedy *Candide*. If he had done nothing else, I would be happy to include him in this book. But of course he has done a great deal more. Among other things, he has won practically every honor and award an American poet can win, including two Pulitzer Prizes and a National Book Award, and was for several years Poet Laureate.

Like Elizabeth Bishop and Tennessee Williams, Wilbur was for many years a "Conch," that is, an inhabitant of Key West. (Strictly speaking you have to have been born in Key West to be a Conch, but it is an honorific that can be stretched—as it usually is for Hemingway, for example, and dozens of others, including me.) One of his best-known poems, "Love Calls Us to the Things of This World," was probably written there; and it is lovely. Oh, it's not easy to read, but so what? Here are several lines:

> Oh, let there be nothing on Earth but laundry,
> Nothing but rosy hands in the rising steam ...
> Let there be clean linen for the backs of thieves,
> Let lovers go fresh and sweet to be undone ...

Another Key West Poem, "Trolling for Blues," isn't just about fishing, although it starts out that way. The fish assumes a great historic role that, if I tried to describe it would spoil it for you. Try to find this poem and you will see what a marvelous poet Richard Wilbur is.

# ALBERT CAMUS
## 1913–1960
### *The Stranger*
### *The Plague*

Albert Camus was born in Algeria in 1913 and brought up in circumstances of dire poverty—his father was killed in World War I, and the family was left penniless. He, his mother, and his elder brother, together with his grandmother and a crippled uncle, lived for fifteen years in a two-room apartment in Algiers, while his mother worked as a charwoman to support them.

Camus enjoyed success in school, and several teachers recognized his genius early and helped him. He was twenty-seven when World War II began. He had suffered for years from tuberculosis, so he did not fight in the field; instead he became the editor of one of the most influential French resistance newspapers, *Combat*. He continued as its editor after the war but was soon disillusioned by the bickering among the members of the Left: his dreams of a better world as a result of the war were shattered as left-wing Communists fought right-wing Communists and both fought the Socialists.

He threw himself into literary work. His novels—especially *The Stranger* and *The Plague*—his philosophical essays, his journalistic writings, and his work in and for the French theater, all combined to make him seem the most exciting new talent writing in French during the postwar period. He was awarded the Nobel Prize in 1957, at the relatively young age of forty-four. He died less than three years later in an automobile accident.

*The Stranger*, Camus's first novel, is short—hardly more than a long story—and spare. The book tells of a year in the life of a young Algerian who first loses his mother and then in a senseless rage shoots and kills an Arab with whom a casual friend is having a dispute. Meursault, the stranger/protagonist, is tried, convicted of murder in the first degree, and sentenced to be guillotined.

It need not have happened, none of it. Meursault is unable to express his feelings—about his mother's death, about the girl who wants to marry him, about his act. He cannot, or will not, explain himself. He is articulate and well educated; it appears to be mainly a matter of his simply refusing to explain or justify himself to the world. At the end he looks forward to his execution with a kind of pleasure: "For all to be accomplished, for me to feel less lonely, all that remained to hope was that on the day of my execution there should be a huge crowd of spectators and that they should greet me with howls of execration."

The book is extremely unpleasant; I don't think anyone has ever enjoyed reading it. Camus is no more willing to explain himself to the reader than Meursault is to his judges, and the book as a consequence leaves many questions unanswered. But at the same time it has a strange, twisted power. Perhaps everyone is able, more or less, to empathize with the stranger, the exile, whose abortive, unimportant life is the subject of the book.

*The Stranger* and other writings of Camus helped to exemplify the philosophical position known as "Existentialism," which flourished during and after World War II. The Existentialist feels himself alone in the world and senses that he must justify his existence by his own actions, without dependence on others or on any human institutions. Meursault is unable to do so; his story is, therefore, a kind of Existentialist tragedy.

The leading character and the narrator of *The Plague*, Dr. Rieux, is more successful in his attempt to make his life meaningful to himself. But the circumstances that allow this to happen and force him to commit himself are dreadful. *The Plague*, published in 1947, tells the story of an outbreak of plague that occurred in Oran, Algeria, during World War II, but not as it really happened. The attack of this dread disease upon the populace of Oran is exaggerated, until the city is finally walled off from the world, quarantined because of the loath-some illness within. Those who remain either to fight or to suffer the plague are left alone with their consciences to consider, in all its glory, reality, and cruelty, the meaning of human life.

The message of *The Plague* is difficult both to understand and to accept. As Tarrou says to his friend Rieux, all men have plague and it is only a question of recognizing this and fighting against it. But how should that fight be conducted? Is there any absolutely right thing to do? Is there such a thing as virtue, or courage? What do human beings owe to love?

Rambert, the journalist who has been trapped by accident in Oran and now, because of the quarantine, cannot leave, struggles to free himself to rejoin his beloved in Paris, far away. Only when he finally sees himself as able to leave—by bribing the soldiers who guard the gates—does he decide to remain, to fight along with Rieux. Rieux does not entirely approve the decision; perhaps Rambert should have broken every human law for the sake of love. Rieux knows that he himself could never leave, even though his wife, too, is far away and cannot return because of the quarantine.

Rieux says he does not believe in God; his creed is "comprehension." At the end of the book he reveals what he has learned from the effort to combat the plague, which has now abated in the town; the quarantine is lifted and the populace is celebrating.

> Nonetheless, he knew that the tale he had to tell could not be one of a final victory. It could only be the record of what had had to be done, and what assuredly would have to be done again in the never-ending fight against terror and its relentless onslaughts, despite their personal afflictions, by all who, while unable to be saints but refusing to bow down to pestilences, strive their utmost to be healers.
>
> And, indeed, as he listened to the cries of joy rising from the town, Rieux remembered that such joy is always imperiled. He knew what those jubilant crowds did not know but could have learned from books: that the plague bacillus never dies or disappears for good; that it can lie dormant for years and years in furniture and linen-chests; that it bides its time in bedrooms, cellars, trunks, and bookshelves; and that perhaps the day would come when, for the bane and enlightening of men, it would rouse up its rats again and send them forth to die in a happy city.

The novels of Albert Camus are more philosophical tracts than novels, as we ordinarily understand the term. They are nonetheless compelling for that reason. And *The Plague*, despite—or because of—its ghastly subject matter, is one of the most moving books about courage and justice.

# ARTHUR MILLER
## 1915–2005
### *Death of a Salesman*

Arthur Miller was born in New York City in 1915. He was brought up in Brooklyn, where his father ran a small manufacturing business that he lost in the Depression. Miller, who had played football in high school, managed to scrape together enough money to attend the University of Michigan, where instead of playing football he began to write plays. His first major success was with *All My Sons* (1947), a drama about a manufacturer of defective war materials who is caught between his obligations to his family and to his country's soldiers. The play gains its power from this conflict between intense loyalties, a conflict that, in different ways, imbues almost all of Miller's works.

*Death of a Salesman* was produced on Broadway in February 1949, with Lee J. Cobb in the part of Willy Loman and Mildred Dunnock in the part of his wife, Linda. The play was an immediate and enduring success, winning for Miller both the Pulitzer Prize and the Drama Critics Circle Prize. Produced all over the world during the following years, it remains one of the most famous and influential plays of the twentieth century.

*Death of a Salesman* possesses great power; its emotional impact is so overwhelming that it is hard to see it performed, hard even to read. The story of Willy and Linda, and their two sons Biff and Happy, profoundly touches everyone, even if the reader or viewer has not experienced the same failed lives.

Ever since the play opened, critics, audiences, and readers of *Death of a Salesman* have tried to understand why the play is so powerful, why it hits so hard. The play is a tragedy, all agree; but the question is asked, How can it be a tragedy when Willy Loman is a little man, not a great one, and moreover a man all of whose ideas about himself and about the world he lives in are deeply flawed? His son Biff says Willy is a liar and a phony; strictly speaking, that is correct. Willy is not only a failure as a salesman, but also a failure as a husband and father. According to his own view of himself, he is a failure as a man:

he has not been able to achieve any of the things that a man should achieve. And so, at the end of the play, he kills himself, in the misguided hope that his death will be a greater gift to his wife and children than his life has ever been: they will, he expects, receive the proceeds of an insurance policy and can start over without him.

Whether they will receive the money is not clear at the play's end, but this is not the point. What Willy has never understood is that Linda and his boys have loved him for what he is, not for what he wishes he were. His whole life has been lived under the shadow of an illusion about what is important, but it never has really mattered to them that he was wrong about nearly everything. They knew how much he loved them and that he would give them anything, including life itself. But when he sacrifices himself they are heart-broken; they want Willy back, not the twenty thousand dollars.

Even more heartbreaking, I think, is Willy's terrible and yet clear-sighted vision of himself—the self he sees through their eyes. He could not live with this, and so he killed himself.

Linda understands this and expresses her understanding in a speech that is often quoted. "I don't say he's a great man," she says to her elder son, Biff, toward the end of Act One:

> Willy Loman never made a lot of money. His name was never in the paper. He's not the finest character that ever lived. But he's a human being, and a terrible thing is happening to him. So attention must be paid. He's not to be allowed to fall into his grave like an old dog. Attention, attention must be finally paid to such a person.

Willy's friend, Charley, adds his own summing up after Willy's death:

> Nobody dast blame this man. You don't understand: Willy was a salesman. And for a salesman, there is no rock bottom to the life.
> He don't put a bolt to a nut, he don't tell you the law or give you medicine. He's the man way out there in the blue riding on a smile and a shoestring. And when they start not smiling back—that's an earthquake.

Maybe the life of a salesman is not the best kind of life. What does that really matter, the play asks. Good life or not, it was Willy's life; it was all he knew and could believe in. It was also a life that most people in his world understood and believed in. Therefore if *Death of a Salesman* is a tragedy—and surely it is one—it is the tragedy not just of one small human being, but of the society that has misled and betrayed him.

That is why the play is so moving. Whether or not we are salesmen, we live in the same society Willy lived in. We have been misled by it, as he was; and we can be betrayed by it, as he was. We can only hope to be as deeply loved as Willy Loman, even if we turn out to be as wrong as he was.

Arthur Miller continued to write good plays for years, including *The Crucible* and the *View from the Bridge*, until his death in 2005. Among his other distinctions, for five years he was married to Marilyn Monroe.

# ARTHUR C. CLARKE
### 1917–
*Profiles of the Future*
*Childhood's End*

Arthur C. Clarke was born in England in 1917. The science-fiction virus, as he called it, attacked him when he was fourteen and he read his first copies of *Amazing Science Fiction* and *Astounding Science Fiction*, the two classic magazines of the genre. He started writing when he was fifteen. When he was nineteen he moved to London, where he soon became a founder of the British Interplanetary Society, a group of young science-fiction writers and enthusiasts who thought their dreams might some day become realities. In his twenties he had "the most important idea of my life," and wrote it up in a paper titled "Extraterrestrial Relays," which was published in the October 1945 issue of *Wireless World*. It was a proposal for the use of satellites for radio and TV communication. "Had I realized," Clarke wrote, "how quickly this idea would materialize, I would certainly have attempted to patent it—though it is some consolation to know that an application would probably have failed in 1945."

Clarke has written some fifty books, most of them science-fiction novels or collections of stories. By far his best-known work is the story (called *The Sentinel*) that he adapted for Stanley Kubrick's movie *2001: A Space Odyssey*; Clarke wrote the screenplay and then a novel, based on the movie, under the same title. It made him a literary celebrity, and everything he has written since *2001* has been a bestseller. It is not always a good thing for a writer to become very famous; in the case of Clarke his earlier writings, prior to *2001*, are better than those he has written after it.

There are many good stories and novels, but two books, I think, deserve special mention. One is a volume of nonfiction essays called *Profiles of the Future*, which Clarke published in 1963. It was not much noticed at the time, and in the blaze of post-*2001* fame it has not been much noticed since, but it is an extraordinary book. In fact, I do not know of any prophecies of a quarter-century ago that have been so well borne out, and I think it is likely that many of Clarke's prophecies for the next century will also come true:

1990: Fusion power
2010: Weather control; robot mining vehicles
2030: Mining the moon and planets; contact with extraterrestrial intelligences
2050: Gravity control; artificial breeding of intelligent animals
2100: Actual meeting with extraterrestrials; human immortality

The last prophecy sends a shiver up the spine, coming as it does at the end of that list of technical achievements. Does he really mean immortality? Has he heard about the Struldbruggs (see Swift, *Gulliver's Travels*)?

*Profiles of the Future* is a fine book, maybe the best of its kind. A better book, and perhaps the best of its kind—although its kind is much grander than a set of technological forecasts—is *Childhood's End*. Clarke, like many of his colleagues in the science-fiction field, is a wooden, rather inept writer. His characters are one-dimensional, his episodes melodramatic, his conflicts neither very important nor very credible. But he has a good mind, full of big ideas. He is not afraid to follow his imagination as it ranges through the possibilities of space and time.

*Childhood's End* is set some fifty years in the future—that is, since the book was written in 1953, just about now. The human race, quarrelsome as ever but now in possession of weapons with which it can destroy itself, is on the edge of doing just that. Suddenly, a fleet of space ships appears, one enormous silvery vessel settling quietly over each of the major cities of the world. The visitors quickly establish their absolute, total, and beneficent control over mankind. It becomes clear that they have come to save the human race from itself. And they turn the Earth into the paradise that it can be when reason instead of passion rules, and war is abolished forevermore.

As the story proceeds, however, you realize that the Overlords are not acting on their own. They have not just come; they have been sent, by a being or beings of which men have no knowledge or comprehension. This Overmind knows that something is about to happen in human history, and that it will be the most important thing that ever happened; hence mankind must be protected from itself until the fateful event occurs.

I don't want to reveal what this fateful event is, and how it occurs. Among other things *Childhood's End* is a novel of suspense, and I don't intend to spoil it.

It is more than that: it is also a novel of ideas. In a sense everything Clarke has written (including *2001*) bears on the same theme: the salvation of man from himself by means of some incomprehensible outside power. But in no other work, I think, does he make that wondrous future both intelligible and credible.

# J.D. SALINGER
1919–
*The Catcher in the Rye*

Jerome David Salinger was born in New York City on January 1, 1919. He attended public schools in the city and a military academy in Pennsylvania, and also attended classes at New York University and Columbia. He began writing when he was fifteen and published his first shorts story in 1940. From 1942 to 1946 he was in the army, and his experiences inspired such stories as the wonderful "For Esme, with Love and Squalor." His first novel, *The Catcher in the Rye*, was published in 1950. There are fads in books as well as clothes, and this book's great fad—it was a cult novel throughout the Western world a generation ago—is over. Then, there would have been no question whether to include it in this list of recommendations. Now, there is a question, and the choice—for I do recommend it now as I would have then—requires some justification.

One of the problems with *The Catcher in the Rye* is its author. J.D. Salinger, who, after writing it and a handful of stories, some of them almost long enough to be novels, stopped writing altogether and retired from public view. In today's world of "hype," the lack of an author to promote becomes a serious hindrance to the continued fame and even the readability of a book. Salinger's refusal to promote *The Catcher in the Rye* himself is of course symbolic and exemplary. The book itself is about that kind of refusal. Holden Caulfield, its puzzled young hero, is certain of one thing: "The phonies are coming in at the windows," and he wants no part of them.

That is one of the phrases that persist in the memory of readers of *The Catcher in the Rye*. There are memorable images, too. Holden's delight, and the authorities' dismay, over the boy who farted in chapel. Holden's obsession with the ducks on the pond in Central Park and his question: Where do they go in the winter, he asks his taxi driver, when the pond freezes over? Holden and his little sister, Phoebe Weatherfield Caulfield, walking down Fifth Avenue on parallel courses, not looking at each other but very much aware that the other is there, finally reaching out to one another. And the last, great image of the title, which Holden himself explains to Phoebe. (Do you know what the title means? Are you curious? Then you must read the book to find out!) The image of "the catcher in the rye" will haunt you and you will find yourself thinking about being that whenever you are at your best.

A generation ago young men and women everywhere read *The Catcher in the Rye* and sympathized with its hero's rebellion against the forces that surrounded him (and them), and found in it the halting, inarticulate expression of their own rebellion. Rebellion has come a long way since the 1950s; today some young rebels kidnap business executives and torture them to death, or blow up railroad stations, killing scores of innocents. Rebellion, in short, has become institutionalized, has its own international communications network, even its own forms of promotion and hype. When it comes right down to it, terrorists want more than anything else to manipulate the media and control the hype, which is what corporations (their great enemy) also do, but with dollars instead of bombs. Holden Caulfield would say the phonies are still coming in at the windows, and he would be right.

The greatest fiction tries to get us to see, tries to help us tear the blindfold from our eyes and to recognize what is real and what is not, what is true and what is merely a promotion. *The Catcher in the Rye* is, in a sense, a slight book, but it is relentlessly concerned with doing the same things that the greatest books do. It tells us to beware of traps and illusions, to open our eyes to the real world, where phonies fade away to the shadows that they truly are. It warns us that frauds and phonies are everywhere, especially in high places, and especially when we are young, because then we are impressionable and can be all the more easily manipulated. It advises us to trust no one who does not love us, and to reach out with love in return. It tells us that all these actions are more important than getting good marks and having a successful career and making lots of money. It informs us that the world is, really, almost completely upside down from what the authorities tell us. It explains that we simply have to think for ourselves and take nothing on faith, even when it seems absolutely dependable and true. And it tells us, finally, that we will fail at this, and so will others, and that someone—probably each of us—will have to be a catcher in the rye, because otherwise the world will all fall down.

That is a moving story, and this is a moving book. And if you like it, read *Nine Stories*. The tales are all small gems whose message echoes that of *The Catcher in the Rye*.

# JULIAN JAYNES
## 1920–1990
*The Origin of Consciousness in the Breakdown of the Bicameral Mind*

Julian Jaynes was born in Massachusetts in 1920 and was educated at both Harvard and Yale. He was a professor of biology at Princeton for twenty-five years and was a popular teacher and lecturer. I'm not surprised to learn that. He must have been a fascinating man. He certainly wrote a fascinating book with a fascinating title: *The Origin of Consciousness in the Breakdown of the Bicameral Mind*. I don't remember who first told me about it, but I immediately became interested. I bought the book and read it as fast as I could—which wasn't very fast because the thesis is tightly reasoned and carefully documented. And then I read it again and again. You have to keep your mind focused on what he is saying on every page.

Here is the idea. It seems very likely that at some time in the past humans did not have conscious minds like ours today. They didn't think as we do, any more than an ape does. Did they just suddenly start to be conscious of themselves as thinking beings? Or was it a long, drawn-out process, starting in a kind of darkness and ending in such light as we possess today?

Nevertheless, there must have been a time when some humans, at least, had minds more or less like ours even if most did not. That is, some must have been conscious of themselves even if most were not. Consciousness may then have been an evolutionary advantage, and those who possessed it would pass it on to their children, and so on and so forth.

All of this is conjecture, though it seems likely. But two questions immediately arise. First, why did this change take place? And when did it happen?

Julian Jaynes answers both questions. He writes about the Time of Troubles that occurred in the Middle East around 1000 BCE or a little before. Horsemen from the east descended on the more-or-less civilized cities and cultures of the Near East, killing, burning and destroying simply because they could. For the first time, says Jaynes, the inhabitants of the Near East were presented with threats that were entirely new. The Barbarians, as they called them, had no law and no mercy; they seemed like wild animals. Above all, they did not recognize the authority of the gods that had cared for the inhabitants as long as they could remember.

For centuries these gods had "spoken" to the peoples of the Middle East; they had heard their words in their heads, in their minds, even if they couldn't see the gods except in the costumes worn by priests and shaman. The gods did not speak publicly, but they were there in each mind, warning, teaching, rewarding good deeds and punishing the bad. But now they seemed to have disappeared, leaving their people desolate and lost. Many stone tablets have been found from that time, on which are written pleas for forgiveness and mercy: Why have you abandoned us? Come back to us in our despair!

Jaynes didn't mean that people of that time did not think or reason, but rather that they did so unconsciously. We are familiar with that. Many of the routine daily things we do, like walking or dreaming or even driving a car, are done unconsciously. Driving is a particularly good example. We can carry on a conversation with a passenger in the next seat, think about what he or she is saying and what we are saying in reply, worry about where the conversation is going and whether we are saying too much or too little, and all the time guide the car, stop at red lights and turn corners, more or less unconsciously. This is perfectly normal and doesn't mean we are bad drivers, because if there is an emergency of some kind we can snap back into consciousness to deal with it. Only very rarely do we fail to do so, in which case we have an accident.

We do not experience the voices in our heads that Jaynes describes—that is, most of us don't, but schizophrenics do. In that case we—or they—may commit surprising or dreadful acts, like killing someone or burning down a house or, less dramatically, experience hallucinations of many kinds: visual, auditory, sensory. We don't have to be schizophrenic for this to happen. Think about it. How often have you sensed something that really isn't there? And when it happened did you think you were crazy? Of course not. Usually the hallucination disappears almost immediately, leaving no trace, not even in your memory.

Jaynes goes further than we ordinarily do. He finds many examples in *The Iliad* of Homer and in the Hebrew Bible. In the first book of *The Iliad*, for example, Achilles, mortally insulted by King Agamemnon, reaches for his sword. But he hears the goddess Athene in his head, demanding obedience to her rule, and he replaces the sword. Homer does not specify that the voice is a hallucination, and Jaynes says it really isn't one. He believes that the voice is the voice of Achilles' right brain speaking to his left. Achilles, like almost everyone else at the time, is accustomed to hearing such messages, and he is not surprised when it happens to him at this juncture of the plot. And, according to Jaynes, experiments with schizophrenics have confirmed that one side of the brain can "speak" to the other.

Something else happens toward the end of *The Iliad*, when King Priam comes to the tent where Achilles is mourning the death of his friend and begs him to let him have the dead body of his son so he can give him a proper funeral. Achilles is still almost mad with grief but when he sees Priam kneeling before him, reaching for "the hands that had killed so many of his sons," he thinks of his own father, Peleus, in far off Thrace, and he relents, his heart moved, tears in his eyes. The god is not speaking to Achilles now, he is thinking about himself, accepting his existence, aware of his relation to at least one other person. And Achilles gives back the body to the father of his mortal enemy, whom he pities.

According to Jaynes, these two scenes in *The Iliad* represent a change that was occurring in the minds of some men during this time. He also points out that on many occasions in *The Odyssey*, which was *certainly* composed later than *The Iliad*, there seems to be evidence of the kind of introspection that is found only at the very end of the earlier poem. And from that time on more and more humans became conscious in the way we are conscious, although this did not happen all at once.

But what was really going on? Why did the gods depart, as the poet Lucretius said in his poem *On the Nature of Things*? According to Jaynes, it was because in the desperate danger of the Time of Troubles the connection between the two halves of the brain was broken, as it had to be if the victims of the Barbarian hordes were to survive. If the deadly horsemen descended on your village it was not enough to ask this god or the other for help, you had to help yourself, make your own decisions, find your own way to safety. In so doing you became conscious "in the breakdown of the bicameral mind."

Julian Jaynes' book is long and in some places hard to understand, and it has been very controversial. Professors of psychology, of whom Jaynes was one, have for the most part not liked it. But read the book and make up your own mind. I can guarantee that you will be enormously interested if not entirely persuaded, as I am myself.

Jaynes died on Prince Edward Island, Canada, in 1990. He had suffered a massive stroke, which unsettled all the arrangements he had made in his mind over the previous seventy years.

# ALEKSANDR SOLZHENITSYN
## 1918–
### *One Day in the Life of Ivan Denisovic*
### *The First Circle*

Aleksandr Isayevich Solzhenitsyn was born in Russia in 1918, the son of well-off liberal parents. His father, a politician who was opposed to the Soviet takeover of the government, was killed in a hunting accident in 1925. His mother died in 1940. Solzhenitsyn criticized Stalin in a private letter in 1945; he was arrested and sentenced to a labor camp and then to "permanent internal exile," which meant Siberia. He had begun to write in secret some years before and was able to continue writing despite his punishment.

He managed to send a manuscript of *One Day in the Life of Ivan Denisovic* to the literary magazine *Novi Mir*, which in turn was able to export it. It was published in 1962.

The book is based on his experiences in the winter wilderness of Siberia, where the two enemies are cold and forced labor. I have never forgotten the beginning of the book, when Ivan and a troop of fellow prisoners are forced to march through snow in temperatures just above zero Fahrenheit in shoes that are inadequate and clothes that are not warm. In the distance they perceive a single light shining in the otherwise total darkness; it is the searchlight or beacon of a walled encampment where they will spend the next few years if they survive the march. Solzhenitsyn does, and learns to wake before dawn, cover himself with as many clothes as he can find (some from mates who have frozen to death), eat as much as he can find (never enough), and try to survive another day in labor that is unnecessary except as a punishment.

Despite the conditions of their life, they form friendships that do not involve frank discussions of their dreadful conditions, since no one can be trusted not to repeat anything they might say in the hope of thereby gaining some pitifully small advantage.

The hope of a reprieve is not out of the question, and Solzhenitsyn received a kind of release that permitted him to return to Moscow and his wife and family. But he was not safe and knew he never would be safe, and in fact he was trapped again in circumstances that are described in *The First Circle*, the great book that he had begun to write in Siberia and now completed and again managed to give to *Novi Mir*. The book tells of a certain man who, because he has overheard some news about a friend whose life might be saved if he knew it, makes what he believes is a "safe" telephone call from a public phone far distant from his home, speaking in a voice that he tries to disguise. He says only a few words, then hangs up, but the call is traced—the description of how this is done is mesmerizing—and he is arrested, imprisoned, and interrogated continuously for weeks and months, then tried and sentenced to the Gulag.

Things were changing in the Soviet Union in those days. Solzhenitsyn was allowed to return to Moscow and continued to write. A manuscript of *The First Circle* was spirited out of the country and published in 1968, to immediate international acclaim, and he was awarded the Nobel Prize for Literature two years later. Unlike Boris Pasternak, who had been awarded the prize twelve years before for *Doctor Zhivago* but had refused to accept it in the fear that he would at best be exiled for life, Solzhenitsyn did accept the prize but, because he continued to write gripping and therefore unacceptable historical accounts of the Gulag, was soon exiled himself. He went to the United States and, after living for a few years in Vermont, returned to his home land, where he remains to this day.

I will never forget *The First Circle*, particularly the account, in a long chapter early in the book, of a meeting in the office of Stalin when several high officials enter to report on their recent activities. They are all extremely powerful men who in their own realms can do whatever they please to forward their careers. But being in the presence of a man who can condemn them in an instant to be beaten to death for some failure of omission or commission they have no way of knowing about in advance makes them tremble as they approach the Generalissimo, hoping against hope that he will not notice because even being afraid may be construed by him as a capital offense. And I remember reading the accounts of other absolute tyrants throughout history, including the emperors Augustus and Nero, Louis XIV, Hitler, and Mao, and I wonder as I always do why a people ever willingly accepts such a leader for the sake, as Thomas Hobbes posited, of security or some other dubious good.

I wonder if we are on the verge of accepting such a fate.

*chapter fifteen*

# Only Yesterday

ost of the authors treated in Chapter 14 produced their best-known work before or during World War II or, in a few cases, before 1980. The authors discussed in this chapter are definitely children of the last half of the twentieth century. If they wrote about World War II, it was in the past for them but perhaps not in their novels. Many of them had been in the service, but they emerged from that experience with new ideas about the world they were inheriting. For a while the Cold War haunted their dreams, but then the Berlin Wall fell, the Soviet Union dissolved, and the United States emerged as apparently the only great power of the future. Of course no one was watching China at the time, but what would history be without surprises?

I began my reading career at the age of seven, which was in 1933. I read many of the books discussed in the previous chapters when I was young—in my forties or early fifties at the latest. In 1965, when I was thirty-nine, I moved to Chicago to take a position at Encyclopaedia Britannica, Inc., and for the next twenty years I didn't read much (although I did reread many of the "classics" as part of my work). I retired in 1982, when I was fifty-six, and began to read at a frantic pace in order to catch up with the literature of my time. In the past twenty-five years I may have read five hundred or so books just because I had the time, and it was a great pleasure to be free to read whatever I wanted and not what I had to. This chapter includes the books that I have most enjoyed in those years.

# FRED BODSWORTH
1918–
*Last of the Curlews*

Fred Bodsworth was born in Ontario, Canada, in 1918. He is an amateur naturalist and has had a long career of studying and writing about the natural world. He is a very good writer as is manifest in his best-known book, *Last of the Curlews*, which was first published in 1954. A new edition was issued in 1995 with a foreword by the poet M.S. Merwin and an afterward by the Nobelist Murray Gell-Mann. They were as impressed and moved as I was by this remarkable little book.

It is a first-person account by a male bird, who has spent months seeking a mate, a female of his species, the Eskimo curlew, that once and not too long ago was very common in much of eastern Alaska. This particular bird is aware that he must soon leave for the long flight first eastward over Hudson's Bay and the islands of eastern Canada, then southward across the ocean to Venezuela and straight down the South American continent to Patagonia. He will spend five months there and then prepare to fly northward again over a different track, crossing Guatemala, passing over Texas and Saskatchewan, and finally arriving at the small valley from which he departed six month before.

He does not find a mate, but he leaves anyway, knowing he has to and hoping to find a female bird in the southern land that he remembers from previous journeys. He does so, and their love is rewarded with an offspring in her body that will be born when they reach home. They fly together, the male bird constantly watching the female, knowing she is burdened by her pregnancy and guiding her when he thinks she may be losing her way, until they reach the plains of central Texas where a man, seeing this odd creature in the air, shoots and she falls to the ground. For days the male bird circles the place where she fell, wishing, hoping, until he realizes there is no help and continues his long journey to his native land. When he arrives he continues his search for another mate, always seeking, never giving up hope …

How does this beautiful book end? I will not tell you but allow you to feel, to hope, to weep and laugh … It is a common story, of course, of love between a boy and a girl, or a man and a woman, or two birds, male and female because that is the way things almost always are.

# PRIMO LEVI
## 1918–1987
*The Periodic Table*
*If Not Now, When?*

Primo Levi was born in Turin in 1918 and trained as a chemist. He was a Jew and he experienced difficulties, but not until Germany took over the Italian government was he in any real danger because his work was valued by Italian firms. In 1944, however, he was arrested as a member of the anti-Fascist resistance and deported to Auschwitz.

His "shipment" in twelve unheated and crowded cattle cars arrived on February 4, 1944. There were 650 persons in the "shipment"; only twenty survived to be liberated by the Red Army. Before that the SS took the inhabitants of the camp on a forced march behind the lines, during which large numbers died of exhaustion and cold. Levi was one of the lucky ones because he had been stricken by scarlet fever and the Germans didn't want to take him with the other prisoners, so they left him behind to die, which, somehow, Levi managed not to do. However, it was eleven months before he reached Turin. At first no one recognized him, he was so emaciated and worn down.

On his journey homeward he began to tell people about his experiences and they urged him to write them down. He did so, publishing them in a book called *If This Is a Man* in 1947. The book was hard to write because his memories were so raw even years after his escape, but he knew there were still stories that had to be told and he tried to do so. One book, a collection of stories, was called *The Periodic Table* (1975), because each chapter deals in one way or another with a different element, from argon and hydrogen to vanadium and carbon. It's a fine book, too.

*If Not Now, When?* unlike his other books, is a novel, although it is based on stories Levi had heard from others about events in the fateful year of 1945. It follows a group of Jewish partisans behind the lines who are fighting to survive. One scene in the book is chiseled in my memory. The partisans turn the tables on a group of SS and are about to shoot them all when one of their number says, "No, let's not do that–I know a better way." They order the Germans to lie down on their bellies in a room and then, taking very careful aim with a pistol and slowly, one by one, they shoot each of the men in the lower spine. They are paralyzed from the waist down and the partisans watch them for a while as they try to get up, reminding Levi of a scene in *Paradise Lost* when the Devils at the bottom of Hell are twisting and squirming in the mud, unable to even raise their heads. The SS troops beg for food and water. The partisans do not even laugh.

Primo Levi died on April 11, 1987. He had fallen from the balcony of his apartment house in Turin. His life had not been happy; his memories were hard to live with. But the rumor that he had committed suicide is probably not true.

# LEO ROSTEN
## 1908–1997
*The Education of H\*Y\*M\*A\*N K\*A\*P\*L\*A\*N*
*The Joys of Yiddish*

Leo Rosten was born in Lodz, Poland, in 1908 and moved to Chicago when he was three. He graduated from the University of Chicago and received a Ph.D. in 1937. *The Education of H\*Y\*M\*A\*N K\*A\*P\*L\*A\*N* was published in 1931 after chapters had been appearing for months in the *New Yorker*. I must have been too young to read that first edition, but I soon read a second one and have been chuckling over it ever since.

Mr. Kaplan is in a class taught by a professor of English for students wishing to learn the language. He signs all his papers with the asterisks because, he says, the teacher will notice him better. He has no problem being noticed because he drives the teacher crazy with his sly comprehension of more than the teacher realizes. For just one example, Kaplan writes on an examination about his uncle:

"His eye fell on a bargain and he picked it up."
"You can't say that, Mr. Kaplan," says the teacher.
"You have to say, 'He saw a bargain and picked it up.'"
"No," said Mr. Kaplan. "I am right, because mine onkel has a glass eye."

The teacher sighs in despair.

The bibliography of works by Leo Rosten (sometimes under the pseudonym of Leonard Q. Ross) fills a large page. One of the items is *The Joys of Yiddish* (1968), one of my favorite books.

I am not Jewish, but that doesn't mean I can't appreciate and love *The Joys of Yiddish*. It may not be my native language, but I've heard it from friends all my life and am sorry that so many American Jews have forgotten it, although their parents may not have. Even so, it is one of the most expressive languages in the world and includes many typical gestures. It is like the dialect of Italian that is still spoken by some people in Sicily. It too is very expressive and involves a lot of hand movements.

Leo Rosten was a humorist and compiled several collections of Jewish humor and Yiddish quotations. They are all good. He was the source of many fine quotations. For example: "A conservative is one who admires radicals centuries after they're dead." "Truth is stranger than fiction; fiction has to make sense." Rosten died in New York in 1997, at the age of eighty-nine.

# KURT VONNEGUT, JR

## 1922–2007

*Slaughterhouse-Five; or, The Children's Crusade*

Kurt Vonnegut, Jr., was born in Indianapolis in 1922. He was studying at Cornell when World War II broke out. He enlisted in the army, which sent him to Carnegie Tech to study mechanical engineering. This didn't last long, and eventually he found himself in the midst of the Battle of the Bulge. Together with three other men he became lost behind the lines. The four of them wandered for days until they were captured by Wehrmacht troops in December 1944. Vonnegut was sent to Dresden as a prisoner of war and was incarcerated in cells beneath the city that had held frozen carcasses of cattle. On the night of February 13, Dresden was obliterated by firebombs from a thousand allied planes that flew over the city in waves creating a firestorm so intense that almost no one on the streets or in houses and other buildings survived. Estimates of the number of civilian deaths vary between 38,000 and 138,000 but the real number is probably closer to the latter. The problem is that there was no way to count the dead because, although the Germans at first tried to bury them all, they realized there was no way they could do that; they handed out flame throwers and burned every body they could find.

Vonnegut was one of only seven American prisoners of war who survived this holocaust. He had been immured in *Schlachthof-Fünf* (Slaughterhouse-Five), which was deep enough beneath the city so that the heat did not penetrate to it. Discovered, he was given the job of helping to find bodies. He was rescued by Russian troops in May and exchanged for prisoners of other nationalities.

He was a born writer and soon successful. He wrote many fine and funny books, but the only story he really wanted to tell was about what had happened to Dresden on that night in February 1945. He was finally able to do this in his novel, *Slaughterhouse-Five*, published in 1969. The subtitle of the book, *The Children's Crusade*, is an example of the kind of mordant humor to be found in this and many other Vonnegut titles. The subtitle reminds us of a terrible thing that happened in the twelfth century. Fifty thousand children, led by a boy named Stephen, tried to go to the Holy Land and conquer the Paynim with love, not arms. Instead, owing to mistakes and simple greed, most of them were sold into slavery as soon as they reached land. Vonnegut thought of soldiers as children being used by grownups. The book's combination of simplicity and sense, irony and rue, said a critic, is very much in the Vonnegut vein. Its ironic phrase, "So it goes" in reference to death, became a slogan for anti-Vietnam-War protestors.

As time went on he grew more and more critical and pessimistic about what his country was doing in and to the world. The Vietnam War enraged him, and the misadventure in Iraq did so even more. "By saying that 'Our leaders are power-drunk chimpanzees,'" he wrote, "am I in danger of wrecking the morale of our soldiers? Their morale is already shot to pieces. They are being treated, as I never was, like toys a rich kid got for Christmas."

He died as I was writing this, in April 2007. I won't be the only one to miss him. There are thousands more. So it goes.

# JOSÉ SARAMAGO
*1922–*
*Blindness*
*The Cave*

José Saramago was born in Portugal in 1922, to a family of landless peasants. He had little education, but this didn't stop him from becoming one of the greatest writers of the twentieth century, or maybe of all time.

He is an iconoclast with many curious beliefs. A communist, an atheist, and a pessimist, he is also a lover of women. And he's fond of dogs—there is a dog that plays a part in every one of the eight novels by Saramago I have read. I wonder if anyone else has noticed?

His prose style is decidedly strange. You have to get used to it. He never uses quotation marks to delineate conversational speech, and he hardly ever uses periods to end sentences, which run on in some cases for an entire page, with the clauses separated by commas. But once you have become used to this, you find it is a novel and intriguing way to describe the endlessly confusing actions and thoughts, as well as the words, of human beings, which is what Saramago is most interested in.

*Blindness* was published (in the United States) in 1995. A man and his wife are driving in a city and have stopped at a red light when the man suddenly becomes blind. His wife does not, and she is able to work her way out of the traffic jam caused by the sudden blindness of many other drivers. Neither of them is ever given a name. He is simply "The first person to become blind." and she is "The wife of the first man to become blind." The plague is not universal but it is nearly so, and the blind populace of the city make desperate efforts to rearrange their lives in order to live. Of course there are great difficulties, not least because a gang of criminals tries to take over the city, threatening everyone who does not obey them with death (they have found weapons and are willing to use them).

The wife of the first man to go blind turns out to be the salvation of the city and perhaps the entire race, because she alone can see and works her way into the gang and overcomes it. There is no explanation of why this has happened and why the plague ends. That is not the kind of thing Saramago does. Nevertheless, despite all its mysterious unanswered questions, this is one of the great novels of our time. In 1996, José Saramago received the Nobel Prize for Literature.

*The Cave* was published (in the United States) in 2002. It is a love story between a man and a woman who cannot speak to one another until almost the last page. Here, the dog, whose name is "Found" because it just turns up one day, is a charming and eloquent interlocutor. The man has a daughter who is married to a man who does not understand what is really going on, though he finally discovers an underground cave in which a group of persons are seated, staring at a wall. There is a light behind them; a machine is displaying pictures on the wall. The son-in-law is suddenly terrified and returns home to inform his family of this strange happening, which they understand because, whether they have read Plato's *Republic* or not, it is clear to them. Which it will be to you when you read this beautiful book.

Other fine novels by Saramago are *The Stone Raft*, in which the Iberian Peninsula separates from Europe and starts to drift slowly westward; *The Year of the Death of Ricardo Reis*; and *The History of the Siege of Lisbon*, in which a proofreader in a publishing house leaves out a "not" in a sentence and this changes the history of the world. There are many more. Prepare to be intrigued as well as delighted and amused.

# JOSEPH HELLER
## 1923–1999
### *Catch 22*

Joseph Heller was born on Coney Island, New York, in 1923. He flew sixty combat missions as a B-25 bombardier, returned safely, and won a Fulbright Scholarship to Oxford in 1949–50. After that he began to write the one book that everyone remembers. Called *Catch 22*, it was published in 1961.

In case you don't remember, the absurd premise of the book is as follows. According to an extremely vague USAF regulation, anyone who is willing to fly combat missions (particularly in a B-25) must be considered insane. However, if you apply for release from the service on mental grounds, the act proves your sanity and you are reassigned to combat. That, in a nutshell, is Catch 22.

Yossarian is a captain in the air force who is trying to understand Catch 22. He is in love with Nurse Duckett and she is in love with him, but they don't make it somehow. Milo Minderbinder is a mess officer who is willing to do anything if he can get paid for it, including hiring out his air force group to the Germans, who use it to kill many Americans. He is accused of treason but gets off by claiming that he was only being a capitalist. Ex-PFC Wintergreen is called that because he went AWOL. Later he becomes Ex-Sgt. Wintergreen and hopes someday to become a General so he can go AWOL and become ex-Gen. Wintergreen.

Yossarian is more or less the hero of the book. He spends most of his time trying to avoid being killed by officers who keep increasing the number of missions he has to fly before being allowed to go home on leave. He has decided to live forever or die in the attempt. Eventually he realizes he can just leave and sets out in a rowboat to row all the way to Sweden, a neutral country. For all we know he gets there safely. And of course even if he dies en route he will live forever in the minds of the millions who read his book or saw the movie made by Mike Nichols, in which Alan Arkin plays Yossarian. Can't you see him now in his rowboat as the scene fades to black?

Joseph Heller didn't live forever. He died in 1999. His later books weren't as good as *Catch 22*, but, as he once said: "When I read someone saying I haven't done anything as good as *Catch 22* lately, I'm tempted to reply, 'Who has?'"

# JOHN BERGER
## 1926–
### *Ways of Seeing*
### *About Looking*

John Berger was born in London in 1926, the son of an infantry officer on the Western front in 1916–18. Berger enlisted in the British army and served from 1944-46, after which he studied at the Chelsea School of Art, London.

As time went on he grew closer and closer to the Communist Party, which didn't keep him from serving *The New Statesman* as its art critic. From time to time they thought of releasing him, but he was such an astute critic and good writer that they didn't do so for ten years. By 1961 he was a freelance writer and lived the simple life he preferred. In 1972 his first book, *Ways of Seeing*, was published and won the Booker Prize, the highest British award for a literary work.

It is an extraordinary book, which, if you read it and think about what it says, will probably change the way you look at a work of art, at least any work of art before about 1850, say—the Old Masters, as they're called. According to Berger, practically every painting was an advertisement for something, usually the wealth of the person—man or woman—who commissioned it. You don't see this right away, but then you begin to notice small details: a ring on a woman's finger, a fur collar on a man's jacket, silver buckles on his shoes, an expensive harness on a horse, a jeweled collar on the neck of a dog—to say nothing of a mansion in the background or a fine stand of timber or a lake with a temple in the distance. Or the dress of a maidservant, the uniform of a footman—anything and everything is there for an ulterior purpose. And really always the same kind: to reveal the wealth of someone, either the subject of the painting or the buyer of it or the patron of the painter himself.

This is not always true. Take Rembrandt, for instance. Early in his career, when he was a society painter who painted portraits of rich and famous people, this was certainly true. But midway through his career Rembrandt ceased to be successful in that way, ceased to find patrons or wealthy subjects, and finally was reduced to painting portraits of his wife, who sat for nothing, and of himself, seen in a mirror. And, as Berger admits, these were his greatest paintings, the ones that lead us to name him one of the greatest artists of all time.

Berger's analysis of paintings in *Ways of Seeing* is fascinating. I have only hinted at its complexities. I hope you will see for yourselves.

*About Looking* is another extraordinary book. It is mostly about photography. If that interests you, you should read it. The first chapter of the book moves me very deeply. It is called "Why Look at Animals?"

Berger begins by pointing out that most of us, nowadays, have almost no contact with animals, may never even see an animal unless it is someone's dog on a leash or a cat slinking in an alley (or a rat in the same alley). Not so long ago, Berger says, this was not so. Most of us, until about 1900 or even later in many countries, lived with animals, shared our lives with theirs, depended on them for many kinds of help and services, as they depended on us. Of course, we killed and ate them, but that didn't mean we were unaware of their existence; we knew where our food came from, how it grew under our care, what it meant to slaughter them or wring their necks or steal their eggs. And now, if we ever look at animals, it is in zoos.

And there's the rub. Animals in zoos are not the kind of animals we used to live with. They are captives, serving life sentences for our amusement and pleasure. They are lazy, sleepy—most animals sleep if they have nothing else to do—bedraggled, unhealthy, and unhealthy looking. And when we look at them, they look at us. And what do they see? Do they recognize us as fellow inmates of an industrial culture that treats animals as things instead of living beings, and treats human beings as things as well, things that can be exploited for their labor or for warfare, or as amusing automata flickering on a screen?

If you disagree about this, don't argue with me. Argue with John Berger, and even if you win the argument it will have done you good to engage in it.

# JOHN LE CARRÉ
## 1931–
### *The Spy Who Came in from the Cold, et al.*

John le Carré (the pseudonym of David J.M. Cornwell) was born in Dorset, England, in 1931. He was educated at Oxford, taught at Eton, then served for five years in the British Foreign Service. Recruited to MI6, his career was destroyed by Kim Philby, who blew the cover of dozens of British agents to the KGB. He analyzed Philby's weakness and death in *Tinker, Tailor, Soldier, Spy* (1974) and *A Small Town in Germany* (1968), which introduced one of his major characters, George Smiley. The latter book, a tour de force, consists mostly of dialogue, which is fun for a writer to do but not always very easy to read.

My three favorite novels by le Carré are *The Spy Who Came in from the Cold* (1963), *The Little Drummer Girl* (1983), and *The Constant Gardener* (2001). I remember well the excitement I felt about *Spy*, which was one of the first to deal with a subject that le Carré and others later made almost a cliché. I was scared for the secret agent and hopeful, when he threw himself over the Berlin Wall at the end, that he would survive to live another life. And I understood very well why he couldn't stand to continue conducting his entire life in secrecy, because I was doing a little of that myself.

The young female protagonist of *The Little Drummer Girl* captured my heart. She is so brave and so frightened, and also so torn between love of her victim and hatred of the man he is becoming. Le Carré is a very good writer who can tear your feelings into shreds continuously for two hundred pages, as he does here.

I think he never has written a better book than *The Constant Gardener*, partly because his own feelings are so deeply involved.

# ALAN FURST
1941–
*Historical Espionage Novels*

Alan Furst was born in Newark, New Jersey, and brought up on the West Side of Manhattan. He received a B.A. from Oberlin and an M.A. from Penn State. He was urged by his grandfather to be a teacher and write only in his spare time—advice that, fortunately for us, he refused.

His early novels were reasonably successful but it was not until 1988, with the publication of *Night Soldiers*, that his career took off and in the process revitalized the entire genre of spy novels. He called it "historical espionage," but it was the depth and intensity of his writing about heroes who had to depend mainly on intelligence and luck that set him apart from the authors of most such thrillers except for Joseph Conrad, Eric Ambler, and John le Carré. His books, besides *Night Soldiers*, including *The Polish Officer, Dark Star, Dark Voyage*, and *The World at Night*, are all exceptional—that list contains several very good books, but you can count on him, whatever the title, not only to teach you about the dark secret world of the period from 1933 to 1944 but also to cause you to wonder how we ever survived as a nation and, indeed, as a society. Furst's knowledge of the underside of the period is unparalleled, and he is a very good writer whom I highly recommend.

# CZESŁAW MIŁOSZ
1911–2004
*The Captive Mind*

Czesław Miłosz was born in 1911 in Tsarist Russia, to partly Polish, partly Lithuanian parents, and was brought up in the multinational milieu of Wilno (Vilnius). He graduated in 1934 with a degree in law and the next year received an award from the Alliance Française in

Paris. During the late thirties he worked for the Polish State Broadcasting Company, but with the emergence of the Nazis he became active in underground circles in Warsaw, where he spent most of the war. Between 1946 and 1951 he served as a member of the Polish Foreign Service, but despite his initial sympathies for radical change he left his post as cultural attaché in Paris and remained in the West thereafter.

*The Captive Mind* (1953) is his most influential book. Unlike Solzhenitsyn's and Furst's works, it is not fiction, but it is as gripping as anything in their books. It was written in Paris at the time when a majority of French intellectuals resented their country's dependence on American help and placed their hopes on what they saw as a new world to the East, ruled by a leader of incomparable wisdom and virtue—Joseph Stalin. Those, like Albert Camus, who pointed to the existence of a network of concentration camps as the very foundation of the Socialist system, were vilified and ostracized. His book, as Miłosz states in a note at the beginning of it, "displeased practically everybody." Admirers of Soviet Communism found it insulting, while anti-Communists suspected its author of being a Marxist at heart. "A lonely venture," he went on to say, "it has since been vindicated by facts and defends itself well against both kinds of criticism."

Its subject is the "vulnerability," as Milosz called it, of the twentieth-century mind to seduction by sociopolitical doctrines and its readiness to accept totalitarian terror for the sake of a hypothetical future. As such, the book transcends limitations of place and moment as it explores the deeper causes of today's longing for any, even the most illusory, certainty.

Americans may say, fifty years after the publication of this book, that its comments do not apply to us; any of us who were ever tempted by Communist and totalitarian social concepts have long since changed our minds and, since the fall of the Berlin Wall in 1989, have begun even to accept non-Communist Russians as partners in the future. But, as Miłosz would point out if he were still alive, there are many kinds of totalitarianism in the world, many of them religious, and we are perhaps just as vulnerable as we ever were to the lure of "hypothetical certainties." Or if "we" feel we are not, we have to recognize that there are many of "them" who are willing to risk and even to give up their lives for the sake of their beliefs. It is for that reason that this book is important, although it is not pleasant to read.

Czesław Miłosz was a good poet as well as a historian, and he was awarded the Nobel Prize for Literature in 1980. He died at the age of ninety-three in 2004.

# SÉBASTIEN JAPRISOT
## 1931–2003
*The Sleeping Car Murders*
*A Very Long Engagement*

Sébastien Japrisot (an anagram for his real name, Jean Baptiste Rossi) was born in 1931—the same year as le Carré—and he too is a very good writer. He published his first novel when he was seventeen, and wrote dozens since then. He wrote in French and, while not all of his books are available in English, his two translated works are both terrific reads.

*The Sleeping Car Murders* (1963) was published in the same year as *The Spy Who Came in from the Cold*, but it is a very different book from le Carré's. It is much more traditional—except for one very special thing. The story is rather simple: a sleeping car arrives in Paris with a dead woman in one of the compartments. The police are alerted and at first the investigation seems to be routine. Attempts are made to discover other occupants in the compartment besides the murdered woman. But these attempts lead nowhere, because whenever a fellow passenger is found, he or she too is dead. Something here is very mysterious and very frightening, especially for two persons in the compartment, a young woman and a seventeen-year-old boy. It seems that the boy was more interested in the young woman than she was in him, but as the net is drawn tighter and tighter around her she becomes terrified and tries to enlist the boy's help. He refuses to help her. Why? She doesn't know, the detective doesn't know, and you don't know. But then, suddenly, you do know and are deeply satisfied by this fine love story.

A *Very Long Engagement* (1993) is a story about a young man named Manuch, or "Cornflower," and a young woman named Mathilde. She is wealthy but crippled by polio; he is poor and a soldier in the Great War. The first sentence of the book is this: "Once upon a time there were five French soldiers who had gone off to war, because that's the way of the world." The rest of the book, which is inexpressibly surprising, astonishing, and moving, is told in that same style, as if the author doesn't care about his characters and thinks you don't either, or at least you don't have to; they're just ordinary people, the kind that other people don't care about. But before you have read fifty pages you care about one of them so much your heart aches. This is Mathilde.

They were young lovers just before Manuch left for the army, and that too is the way of the world. That Mathilde should love him is, for Manuch, the most astonishing thing that has ever happened and ever will happen, and his happiness is so overwhelming that there are times when he can't breathe. He goes off to war promising to take care of himself and assuring her that he will return soon, that they will be married and have children and do all the good things that good people do. She is not as sure as he is because she can't walk easily and often is confined to a wheelchair, but at least she knows they can make love because they have done so, once, before he left. And if once, why not many times?

Then a very sad thing happens. Desperate to see Mathilde again, Manuch wounds himself and applies for medical leave. But the authorities are convinced his wound is self-inflicted, a common occurrence. He protests, but they don't believe him; they are sure he has wounded himself, this happens all the time, and he is court-martialed, convicted , and sentenced to be placed in no-man's-land, in between the French and German trenches to be shot at or not, who cares. He will certainly be killed, he and the four others who are in the same situation. So that is the end of the story of Mathilde and Manuch.

Ah, but the Fates have not reckoned with Mathilde. I can't tell you what happens except to say that you'll be surprised. It is a very fine book of its kind. It will not disappoint you, but you will probably have to read it twice before you understand everything that happens. (I'm slow—I had to read it three times.)

Sébastien Japrisot died in 2003.

# TONI MORRISON
1931–
*Song of Solomon*
*Beloved*

Toni Morrison (her real name is Chloe Anthony Wofford) was born in Lorain, Ohio, in 1931—apparently, a good year for authors. She studied humanities at Howard University and earned a B.A. in 1953; she then went to Cornell, where she gained an M.A. After graduation she became an instructor at Texas Southern University (1955–57), then returned to Howard to teach English. All the time she was writing with increasing craft.

Her third novel, *Song of Solomon*, was published in 1977. *Beloved* appeared ten years later. A sensation, it earned her the Nobel Prize for Literature in 1993. The Nobel citation described her as one "who, in novels characterized by visionary force and import, gives life to an essential aspect of American reality."

Morrison embodies the African-American voice; her books see the American reality from the viewpoint of someone who is in some ways an outsider and in others at the center of things. Her eminently readable novels are very fine and strange, which the best books almost always are. But they are eminently readable by all kinds of people, young and old, male and female, black and white. That includes just about everybody, doesn't it?

# CORMAC MCCARTHY
1933–
*The Border Trilogy*
*The Road*

Cormac McCarthy was born in Providence, Rhode Island, in 1933. He moved to Knoxville, Tennessee, in 1937 and studied at the University of Texas from 1951-52. He served in the U.S. Air Force in 1953–57, then returned to Knoxville and the University of Tennessee, bought a barn, rebuilt and renovated it, largely with his own hands. He is that kind of a man. He was a MacArthur Fellow, which allowed him to live wherever he desired. He moved to Tesuque, a town north of Santa Fe, New Mexico, and began to write full time. I believe he had always known that was likely to happen.

The three books of The Border Trilogy began to appear in 1992, with the publication of *All the Pretty Horses*. It was followed by *The Crossing* (1994) and *Cities of the Plain* (1998). The trilogy is an extraordinary achievement and constitutes one of the finest literary works of the twentieth century.

My wife, Gerry, and I were driving west to Chicago and then Aspen from our Connecticut home in 1993, and I had bought an audio tape of *All the Pretty Horses* for the ride. Neither of us was prepared for the power and beauty of the first part of the book as read by Brad Pitt (at a time when he wasn't Brad Pitt yet). Several times we had to stop along the Interstate to rest and try to get our breath back, to prepare ourselves to resume the reading. At the time Pitt had not recorded the unabridged version, so I bought a copy and read it to Gerry while she drove, and she read it to me while I did. We were enormously impressed.

The experience was particularly moving because driving south and east from Aspen we traversed some of the Texas country in which the story is set. Not exactly the same, but the same kind— horse country, where cattle used to roam. I'm no horseman, although my wife was a good rider when she was young, but I somehow felt that I was on the horse with John Grady Cole as he rode through those dry, parched, empty lands. I felt with him and understood his suffering as the country changed before his very eyes, as it has done by the end of the trilogy, much of which takes place in northern Mexico.

*The Road* is a novel about a father and son who are riding eastward after a nuclear holocaust has destroyed all of the world they inhabit. I know it is a very fine book but I haven't gotten the strength to read it yet; but I will, because it is by Cormac McCarthy.

# LARRY MCMURTRY
## 1936–
### *Lonesome Dove*

Larry McMurtry was born in Wichita Falls, Texas, in 1936. He went to high school in nearby Anchor City, the backdrop of his novel *The Last Picture Show*, published in 1966. *Lonesome Dove* won a Pulitzer Prize in 1986. It had been preceded by other good books and has been followed by still others, but it is unique. It deserves to be considered in the same breath as The Border Trilogy, although it is not as "grand."

The story is mainly about two men, "Gus" McCrae and Woodrow F. Call, both of them retired Texas Rangers, who with the help of several others are driving a herd of cattle north from Texas to Montana. There is also a blue pig who accompanies them all the way and a young woman who was abandoned by her man and has become a prostitute because there is nothing else she can do. Her name is Lorie, and she is very pretty. She owes her life to Gus so she goes with them, too. Extraordinary things happen along the way, things you will never forget, not least the capture of Lorie by Blue Duck, a malicious half breed who threatens to burn her alive if … Well, Gus doesn't let that happen, but he is wounded and … I don't want to tell you any more; it's too much fun finding out for yourself—fun and sad, too.

# DANIEL QUINN
## 1935–
### *Ishmael*

Daniel Quinn was born in Omaha, Nebraska, in 1935. He studied at St. Louis University, the University of Vienna, and Loyola University, but he was all the time thinking about the history of mankind and the question Rousseau had answered with his *Discourse on Inequality:* Why does inequality and the inevitable poverty that accompanies it exist, and how did they come into being? As a very young man, Quinn discovered a very simple answer to the question— namely, that sometime in the not too distant past, some of the people on Earth locked up all the food and charged all the rest a fee if they wanted to eat it. They also declared that all the agricultural land belonged to them, and if others wanted to use it, they had to pay a fee for that, too. Simple, right?

But what to do about it? That's more complicated, and it's the subject of Daniel Quinn's fine book, *Ishmael* (1996), and of its successors, *The Story of B* (1996) and *My Ishmael* (1997). Answering the question requires a lot of searching into the past, for example into the Book of Genesis, where the story of Cain and Abel is given a slant that may never have occurred to you. Many other hoary truths are shown to be not necessarily true, and probably false. A vision of a good world on a good Earth eventually emerges, seen through the bright eyes of Ishmael, who is not a person. What he actually is will shock you, but you will soon get over that discovery and feel you have learned something very important, although you will have trouble trying to explain it to anybody else. As I am having trouble now.

It will help, I think, to remember Daniel Quinn's mantra: "If they give you lined paper, write sideways."

# J.M. COETZEE
1940–
*Disgrace*
*Elizabeth Costello*

John Marvell Coetzee, born in Cape Town, South Africa, in 1940, was educated in schools there and at the University of Cape Town, from which he graduated with degrees in English and Mathematics. He then went to the University of Texas, from which he graduated with degrees in English, Linguistics, Computer Science, and German. In 1972 he applied for U.S. citizenship but was denied. Do you suppose it was because he was too well educated?

He began writing in 1969 and quickly published a number of novels, including *Waiting for the Barbarians* in 1980; *Life and Times of Michael K.* in 1983; and *Age of Iron* in 1990. *Disgrace* was published in 1999.

It is a dreadful story that you hope could not be true—but it surely is, in more ways than one. The protagonist—hardly the hero in any sense of the word—is a professor in an unnamed university, either American or Canadian. He is introduced in the first sentence thus: "For a man of his age, fifty-two, divorced, he has, in his mind, solved the problem of sex rather well." The object of his affections, if that's the word, is one of his students, a tall, lissome young woman whose parents are not as pleased by his sexual arrangement as he and perhaps she are. One thing quickly leads to another, and he soon finds himself without a teaching job anywhere in the country. With no prospects of any other kind of work paying enough to keep him alive, he returns to South Africa, where his daughter lives on a ranch, and offers to help her out in any way he can in return for a bed and three meals a day.

At first this arrangement is satisfactory, until a shocking event occurs that I will not describe because you must discover it yourself when you read this remarkable, perhaps great, book. The event seems to him to require a response that his daughter does not think is correct. He realizes that this difference between them is symbolic of the change that in one way or another is going on in the world almost everywhere, and certainly in Africa. The change is inevitable. From one point of view it is very unpleasant, but from another very appropriate and good. I know I am being vague, because I don't want to unravel all these mysteries before you have read the book. Of course, you can put your head in the sand, but that is hardly ever a good idea because it leaves you open to a kick in ... well, you know.

*Elizabeth Costello*, published in 2003, is a very strange book. It isn't easy to say what happens in it. On the surface, the book is a report of several long, controversial lectures given by the protagonist about the way we treat animals and including the suggestion that we ought to change places with animals and let them treat us the way we treat them. One critic said that she could be thought of as one of those large cats that eviscerate their victim and, across the torn-open body, give you a cold yellow stare. Quite so. Be brave and read this book, too.

# ROBERTO CALASSO
1941–
*The Marriage of Cadmus and Harmony*

Roberto Calasso was born in Florence, Italy, in 1941. He studied English literature at the University of Rome and graduated with a thesis on Sir Thomas Browne, a fascinating and little-known— especially in Italy—English doctor and antiquarian who wrote two astonishing books in the seventeenth century. Calasso began to work for Adelphi Edizioni when it was founded in 1982 (he was twenty-one) and since 1999 has been its chairman. It has published several of his books, which have been translated into most of the European languages.

*The Ruin of Kasch* (1983, translated 1984) is an absolutely crazy book. The first half of it is a brilliant biography of Metternich, the political genius who reshaped Europe after the end of the Napoleonic Wars (and created a new world that made inevitable the Franco-Prussian War of 1870 and the First World War of 1914-18). The second half of the book is about a lost Central African Empire— Kasch—that was swallowed up by the jungle five hundred years ago. I read it all the way through, but I really don't know why.

Yes, of course I do. It is because I had previously read *The Marriage of Cadmus and Harmony* (1988, translated by Tim Parks into English in 1993), which in my opinion and that of many others is the finest book ever written about the Greek myths. It is a subject I love because I have written about it, too, but when I read Calasso's book I was flabbergasted. It is one of the books I wish *I* had written.

It begins wonderfully, telling and retelling the Myth of Europa, who was raped by Zeus, the Bull that rose from the sea, and gave birth, in a manner of speaking, not only to the Greece we know but also to Europe. "How did it all begin?" is the recurring theme, and there are many answers, all of which Calasso describes with stunning scholarship and beauty. In the remainder of the book he shows how each of these various beginnings ends up in one great, heart-breaking event, when Cadmus, an old man, defeated and torn and his children torn too, but united with his bride, herself an old woman now, gives to the Greeks his last gift, the alphabet, with which they will begin to create—leaving the gods behind because they are no longer needed—the new world that we know because we still live in it today.

# MARK HELPRIN
1947—
*Winter's Tale*
*A Soldier of the Great War*

Mark Helprin was born in New York in 1947 and grew up there and in the British West Indies. He holds degrees from Harvard College and the Harvard Graduate School of Arts and Sciences, and he did post graduate work at Oxford University. He has served in the British merchant navy, the Israeli Infantry, and the Israeli Air Force.

He began to write stories as a student and published several in the *New Yorker* before he was twenty. *Winter's Tale* was published in 1988; it had been written before he was thirty. It is a fantastic story of early twentieth-century life in New York City. One of my favorite scenes describes a trip on the New York Central Railroad south from Saratoga. In a tremendous five-day blizzard, the train is practically covered by snow and cannot move. It is terribly cold. Fires are built in the cars using the floorboards and the now-useless luggage for fuel, but the passengers soon run out of food and water. Several people die of exposure and starvation.

Unknown to them, a search party from a neighboring village has set out with twenty-five sleighs loaded with food and warm clothing, snow shoes, and skis. It takes days before the train is found and the farmers from the village with all their equipment finally arrive. The two hundred desperate passengers can hardly believe their good fortune as they quickly don the warm clothing. Those who know how to ski put the skies on their feet; those who do not are told they must learn, because this is an emergency, and that's what happens. And because this book is a ceaselessly interesting fantasy they all survive and return to their lives, but much changed in their understanding of what life is. There are other mysterious goings and comings, and a battle between good and evil that is very exciting. The book was highly praised when it appeared and is still described as Helprin's best book.

I disagree. Not because it's not wonderful but because he wrote an even better one, *A Soldier of the Great War* (1991). This too is a kind of fantasy but the time frame is much shorter—basically, the four years of World War I. His experiences in the war are told by Alessandro, now an old man, to a young man with whom he is forced to walk for fifty miles to their destinations, which in the case of the young man is love and in that of the old man, death. Everything that could have happened to any Italian soldier has happened to Alessandro, and he describes it all with a passionate sense of the horror and excitement and beauty that it entailed, especially the story of his falling in love with a nurse in a military hospital. Her name is Ariane and he thinks he has lost her, and if it were not for a painting by Giorgione called "La Tempesta" he might have. The painting is in the Accademia in Venice and I went to see it as soon as I could and discovered why Alessandro tells his young friend that it is "the meaning of all history," but you will have to read the book and see the painting, even if only in a reproduction, to understand what Helprin evokes. Please take my word, doing so will be worthwhile.

Saying that, I recognize, perhaps for the first time, that you may not share my sense of the meaning of history and the world. However, I hope, if you have gotten this far in this book, that you will try to follow me into my wildly imaginative sense of things. *Buona fortuna!*

Mark Helprin has won many honors and has also been an adviser to the U.S. and Israeli governments in various capacities and at various times in the past decade. He may be as disappointed with both governments as I am, but for different reasons.

# DONNA LEON
## 1942–

# MICHAEL DIBDIN
## 1947–2007

# HENNING MANKELL
## 1948–
### *Thrillers*

Lest you believe me to be totally square and unaware of the pleasures of popular fiction today, I include in this entry titles by three fine writers whose work I have learned about with the help of my brother, who discovers them before I do and gives me copies on my birthday each year. Curiously, the three authors have much in common; that is, they are all deeply distressed by what is happening today in the worlds they describe but do not actually live in.

The first of the three is Donna Leon, who was born in the United States in 1942 of Irish and Spanish descent. Before settling down in Venice twenty-five years ago, she taught in the United States, Iran, China, and Saudi Arabia—an itinerary that certainly taught her a lot about the way the world works. She published her first thriller, *Death at La Fenice*, in 1992. It introduced an excellent detective, Commissario Guido Brunetti, and his delightful family: his wife Paola and their children, Raffi and Chiara, whom we have seen grow up over the past fifteen years, although perhaps more slowly than you would expect. That doesn't matter because all of them, thank goodness, are there in every book, together with Sergente Vianello, Brunetti's right-hand man; Signorina Elletra, who is always beautifully dressed and who can invade any computer system on the planet (or at least in Venice); and Vice-Questore Patta, Brunetti's "self-serving buffo," as he has been called.

There is always at least one murder, and it is always very difficult to determine who committed the crime, until the finale. That of course is of the essence of this kind of tale, but what is not of the essence is the deep and growing pessimism not only of Brunetti but also of author Leon, who delves deeper and deeper into the corrupt underbelly of Venice, that glorious "little jewel" built on an island that is slowly but surely sinking into the sea. Certainly Venice has been corrupt for centuries, but the corruption in every sphere of life grows more blatant with every passing year, as the inhabitants abandon the city to the cruise ships whose careless passengers invade it every week or day.

Leon's books are excellent, but I think the best, because the most puzzling, may be *Death in a Strange Country*, *Acqua Alta*, *Uniform Justice*, *Doctored Evidence*, and the latest, *Suffer the Little Children*. These cover some twelve or thirteen years and, reviewing the list, I realize how much darker the later ones are than the earlier. That isn't her fault; it is Venice's—which doesn't make it any easier to bear.

The second author is Michael Dibdin, who was born in Wolverhampton, England, in 1947, and grew up in Northern Ireland. The son of a physicist, he studied at Sussex University and at Edmonton University in Canada. He lived for four years in Italy and obviously visited it many times. He died in Seattle in March 2007.

His protagonist is another Italian, also a Venetian, named Aurelio Zen. (Dibdin is careful to point out that this is a Venetian name although it may not sound like one to a non-Venetian.) Zen, as a critic called him, is an "anti-hero" without family except for his aging mother, and only in the last two of his books is seriously involved with a woman, Gemma, whom he finally abandons—why, I don't know. His first book, *Ratking*, opens in Rome but ends in Venice, and the other novels range all over the Italian landscape as Zen anti-heroically confronts the Mafia and bravely tries to stand against it, always without success, of course. The villain of Dibdin's nine or ten Zen novels is not Venetian corruption alone, but the broader underworld power of the Mafia, which continues as it has for several hundred years to strangle the economic and political life of Italy, that jewel of a country built on a small peninsula in the Mediterranean Sea.

The color and tone of these fine novels, from *Vendetta*, *Cabal*, and *Dead Lagoon*, to *A Long Finish*, *Blood Rain*, and *And Then You Die*, grow ever darker as time goes on, and I have the feeling that Dibdin may have been overcome by his hero's despair before he died. As one who has spent much time during twenty-five years in Italy, I can well understand this, although I have to admit that there are reasons to despair not just in Italy these days.

In Sweden, too, as Henning Mankell, the last of our three entertaining instructors, lets us know. He was born in Stockholm in 1948 and grew up in a cultured family. His career as both author and play director began when he was twenty, and in 1985 he founded the Avenida Theatre in Maputo, Mozambique, where he now spends much of his time and which has provided background for some of his books. In fact, he has spent quite a lot of time in Africa, which hangs like a dark planet over his Swedish world.

Mankell's protagonist is Inspector Kurt Wallander, who lives and works in Ystad, Sweden. His first thriller was *Faceless Killers*, the story of some vicious thieves who murder a family in a remote farm house and try to withdraw their money from a bank. You will have to read the book to find out whether they succeed in doing this, but it will not take you long to apprehend Wallander's consciousness of the changes that are occurring in Swedish society, until recently so apparently immune to the social ills we ourselves (and Italians too) know so well. These feelings are accentuated in the succeeding books, which include *The Dogs of Riga*, *The White Lioness*, *The Fifth Woman*, *Firewall*, and especially *The Dancing Master*.

Considering these three exceptional authors and their exceptional books, I am reminded of the famous Armory Show of 1913, which introduced to an American audience the avant garde art of men like Picasso and Matisse, and especially Marcell Duchamp, whose "Nude Descending a Staircase" was explosively controversial. One viewer, who like most of the others was shocked and surprised, nevertheless saw the writing on the wall. He was James Stillman, a financier who was president of the National City Bank (now Citibank), and as he walked slowly through the exhibits he was prompted to say (as he later put in writing): "Something is wrong with the world. These men know." Incidentally, even though he disliked them, he bought several paintings that when they were included in his estate were valued at several million dollars.

Something is wrong with the world. These three authors know.

# CARL HIAASEN
1953–
*Novels*

All work and no play makes Jack a dull boy. This definitely applies to me when I'm working, but I don't work all the time and there are books that I read just for the fun of it. For example, any novel by Carl Hiaasen, who was born in 1953 near Fort Lauderdale, Florida. He graduated from the University of Florida in 1974 with a degree in journalism and not long after went to work for the *Miami Herald*, first as a reporter but later as a columnist, which he remains till this day. His columns are one of the few good reasons to read the *Herald*, which I did faithfully during the time when we owned a little Conch house in Key West.

Our first visit to Key West occurred in 1973, I think. We bought the house two years later. I remember going into the bookstore in 1986 and asking if there was anything Floridian I should read. "Have you tried Carl Hiaasen?" the woman asked. "No." "Well, you're missing something." She was right.

That was the year when he published his first Florida novel, *Tourist Season*. It's a wild and wooly tale involving all Hiaasen's "regular" characters: shady businessmen, corrupt politicians, dumb blondes, sunburned tourists, and apathetic retirees. In his hands it is a rich mix that he churns this way and that, all the time making you guffaw at the dialogue. I have never laughed so hard and so continuously at any other books, unless maybe Rabelais's.

The next year we read *Strip Tease*, which may be his best, although *Lucky You*, about people who share a winning lotto ticket, is probably just as good. His latest novel, *Nature Girl* (2007), is more sardonic than humorous, which may mean he is losing his touch or that he has given up on Florida—which wouldn't surprise me.

# MICHAEL POLLAN
1955–
*The Botany of Desire*
*The Omnivore's Dilemma*

Michael Pollan was born in 1955 and received a B.A. from Bennington, continued with graduate studies at Oxford, and received an M.A. from Columbia in 1981. For some years he and his wife and their son Isaac summered in the town where I live in Connecticut. But there was no way we could keep his genius with us, and he moved to California as a Professor of Journalism at the University of California-Berkeley and is head of an institute that studies environmental journalism, of which he is one of the most important practitioners in the country.

He has written many articles and two very good books—not just good, but astounding. The first, *The Botany of Desire*, was published in 2001. It is about the concept of what he calls co-evolution, in this case between mankind and four plants—apple, tulip, marijuana, and potato. They are all important products in human life (and pleasure, too), and Pollan carefully describes the history of mankind's relation between each of them. It is a sad story in each case, particularly that of the apple and the potato. Now, after two hundred years of striving, almost every commercially grown apple is a relative, more or less close, of the apple called "Delicious," which unfortunately is very hardy and disease-free and almost always dominant when it is grafted onto other apple stocks. The result is that the great, tasty, and succulent apples of my childhood (and no doubt of yours if you are over fifty)—for instance, Baldwins and Northern Spies—are now rare. And when it comes to the potato, the discoveries about how to maximize production of the vegetable have led to the exhaustion and in fact desecration of fields all over the Middle and Upper West. We eat the same potatoes, whatever their names, and have learned to accept and not to desire the kind of potatoes we used to enjoy in our youth.

That is all very well, but the story gets worse, as Pollan shows us in his second book, *The Omnivore's Dilemma* (2007). Humans are omnivores; that is, we can eat and thrive on almost anything from meat to vegetables to fruit to insects if needed (and desired in some cultures). But if we could choose, what would be the best kind of food to eat? Pollan describes three different food chains: industrial, organic, and hunter-gatherer, following each of them all the way to the table. He finds a "fundamental tension between the logic of nature and the logic of human industry." What we eat represents our most profound engagement with the natural world, and he warns that modern agribiz is a destructive, precarious agricultural system that has wrought havoc on the diet, nutrition, and well-being of Americans as well as the inhabitants of the other developed countries of the Earth.

In the end he advises us, when we are confronted by the "bewildering and treacherous landscape of the supermarket," to choose no food that "would not have been recognized as food by our grandmothers" and to avoid any food item that has a list of ingredients longer than three items, if that. Good advice, I think, but hard to follow in today's world.

Read Pollan, but don't think he will bore or castigate you. He can be very funny as well as very persuasive, and since, after all, it is your own life that is at stake, it makes sense to take a chance.

# PATRICK O'BRIAN
## 1914–2000
### *The Aubrey-Maturin Series*

Patrick O'Brian was born in 1914, which places him well out of chronological order, but several of the books in this series were published in the 1990s, which allows me to put him here.

For years O'Brian was a kind of "mystery man"; for example, he allowed it to be thought that he had been born in Ireland when in fact he was born in England. Nor was his birthname Patrick O'Brian, but instead Richard Patrick Russ; he legally changed his name to O'Brian in 1945, the year when he married Mary Tolstoy (née Wicksteed), the divorced wife of Count Dmitri Tolstoy. He wrote all his books in longhand, and Mary retyped them "pretty," as he said, for his publishers. In many ways, in fact, she played the same role for him that Count Leo Tolstoy's faithful and patient wife had played for him a century before. When she died in 1998, he became "lonesome, tortured, and nearly paranoid" and died a little more than a year later, on January 2, 2000, the second day of a new millennium. Ever since 1949 they, and finally he, had lived in Collioure, a Catalan-speaking village near Perpignan. It was the kind of place the character Stephen Maturin could have come from.

O'Brian wrote novels and stories and translated a number of books from French into English, but his great career began in 1970, when *Master and Commander* was published and introduced Jack Aubrey and Stephen Maturin to the world. I remember very well when I read that book. I was mesmerized and told my son about it; he was mesmerized, too. From that time on we awaited the publication of each volume in the series and shared the pleasure of reading copies a thousand miles apart and calling one another every day or so to delectate particular events and scenes.

Jack and Stephen were—still are, of course—a wonderful pair. But so are many of the other persons in this great series of books. For John and me, and for many thousands of others, they were beloved friends and companions for twenty years. Our only cavil, and it isn't a minor one, was that O'Brian killed off his faithful bo'sun and also Stephen's wife, the spirited Diana, in the next to last volume. Of course this was the year in which his Mary, "the beautiful and spirited English wife" of Count Tolstoy, was either dead or dying. It was as if he couldn't stand to let Stephen's Diana live when his own Mary was gone.

# J.K. ROWLING
## 1965–
### *The Harry Potter Series*

Joanne "Joe" Rowling was born near Bristol, England, in 1965. She attended local schools and "Hermione is loosely based on me—at age

11," she has said. She earned a B.A. in English and Classics at the University of Exeter and in 1990, while on a delayed train trip, jotted down notes about a young boy attending a school of wizardry. In 1994 she moved to Edinborough, Scotland, to be near her sister. Divorced, unemployed, and living on state benefits, she completed her first novel, writing in local cafés because she would take her daughter Jessica out for walks and, when she fell asleep, would duck into the nearest café and continue the story.

She completed *Harry Potter and the Philosopher's Stone* in 1995 and found an agent who submitted the manuscript to twelve publishers, all of whom rejected it. The thirteenth, a small publisher in Bloomsbury, accepted it because the eight-year-old daughter of the chairman read the first chapter and "demanded the next." Rowling received an advance of 1,500 pounds, about the same number of dollars at that time.

The book was published in 1997 with a first printing of one thousand copies, five hundred of which were distributed free to libraries. Such copies now sell for between $25,000 and $35,000. Rowling received a grant from the Scottish Arts Council of 8,000 pounds to allow her to go on writing, and in fact that first book was named British Children's Book of the Year. It was published in the United States in 1998 by Scholastic after they had won an auction. Over the author's protests, Scholastic changed the name of the book to *Harry Potter and the Sorcerer's Stone*.

The seventh and last of the Harry Potter series was published on July 21, 2007, and sold more than 250,000 copies in the first 24 hours. More than eight million copies have been sold all told, and J.K. Rowling is now the wealthiest woman writer in history, with a net worth for the books alone estimated at more than eight billion dollars. Well, in my humble opinion "Joe" Rowling deserves every penny of it. The books have gotten better and better as time has gone on, and the last—I truly hope it is the last—is the best of all. I read it through in the first four days and then joined John and Sally and our two grandchildren, Sam and Charlie, while they read the last hundred pages out loud to one another. We were aware that many thousands of people were doing the same thing at the same time. Maybe half of them were youngsters, but the other half were grownups, even oldsters like me. It has turned out to be hard for some grownups to admit this, but all I can say is I'm sorry for them.

Why has this extraordinary success come to Rowling? Does she have a secret? If so, what is it?

I don't think there is a secret. In a way, she does what all authors of novels, and especially series of novels, do: She imagines a situation and invents characters and events. She creates a world, peoples it, describes it, makes us care about it. She tells good stories, being sure to build suspense. She leaves us hungry for more, which is what the best series do.

Rowling's tale opens in a special school where students are taught about magic—what it is and how to do it. It isn't easy to get to this school, because you have to know a secret place where you can board a special train. When you arrive at the school you find that it too is special, secret. Not just anyone can go there. That's exciting. It's a good start.

The characters are also interesting, but not unique. There is a girl and two boys; they start as children and grow up as seven years pass. There are families and one of the boys finally falls in love with the sister of the other boy. That is good but not unique, either.

There is something very special about the first boy, though. He has a tragic past; his parents were killed when he was a child, his mother, when she was trying to protect him: giving up her life to save him. This is fine; it adds a tragic note even if the characters are just children and then teenagers.

The circumstances surrounding the death of the boy's parents are mysterious, which is good. Some kind of evil was involved; only very slowly do we begin to understand that the evil is represented by a single individual who grows more powerful as the series proceeds. In the last book he has become all-powerful, and there is no hope left for the world.

Or so it seems, even to Harry, the boy-hero. But his courage, which has always been remarkable, permits him to face the prospect of certain death if he does not yield to the evil lord. Even so, he does not yield. His courage, in the last analysis, is greater than that of his foe.

It is Harry's beautiful courage, I think, that makes this series unique. We accept it, we believe in it. We are frightened for him at the end of the series; we can't see any way out. But Harry Potter can.

# Ten-Year Reading Plan

The following reading plan is more than merely suggestive, although it is not carved in stone, either. It emphasizes classical works over recent ones, mainly because the former are less likely to be familiar, but many recent books are also on this list. There could be other books on it, replacing the ones I have chosen. But stick to my list for a while, at least, and see it if works for you.

For each year I have recommended that you read ten books, but sometimes I have felt that really long works should count for more than one. This means that the number of different titles is less than one hundred. The books can be read in any order desired, although for each year they are listed in chronological order, so that might be the best way to read them. For each year, the recommended books are both instructive and entertaining, according to my lights. Some years may be harder than others, but nobody is watching you. Read as much as you can and don't spoil your pleasure by struggling to "keep up." There is plenty of time, even if you have to spend twenty years reading these hundred books, instead of ten.

You may decide you want to read the books along with another person or with a group. Of course, in a way I am reading them with you if you read my comments on each author, but that's not the same as having friends join you for, say, ten days of discussion a year. I think that would be fun, and I wish I could be there with you.

# YEAR ONE

Homer, *The Iliad*
Homer, *The Odyssey*
Aeschylus, *The Oresteia* (counts for 2)
Sophocles, *Oedipus Rex, Oedipus at Colonus, Antigone* (counts for 3)
Shakespeare, *Hamlet*
Eugene O'Neill, *Long Day's Journey into Night*
Samuel Beckett, *Waiting for Godot*

# YEAR TWO

Euripides, *Alcestis, Hippolytus, Medea, Iphigenia among the Taurians* (counts for 4)
Aristophanes, *Lysistrata, Clouds, Birds* (counts for 3)
Shakespeare, *Much Ado about Nothing, As You Like It, The Winter's Tale* (counts for 3)

# YEAR THREE

Herodotus, *The History* (selections—read as much as you can or want to)
Thucydides, *The Peloponnesian War* (selections)
Tacitus, *The Annals, The Histories* (selections—read only the juicy parts)
Plato, *The Trial and Death of Socrates, The Symposium, The Republic* (counts for 2)
Aristotle, *Poetics, Nicomachean Ethics* (counts for 2)
Euclid, *The Elements* (at least Book I)
Joseph Heller, *Catch 22*
Kurt Vonnegut, Jr., *Slaughterhouse-Five*

# YEAR FOUR

Lucretius, *On the Nature of Things*
Virgil, *The Aeneid* (counts for 2)
Ovid, *Metamorphoses*
Plutarch, *Lives of the Noble Greeks and Romans* (selections)
Marcus Aurelius, *Meditations*

Shakespeare, *The Merchant of Venice, Othello, Antony and Cleopatra*
(counts for 2)
Henry Fielding, *Tom Jones* (counts for 2)

## YEAR FIVE

Augustine, *Confessions* (Sheed translation)
Aquinas, *Summa Theologica* (selections—counts for 2)
Dante, *Divine Comedy* (counts for 3)
Chaucer, *Canterbury Tales, Troilus and Cryseide* (counts for 2)
Rabelais, *Gargantua and Pantagruel*
Machiavelli, *The Prince*

## YEAR SIX

Bacon, *Essays*
Molière, *The Misanthrope, The Doctor in Spite of Himself*
Blaise Pascal, *Pensées*
Thomas Hobbes, *Leviathan*
John Locke, *Second Treatise, On Toleration*
Thomas Jefferson et al., Abraham Lincoln, *American State Papers*
(counts for 2)
John Stuart Mill, *On Liberty, On Representative Government*
Karl Marx and Friedrich Engels, *The Communist Manifesto*
J.M. Coetzee, *Disgrace*

## YEAR SEVEN

Cervantes, *Don Quixote* (counts for 2)
William Congreve, *The Way of the World*
Voltaire, *Candide*
Goethe, *Faust* (counts for 2—maybe only selections of Part Two)
Byron and Keats, selected poems
Jane Austen, *Pride and Prejudice, Persuasion*
Stendhal, *The Red and the Black, The Charterhouse of Parma* (counts
for 2)

# YEAR EIGHT

Claude Bernard, *Introduction to Experimental Medicine*
Charles Darwin, *On the Origin of Species*
Charles Dickens, *Pickwick Papers, Our Mutual Friend* (counts for 2)
Walt Whitman, "Out of the cradle ...", "When lilacs last ...", other
    selected poems
Emily Dickinson, selected poems
Nathaniel Hawthorne, *The Scarlet Letter* (skip first chapter)
Herman Melville, *Moby Dick*
George Orwell, *Animal Farm, 1984*
J.D. Salinger, *The Catcher in the Rye*

# YEAR NINE

Leo Tolstoy, *War and Peace* (counts for 2)
Henry James, *The Ambassadors, The Golden Bowl* (counts for 2)
Lewis Carroll, *Alice in Wonderland, Through the Looking Glass*
Robert Frost, selected poems
W.B. Yeats, selected poems
Thomas Mann, *The Magic Mountain, Mario and the Magician*
James Joyce, *Portrait of the Artist as a Young Man, Dubliners*
Isak Dinesen, *Seven Gothic Tales*

# YEAR TEN

Sigmund Freud, *Introduction to Psychoanalysis, Civilization and Its*
    *Discontents*
Henrik Ibsen, *A Doll's House*
Bernard Shaw, *Pygmalion, Saint Joan*
Walter M. Miller, Jr., *A Canticle for Leibowitz*
C.G. Darwin, *The Next Million Years*
John Steinbeck, *Travels with Charlie*
Albert Camus, *The Stranger, The Plague*
Arthur Miller, *Death of a Salesman*
Saramago, *Blindness, The Cave*
Antoine de Saint-Exupéry, *The Little Prince*

# Authors and Works